"This new book on Christology dares to break new ground in our understanding of Jesus. Dr. Hill manages to arrange a perfect marriage between historical scholarship and contemporary concerns, addressing such questions as the relationship of Jesus to questions of gender equality, environmental issues, and Jesus' solidarity with the poor and the oppressed.

"Brennan Hill has the uncanny ability to synthesize oceans of complex theological material and present it to the reader in a style that is as clear as a mountain stream. One sees this, for example, in the section on Rudolf Bultmann where Dr. Hill ably sums up form criticism and demythologization in two succinct pages. Dr. Hill is absolutely sovereign vis-à-vis his material, much the way an eagle easily glides over the highest pinnacle of a mountain."

Richard Penaskovic
Auburn University

"Professor Brennan Hill is a master communicator. His research is comprehensive and completely up-to-date. He offers a Christology focused on the historical Jesus, respectful of tradition and engaged in contemporary issues of justice regarding the poor, women, and the environment. On questions on which scholars differ, his approach is modest and judicious. On values issues, his commitment is strong but calm, never strident. Hill's clear, direct prose renders this introduction to the revolution that Catholic Christology has undergone in the past four decades wholly accessible to a wide circle of readers."

William Loewe, Associate Professor
The Catholic University of America

"Amidst the summaries of much New Testament and later Christological scholarship, certain insights into the teachings of Jesus stand out. I find those that relate his words to God's creation and the care of the earth and to human liberation most valuable."

Gerard S. Sloyan
Author of *Jesus in Focus*

"Pedagogically and theologically, *Jesus, the Christ* is a highly accessible book for those groups too often overlooked in the writing of texts on Christology, namely, theologically unsophisticated college undergraduates, adults in religious education programs, and the ordinary lay/clergy person trying to keep abreast of current Christological perspectives.

"As an instructional tool the text is refreshing. The author writes clearly and candidly...gets to the point, and does not presume knowledge when he shouldn't.

"Besides offering a lucid historical and biblical overview of Christological developments, the text also confronts some of the most pressing issues surrounding the contemporary Christological debate: Jesus and sexism, Jesus and ecology, what it means to call him 'Savior' and 'Liberator' in a suffering, complex world.

"This book will prod and provoke the ordinary folk in Christian churches and educational institutions."

Mary Hembrow Snyder
Mercyhurst College

Jesus the Christ

CONTEMPORARY PERSPECTIVES

Brennan Hill

XXIII

TWENTY-THIRD PUBLICATIONS
Mystic, Connecticut 06355

Twenty-Third Publications
185 Willow Street
P.O. Box 180
Mystic, CT 06355
(203) 536-2611
800-321-0411

ISBN 0-89622-492-9
Library of Congress Catalog Card No. 91-65739

Map and frontispiece by Robert McGovern.

Acknowledgments

I would like to offer my gratitude to a number of people who assisted me in this project. First, I would like to thank my students at Xavier University in Cincinnati and at St. Bernard's Institute in Albany, New York, for inspiring me and challenging me to write this book. My thanks to Rev. Kenneth Overberg for his support and for his encouragement to apply for a sabbatical research semester. My thanks as well to Xavier University for granting me this time to do research and write. I wish to acknowledge Ken McAuliffe for his dedicated bibliographical searches, as well as Dr. William Loewe and Dr. Gerard Sloyan for their valuable critiques and suggestions.

My gratitude to Stephen Scharper, John van Bemmel, and Daniel Connors for their marvelous editorial assistance. Also, my thanks to Betti Glynn for her perceptive proofreading. Finally, I want to thank my family for bearing with me during this challenging time, especially my wife Marie, who encouraged and supported me, as well as helped me greatly through her proofreading and indexing.

Contents

CHAPTER ELEVEN
Savior   229

CHAPTER TWELVE
The Liberator   252

Dedication

To my family,
Marie, Ami, B.J., and John,
and in special memory of my beloved mother, Elva,
who passed away with His name on her lips.

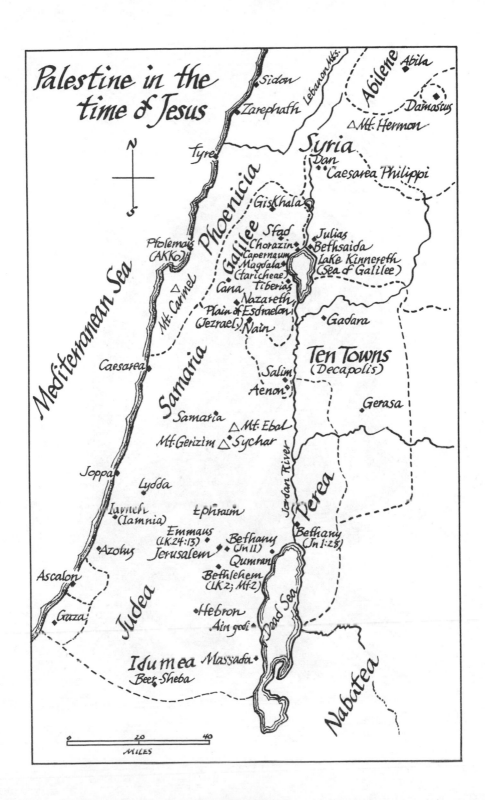

Palestine in the time of Jesus

Mediterranean Sea

Sidon
Zarephath
Lebanon Mts.
Abilene
Abila
Damascus
Mt. Hermon

Tyre
Syria
Dan
Caesarea Philippi

Phoenicia
Giskhala
Safed
Chorazin
Julias
Bethsaida
Ptolemais (AKKO)
Galilee
Capernaum
Magdala (taricheae)
Lake Kinnereth (Sea of Galilee)
Cana
Tiberias
Mt. Carmel
Nazareth
Plain of Esdraelon (Jezrael)
Nain
Gadara

Caesarea
Samaria
Salim
Aenon
Ten Towns (Decapolis)
Gerasa

Samaria
Mt. Ebal
Mt. Gerizim
Sychar

Joppa
Lydda
Jamnia (Iamnia)
Ephraim
Perea
Jordan River
Emmaus (LK 24:13)
Bethany (Jn 11)
Bethany (Jn 1:28)
Azotus
Jerusalem
Qumran
Bethlehem (LK 2; Mt 2)
Ascalon
Judea
Hebron
Ain gedi
Dead Sea
Gaza

Idumea
Massada
Beer-Sheba
Nabatea

0   20   40
MILES

Introduction

A colleague of mine recently lectured around the United States on Jesus Christ. In our conversations, he noted that he was rather surprised at the large turn-outs and enthusiastic response to his presentations. All this convinced him that too often the Catholic emphasis is on doctrines and church matters, rather than the "center of it all," Jesus Christ and his call to discipleship. This conviction was further confirmed as he observed throughout his tour the lack of courses on Christology in the curricula of lay ministry programs, colleges, and, perhaps most surprisingly, in seminaries. As a result of this neglect, he observed, there seems to be a deep hunger among Christians of all ages to learn more about the person of Jesus, to relate to him more intimately, and to somehow connect all this to everyday living.

My own work among undergraduates, college students, graduate pastoral ministers, and adults in parish programs has brought me to this same realization. Our people do want a more comprehensive knowledge and deeper understanding of Jesus, and a closer relationship to him. Preachers or teachers who doubt this need only to pause in their presentations and say, "Now let us reflect on the person of Jesus," and observe how the level of attention is raised.

My work among teachers and pastoral ministers has also made me aware that there is a need for more resources in Christology. Even though there is an on-going and abundant flow of articles and books on Jesus, much of this material is either too devotional for educational purposes or it is too specialized for the increasing number of students not familiar with technical theological language. There is a need for more resources that can bring the best of modern scholarship on Jesus Christ to students in a "user-friendly" fashion. This is the kind of book I have set out to write.

The first lesson one learns in going through the vast amount of research on Jesus is that this is an area with a wide range of points of view. Although there are some doctrinal questions that have been settled definitively by solemn councils, there are many historical, biblical, and theological questions that are highly controversial. One soon learns that with many issues it is a matter of dealing with probabilities, possibilities, even "educated guesses." The more one delves into the issues, the more one encounters complexity, as well as a broad spectrum of scholarly opinions. Although it is important to eventually take one position, this needs to be done with the awareness that there might be other points of views that are equally convincing. As one of my colleagues recently put it, "You simply have to study and reflect as much as you can, and then 'place your vote.'" In the following pages, you will read the results of my research and reflection; often you will observe where I have placed my ballot, and you will have the opportunity to place yours.

Jesus, the Christ begins with context and background, in a discussion of the places and people that were a likely part of Jesus' experiences. The sources are limited and generally later than his own times. Yet even in this "dim light of historical research" it is possible to recreate at least a reasonable semblance of what life must have been like for this man from Nazareth. We can speculate on the kinds of people that might have influenced him as he grew up and worked in Galilee, as well as during the brief period in which he carried out his ministry throughout some of the areas of Palestine.

Next we consider the foundational questions regarding the search for the historical Jesus. Is it useful or even possible to dig beneath the various layers of story, theology, and proclamation in the gospels and discover that uniquely sacred layer wherein we meet the man Jesus? Is it possible to get at least a glimpse of this preacher and healer from Nazareth, the "vintage Jesus" who was seen, heard, and known by the people of this time?

Chapter three explores the pedagogical and prophetic dimensions of Jesus' ministry. Here we attempt to view what may have been his style and to consider the content of this teaching as compared with other teachers of that time. Then Jesus is considered in the context of the prophetic tradition of his Hebrew people, a tradition that challenged corrupt leadership with the authentic revelation of God. Jesus' prophetic teachings on the kingdom and his unique presentation in parables will be given special consideration.

The next chapter on miracles deals with how our post-scientific mentality might relate to the historicity as well as the meaning of the gospel stories of "wonders and cures." Jesus is here considered as a worker of miracles, as one who brought physical, psychological, and spiritual healing to many, especially to outcasts of society. In this phase of his ministry, Jesus revealed not a God of plagues and punishing handicaps, but a God of compassion and mercy who wants people to be whole. Here Jesus sets out to reveal not a God who needs to "prove" anything through miracles, but rather a God who offers convincing signs of divine presence and power to those who have faith.

Chapter five deals with what seems to be Jesus' uniquely unprejudiced attitude toward women, as well as his unprecedented practice of choosing them for his disciples. This recollection of Jesus apparently served as a basis for women to play a central role in the early communities, as well as for their claim to the same kind of roles in today's church.

Midway in the book, chapter six, consideration is given to how disciples of Jesus might approach the pressing environmental issues of our time. Without anachronistically attempting to make Jesus into an environmentalist, we discuss how the Jesus tradition might be better linked to our present-day understanding of our universe and world. This means looking at both the cosmic dimension of Jesus Christ, as well as considering how he was historically a man who viewed all of creation as sacred and under the compassionate care of "Abba." Attention is also be given to the gospel parables, miracles stories, as well as the Christian mysteries of incarnation, salvation, and resurrection to see how these areas might be reinterpreted to move Christians toward an ecological spirituality.

Chapters seven, eight, and nine will explore the gospel stories of Jesus' birth, death, and resurrection. The focus in these is on how the sacred texts reveal the various interpretations the early Christian communities gave to these key events in Jesus' life. These stories also resound with the original Christian proclamation and celebration of "post-resurrection" faith in Jesus as the Son of God, the Christ. In these treasured narratives one can discover the amalgam of historical memory, faith experience, and theology that is the very foundation of the Christian tradition.

In chapter ten the stages of the development of the early Christian doctrines on incarnation are examined. Attention is given to the earliest controversies on Jesus, as well as to how the early apologists, the church fathers, and the first church councils of Nicea and Chalcedon addressed these controversies.

The final two chapters deal with two central titles given to Jesus. One title, "Savior," is an ancient title that over the centuries Christians have assigned a variety of different meanings. Scriptural interpretations, some views in later centuries, and then contemporary explanations of this title are explored. Chapter twelve deals with what is perhaps the most important contemporary image of Jesus, that of Liberator. This is a perspective that came originally "from the people," from the oppressed in Latin America. This "model" reflects their view of Jesus as one who historically, as well as in "resurrection," confronts injustice and violence. This radical image of Jesus emerges out of liberation theology and thus interprets the Jesus of history, his teaching, death, and resurrection in such a manner as to give hope to those who need to be freed from degradation and oppression. It is a perspective that is rapidly spreading to other countries of the world and has inspired many who have suffered injustice for such reasons of nationality, ethnic background, sex, religion, age, or economic status.

Other great historical figures have had it said of them: "We will never have another like this person," but this epitaph seems to apply most appropriately to Jesus of Nazareth. Ironically, neither his background nor education were impressive. He was a Jewish commoner who spent most of his life working with his hands. His public ministry as teacher and healer was brief, and ended with his execution as a criminal. Yet there were extraordinary, often astounding, aspects of this man's life. To his disciples and to many others, he was perceived to be a superb human being who seemed to be able to bring the very presence of God into their lives. So vivid were their memories of the magnificent things Jesus said and did in their midst that after they began to experience him as "raised from the dead," they were able to come to believe that he was in fact their Savior, their Lord and God. This book is about this man Jesus, whom countless followers have come to know and love as "the Christ."

CHAPTER ONE

Places and People

All people are shaped and influenced by the locale in which they grow up, by the political and social forces that surround them, and by the religious milieu in which they are raised. Jesus was no exception. He was a Jew who grew up in a tiny Jewish ghetto village. He was surrounded by parents and neighbors who were deeply committed to their religious tradition. He lived during a time of political and social unrest. All this surely left its mark on him.

Jesus was also surrounded by significant political and religious figures. By looking at these people and by comparing and contrasting them to Jesus, we can perhaps come to a better understanding of who this Galilean was and how uniquely he stands out among his contemporaries.

Much of history, especially ancient history, has to be described and discussed in terms of possibility, probability, and even conjecture because the resources are limited. This is true of any attempt to describe the times in which Jesus lived. We have the gospels, but we know that they were written generations after the time of Jesus and are often colored by later theological, social, and political concerns. Then there are the historical writings of the Jewish historians Philo and Josephus. Philo (d. 41 C.E.) was a contemporary of Jesus, but his writings tell us more about what was going on among the Jews who lived among the Greeks than about the people with whom Jesus lived. Josephus (d. 100 C.E.) was born just after the time of Jesus. He claims to have studied with the Pharisees, Sadducees, and Essenes as a young man, fought in the 66-67 revolt against Rome, surrendered, and then lived out the rest of his days writing Jewish history in Rome. He is one of the few extensive resources we have of the times of Jesus, but his accounts of these times were written from his own peculiar bias.

In addition to these Jewish historians, we have the *Mishna*, a second-century collection of Jewish rabbinic writings. Although these materials are valuable, it is difficult to sort out from these writings the information that might apply to the time of Jesus.

Further information on Jesus' times has been gained by the discovery of the many "Dead Sea Scrolls," but here the material seems to apply mostly to a rather esoteric group that was not typical of the Jews in Jesus' Galilee. These manuscripts, others less significant, and the numerous archaeological excavations in Palestine in modern times all have given us useful but still limited information about Jesus' background.

Given these resource limitations, it should be kept in mind that the scholars we use in this chapter are restricted in their conclusions. Much of what is said about the times of Jesus should be taken as tentative and provisional, and yet nonetheless valuable.

Palestine

Jesus grew up in the ancient area of Palestine, where his people, the ancient Hebrews, had lived for thousands of years, since the days of the patriarchs Abraham, Isaac, and Jacob. The establishment of his people as a nation begins with their conquest of Palestine, perhaps a thousand years before Jesus was born. The era that followed the conquest included the glory days of the kings Saul, David, and Solomon, as well as the decline of the nation and the eventual exile of its people under the Babylonians in 539 B.C.E.

The conquest by the Babylonians was only one in a long series of subjugations under conquering nations: Persia, Greece, and, during Jesus' lifetime, Rome. Throughout these oppressions, the Hebrew people somehow kept their identity and clung to their belief in their God, Yahweh. They also maintained their belief that Yahweh had made a covenant with them and selected them to carry out a unique destiny in human history as God's chosen people.

The Romans had occupied Jesus' area and begun dominating his people a little more than fifty years before he was born. Palestine had been incorporated into the Roman Empire largely because of its extensive resources and its strategic position on the Mediterranean Sea. Pompey, who had conquered Palestine in 63 B.C.E., incorporated the area into Syria and placed it under the rule of a Roman legate. The Romans then reorganized the region, took over the coastal areas, and repopulated them with Phoenicians and Syrians. The Jewish population from these areas was pushed back into the hinterlands, and many were forced to eke out an existence as landless peasants.[1] Pompey placed the coastlands and most of Samaria under the direct control of a Roman governor, while the other provinces gradually came under the control of local aristocrats in the Herodian family.

After much intrigue between the Herodian family and the Roman leaders, who feuded among themselves, Herod the Great was ultimately declared the King of Judea and became the undisputed ruler of Palestine.[2] The Emperor Octavian gave Herod full domestic power, and Herod was subject to Rome only in matters of war and foreign policy. He ruled from 37 B.C.E. until around the time Jesus was born.

As Jesus grew up, he no doubt would have experienced a great deal of hostility toward Herod the Great and his family. Most Jews did not accept the Herodians as authentic Jews because they were considered to be "half-breeds" from Idumea. Most Jews resented the lavish lifestyle of Herod the Great, which included a series of ten wives and a sumptuous life in the palaces he built for himself.[3]

All this, of course, as well as Herod's enormous building program of monuments to himself, temples for emperor worship, theaters, sports arenas, baths, fortresses, and even entirely new cities, was supported by a tax program that heavily burdened the people and caused deep resentment and hatred toward Herod. Herod did make some attempts to appease the Jews, especially through his project of rebuilding the Temple in Jerusalem. This was the so-called Second Temple, and was built to replace the magnificent structure that had been destroyed by the Babylonians. But, again, the heavy taxation to provide lavish materials of gold, alabaster, and marble for the Temple, as well as Herod's ruthless activities (including the murder of his own children to maintain power), only gave the Jews more reasons to hate and resent him.

When Herod died, he willed that his kingdom be divided among his three sons: Archelaus, who was given Judea, Samaria, and Idumea; Herod Antipas, who took over in Galilee and Perea; and Philip, who was given the areas north and east of the Sea of Galilee. Because Jesus was a Galilean, it was Herod Antipas who would play a role in his life. This was the Herod who executed Jesus' mentor, John the Baptist, and who mocked and ridiculed Jesus when Jesus was brought to the palace before his crucifixion. At one point in the gospels Jesus refers to Herod as "that fox" (Luke 3:32).

Archelaus turned out to be a disastrous and cruel leader in the southern province of Judea. In protest, the Jews sent a delegation to Rome and were able to persuade the authorities there to depose Archelaus and have him sent into exile. Judea would now be ruled by a Roman prefect, who would reside in Herod's palaces at Caesarea or Jerusalem. The prefect held ultimate authority over the public order and over the collection of tariffs for Rome.

One such administrator, Pontius Pilate, has gone down in history as the one who decreed the execution of Jesus. History has given Pilate a reputation for cruelty and brutality. In the gospels Jesus hears of how Pilate had some of Jesus' fellow Galileans killed while they were offering sacrifices (Luke 13:1). On another occasion Pilate had Jews beaten to death for protesting the use of Temple money to build aqueducts. Pilate eventually went too far in his barbarities, was reported to Rome and summoned there for an account of his atrocities, and then disappeared from history. There are legends that he committed suicide or even that he was executed under Nero.[4]

The Man from Galilee

Jesus was known as a Galilean, and all of the apostles that he chose, with the possible exception of Judas, were from the same northern province of Galilee. People from Galilee had the reputation of being independent. As we have seen, the province was not under direct Romans rule as was Judea, and although Herod was not liked by the Galilean Jews, his reign over them gave them relative autonomy. Moreover, Galilee was a distance from Jerusalem, the center of Jewish religious and legal authority, and therefore somewhat out of reach of the Sanhedrin, the Jewish ruling body. Being rich in resources also helped to give Galileans an attitude of self-sufficiency.

Galileans also had the reputation in some quarters of being proud and rebellious. Many felt that it was in Galilee that the later revolutionary movement was born. Jesus no doubt was well aware of several incidents of rebellion during his infancy and youth.

Around the time of Jesus' birth, the Emperor Augustus sent his general Sabinus to arrange for a successor for the deceased Herod the Great. The Jews perceived that Sabinus was intimidated by them, and some of the more aggressive ones attacked his forces in Jerusalem. In the north a famous rebel called Judah the Galilean broke into the royal arsenal in Sepphoris, the capital of Galilee, stole weapons, and led an uprising. The Romans retaliated by burning Sepphoris to the ground, selling its inhabitants into slavery, and crucifying thousands of rebels.[5] When Jesus was about ten, Judah led another rebellion, this time against the census ordered by the Roman Quirinus, because many believed that the census would only result in heavier unjust taxes.

Although matters were rather quiet in Galilee throughout Jesus' teen years and young adult life, the spirit of rebellion seemed to fester within, and forty years after Jesus' death another Galilean, Menachem, a descendent of the rebel Judah, seized the fortress at Masada during the great uprising against Rome in 66 C.E. And it was Menachem's nephew Eleazar who led the last stand of the Zealots at Masada, where nearly a thousand Jews committed suicide rather than submit to the domination of the Romans.[6]

Jesus grew up in a province known for rebellion, but this does not mean, as some have implied, that he himself encouraged violence.[7] First of all, there is a growing consensus that Galilee was peaceful and stable for most of Jesus' life.[8] More important, there is little in Jesus' teaching or actions that would indicate that he ever advocated violent rebellion. Of course, as a Galilean he had experience with economic, political, and religious oppression and with the resentment and frustration among his people that so often leads to violence. Still, his "revolution" was one born in forgiveness and love, in a non-violent but active struggle for justice for the poor.

Even though Jesus was not himself an advocate of violence, he carried the reputation of being from Galilee, the main seat of anti-Roman feeling, messianic hopes, and an area where bands of brigands and robbers roamed looking for victims.[9] Once Jesus became a public figure it would be convenient for his enemies to use these unfavorable Galilean images against him. This will be discussed in much more detail in the chapters where we deal with Jesus' trial and with his role as Liberator.

Because many of the Galilean Jews lived in the rural areas, they often had the reputation of being "hicks" or "country types." There were significant Jewish populations in the larger northern towns of Tiberias, Sepphoris, and Joppa, but Galilee had no urban area comparable to Jerusalem. Most Galilean Jews were peasants living in small towns and villages and working as tenant farmers for the rich landowners. Many others had been dispossessed or even sold into slavery because of their inability to pay exorbitant taxes and rent for land, and these usually lived in extreme poverty.[10]

The Galileans also had a reputation for being poorly educated. Those in the south looked upon the Galilean schools as backwoods schoolhouses where there was little record of any famous teachers. And because education was the way that the Jew learned the Torah, Galileans were thought to be careless and even arrogant about following the legal details of the scribal laws. The Pharisees, who prided themselves on how they led and influenced the common folk in practicing the law, did not seem to make a serious impression on many Galileans. The Galileans also spoke with an unusual accent, in some cases so heavy that they were not permitted to read in the synagogues when they were traveling.[11] The gospels note that Peter was singled out as Jesus' follower because of his Galilean accent.

Although Jesus grew up in the rural area among many peasants, he would not have been viewed as coming from peasant stock. He was known as the son of a tradesman, a carpenter, and most likely followed this craft himself. Jesus' work with wood probably offered him more opportunity for travel and commerce than the peasant farmer would have had.

At the same time, the rural images and people in Jesus' parables indicate that he was most at home among the common folk. Jesus would have known how the rich absentee landowners oppressed the local farmers, and he had empathy for the plight of the people of the land. This is certainly one of the dimensions of Jesus' life that today gives endurance and courage to the poor peasants in Central and South America, who experience similar oppression from the wealthy landowners in their countries.

That Jesus spent most of his life, even his public life, among the common folk is another indication of his preference for rural life. He seems to have lived most of his early life in the small, insignificant village of Nazareth, and moved as a young adult to the fishing village of Capernaum. Most of his preaching seems to have been done there and in other small towns like Bethsaida and Chorozain. He seems to have studiously avoided the aristocratic cities of Tiberias and Joppa. His visits to the great metropolis of Jerusalem were possibly limited to pilgrimages for the feasts.

Jesus was a small-town person who was largely satisfied with carrying on his ministry with common folk. This is not to say that he was alienated from urban life or from those who were well off, for he certainly had his friends among the rich and powerful, and he could hold his own with people from all walks of life and class levels.

Jesus does not seem to have had the opportunity to attend the "finer schools" for rabbinic learning in Jerusalem. Nevertheless, judging from the extraordinary understanding he had of his Jewish tradition as well as his outstanding ability to teach and debate with the learned scholars, he must have had a great deal of natural genius. One also might be led to suspect that there must have been some unusual and gifted teachers in that small synagogue school in Nazareth.

Jesus lived up to the common reputation of Galileans, who were thought to have a lax attitude about adherence to the scribal laws. Though he was obviously a devout Jew who cherished the Torah, he was not given to worry about the details of purification laws and Sabbath practice, especially if they conflicted with service to others. Moreover, he was quite liberal in regard to the laws on associating with others. He seems to have felt comfortable befriending tax collectors, prostitutes, the diseased, the disabled, the poor, and even non-Jews.

Galileans were often looked upon as "impure" by the Jews of Jerusalem. The Romans and other conquerors had repopulated the area with many non-Jews, and the association with these "pagans" from many nations was thought to dilute the Judaism of the north. (It is interesting to note that some scholars, in an attempt to diminish if not to eliminate altogether the Jewishness of Jesus, have stressed the dilution of Judaism in the north. One German scholar in 1941, during the height of that era's anti-Semitism, maintained that Jesus, in fact, was not a Jew at all!)[12] There seems to be much agreement among scholars that during the time of Jesus the influence of these other cultures on the Galilean villagers was not significant. Still, it would seem that being in constant contact with those from many other cultures would have given the Galilean a broader and more liberal outlook than those who remained in "ghettos" would have had.

Jesus, of course, was thoroughly Jewish in his way of life, religion, and teaching. Yet it is likely that his trade would have brought him to market towns where he would have had contact with all kinds of people, Jew and Gentile alike. He possibly knew enough Greek and Latin to carry out business with Greek-speaking Jews and with non-Jewish customers. The gospels show that he was able to converse with Romans and Syro-Phoenicians. We, therefore, might assume that Jesus had no fear of being rendered impure by associating with non-Jews.

At the same time, the gospels give little indication that Jesus was doing anything other than attempting to reform his own religion and carry out a God-given mission to his own people. The one incident with the Syro-Phoenician woman even indicates a certain disdain for the non-Jew, even though we might grant that such terms as "dogs" and "swine" might reflect later hostilities between Christians and pagans more than they portray Jesus' own attitudes. Certainly his view of a God who is universal in love and care would imply that Jesus had love and respect for Gentiles as well as Jews. It is unreasonable to assume that Paul, and ultimately the early Christian community, could move to extend Jesus' message to peoples of all nations if such teaching had not at least been implied in the original message of Jesus.

Nazareth

Jesus grew up in the obscure village of Nazareth. It was situated among the hills of southern Galilee, where farmers grew their crops in great abundance with two harvests in the rich alluvial basins, and where shepherds pastured their sheep on the green hillsides. This Galilean setting is familiar to any follower of Jesus, because it serves as the setting for many of Jesus' teachings and parables.

Even though it was a small country village, Nazareth could not be described as isolated. Sepphoris, the capital city of Galilee, was only four miles away and visible from the hillsides. The bustling city of Tiberias was also nearby, and craftsmen like Jesus could go there for work and to sell their products in the marketplace. To the west, one could have access to the busy ports of the Mediterranean, especially the key ports of Ptolemais, Caesarea Maritima, and the picturesque port at the foot of Mt. Carmel in the bay of Haifa. To the east, one could walk down the rolling hills leading to the blue water of the Sea of Galilee, with its thriving and crowded fishing villages. To the south lay one of the greatest caravan routes in the world, which connected Damascus with Egypt. Many conquerors have used this route over the centuries, including Alexander the Great, Pompey, and even Napoleon Bonaparte.

Even with all the charm and beauty of this area, life in Nazareth was not easy. In the predominantly Gentile Galilee, Nazareth was a Jewish enclave where the lifestyle was extremely simple, if not impoverished. The dirt alleys were lined with square, one-room houses, each having an adjoining yard for a few animals, perhaps a donkey and some sheep and goats. The houses were clustered closely together so that the limited resources could be shared. Such closeness had the advantage of helping to develop close family ties and a spirit of neighborliness and sharing. Some have suggested that it was in this context of closeness that Jesus formulated his later teachings on love of neighbor and on treating others as you would expect to be treated.[13]

The dark side of such closeness was the high frequency of disease and the short life expectancy. Resources were often limited in villages like Nazareth. Water was scarce and had to be brought daily from cisterns. Bathing was not common except during the rainy season when the wadis would fill up. In times of drought, both food and water would be in short supply.

The limited resources and overpopulation also made it tempting to ignore the weak and to expel the sick lest contamination be spread. At the same time these conditions often generated a system of local care for the needy and a sense of compassion for the handicapped and diseased. Could it be this kind of environment where Jesus learned to reach out to outcasts and to bring healing to those afflicted with disabilities?

Jesus most likely learned his trade as a craftsman *(tekton)* in wood from his father, Joseph. Craftsmen would work in their own villages as long as there were things to be made and repaired, but often they would have to go to the neighboring cities, such as Tiberias and Sepphoris, where building projects would be more likely. It is even possible that Jesus moved to Capernaum as a young adult partly because there was not enough work in Nazareth to make a living.

Securing wood would have been a major task for a carpenter in those days. Wood was not easy to come by in Jesus' area. The marauding armies had plundered the woodlands of Galilee, and what was left was often either stripped by the rich landowners to make way for plantations or gathered by poor peasants in their desperate attempt to survive. One might have to go to Carmel, Sharon, or even as far south as Hebron to find the quality oak, terebinth, or pine needed to do solid construction or to fashion fine furniture. The tools were primitive, and the cutting and hauling required grueling labor. A carpenter had to be a strong, hardy individual.[14]

Education was a priority for the Jews, even in the smallest villages. Jesus would have had to attend the village school daily from early childhood until age twelve or thirteen. There he would learn the books of the Bible and the basic knowledge needed to live as a devout Jew. Once this period of formal learning was finished, Jesus and the other students could move on to study with the local sage or teacher of the law and could join regularly in the village with other adults who studied the Torah while working in the fields, in their spare time, or on the rooftops in the cool of the evening.[15]

The synagogue was indeed another forum for studying the Torah. The synagogue was possibly set up by the Pharisees as an alternative to the Temple, and it ultimately prevailed as a religious gathering place for Jews after the destruction of the Temple in 70 C.E. Jews would gather regularly in their local synagogues for liturgical prayer and for study of the sacred texts. The readings would be done in Hebrew, so it was necessary for Jews to have a strong grasp of this language, as well as Aramaic, the living language in which the discussions would be held. Jesus most likely knew both languages well.

The depth of Jesus' understanding of his tradition, as well as the unique originality he was able to give to this teaching, indicate many long hours of study and discussion with the learned in his village. Common sense tells us that he did not arrive on the scene in his public ministry as a master teacher and healer without extensive training and experience in his earlier years.

Jerusalem

In the days of Jesus, Jerusalem was the mid-point of the civilized world, the crossroads where nations converged. The book of Ezekiel (38:12) described Jerusalem as "the navel of the world." Jerusalem was indeed the heart of Judaism, its central city, rich in symbolism and meaning. For the Hebrew, Jerusalem symbolized the Exodus into this promised land, the days of glory when King David ruled the nation from his magnificent court. This was the "Holy City," where Yahweh dwelt in the Temple. It was the center of Hebrew worship, authority, and education.[16]

The Roman eagle dominated Jerusalem, as it did all of Palestine, and the Roman presence was felt here even more than in Galilee, because the province of Judea was under the direct control of a procurator. The troops of the empire, many of them Gallic, German, and Italian mercenaries known for their brutality, were visible throughout the city. Anyone with any doubts about who was in charge had only to look at the crosses outside the city on which hung those convicted of sedition or rebellion.

It is not known how many times Jesus went to Jerusalem. The gospel of John indicates three visits as an adult. The synoptic gospels refer to only one visit, and two gospels speak of a visit with his family when Jesus was twelve. There was a law that required male Jews to make a pilgrimage to Jerusalem three times a year for the feasts of Passover, Pentecost, and Tabernacles.[17] It is doubtful that this would apply to someone who lived as far from the city as Jesus did. It is possible, however, that Jesus, a devout Jew, made the trip numerous times during his life.

Jerusalem was about one hundred winding miles from Nazareth, a trip that would require three or four days. Such a trip always had its dangers. Brigands and robbers lived in the hills, waiting to pounce on the unsuspecting pilgrims bringing their tithes to Jerusalem (the well-known story of the good Samaritan gives an account of such an attack). Moreover, to make the trip one would have to pass through the hostile territory of Samaria, and here skirmishes between travelers from the north and the local inhabitants were common. Another hazard was the presence of wild animals who roamed the deserts. Given all these dangers, travelers usually joined a caravan or traveled in large groups, with some among them armed to protect the group (this might explain why some of Jesus' own disciples were armed with knives and swords).

There were other reasons why those from small villages in Galilee would be reluctant to go to Jerusalem. Many of the rural peasants were suspicious of the metropolitan area, for here lived many of the rich absentee landlords who held heavy mortgages against the tenant farmers. In the marketplace the Jewish visitor would encounter the infamous customs officials and tax collectors, taking in the levies for the Temple and the Roman coffers, and collecting the mortgage money for the land and crops of the tenant farmers. The poorer visitors, who could barely make ends meet back in their villages, would also come face to face with the sumptuous lifestyle of the rich. For the Jews, Jerusalem was also the place of the Sanhedrin, the "supreme court," which could make edicts and enforce sanctions that often deeply affected their lives.

In spite of these negative features, however, Jerusalem had the attractions of "the big city." Going there for the feasts was an opportunity to get away from the humdrum life in the country and to experience the excitement of the marketplace. Here merchants sold their wares in the hundreds of shops that lined the streets. The fish merchants sold dried fish from the Sea of Galilee. Traders from the great port of Tyre displayed precious glassware and the renowned purple dyes. One could shop for fine white linen and scarlet woven materials from Babylon. Huge caravans of hundreds of camels moved into the city laden with spices and exotic products from Mesopotamia. On auction stones throughout the marketplace slaves were being sold to the highest bidder. If one wanted entertainment there were chariot races, gymnastics, and shows with lions and other wild animals from the Arabian deserts taking place in Herod's Hippodrome. Or there were the latest musical and dramatic performances showing in the theater.

And, of course, there were many occasions to visit friends and relatives from local towns and villages or from distant *diaspora* areas. Hundreds of thousands of pilgrims would converge on the city for the big feasts. There would be opportunities to renew old acquaintances and to listen to the intrigues of the city. If one were fortunate enough to have a relative or friend in one of the towns surrounding the city, there might be the opportunity to stay with them during the pilgrimage. If one did not know a friend or relative in Jerusalem, it would be necessary either to tent outside the city or battle the crowds for the jammed accommodations in the city itself.

If one had political or legal matters to attend to, Jerusalem was the place to do it. The Sanhedrin was the chief agency for Jews both inside and outside of Palestine. This was the major political body, as well as the "supreme court" for all of Judaism, with the power to exercise authority in matters of justice and finance.[18] This body could make laws, enforce them, and hand down punishments for the Jewish people. It was this court, according to the gospels, that passed judgment on Jesus and requested his execution by the Romans.

Jerusalem was also the educational center of Judaism. Scholars from all parts of the world were attracted to the famous rabbinic schools in the city. Talented and ambitious students would come to attend these schools and learn from the masters.

There is no evidence that Jesus ever had the opportunity to attend any of these renowned rabbinic schools, but the respect and (sometimes) hatred that he earned from the religious leaders in Jerusalem might be an indication that he had the reputation in Jerusalem of being a formidable and (to some) threatening scholar and teacher. The gospel story of the adolescent Jesus dazzling the elders in the Temple school might well relate to the memory of Jesus as an outstanding student and teacher of the Torah.

The central attraction in Jerusalem for the devout Jew was, of course, the Temple. This was the cultic center of Judaism, "the place of the presence of God on earth."[19] Jews came from all over the world to worship at the Temple and offer sacrifice through the priests. Here Jews came in hopes of having their prayers heard. They would bring the first fruits of their harvest and make amends for their offenses. Mothers came to the Temple to be purified after the birth of a child, and Gentile proselytes came to repent their past lives, be baptized, and become part of the chosen people.

The Temple that Jesus visited is called the Second Temple. The First Temple of Solomon was destroyed by the Babylonians in 587 B.C.E. Although there was an interim Temple dedicated in 515 B.C.E., the one in Jesus' time was officially called the Second Temple. It was built in grand style by Herod the Great as a futile effort to be recognized as more than a "religious pagan" by the Hebrew people. The structure of this magnificent edifice was completed as a structure about ten years before Jesus was born, but the luxurious decorating went on for years to come, and was not actually finished until about six years before the Temple was reduced to rubble by the Romans during the revolution in 70 C.E.

It was at the Temple that Jesus would observe the high priests, men appointed by Rome and often known for their corruption, as they walked about dressed in the finest materials from India and bedecked in precious jewels from all over the world.[20] The revenues poured into the city from taxes, from the bounty gained from the sale of sacrificial animals and from the required exchange of "unclean" foreign money for the half-shekels required for the Temple tax. These monies enabled the high priests to live extravagantly in luxurious homes, support one or even several wives, and have huge numbers of slaves and servants.[21]

The sight of all this opulence as well as the spectacle of the sumptuous banquets with free-flowing wine and exotic dancing throughout the city during the time of feasts must have been a disturbing sight for Jesus. After all, he was a simple craftsman from the north whose hard labor, along with the labor of so many of the struggling peasants from his area, served to support all of this decadence. More than likely the nepotism, bribery, greed, and corruption that Jesus witnessed on these trips disillusioned and even infuriated the young idealistic preacher from Galilee.

The gospels recall one incident when the chaos of the Temple court, with all the exchange of money and the sale of thousands of doves and small livestock for sacrifice, finally pushed Jesus to the edge. In the only act of violence recorded in his life, he drove the animals out of the court, overturned the tables of the money changers, and drove out those who were selling birds for sacrifice. The gospel of John tells us that this incident brought on Jesus' death. (We will deal more with the significance of this event in the chapter on the trial and execution of Jesus.)

Thus far we have been looking at some of the places and historical background of Jesus' times. We have been able to make some conjectures about some of the events, people, and places that might have influenced Jesus as he lived in Palestine, in the province of Galilee, in the town of Nazareth, and throughout his visits to Jerusalem. Now we are going to examine some of the religious groups that were contemporary with Jesus. By describing these groups and then comparing and contrasting them with Jesus, we hope to gain further insight into the uniqueness of his personality and message.

The Essenes

The Essenes were a group of sectarian Jews, some of whom lived an intense monastic life. Josephus and Philo, both significant Jewish historians, mention the Essenes, but, except for a few existing fragments, we knew little about them until 1947, when manuscripts were discovered that most agree belonged to the Essenes. In that year several Arab shepherds came upon a collection of scrolls in a cave near where the Wadi Qumran flows into the Dead Sea (thus the documents have been called the Dead Sea Scrolls). Many more manuscripts relating to the Essenes were found in nearly a dozen other caves, and these documents have revealed a great deal about this fascinating group.

Some think that the Essenes had their origin in the Hasidim during the time of the Maccabean revolt. The group broke off from mainstream Judaism because they did not recognize the legitimacy of the Temple priesthood that was established at that time, and they established themselves as the true remnant and last generation of Israel, expecting that the "Messiah of Aaron" would come to them in the final days. They settled in the Qumran area, where they built a monastery and established their own priesthood and rituals. It is estimated that during Jesus' time there were perhaps 4000 Essenes living in Palestine, with about 300 living at Qumran, and the others living in small communities in the towns and villages.[22] (We can presume that Jesus was at least familiar with the existence of these latter communities, although the gospels make no mention of the Essenes.)

The Essenes apparently lived in a very closed kind of community, with very strict rules limiting their association with outsiders. The white robed "monks" lived a highly organized life that was both clerical and priestly, and subject to a strict hierarchical authority. It was only possible to enter one of these communities after a three-year trial period. If, after that time, the authorities were convinced that the candidate was totally committed to the Essene ideals, a solemn oath was administered and the candidate was admitted to the common table. Members usually were male, and were expected to be celibate, although there is some evidence that there was one branch that did allow marriage.[23] Cripples, the blind, and the lame were not permitted to enter the communities.[24]

Community members were expected to keep the Essene teaching secret and to carry on a strict daily routine of prayer, work, ritual washings, and common meals. The Essenes had no use for wealthy people and demanded that their members live a simple life, sharing all their possessions. They were careful to make provisions for the needy among them, and they held fellowship meals of bread and wine that looked forward to the end of time.

Although there are striking similarities between a few elements of the lifestyles of the Essenes and that of the early Christian communities, there is no evidence of influence. Many of these practices were common in other Jewish communities, and any of these communities could thus have been the source of influence upon early Christians.

In many of their beliefs the Essenes were similar to other Jews of the time. The Essenes were dedicated to the one God, Yahweh. They stressed the importance of Moses, held faithful to the Torah, and were committed to a life of truth, humility, and justice. In apocalyptic fashion they warned of the power of Satan, the coming of the end-time, and the ultimate righteousness of the poor in a new age of eternal life and everlasting joy.

The Essenes did, however, have their own unique beliefs. They did not accept the legitimacy of Temple sacrifice or priesthood. In true sectarian fashion, the Essenes believed that the righteous would be from their membership alone, and they rejected all those who were considered to be unclean or sinners. They anticipated persecution for themselves and for their mysterious leader, whom they referred to as The Teacher of Righteousness.

There was a certain militancy among the Essenes. Some think this militancy was more symbolic than anything else, but they *were* taught to hate their enemies. They were very strict in the Sabbath observance, even going beyond some of the most rigid of the Pharisees. On Sabbath they would neither lend anything to a friend, pull a beast out of a cistern (an example mentioned by Jesus in Matthew 12:11), pick up even a pebble, or even brush away dust. They were also extremely strict about ritual purification.

The Essene community apparently was annihilated by the Romans during the revolution in the 60s C.E. There is some evidence that a number of them fled with the Zealots to Masada and died in the mass suicide there. Most of their traditions remained a secret for nearly two thousand years until their manuscripts and monastery were uncovered in 1947.[25]

Jesus and the Essenes

Comparing and contrasting Jesus and the Essenes is a useful way of further coming to an understanding of who Jesus was and what he taught. If he ever did meet an Essene (and it is possible that he did, because they were allowed to travel from one community to another),

Jesus would have had a great deal in common with him. Both would be devoted Jews committed to Yahweh. They would hold Moses in high esteem and would be dedicated to the Torah and to a life of truth, humility, and justice. They would share concerns about the struggle against Satan, the coming of the messiah, and of the end-time (perhaps in their own lifetimes), and both would hold for the ultimate blessedness of the poor. Similarly, both would value the table fellowship, helping the needy, and the importance of prayer and hard work. Jesus, like the Teacher of Righteousness, seemed to anticipate persecution for himself as well as for his followers.

But there are also striking contrasts. Jesus did not share the exclusivity of the Essenes. He did not isolate himself from everyday life, nor did he encourage his disciples to limit their association with outsiders or avoid outcasts and sinners. On the contrary, Jesus was known for extending compassion to the handicapped, and for befriending such outcasts as prostitutes and tax collectors. He spoke of a God who loved sinners as well as the righteous,[26] and he encouraged his followers to love their enemies and pray for those who persecuted them.

Unlike the Essenes, Jesus recognized the legitimacy of the Temple and its priesthood, and journeyed to Jerusalem with his family and fellow Jews to celebrate the feasts. After his death his followers continued to go to Temple as devout Jews. It was only when there was a historical break with Judaism, and after the destruction of the Temple and the disappearance of the Jewish priesthood, that the disciples of Christ over a long period of time began to develop their own priesthood and hierarchical clericalism. Jesus did not refer to himself as a priest and did not encourage his followers to see themselves in the role of priest or cleric. Unlike the Essenes, Jesus was a layman and invited a following of both women and men who continued to recognize the legitimacy of the Temple priesthood. He also differed from the Essenes in that he neither required celibacy of his followers nor denigrated marriage.

Jesus did value simplicity and poverty but, unlike the Essenes, he did not abhor wealthy people. True, he warned of the dangers of riches, but he taught and befriended the rich, just as he did the poor, and would not have had a tomb when he was crucified had it not been for a wealthy and generous follower, Joseph of Arimathea. Jesus also went beyond meeting the needs of his followers and extended himself to anyone in need, Jew or Gentile.[27]

Jesus did not encourage his disciples to be sectarian. Though Christians have historically cut themselves off from others, Jesus' message of the universal love of the Father, as well as the essential mission mentality of Christianity, and its concern for all the needy of the world, is strikingly different from the Essene perspective. Jesus did not preach a secret esoteric message, nor did he ask his followers to keep his good news a secret. The gospel of love would eventually be for all nations to hear.

Finally, there is a striking difference between Jesus and the Essenes with regard to the legalities of Judaism. He was noted for his flexibility on issues of Sabbath observance and ritual purity. He was faithful to the Torah and its prescriptions, but the service of others and the goodness of intention were at the heart of his teaching, not the legal casuistry of the Essenes.[28]

The Zealot Movement

Many scholars have believed that there was a well-organized Zealot party during Jesus' lifetime that advocated terrorism and violence against Roman occupation. It has even been proposed that Jesus himself was sympathetic toward the Zealots because he had one or two Zealots for apostles, allowed his apostles to be armed with knives and swords, and was himself crucified as a seditionist.[29] Among many scholars today, however, there seems to be a growing consensus that the Zealots were not an organized group until the 60s C.E., when a major revolution broke out in Palestine that resulted in the destruction of Jerusalem and the Temple and the ultimate elimination of Jewish parties or groups, with the exception of the Pharisees.

Even though the Zealots do not seem to have been an organized party until the 60s C.E., there was, at least from the time of Judah of Galilee (a contemporary of Jesus), a movement among the Jews that advocated terror as a means of eliminating collaborators with Rome and driving Rome out of Palestine. This movement became violent periodically, but it smoldered underground during most of Jesus' life. By the 60s, the oppression of the Jews was so intense that organized revolution and resistance broke out and lasted until the final stand of the Zealot party at Masada in 74 C.E.

While this movement included gangs of slaves, hoodlums, and criminals, its mainline members, for whom the movement was named, were ardent patriots and Jews filled with "zeal for the Lord."[30] This zealous spirit is described in the book of Kings by Elijah the prophet: "With zeal am I zealous for the Lord God of Hosts."

Some think that the Zealots were a branch of the Pharisees, aligned with them in the belief that there is only one God, Yahweh, the master of Israel, and that there should be no collaboration with the pagan Roman occupiers who viewed Caesar as their God. Jews with this view ardently ruled out payment of tribute to the empire as well as worship of the emperor and the false gods of Rome.[31]

The Zealot movement agreed with the Pharisees that the Jews should be vigorously dedicated to opening the way for the kingdom of God.[32] The two groups went their separate ways, however, when it came to the understanding of God and the means for preparing for God's kingdom. During the time of Jesus the Pharisees were growing in their conviction that personal acts of love and mercy were the way to grow in an intimate relationship with God. These acts would open the way for God's kingdom.[33] The Zealot movement, however, held that force was the only way to overcome oppression and open the way for the kingdom. Theirs was a God of vengeance, who destroyed the enemies of his people. In their acts of terrorism and violence against the Romans and those who collaborated with them, the Zealots believed that they were carrying out the will of God. One sees a parallel today in extremist Arab terrorists, some of whom actually believe that by blowing up an airplane and killing hundreds of innocent people they are, in fact, carrying out the will of Allah.

The Zealot movement saw rebellion against heathen rulers as a prelude to the redemption of Israel, and they viewed their violent actions as a means of helping bring this redemption about. As long as there was toleration of heathen domination, Yahweh would remain angry and the kingdom of heaven would be delayed. By their actions and their martyrdom they were paving the way for the imminent coming of God's kingdom. They opposed those among the Jews who held for predestination and the acceptance of occupation as God's will. The Zealots insisted that deliverance would come only after a "holy war" of resistance against the pagan Roman Empire.[34]

Jesus and the Zealot Movement

If it is true that Zealotism was an informal movement and not an organized party during the time of Jesus, then it is futile to attempt to make the case that Jesus was sympathetic toward such a group or died mistaken for one. It also rules out the argument that Jesus had chosen Zealots to be among his followers. One apostle, Simon, is listed in the gospels as a "zealot," but it is possible that during Jesus' time this meant nothing more than someone noted for being "zealous for God."[35] Some have suggested that Judas' surname, Iscariot, is derived from the Latin word for "dagger" (sica) and that he was associated with a group among the Zealot movement called "sicarii," or "dagger men." These terrorists specialized in the terrorist stabbing of prominent Jews who collaborated with Rome. Others hold that the surname might just as well refer to the place where Judas came from: Keriotes.

There is, in fact, no hard evidence that Jesus chose violent revolutionaries to be his followers. And if he had chosen individuals who had been so inclined, they would have surely found their positions on violence in conflict with Jesus' central teachings on love, forgiveness, and the value of peacemaking.

Comparing and contrasting Jesus with those who espoused the spirit of Zealotism can help us see the historical Jesus a little more clearly. Jesus would have agreed with their zeal to worship, with their paying tribute to but one God, and with their dedication to bring about the kingdom of God. We can assume that he would have shared their indignation toward the Roman occupation and toward those who would collaborate with the Romans.

On the other hand, Jesus' message of love of all, including enemies, his teachings on gentleness, compassion, and forgiveness, as well as the absence of violence in his own life, would stand in stark contrast to the ruthless and violent actions of those with the "Zealot" mentality. This was not to say that Jesus was not aggressive or confrontational. His conflicts with some of the Jewish leaders throughout his ministry, as well as his outburst in the Temple, certainly indicate that Jesus was a man of feeling and would stand up against corruption and oppression. But none of these incidents, including the one in the Temple, could be classified as acts of terrorism or as acts that brought personal physical harm. The "dagger men," the "bandits," and other terrorists of the time, who eventually formed into the Zealot party in the 60s, killed, maimed, looted, and torched houses all in the name of Yahweh and his kingdom of justice. Nothing could be more foreign to the messages and deeds of Jesus.

Jesus would have differed significantly in other areas from those within the Zealot movement. Even though the gospel words about repaying to Caesar what belongs to Caesar (Luke 20:20–26) may reflect a later conflict for early Christians, it might also indicate a tradition of pragmatism on the of part Jesus regarding minimal cooperation with the Romans. For him, then, paying taxes does not symbolize a recognition of Caesar's "divinity," for such tribute is only to be "rendered to God." To pay taxes is simply to accept the fact that tax resistance will bring about brutal retaliation from the Romans. If this were Jesus' position, it would have gained him a great deal of animosity from terrorists. For them, paying taxes was nothing other than giving tribute to a false god, the Roman emperor.

Nor would Jesus agree with the Zealot mentality that Yahweh is a

God of vengeance and that violence is a means of carrying out God's will and the means of opening the way for the kingdom. Jesus spoke of a God who was a loving, caring, and saving Father. The will of this Father is to be carried out in self-sacrifice and service of others, for this truly is to be a kingdom of peace, justice, and loving intimacy.

It is true that Jesus was crucified because he was perceived as a threat by both the Roman authorities and by the Jewish leaders who collaborated with those authorities. He was chosen to die over another seditionist (Barabbas), and was hung between two men who had been rebels. Yet, as we shall see in much more detail in the chapters on Jesus' trial and on Jesus as Liberator, those who "convicted" Jesus had to lie and even change the charges against him in order to have him executed.

There is no evidence in the gospels or elsewhere that Jesus was accused of violent terrorism, and there is no evidence that he encouraged his followers to act in such a manner. If indeed he had been a leader of terrorists, his apostles and disciples would have been killed along with him. Neither is there any evidence that Jesus had any association with Barabbas or the two men on either side of him at Calvary. If anything, he is portrayed in stark contrast to them, and as effective in bringing one to conversion. As for his disciples carrying weapons, it would seem that these would be nothing other than the normal weapons many carried to defend themselves from the dangers of traveling during those times.

The Sadducees

The Sadducees were the aristocracy in the Jewish society in Jerusalem. They included the chief priests, elders, and lay nobles of the Hebrew community.[36] These were the patrician families who controlled the Temple as well as much of the land in Judea and Galilee. In many ways they were like today's wealthy families in Central and South America (as well as in South Africa and in other countries throughout the world) who control the wealth and live off the labors of the underclasses and minorities.

The Sadducees looked upon themselves as the guardians of the Hebrew tradition, holding absolutely and literally to the Torah and with no acceptance of the oral interpretation of the laws. In fact they resented the scholarship of the scribes and Pharisees, the latitude of their interpretations, and how the Pharisees were followed so loyally by the common masses. Josephus describes them as heartless individuals who strictly followed the letter of the law and imposed harsh sanctions on those who disobeyed the laws of the Torah.

In practice, the Sadducees seem to have been secular in their approach to religion. Justifying their own wealth, opulence, and material success in the here and now, they rejected the resurrection of the dead as not justified in Scripture. Nor did they believe in angels or devils, divine providence, or any clear messianic beliefs. They resented any modernization of Jewish teaching and any intrusion of lay points of view in their priestly perspective.

The Sadducees were politically conservative and pragmatic. They held that collaboration with the Romans was the best way to keep the system stable and to protect the great wealth and power over which they had control. The high priest of the Temple, who was appointed from among their midst, was named by the Romans and thus was under the control of the imperial authority.

The Sanhedrin, the highest political and religious body in Judaism, was for the most part under the control of the Sadducees, largely because their representative high priest served as head of the Sanhedrin. Other ordained members, among them some Pharisees, were on the Sanhedrin and could at times vie for power, but they were generally no match for the more wealthy and politically powerful Sadducees. Still, the Pharisees had the support of the common people, and this made the Sadducees cautious and wary of offending the Pharisees.

Jesus and the Sadducees

Jesus stands more in contrast to the Sadducees than he does perhaps to any other group of his time. Jesus was not an aristocrat with great power or wealth. He was a working man from Galilee who placed little value on material wealth and even warned that riches could be a serious hindrance to entering the kingdom. He was not a priest, but a layman, and yet he spoke with a personal authority on religious matters concerning the Torah as well as the oral tradition that was so vehemently rejected by the Sadducees. He even took it upon himself to make priests and levites look bad in the story where they pass by the beaten and robbed man and are surpassed by the mercy and compassion of the hated Samaritan. Jesus was openly critical of the religious hypocrisy and corruption that he saw among the religious leaders. His liberal interpretations of the Sabbath and purification laws must have also alienated the Sadducees.

Just as the Sadducees resented the Pharisees' following among the common folk, they similarly must have been threatened by the popular response Jesus often received from the masses. No doubt his befriending of sinners, the poor, the disabled, and others whom the Sadducees viewed as unclean must have intensified their hatred for Jesus.[37]

There were many other reasons why the Sadducees were unhappy with Jesus, including his emphasis on the afterlife, his open struggle with the powers of evil, his deep faith in Providence, and his messianic and prophetic emphases. Who did this Galilean think he was, criticizing and lecturing the priestly aristocrats from Judea? It is not difficult to understand why Jesus had deadly enemies among the Sadducees of Jerusalem. They had many more reasons to see him done away with than did the Pharisees of the time. The Sadducees are the most visible group in the gospel accounts of Jesus being brought before Pilate.

The Scribes

During the time of Jesus the scribes were the intellectuals and scholars, the "theologians" of the community.[38] The scribes did not make up an official "party" of their own among the Jews. Most of them belonged to the Pharisee sect and a good number of them were priests. The scribes viewed themselves as successors to the prophets, and they served as master teachers, gathering students around them in order to pass on the secret and esoteric knowledge they had gained from their years of study. Their students sat in awe of the scribes as they expounded on quotations from the law and the interpretations of the outstanding elders and scribes. They were also venerated in the communities of Pharisees in which they lived. They would proudly walk through the streets in the long scribe's robe; as they passed by, people would rise and greet them with titles of "Father," "Rabbi," and "Master." Crowds would often follow them, venerating them with superstition and awe, and clamoring to hear their teachings on the law. And when the scribes appeared at synagogue or at a feast, they were given the highest places of honor.

It was not easy to become a scribe. One had to study for several years under a master from whom one would learn the theory and practice of Jewish law. Upon completion of studies, the student would be ordained as a scholar and would now be eligible to both create and teach the oral tradition. This oral tradition, according to the pharisaic tradition, was equal to the Torah. The scribes were also eligible to be on the Sanhedrin along with the Sadducees and the chief priests. (It would seem from this that the Pharisees on the Sanhedrin who opposed Jesus were, in fact, scribes.)

Jesus and the Scribes

Jesus differed from the scribes in many ways. As with the Sadducees, it is understandable why he generated so much resentment and hatred from some of them. Jesus of Nazareth did not belong to any sect or party, apparently did not sit at the feet of any of the famous scholars, and had never been an official scholar or priest. Yet, from the scribal perspective, he had the "audacity" to gather students about him, both women and men, and to teach them—and the lowly masses as well. In addition, his teachings were not generally the standard quotations of the elders or the latest scribal interpretations of the law, but were often his own commentary on the Torah. And when he did use some of the current interpretations, he felt free to interject his own teaching on the matter. The scribes must have thought, "Where are this carpenter's credentials and how dare he teach with such authority?"

It also must have infuriated some of the scribes that Jesus had his own untraditional way of relating to his disciples. He related to them as friends, not as servants. And rather than teaching his disciples to lord it over others in the manner of the scribes, Jesus taught them a spirit of humility and service.

More fuel was undoubtedly added to the scribes' fires of wrath when Jesus criticized them for their pride, their desire for highest places in synagogue and at feasts, and their hypocritical behavior. While Jesus granted that the scribes did have the "authority of Moses," at the same time he pointed out that they were too strict in their interpretation of the law, excessively heavy-handed in the way they dealt with people, and both close-minded and exclusive when they spoke of who would enter the kingdom of heaven. No doubt further fury was aroused when the scribes heard Jesus speak of himself in prophetic or messianic tones, and when he was addressed with the titles of master and rabbi, which they felt should be applied only to them. They also were scandalized by how Jesus freely forgave sins, acted liberally with regard to the scribal laws of Sabbath and purification, and openly befriended outcasts and sinners.

The animosity of the scribes comes out in the gospel stories. They slander Jesus and attempt to trick him in debate. They were among those in the arresting party at Gethsemane, and in the group who presented Jesus to Caiaphas for judgment. Scribes accused Jesus before Herod, mocked Jesus before he died, and later persecuted his followers (Mark 14:53; 15:31; Matthew 26:57; 27:41).

It should be noted, however, that not all the scribes were hostile toward Jesus. In the gospels, one scribe addresses Jesus as "Teacher" and offered to follow him as a disciple. Another admires Jesus' answers to the Sadducees who tried to ridicule his teaching on afterlife with a question about a woman who had been married seven times. Jesus commends the scribe for his insights and then says that the scribe is "not far from the kingdom of God." These and other stories would indicate an underlying tradition that while Jesus had deadly enemies among the scribes, some of them were his admirers.

The Pharisees

It is unfortunate that the Pharisees have had such a bad reputation over the centuries. The standard dictionary definition of "pharisee" is that of a hypocritical, self-righteous person. This negative image is derived largely from the gospels, where the Pharisees are described as "blind guides," "frauds," "white sepulchers," and even as those doing the work of the devil. Yet Christians were not their only critics. Even the later rabbinic literature presents a disparaging picture of the Pharisees, putting them into seven categories and praising only the last type. Some are described as those who parade their good deeds, others as those who cower in the face of an avenging God, or walk with face down with a false humility. Some are described as being so foolish in their attitude toward women that they would prefer to walk into walls rather than stare after a woman.[39]

There is a growing consensus among scholars today that, while Jesus did have enemies among some of the Pharisees, the types who are attacked in the gospels seem to be those who ruled Judaism and persecuted the Christians after the destruction of Jerusalem in 70 C.E. The Jewish state was all but destroyed during this period, and the Temple, the Sanhedrin, and all the significant parties and sects with the exception of the Pharisees were wiped out. At that time the Pharisees became much more politicized than they were during the time of Jesus, and they persecuted Christians for their betrayal of the Torah and for supposedly bringing the Romans down upon Judaism through their messianism and their following of Jesus as Savior. As a result, the gospel of Matthew portrays Jesus as condemning all the Pharisees as hypocrites. In fact, this seems to be an attack on the Pharisees of a later period.[40]

Of all the religious types who surrounded Jesus, it is possible that the Pharisees bore considerable influence on him.[41] The Pharisees who did come into conflict with Jesus were most likely the extremists among them, especially those who were also scribes. While saying all this, we must admit it is difficult to get a clear picture of the Pharisees during the time of Jesus. Most of the information that we have on them is from later rabbinic literature, and even here there is not a consistent picture.

The word "Pharisee" is derived from the Hebrew word *perushim*, which means "the separated ones." This has been commonly interpreted to mean that the Pharisees kept themselves aloof from others. On the contrary, the Pharisees of Jesus' time seem to be the party of the common people and generally had the support of the masses. Their separatism was actually more associated with how they historically set themselves aside from the high priests and Sadducees, both religiously and politically. Unlike the high priests and Sadducees, the Pharisees held for the validity of the oral law in addition to the Torah. In contrast to the Sadducees and scribes, who were rigid legalists, many of the Pharisees had learned a flexibility during periods of exile and domination and were willing to adapt Jewish law to other cultures and to modern developments.[42] Indeed, they were hardly the inflexible legalists they are often made out to be. They held that life experience was also a source of revelation and were, therefore, willing to accommodate themselves to history and changing circumstances.[43]

The Pharisees varied in their degree of political influence throughout their history. At times they were advisors to the ruler. During Herod the Great's reign they were held in great favor until just before his death, when he broke with them over intrigues within the court. It seems that few of the Pharisees had much political involvement during Jesus' time. Although the common people whom they represented were under the domination of the empire, there was still considerable religious freedom for the Jews. The Pharisees did not tend to get politically involved unless the practice of the Torah was actually threatened.

The Pharisees seem to have disagreed among themselves on how to deal with Roman domination. Some felt that subjugation was indeed a punishment for sin that had to be endured until repentance and fidelity to the law would restore freedom. Others felt that all foreign domination was against the will of God, and they strongly opposed the collaboration of the Sadducees. Most did not concede to the violent approach of the Zealot mentality, nor did any of them agree with the withdrawal approach of the Essenes. Many of the Pharisees during Jesus' time proposed to redefine the covenant and design a way of following the law that would restore harmony and freedom.[44]

The pharisaic perspective prevailed among the masses of the Jews. In order to shift power from the priestly class in the Temple, the Pharisees had promoted the system of synagogues throughout Palestine. The synagogue was set up as an alternative house of prayer and study, as well as a center for the works of mercy. The Pharisees established themselves in closed communities wherein some members were priests and some were scribes. Through the latter individuals, they were able to keep their influence in the Jerusalem Temple and Sanhedrin, while through the synagogues they were able to deeply influence and keep the sympathy of the common lay people, especially through their projects for charitable care of the needy.

After the destruction of the Temple in 70 C.E., this structure of synagogues prevailed, and priesthood was replaced by the rabbinic model. The home, with the father of the family presiding, became the main setting for Sabbath celebration, and the Pharisees firmly established themselves as the main authority in charge of Jewish practice.

While the Pharisees of Jesus' era lived within closed communities, they stayed close to the people, and in this they differed from isolated groups such as the Essenes. Their table fellowship apparently was open to someone like a rural preacher from Galilee, as is evidenced by Jesus' presence at Simon's house for a meal. Many of the Pharisees were simple men without formal learning who had to support themselves by working a trade; they could easily relate to someone like Jesus of Nazareth.[45] It should be noted that it was a Pharisee who warned Jesus of the dangers from Herod, and another, Nicodemus, who came to learn from Jesus.

While the scribes among them were scholars, most of the Pharisees saw themselves as practitioners of the written and oral tradition. Many of them personalized the relationship with the divine, referred to Yahweh as Father, and, in the spirit of the prophets, opted to serve the poor and the oppressed. Many of them lived a simple lifestyle, saw the importance of conversion of heart, and viewed acts of both love and justice as a higher experience of religion than the priestly cult in the Temple.[46] All this is a far cry from the common stereotype of the Pharisee.

Jesus and the Pharisees

Jesus had much in common with the Pharisees. Like most of them he was a layman who had to work with his hands to support himself. He also valued simplicity of lifestyle, community, and identification with and service to the poor. He also seems to come out of the tradition of synagogue rather than Temple and the priestly cult. He found himself "separated" religiously and socially from the priestly and aristocratic caste, and was apparently little interested in political power.

Still, Jesus' position differs significantly in some key areas. While he opted for the oral tradition, he seemed often to bypass the scribal interpretations of this tradition and was free to authoritatively teach his own perspective. And while Jesus displayed the pharisaic flexibility and adaptability with regard to the law, even the most open Pharisees might have had difficulty with his liberal views on Sabbath observance and ritual purity. Moreover, his sense of community and table fellowship went considerably beyond that of the Pharisees and was open to women, outcasts, and even sinners. The story of the sinful woman showing up while Jesus was dining at Simon the Pharisee's table is certainly a moving example of how Jesus was uniquely free in his associations with others.

Jesus went beyond the Pharisees' personalization of the covenant with the Father. He referred intimately to Yahweh as Abba, taking the radical position that God loved not only the righteous, but also sinners who had not yet repented.[47] He taught of a God who willed wholeness, not of a God who would send disease and disability as punishment for sin. In addition, Jesus himself claimed to actually bring this divine power of healing into the lives of many. He extended the love of God universally to all, Jew and Gentile, and radically commanded his disciples to love all, even their enemies.

Jesus also went beyond the Pharisees in his emphasis on the nearness of the kingdom of God, and he taught that God's action of forgiveness was actually available independently of the observance of the Torah and scribal law. And where the Pharisees gave the Torah and the oral tradition a central place and used parables as examples, Jesus made the parables containing his oral tradition the very core of his teaching. Ultimately, Jesus' teaching would replace the Torah and the scribal tradition. This explains the eventual break and hostility between the Christian community and the Pharisees. It is this later hostility that seems to come through in the gospels and is responsible for the horrible reputation that has been given to the Pharisees for thousands of years.

It is time to eliminate the stereotypes that we have of the Pharisees as portrayed in the gospels. Christians must come to realize that much of the negative view of Pharisaism is derived from later clashes between the early church and the Pharisees of that time. Though Jesus seems to have had clashes with some Pharisees, his views are often close to theirs. In fact, at its best, the pharisaic tradition of Judaism represents one of the finest interpretations of Hebrew living.

Summary
Jesus of Nazareth was a man of his time, a Jew who grew up in Palestine during the difficult times of occupation by the Roman Empire. As a Jew he seems to have shared in the devotion and fidelity of his people to Yahweh and the Hebrew tradition. At the same time, he was probably deeply affected by the oppression, unrest, and periodic rebellion in

his native province of Galilee. The small village of Nazareth where he was raised, the surrounding towns and cities where he perhaps went to find work as a craftsman, the big city of Jerusalem with its great market and magnificent Temple, all played their role in his formation.

Though he seems to have had some things in common with all the typical individuals of his time, including the Essenes, radicals of the Zealot movement, Sadducees, scribes, and Pharisees, Jesus stands uniquely on his own, in one sense beyond comparison, and yet deeply rooted in and related to his culture and religion.

Questions for Reflection and Discussion

1. During Jesus' time Galileans had a unique image. How might Jesus of Nazareth have measured up to this image of the Galilean?

2. In what significant ways might growing up in Nazareth have affected the young Jesus?

3. Compare and contrast Jesus with the Essenes, scribes, Sadducees, and Pharisees of his day.

4. Do you think Jesus would have shared some of the views of those in the Zealot movement? In what ways would he have differed from them?

CHAPTER TWO

The Jesus of History

Christians have had an enduring curiosity to discover Jesus as he was two thousand years ago in Palestine. There has always been a drive to reach beneath the myth, the doctrines, and the theology to find the Jesus who walked along the dusty roads of Galilee or sat at table in Bethany. Scholars have studied the Scriptures and other manuscripts of the time, archaeologists have dug beneath the earth into times past, and many have searched their imaginations and their souls to try to come to a deeper understanding of this man's identity.

There is surprisingly little factual information to go on. We don't have any statues or drawings of Jesus, so we really do not know what he looked like. We know nothing for certain about the first thirty years of his life, and we are really not sure how long his public ministry lasted. Even the gospels differ on this, with the synoptics describing it as one year and the gospel of John giving an account of three years. We have no written words of Jesus, and we have very few of his exact spoken words.

We do know that Jesus was a Jew, that he was born during the reign of Caesar Augustus around 4 B.C.E., and that he grew up in Nazareth in Galilee, the northern province of Palestine. His parents were known to be Mary and Joseph, and the latter worked as a carpenter, a trade he most likely passed on to his son.

In his public life Jesus was known as an itinerant preacher who spoke about the reign of God and called people to conversion of heart.

He was also known to be a miracle worker, an exorcist, and one who befriended the marginal and outcast in society. Somehow his teaching and behavior became controversial and alienated some of the religious and political leaders of his time. He was arrested in Jerusalem and was crucified outside the city. After his death, his followers, many of whom he had chosen himself, began to experience him as raised from the dead, and they started a movement that came to be known first as the Way, and then as Christianity.

Our primary sources for information on Jesus are the gospels that were written by his followers. There are a few outside sources, such as the Roman historians Pliny the Younger, Tacitus, and Suetonius, as well as the Jewish historians Josephus and Philo. These sources, however, tell us little other than that Jesus existed and had followers. There are some elaborations on the religious identity of Jesus in Josephus, but these are thought to be later additions by Christian editors.[1] Therefore, if we are to discover any real insight into the so-called historical Jesus, we have to rely on the four gospels that were written by his followers decades after his death.

In this chapter we will be discussing some of the different approaches to the gospels and how these affect attitudes toward the Jesus of history. Reasons will be proposed for placing value on the historical Jesus, and then a composite portrait of Jesus will be drawn from the work of modern biblical critics.

Literalist Approach

Those who interpret the Scriptures literally generally have certain basic assumptions about the gospels. The first assumption is that the gospels were written by eyewitnesses (the apostles Matthew and John) or those who had access to such accounts (Mark, an associate of Peter, and Luke, a companion to Paul). Thus, what we have in the gospels are exact historical accounts of what Jesus said and did.[2] The quotations of Jesus are considered to be verbatim and are shown in red in some bibles to set them off from the rest of the text.

Those who have approached the gospels in this fundamentalist fashion have usually assumed that the gospels were all written independently. Therefore, the gospels can be used to corroborate each other, and any discrepancies can be overcome by merely putting the varying accounts together in what is known as a "harmony." Efforts to harmonize the gospels in this fashion were made as early as the second century by Tatian and later church fathers.

This literalist perspective makes no distinction between the Jesus of

history and the Christ of faith. It is assumed that the Jesus who is portrayed in the gospels as the messiah, the Son of God, and the Savior, is
the Jesus who was experienced by his disciples during their time with
him in Palestine.

From this perspective, then, the gospels are divinely inspired and literally accurate accounts of everything that Jesus said and did during
his life. The accounts of his birth, miracles, death, and resurrection are
to be accepted exactly as they are told in the divinely inspired accounts
of eyewitnesses. This perspective accepts the gospels as biographies of
Jesus that give us clear and factual information about what Jesus said
and did.

Historical-Critical Method

The modern scientific approach to the Scriptures dates back to the seventeenth century, and it has radically affected the way many Christians
view the gospels accounts of what Jesus said and did. The method is
called historical-critical because it places the Scriptures in their historical context and uses the critical tools of scholarship to study these writings.

The Reformation prepared the way for this movement by shifting
priority from tradition to Scripture and by making it possible to interpret Scripture independently of the teachings of the church. But it was
the Enlightenment with its emphasis on reason, research, and scientific
analysis that gave the most impetus to biblical criticism. Once scientific
scrutiny was turned on all levels of knowledge, it was inevitable that
such probing would eventually be applied to the Christian gospels.

As a movement, biblical criticism seems to find its beginnings in the
work of a French priest, R. Simon (1638–1712), who challenged Moses'
authorship of the Pentateuch (the first five books of the Hebrew Scriptures), and who was the first to apply a critical method to the Christian
Scriptures. The biblical movement really began to flourish in the nineteenth century, especially in Germany where there was an intense interest in linguistics, in the history of religions, and in examining the vast
amount of new knowledge that was uncovered in the Middle East
following French and British conquests there.[3]

As with any scientific movement, discoveries and insights came
slowly and in gradual stages. Some of the earliest biblical critics proposed that the gospels are not eyewitness accounts of Jesus' words and
deeds, but are, rather, later doctrinal statements of the beliefs of the
first Christian communities. Scholars from the Protestant camp, such as
F.C. Baur (1792–1860) and David Strauss (1808–1874) who were often

perceived to be rationalists, regarded the doctrinal material as later distortions and attempted to peel it away in an effort to discover the real
Jesus. It was at this point that the first wedge was driven between the
Jesus of history and the Christ of faith. From then until the present day
that distinction has been one of the most basic issues in biblical studies.

Before we go on to examine how this issue of the historical Jesus has
been dealt with in biblical research, we will first look at some of the
more specific approaches taken in studying the Bible. Each of these
approaches in its own way affects the way the Jesus of history is understood.[4]

Source Criticism

Major breakthroughs were made in nineteenth-century biblical scholarship by those associated with source criticism. These scholars challenged
the traditional views that the gospels were written independently by
eyewitnesses. Instead, they asserted that the gospels were later documents that had their origin in the early Christian communities.

Linguistic and literary analysis showed that the gospels were influenced by a number of other sources, including Greek, Hebrew, and
Aramaic religious thought. It was eventually discovered that the gospel
of Mark was written first and provided a source for the authors of both
Matthew and Luke.

Another source also was found to be operative in the gospels.
Though the manuscript itself has not been found, it was evident that a
source designated as "Q" (for the German word for source, *Quelle*) was
widely used by gospel writers. This source, in fact, seemed to be a collection of "sayings of Jesus."

Other sources for the gospel material came to light as these scholars
came to know more about the religious and cultural background of
Jesus' time. It was becoming evident that the gospels were highly complicated literary and theological statements written decades after Jesus
had lived, and that the gospels were not biographical accounts of what
Jesus said and did. One could not count on the gospels as such for a life
of Jesus of Nazareth.[5]

Form Criticism

Source criticism's main contribution to biblical studies was the discovery that the gospels were, in fact, literary creations by authors who
were using other written sources (the authors of Matthew and Luke
were using Mark and "Q" as their sources). Form criticism took the biblical movement one step further when it proposed that still earlier

Approaches to Biblical Criticism

	Focus	Goal
Source Criticism	the origins of biblical materials	rediscover the original authors, as well as the composition of the texts
Form Criticism	the literary "forms" used by the biblical writers	uncover the message that is conveyed by the forms
Redaction Criticism	the arranging and editing of the traditional material	study the theological motivations of the authors
The Literary Method	the biblical text as a literary genre	locate the meaning that is in the text itself, or is then generated in in the reading
The Liberation Approach	themes of justice and peace	inspire Christians to resist oppression and struggle for freedom
The Feminist Perspective	patriarchal themes as well as themes on equality and liberation	critique sexual oppression and restore Jesus' inclusive perspective

sources were evident in the gospels: the oral stories that were passed around in early Christian communities.

Form critics asserted that the gospels are disconnected collections of anecdotes about Jesus that were circulated orally among the early Christians. The stories appear in the gospels in certain literary "forms," and it is the task of the form critic to analyze these forms and, thereby, be able to explore the religious beliefs and needs of the early Christians.

Especially in its earlier days, form criticism held that most of the gospel stories and sayings were largely unhistorical. If this be true, one could not expect to discover much about the Jesus of history from these largely fictional accounts in the gospels.

Rudolph Bultmann (who will be discussed in more detail later in this chapter) became the major leader of form criticism. Bultmann maintained, especially in his earlier work, that little or nothing could be learned about the historical Jesus. For him, the gospel "kerygma," or proclaimed message, was of central concern, not Jesus of Nazareth. The thrust of Bultmann's work was to "de-mythologize" the gospels, that is, lift away the outmoded myths that carried the message in the past, and provide contemporary language whereby the people of today might hear God's Word. From this perspective, it appeared futile to attempt to discover Jesus as he was.[6]

Redaction Criticism

The form critics tended to view the gospel writers as collectors and organizers of earlier oral stories. Those who approach the gospels through redaction criticism view the gospel writers as creative authors in their own right, authors who left their own literary and theological mark on the material at hand. The focus here is not on analyzing literary forms, but on closely studying how the gospel writers edited (redacted) their sources. A study of this "editing" process can reveal the unique theological concerns of these authors and of their communities. It is also possible to dig deeply beneath the editings to find original material, some of it going back to the person of Jesus himself. It is this school of biblical criticism, more than others, that has opened new paths for searching for Jesus' own words and deeds.[7]

Other Approaches to the Gospels

The critical approaches mentioned so far are the most prominent, but there are additional methods that also have had an impact on the search for Jesus as he was. Canonical criticism receives its name from the "canon" of the Scriptures—the collection of sacred writings that is officially recognized as authentic. It is now accepted that there are a number of other "gospels" and fragments of gospels that never found their way into the collection we call the New Testament. Canonical critics study the criteria used in the early centuries for officially including or excluding certain documents.[8] These criteria, as well as the ultimate decisions made in compiling the New Testament, can tell us a great deal about the beliefs the earlier Christians held to be authentic or inauthentic. Such insights have obvious importance in helping us come to an understanding of what Jesus actually said and did.

The literary method of studying the Scriptures also offers some valuable insights. This method does not place as much importance on sources, forms, or editings as the other methods do. Instead, it is most concerned with *meaning*, either as it is in the text itself or as it "happens" in the reader.

Advocates of New Criticism, which originated in Britain and the United States in the 1940s, focus on objective meaning. Such meaning is best discovered in all literature (and, in this case, in Scripture) through a close study and explication of the text itself.[9] Another group, called literary structuralists, maintains that the genuine meaning of a text is produced as the reader encounters the deep structures of meaning within the writing. Both of these approaches have gained popularity among those who wish to find the reality of Jesus and his message without caring to first master the complicated tools of the historical-critical approach to Scripture.

Finally, three other approaches to the gospels are making radically new contributions to the study of Jesus. Sociologists and anthropologists are uncovering new and interesting information about both Jesus' time and the periods in which the gospels were written. This material has put aside many former misconceptions about these periods and has helped us to develop a more accurate understanding of Jesus' own religious and cultural experience, as well as the background against which the gospels themselves were written.[10] For example, we saw in chapter one that the Pharisees who are excoriated in the gospels are really of a later period than those whom Jesus would have known.

Another approach to the gospels, one that will have radical religious and political implications for some time to come, is that of the liberation theologians. These theologians have given unique significance to Jesus as he is known and experienced in the reading of the gospels by the poor and the oppressed. Moreover, it is their conviction that the historical Jesus in the gospels was committed to freedom and justice for the marginalized.

Related to this liberation school is the growing number of women biblical scholars who have brought to light Jesus' radical views on the liberation of women, and who wish to retrieve this authentic material while at the same time revealing how male dominance and patriarchal structures both past and present have suppressed Jesus' teachings on freedom and equality. We will be discussing this perspective in detail in a later chapter.

Approaches to the Historical Jesus

There have been a number of trends in the modern search for the historical Jesus. Here we will deal with four of the most significant: 1) the Catholic "Lives of Jesus"; 2) the rationalistic approach; 3) those who diminish the importance of the historical Jesus; and 4) the renewed interest in giving significance to the Jesus of history.

The Catholic "Lives of Jesus"

The lives of Jesus that were written by Catholic authors during the late 1940s and 1950s are examples of literalist efforts to portray Jesus. They were written long after biblical criticism began, and even after Catholic scholars were permitted to approach the gospels critically, yet they were done under the assumption that one could assemble a life of Christ by merely putting the four gospels into harmony. The title itself, "Life of Christ," is indicative of how the authors made no distinction between later Christological faith and the historical person of Jesus of Nazareth.

The most well-known authors of the "Lives," Fulton Oursler, Ferdinand Prat, Giuseppe Ricciotti, and Fulton J. Sheen were all men deeply devoted to Jesus Christ and to their Catholic tradition.[11] Their books are written with great devotion and creativity and have given inspiration to many. Yet these lives are based on an older assumption that Jesus, fully understanding himself as the Christ and recognized as such by his followers, carried out his ministry on earth. These authors sincerely set out to write a sequential biography of Jesus Christ. It would seem that they also believed that, with imagination and creativity, they could at the same time recreate the inner thoughts and feelings of Jesus.

While these lives are inspiring efforts, they are based on assumptions that are no longer accepted by biblical critics. The authors of these lives paid little attention to the actual Jesus who lived a fully human life two thousand years ago. Instead, they projected Christ as he is understood in doctrinal tradition and faith back into the time when Jesus lived. Given current biblical scholarship, it is unlikely that such a life of Christ will ever be attempted again by a Catholic scholar.[12]

Rationalistic Approach

The so-called search for the historical Jesus was given impetus by the appearance of a highly inflammatory work by H.S. Reimarus (1694–1768). In his "Fragments," a work that was published posthumously, Reimarus was the first to distinguish between the Jesus of history and the Christ preached by the early church. In modern times this has become a useful way of distinguishing between Jesus as he existed on earth as a flesh and blood person and Jesus as he was later perceived in faith as the Christ.

Reimarus's views on Jesus and the Christ shocked the readers of the time. He maintained that Jesus was, in fact, nothing other that a deluded failure and that the "Christ" notion was a fraudulent scheme on the part of the first disciples.[13] Reimarus approached the gospels with two assumptions. As a rationalist, he could not accept the supernatural as a reality. Therefore, he had to find a way of explaining away the stories of the supernatural in the gospels. In addition, Reimarus rejected the traditional doctrines about Jesus Christ, and so had to find a way to discredit these beliefs. His solution was this: Jesus was a man who aspired to be a Jewish revolutionary and to found a political kingdom.[14] In fact, he was a dismal failure at this, was arrested and crucified, and died crying out in despair and anger. The Christ tradition was then started by Jesus' followers, who stole the body and made up the stories of the resurrection and the second coming in order to get a following. The stories of the supernatural in the gospels, said Reimarus, were nothing other than fraudulent fabrications of the early followers of a confessed failure.[15]

These theories created a considerable uproar, and resulted in numerous attempts on the part of scholars to reconstruct the historical Jesus and counteract Reimarus's "repulsive caricature." Scholars such as Strauss (d. 1874), Renan (d. 1892), Harnack (d. 1930), and many others attempted to write lives of Jesus. The method was generally similar: strip away the dogmatic teachings about Jesus by the early church and, with what is left, attempt to assemble a portrait of Jesus as he really was.

Because biblical criticism was still in its early stages, the scholars were not very successful in their search. First of all, they were assuming that the gospel of Mark was the historical account of Jesus' words and deeds, and thus they based their portrait and sequence largely on that gospel. This presumption prevailed until 1901 when W. Wrede (1859–1906) demonstrated that Mark's gospel was a highly theological interpretation of Jesus and his mission.

It was the great German musician, theologian, and medical missionary Albert Schweitzer (1875–1965) who combined Wrede's discovery with insights of his own to expose the futility of writing a life of Jesus from the gospels.[16] He pointed out that besides mistakenly accepting Mark's account as historical, the nineteenth-century "searchers" had brought their own assumptions and prejudices to their work. They had, in fact, "projected" themselves and their perspectives back into the gospel times and made Jesus into a nineteenth-century teacher of ethics, or social worker, or even German philosopher.

After saying all this, however, Schweitzer attempted to draw his own portrait of Jesus. Rather than use the ideals of the time, he used the concept that he believed was central to Jesus' mission: the anticipation of the apocalypse. He portrayed Jesus as a heroic but deluded preacher proclaiming the last days. When Jesus discovered he was mistaken in his predictions, he went to his death hoping that this act would somehow bring about the coming of the kingdom.

Schweitzer had put his finger on the reason for the failure of liberal Protestantism to reconstruct the historical Jesus. His cogent arguments, as well as his own futile attempt to portray Jesus, discouraged scholars from the "search" for some time to come.

De-Emphasizing the Historical Jesus

We have looked at the interest shown in Jesus by Catholics who wrote lives of Christ and by liberal Protestants who wrote lives of Jesus. Now we will discuss three scholars who exemplify those who do not place a value on the Jesus of history: David Strauss, a nineteenth-century Protestant biblicist, Rudolf Bultmann (d. 1976), broadly recognized as the most influential Protestant biblical critic of this century, and David Tracy, a renowned contemporary Catholic theologian. These men vary broadly in their approach to the question, but they are similar in their lack of interest in the significance of the historical Jesus. These three scholars have had significant influence, and they help us see how widely nuanced the approach to the historical Jesus has been.

David Strauss   Like so many other biblical scholars of the nineteenth century, Strauss felt compelled to write a life of Jesus. He was not satisfied with the rationalists' approach, which discarded the supernatural stories as irrelevant, and yet neither was he agreeable to accepting the doctrines on Christ found in the gospels. Following Hegel's method of deriving synthesis from extremes, Strauss attempted a synthesis here by explaining the supernatural stories in terms of myth and by portraying Jesus as a preacher of little significance. As a Scripture scholar, Strauss was able to discover a certain historical core in the gospels. He was even able to grant that some of the miracles were historical, but he was unable to accept a supernatural explanation and explained them instead in terms of parapsychology.

Strauss argued that the heart of the gospel was an *idea*: that the divine and human are joined in reality. Jesus was only important because he symbolized that idea. And the gospels are substantially myths about his miraculous birth, deeds, and resurrection composed by the early communities to promote this idea of divine-human unity. For Strauss, Christian faith was not based on a person, but on a philosophical concept. Jesus of Nazareth has little significance in himself other than in being a symbol of this concept.

Strauss came under attack from all sides for his position. He was dismissed from his university post and was never again able to hold an active academic position. For a brief time he conceded that Jesus was a great genius of lasting significance, but his final conclusion seems to have been that Jesus of Nazareth was an insignificant preacher who embodied the great concept of the unity of the human and the divine.[17]

Rudolf Bultmann Bultmann has been extremely influential for both Catholic and Protestant scholars on the question of the importance of the historical Jesus.[18] As we have already noted, Bultmann was one of the architects of form criticism. He maintained that the gospels are largely made up of disconnected anecdotes (forms) and that these forms—rather than the historical content of the words and deeds of Jesus—carry the Christian faith message. Bultmann, at least in his earlier work, argued that it is not possible to determine what is and is not authentic historical material in the myth of gospel writing. But this didn't concern Bultmann because he was much more preoccupied with the kerygma (the Christian message that is witnessed) than he was with the historical Jesus. For Bultmann, it was sufficient that Jesus existed; that existence provides an adequate historical basis for the kerygma.

Taking his cue from Strauss, Bultmann argued that the early Christian communities developed the myths of the gospels as means of conveying the faith that they had in the message of God that came through Jesus Christ. He departed from Strauss, however, when it came to the core of the message. Bultmann said that the heart of the Christian message is not the unity of the human and the divine, but the teaching on how to live an authentic human life. On this point Bultmann was influenced by the great existential philosopher Martin Heidegger (d. 1976) and his insights on authentic existence. Bultmann argued that authentic existence is a gift from God. One opens oneself to this gift by accepting the Word of God as witnessed in the gospels. The gift, the invitation to faith, is contained in the gospel kerygma.

Bultmann's Lutheran notion of faith allowed him to be indifferent to discovering historical material in the gospels or to reconstructing the Jesus of history. For him, faith seems to be a blind leap, an acceptance of the Word of God without the need for historical knowledge. Faith does not depend on facts or on historical proof, so it becomes irrelevant whether or not we know anything about Jesus, other than that he lived. For the Christian, faith is the acceptance of the gospel message of salvation, acceptance of the kerygma.

Bultmann is known for his advocacy of "de-mythologizing" the gospels. This does not mean, as some of his critics have charged, that Bultmann thought of the gospel stories as fairy tales that should be easily dismissed. On the contrary, Bultmann revered these forms as the means the early church used to witness to their faith.[19] He was skeptical, however, about the historicity of much of the gospel material, because it was so heavily influenced by ancient religions, Gnostic sources, and by the theological needs and insights of the early communities.

In his efforts to de-mythologize, Bultmann did not attempt to debunk the gospel myths, as did so many of the rationalists of the last century. Rather, he saw the need to translate them into contemporary language and concepts so that the people of today might hear the gospel message. At the same time, Bultmann viewed mythology as a "worldly language" that can disguise the transcendence of God's Word. Moving it aside opens the way toward one's reception of the divine gift of an authentic life.[20]

In his later days, Bultmann did concede to the pressure of so many of his followers and accepted that there is a fuller historical core about Jesus in the gospels than he had previously thought. He was, though, prepared to accept more of a historical basis for the words of Jesus than he was for the deeds of Jesus as depicted in the gospels. Yet, even with these concessions, the center of faith for Bultmann was the gospel message, not the person of Jesus Christ. For him, God is not an object of the world and cannot be known through historical facts or even through a historical person.[21]

David Tracy   Tracy's views on the value of the Jesus of history are more carefully nuanced than those of either Strauss or Bultmann. For

Tracy, the primary norm of both faith and theology is not the historical Jesus, but the apostolic witness to Jesus as remembered and proclaimed by the original followers.[22] Tracy does recognize, however, that the Jesus of history is a secondary norm that preserves that which is "subversive" and "dangerous" in the memory of Jesus.[23] The Jesus of history keeps us in touch with this radical dimension of Jesus' message, a dimension that can easily be lost as the tradition develops. In addition, the historical Jesus serves as a reference for the reform and renewal of the tradition. The development of the traditions needs always to be measured against the historical words and deeds of Jesus.

Tracy offers different reasons than Bultmann for not giving the Jesus of history primary significance in faith and theology. Bultmann came from the Lutheran perspective and ruled out any historical or factual basis for faith. On the other hand, Tracy, a Catholic theologian, seems to be willing to accept the reasonableness of faith, but does not view the historical Jesus as sufficiently accessible to serve as a rational basis of faith. In other words, there are many versions of the Jesus of history, and much of what we have is tentative and conjectural at best. Therefore, the Jesus of history is too relative and changeable, too susceptible to new discoveries by historians, theologians, and exegetes to ever be the primary norm for faith or theology. For Tracy, then, faith is not primarily a response to a historical person, but to an event, "the event of Jesus" as witnessed in the past and experienced in the present.

Tracy would not agree with Ogden or those who maintain that the reconstruction of the historical Jesus is impossible; nor would he agree with Bultmann that the historical Jesus is inconsequential to faith. He seems appreciative of the work of exegesis and is willing to grant that a certain amount of historical material is recoverable from the gospels. But Tracy does not want to ground Christology in this historical core. His position seems to be that Jesus of Nazareth is best encountered through his witnesses and in the living tradition. For Tracy, it is the confessed Jesus Christ who is the norm for Christology, and only secondarily Jesus of Nazareth.[24]

It follows from what has been said that Tracy does not go to the gospel stories primarily for historical content. For him these stories first and foremost "disclose" human reality rather than give us the words and deeds of Jesus. What we need are not the facts or the verbatim statements of Jesus. Rather, "we need to know what his words, his deeds, and his destiny, as expressions of his office of messiahship, authentically re-present as real human possibilities of genuine relationship with God. In a word, we need to know the existential meaning and truths re-presented for our present human experience by the Christological affirmations."[25]

Importance of the Historical Jesus

It was Bultmann who led the way among modern biblical scholars to de-emphasize the importance of the Jesus of history. Reactions to his position came from many quarters, however. Some British scholars, while appreciating the critical tools of scholarship given to them by Bultmann, claimed to find much more historical material in the gospels than he did. Some of Bultmann's own students and disciples, led by Ernst Käsemann, eventually launched their own "new quest" for the historical Jesus.

In 1953, Käsemann announced his position that, without the historical Jesus, Christianity could easily become a myth without a history. For him, the Christian faith requires not only the glorified Lord, but also Jesus of Nazareth. Käsemann maintained that, although the early Christians proclaimed a Christ of faith, the gospel writers display considerable interest in the history that lay behind this belief. He offered scholars new critical criteria for reclaiming this historical material and initiated a new era of searching for Jesus as he lived and taught.[26]

The enormous amount of biblical research on Jesus during the latter half of this century has profoundly influenced Catholic theologians.[27] For example, Karl Rahner, recognized by both Protestant and Catholic theologians as one of the most outstanding Christian scholars of this century, maintained that faith is indeed grounded in the historical events in Jesus' life, death, and resurrection. Otherwise, these events become mere objects or myths created *by* faith. Christians, according to Rahner, need a personal Christ who sustains faith, not a Christ who is simply a myth or an idea that has been created by faith. The miracles and the resurrection are not, therefore, events created by faith, but events that are the very foundation of faith.

Early Christian faith, said Rahner, was a new grasping or comprehension of historical events in terms of transcendence. Our faith is linked to the testimony of these original witnesses who after the resurrection were able to truly understand the earlier experiences they had of Jesus of Nazareth. Early Christian faith "was related to a definite historical event, which did not simply posit this event or create it in faith, but rather receives its justification and foundation from this event."[28] Historical knowledge of Jesus, from Rahner's point of view, does not generate faith, but it certainly provides a ground for such faith.

Hans Küng, another highly influential contemporary theologian, points out the historical limitations of the gospels. He is fully aware that the gospels are primarily testimonies of faith rather than historical accounts. These gospels ask us to believe and be saved, not to investigate the facts of what really happened during the time of Jesus. At the same time, these faith accounts are based on real memories of what Jesus said and did. In the gospels we hear the still living memories of Jesus' teachings and actions, now reflected upon in faith. The early Christians did not arbitrarily invent Jesus' words and deeds. They were, in faith, "convinced that they now know better than in Jesus' lifetime who he really was and what he really signified."[29]

Küng argues that the early Christians felt free to attribute everything that had to be said about him in faith to Jesus himself, even to the point where they would create "sayings" and stories that would reflect their faith. But in all of this they were being faithful to the original experience they had of Jesus of Nazareth. Beneath the stories and sayings there is authentic historical experience that can at least in part be reconstructed through biblical criticism. There is a continuity between what was preached and what really happened.

Küng does not say, however, that this historical material provides a reason for faith. He does say that history helps us take stock of our tradition, maintain our faith concretely, and share it with others. And though our primary concern is how Jesus meets and challenges us here and now, we remain also linked to Jesus as he was in actual life.

Edward Schillebeeckx, who has written the most extensive Catholic account of Jesus Christ in modern times, is deeply concerned about the value of the Jesus of history. It is his position that, when the early Christians speak in their language of faith in Christ, they are at the same time referring to the memory of Jesus of Nazareth. The magnificent images and titles that they attribute to Jesus are in the light of both past and present experiences.

For Schillebeeckx, the "matrix" of the gospels is both the firsthand experience of the followers of Jesus as well as the continuing fellowship that was being experienced with his Spirit. Consequently, all faith articulations about Christ, whether they be by councils, theologians, or the faithful, must somehow be based on the original memories of Jesus of Nazareth.[30]

Schillebeeckx has a profound regard for modern biblical criticism and uses its findings as a basis for his own Christology. He cautions, however, that in our search for the Jesus of history we should not attempt to find some "neat" core of historical material that is untouched by dogma. At the same time, if the dogmatic tradition of the church is set aside, as was done by the nineteenth-century rationalists, we are left with a kind of vague phantom-like Jesus. The Jesus of the gospels is always Jesus confessed as the Christ.[31] Jesus of Nazareth and Jesus the Christ are one and the same person. The historical material is important for Schillebeeckx, and he holds that a significant portion of it is recoverable. But it should never be separated from the tradition of the community.

The driving message behind Schillebeeckx's theology of Jesus seems to be that Christian faith is not a commitment to an ideology or even to a faith message, but to a person, the person of Jesus Christ. This faith commitment is made to the glorified Jesus of today, but it is also linked to the Christ event of the early communities and to the experience that many had of the earthly Jesus. As Schillebeeckx observes : "... the Christian faith entails not only the personal presence of the glorified Jesus, but also a link with his life on earth; for it is precisely that earthly life that has been acknowledged and empowered by God through the resurrection."[32]

Key Reasons for Stressing the Jesus of History

One of the underlying assumptions in this book is that a great deal of historical material about Jesus as he was can be recovered both through biblical study and through research into the social, religious, and political background of his times. In the next chapter we will be looking at the person of Jesus against this background. In other chapters the historical material will play a role in helping us understand Jesus as teacher, prophet, miracle worker, liberator of the oppressed, and risen Savior of the world.

Throughout our discussions it should become more clear how the doctrinal traditions of the church are rooted in history. And because the Jesus of history is the foundation of our study, we need to consider why the historical Jesus is important today. Here are five such reasons.

1. The appeal to the contemporary mentality. Even though we are poised to enter a third millennium, we are still heirs of the Enlightenment and the beginnings of the scientific era. This is an age of science and technology. We value information, a reasoned approach to the solution of problems, and possession of the truth of history. For many today, faith is reflective and analytic, not merely a blind leap into the darkness. Although Christian faith can still be viewed as a gifted invitation to respond to a relationship with God, the response can be made reasonably and reflectively. Many today would resist following Jesus unless they could be reasonably certain about the authenticity of his life and teaching.

This has also been described as an age of personalism, which values intimacy, relationships, and community. Perhaps nineteenth-century rationalists could be satisfied with following an ideology, a message, or even an institution. Many today are more inclined to view faith as following a person who has founded and who is found in a historical community. Many today would not be satisfied with Jesus as a vague phantom of the past; they want to be assured that they are following a real person who lived a fully human life in history.

2. To provide continuity and wholeness to our understanding of Jesus Christ. Biblical scholars and theologians have made so many distinctions about Jesus that one might get the impression that we are dealing with a number of different persons. They speak of the actual Jesus as he lived in Palestine, the historical Jesus as he has been reconstructed by biblical scholars, the post-resurrection Jesus as he was uniquely experienced by a number of his followers, the Christ of faith as he has been described in the doctrines and theology of the community and as he has been worshiped through the centuries, and the Christ of glory who is to come in the final days.

This can all be confusing to the ordinary believer who perhaps wishes to follow Jesus as a friend and personal savior. Without the Jesus of history, a real flesh and blood person like ourselves, the doctrines and titles can well become an ideology. Jesus of Nazareth must be known in order to keep our understanding of Jesus Christ in continuity with reality. It is all of a piece: following Jesus whom we recognize to be the Christ.

3. To provide a basis for myth and doctrine. The myths and doctrines of the gospels can certainly be reduced to mere fairy tales and religious fabrications unless they can somehow be rooted in the words of Jesus himself. The faith of the early church did not begin spontaneously from a vacuum after the resurrection. Post-resurrection faith is a validation of what had been experienced earlier in Jesus of Nazareth. During his life many "believed" in him, trusted him, loved him, and decided to answer his call to conversion and discipleship.

All this was transformed into Christian faith after the resurrection, but it is nonetheless real and historical experience.[33] It was the new light that had been shed on this experience that the early followers were attempting to share first in oral and then in written accounts. Myths are usually bigger than life, and they can become useless unless we keep in touch with the life on which they are based.

4. To keep us in touch with the uniqueness of Jesus. Reducing

Jesus to some vague figure in the past misses the point that, in Jesus, we are encountering a unique human being, a profoundly distinctive individual with a genius beyond compare. It would be preposterous to assume that the phenomenon of Christianity as it has been known for over two thousand years in its traditions and people could be traced back to a rather ordinary carpenter from Galilee. It would be equally unacceptable, as some scholars have set out to prove, that Jesus was a typical teacher, Pharisee, miracle worker, or sage of his time. While it is useful to compare and contrast Jesus with other people of his time, he stands out as unique and incomparable. Even among other great religious leaders, such as the Buddha, Muhammad, and Moses, Christians find no one who can be put on the same level with Jesus, both as he was in history and as he is held in faith.

5. **To provide a norm for evaluating interpretations of Jesus.** Many biblical scholars, theologians, artists, writers, poets, filmmakers, mystics, and musicians have sought to portray Jesus. We have already seen how persons in the nineteenth century portrayed Jesus as a deluded revolutionary or as an insignificant preacher. In modern times he has been described as an anti-hero, a flower child of the 1960s, a deviant prophet hatching his own "passover plot," or even the product of hallucinatory fungus taken by some early cult figures.[34] Some have proposed that Jesus never existed at all. Others have argued that he was not, in fact, a Jew.

Much of this can be dismissed as the fantasies of misguided people who simply don't understand the person of Jesus. Nevertheless, it does seem valuable for the Christian community to have a substantial understanding of the real identity of Jesus of Nazareth, a norm that can be used to critique such distortions.

Even more important, such a norm is needed to evaluate intelligently the more radical and challenging interpretations of Jesus that are arising out of liberation theology and the feminist movement. Was Jesus of Nazareth truly a liberator of the poor and the oppressed? Was he indeed radical in his views on women and in decisions to give them equal place among his disciples? Unless these interpretations can be linked to Jesus himself, they will never have the force that their proponents intend. If these interpretations can indeed be linked to him, this will indeed revolutionize the way Christians in the future will think and act socially, politically, and ecclesiastically.

The Emerging Portrait

After two centuries of scholarship, biblical criticism has matured, moved away from the rationalism of the last century, and become much more ecumenical in its undertakings. Much of the former skepticism about the historical value of the gospels is gone, and many scholars are prepared to admit that the early Christians did have a concern for historical detail.

This is not to deny that a great deal of the gospel material is myth, religious image, and theology. Underlying this fictional material, however, scholars often discover historical material that seems to go back to Jesus' time, if not to his actual person. A considerable amount of "authentic" material has been discovered, and often the material classified as "inauthentic" seems to be faithful to the person and teachings of Jesus.

The following is a composite portrait of Jesus that seems to be emerging among exegetes and theologians. It must be admitted from the outset that most of the elements in the portrait have one degree or another of certainty, probability, or possibility. Often these are "guesses" about Jesus, but they are extremely well-educated guesses that are based on competent research.

Jesus of Nazareth

Jesus of Nazareth was a real human individual, a person of flesh and blood who lived for thirty-some years in Palestine during a time that can be historically verified. As a human being he shared the same emotions, physical pleasures, thought processes, and ability to choose that are common to all people. He had the human limitations of intelligence, and he experienced the struggle to learn and discover the truth. He also struggled with confusion, doubt, and even error. All of these human characteristics are reflected in the gospel stories about what Jesus said and did. Underlying the myths, theology, titles, liturgical prayers, and other forms, there exist actual memories of Jesus as a real person.

Jesus was a Jew who accepted and cherished the religion of Israel and its tradition as the will of God for him and for his people. He took part in the religious life of his time, which included learning the Torah, attending synagogue, making pilgrimages to the Temple, learning from the priests and teachers of his time, and following the laws and religious customs of the Jews. Jesus' life was shaped by the Jewish culture, by his family, by his life in Nazareth and other areas of Galilee, and by his work as a craftsman in wood.

He entered public life for a year or more as a teacher and preacher. His training for this must have been the study of the Torah in the local synagogue and through the usual religious discussion that went on among adults in the villages of Galilee. It does not seem likely that he attended any of the prestigious rabbinical schools or studied under any of the outstanding teachers of the time.

Jesus began his public life as a follower of John the Baptist. After John was executed, Jesus went on his own individual mission. He was similar in some ways to other teachers of his time, but he also had his own unique style and message. Instead of the traditional manner whereby followers choose to follow a leader, he picked his own followers, both women and men. Rather than have a school, Jesus chose to be an itinerant preacher, delivering his message in open fields, by the lakeside, and at table. He taught with an authority that was distinctive, yet confined his teaching mostly to small towns in Galilee.

The central message of Jesus concerned the reign of God. This was a common theme in Israel, but his version was uncommon, for he apparently experienced an unprecedented intimacy with this God, whom he called Abba, and he called others to share in this intimacy with him. Jesus perceived the world about him, both natural and human, as the creation of this loving and saving God. He taught that God's love was extended to all, even to sinners before their repentance. He saw himself as being in radical solidarity with all outcasts and as a liberator of the oppressed. He extended his table fellowship to people of all kinds, rich and poor, virtuous and sinner. He extended the love of God to all, both Jew and Gentile. Moreover, he promised them a time of future fulfillment when the righteous would prevail and evil would be overcome in the end-time.

Jesus called people to a radical conversion, to prepare themselves for the acceptance of the reign of God in their lives. In both his words and deeds, Jesus became the personification of this loving, saving presence of God in the world. He struggled against the current religious legalism that put the law in the place of this loving God, distorting God into a fearsome and manipulative task-master. To demonstrate his rejection of such legalism, Jesus was liberal in his views and practice with regard to Sabbath observance and purity laws, especially when such observances became an obstacle to serving others. Indeed he was dedicated to freeing people from anything that would prevent them from experiencing the love and compassion of God.

Jesus performed miracles, especially healings and exorcisms. Through these miracles he demonstrated that the power of a caring and loving God was active in the world. He did not use these miracles to prove divinity, for he never claimed to be God, nor did he explicitly claim to be the messiah.

At first, the response to Jesus' mission was enthusiastic. There seemed to have been high hopes of his success. But Jesus' words and deeds gradually put him into conflict with the political and religious authorities of the time. This opposition did not, however, move him to abandon his message or mission.

Jesus was arrested in Jerusalem, and was crucified as a seditionist. He died on a cross outside the city, apparently facing death with courage and persistent fidelity to his mission.[35] After Jesus' death, his followers began to experience him as being raised from the dead. They came to have faith in him as the messiah, Savior, and the Son of God. These disciples established a new community within Judaism, but eventually this group became separated from Judaism and became known first as the Way, and then as the Christian church.

This is the portrait of Jesus of Nazareth, who came to be recognized as the Christ, the messiah. Both aspects of Jesus are necessary if we are not to distort the Christian tradition. As the German Scripture scholar Gerhard Kittel wrote earlier in this century: "The Jesus of history is valueless and unintelligible unless he be experienced and confessed by faith as the living Christ. But, if we would be true to the New Testament, we must at once reverse this judgment. The Christ of faith has no existence, is mere noise and smoke, apart from the reality of Jesus of history. The two are inseparable in the New Testament."[36]

Summary

In the early days of the church the memories of Jesus of Nazareth were still etched in the minds of his disciples. At that time, therefore, there was a continuity between the earthly Jesus and the Christ of faith, whose risen and glorified presence they now experienced. In oral and written stories the communities developed gospel stories and theological interpretations around both these memories, as well as around their experiences of the Christ. As the centuries distanced the community from the memories of Jesus, the community began to rely solely on its Scriptures, where the Jesus of history and the Christ of faith seem to be one. Here Jesus Christ the Lord seems to be preaching in Galilee with all the grandeur and power of a divine Savior. Until modern times, this Jesus Christ of the gospels was considered to be Jesus as he lived two thousand years ago.

In modern times, biblical criticism has lifted the veil on the gospels and disclosed their sources, literary forms, and the early editing that took place. The response to these critical approaches to the Scriptures has been varied. Fundamentalists, both Protestant and Catholic, have refused to accept this perspective and continue to accept the gospel stories as biography and history. Rationalists, who refuse to accept the possibility of the supernatural, view the Scriptures as mere imaginative literature, perhaps based on some ordinary person or even on some skullduggery by early disciples. Others accept in faith the message of Jesus and his early communities, but to one degree or another find little possibility of digging beneath the myths to find the Jesus of history.

In this chapter we have allied ourselves with the biblical experts and theologians who are confident that the gospels indeed reflect the kinds of things that Jesus said and did, and that his person and memory can be discovered deep beneath the myths and theology of the early church. They are convinced that Christian discipleship began with people experiencing and listening to a real person of flesh and blood, and that the faith with which they came to accept him as Christ is in continuity with that original experience.

Christians do not primarily follow a message, an idea, or a doctrine. Rather, they first follow a person who, in his life, death, and resurrection was revealed to be their Lord and their God. What they can learn of him when he was alive can help them to both understand and authenticate these traditions.

Questions for Reflection and Discussion

1. How do literalists generally view the historical accuracy of the gospels? How would those who follow the historical critical approach differ from the literalists on this?

2. Why is the distinction between the historical Jesus and the Christ of faith so important for the biblical critic?

3. Explain the differences among source, form, and redaction biblical criticism.

4. What are some of the reasons scholars give for spending a great deal of effort in searching for the historical Jesus?

5. What are some of the outstanding features of the portrait of the historical Jesus that seems to be emerging in biblical research?

CHAPTER THREE

Teacher and Prophet

As they seek to identify Jesus, some scholars have set out to describe him as one of the "types" observable in those ancient times. They often study such figures as "Pharisee," "Zealot," "charismatic," "teacher," or "prophet," and then attempt to show how Jesus of Nazareth fits into the specific classification.[1]

These scholars have offered some interesting parallels between Jesus and the category in question, but, for the most part, they fall short of the mark. Usually overlooked in these studies are the unique characteristics of Jesus Christ that seem to put him beyond any kind of typology or classification with other figures of his time. Jesus of Nazareth seems to have undergone an unprecedented religious experience and displayed an original genius in demonstrating the truth of this experience in his words and deeds. He was not a typical teacher, prophet, healer, or charismatic, but a singular combination of all of these and more.

The purpose of this chapter is not to establish that Jesus was either a typical teacher or prophet. It will attempt, rather, to compare and contrast Jesus of Nazareth with others who functioned in these roles, and, in the process to further delineate Jesus' distinctive identity. We will begin by looking at Jesus the teacher, then examine his prophetic characteristics, and close with a discussion of his central message and the key means he used to proclaim that message.

Jesus as Teacher

In all four gospels Jesus is addressed by both friends and enemies as "teacher," but there are a number of problems with considering him in this role. First of all, the title "Rabbi," or "teacher," might well have been simply a title of respect. It was only in the second and third centuries that this term came to clearly be associated with a formal role of a scholar who instructed others. Second, we actually know very little about what Jewish teachers were like in Jesus' day; most of our descriptions are from much later materials.[2]

Moreover, if Jesus is identified simply as a religious teacher, that role does not adequately explain why he alienated some people so much that they brought him to execution. Apparently he was not crucified for being a teacher. It is also possible that Mark's depiction of Jesus as teacher might well be modeled after later Jewish and Greek teachers, and thus the image of "teacher" might have little bearing on the actual activity of Jesus himself.[3]

All of these problems force us to proceed with caution when discussing Jesus as teacher, but this is still a valuable area for our exploration. Even though much of what we know about Jewish teachers is from later rabbinic writings, it seems safe to assume that there is some continuity between Jesus' time and these later teachers. And although we may grant that the gospel portrayal of Jesus is stylized, this dimension of his work is too central to suppose that it was simply a later addition. Consequently, we will, with due caution, pursue the discussion of Jesus' teaching activity and attempt to compare and contrast him with other Jewish teaching models of the time.

A Non-Academic Teacher

Jesus certainly did not qualify as an official teacher in his own day. He apparently did not attend any of the rabbinic schools or established academies where a potential teacher would be trained to master the Scriptures as well as the traditional oral commentaries.[4] Jesus was not an ordained scribe. As we mentioned earlier, the scribes were scholars who were certified to transmit and create the oral tradition on the Torah and to make legal decisions "to bind and loose." Their prestige provided them with many opportunities to advance in the administration of justice, government, and education.

In contrast, Jesus seems to have acquired his formidable understanding of the Jewish tradition in his ordinary schooling in Nazareth, at synagogue, and perhaps most of all through prayer and intense living among his people. As a result, Jesus' style of teaching was much less formal than that of the scribes. Where other ordained teachers would make their point by quoting other scribal interpretations of the law, Jesus would usually give his own point of view based on his own unique authority. No doubt he had heard many of the expert opinions in his education and at synagogue, but he does not quote these in his teaching. As we shall see in our discussion of Jesus' parables, his major reference seems to be everyday life, rather than academic interpretations.[5]

Jesus Compared to Other Sages

Even though Jesus would not have been recognized as an official teacher of his time, he seems to conduct his teaching within the rabbinic tradition, and some of his points of view are similar to those of other teachers of his time. Jesus' teaching that "the Sabbath was made for the good of man" (Mark 2:27) is found in slightly different form in the rabbinic teaching of his day. His saying that "Sufficient for a day is its own evil"(Matthew 6:34) also is paralleled in rabbinic teachings. Even the golden rule about treating others as you would have them treat you can be found in a modified form in the teachings of the famous Jewish teacher Hillel (d. 10 C.E.).[6]

Hillel was the most prominent of the Jewish sages and he was probably still alive when Jesus was a boy. Even though the "historical Hillel" is quite as difficult to find as the "historical Jesus," he seems to have been a sage who loved people as much as he loved the Torah.[7] He was renowned for his gentleness and charity toward the impoverished, as well as for his dedication to peace. Hillel is also known for his profound teachings on the value of self-respect and on having equal regard for others. He taught: "If I am not concerned for myself, who will be? Yet, if I am concerned only for myself what do I amount to?" He was a teacher who liked to focus on the urgency of the present time. He strongly opposed loners who refused to take part in public affairs, and he objected to judging others until we have been in the same situation ourselves. We can find a number of parallels between Hillel's teachings and those of Jesus.[8]

Although we can draw these parallels between Jesus and other sages of the time, Jesus would not have been accepted among them. He did not share their strict standards of religious behavior regarding fasting, ritual purity, or Sabbath. Nor did he work out of an established "house" of scholarship or "school" of thought. He taught on his own authority and paid little heed to the scholarly interpretations of the day. Jesus also broke tradition by associating with whomever he wished, even with the "undesirables" of the day.

The gospels make it clear that Jesus often engaged in heated debates with the official teachers of his time. This is nothing out of the ordinary, however, for such disputes were common among teachers, and the scribal tradition was open to original opinions.[9] What is significant in these disputes between Jesus and the scribes is that his opponents resent his lack of credentials, his independence, and what they seem to view as a demonic authority that he used in his teaching. Jesus' rejoinder, "Amen, I say unto you," was simply not acceptable in scribal circles.

Efforts have also been made to compare Jesus' teaching style as portrayed in the gospels with those of others of the ancient world. Parallels can be made with the great Greek teachers Plato, Aristotle, and Socrates, who gathered disciples about them and shared wisdom with these pupils. In fact, a good case can be made that Judaism borrowed its teacher-disciple model from the Greeks. Jesus has also been compared to the wandering Sophists and Cynics, who, like Jesus, were itinerant teachers who moved from city to city with few possessions and who gathered followers for the sharing of wisdom.[10] While parallels do exist here, however, the contrasts only serve to further underline the originality of Jesus' teaching mission.

The Academy Approach

The officially recognized scribal teachers of the day no doubt resented this upstart Galilean, Jesus of Nazareth, who had not "paid his dues" by attending formal education at one of the reputable academies of study. These "houses of study" were set up by well-known teachers, and male students would come from great distances to sit at their feet.

A neophyte scholar would spend years at the academy studying the sacred texts and listening to the master's oral commentary. The teacher and his message would be the center of attention. Much of the master's teaching would be committed to memory, and the master's ritual behavior and gestures would be imitated with care and precision. The student assumed the role of servant and would perform domestic services for the master teacher in partial payment for the teaching. Both teachers and students seemed to sustain trades such as carpentry, weaving, or tent-making in order to have sufficient income for subsistence, and the funds were held in common.

Except for the occasional forays into the countryside and towns (where the master would orate to the students in the presence of interested onlookers, and also perform services for the poor or bereaved), the time of learning was a time of being cut off from everyday life. The exclusivity was even sustained when the studies were finished, for the students were warned upon finishing to seek out only like-minded scholars. The many secret and esoteric teachings that the master had shared with the students were only to be repeated within the group of specialists.[11]

Some Parallels and Contrasts

There are some obvious parallels between the formal academies and Jesus' approach to teaching his own disciples. There is a similar fellowship between master and student, as well as a comparable lifestyle of simplicity and shared funds. There is a similar careful transmission of sacred message from master to student in a communal setting. And there is a coinciding movement to the outer community for service and for exposing the message to a larger audience.

There are also, of course, many contrasts that underscore the independence that Jesus had in establishing his own way of doing things. Jesus does not seem to have had an academy or house of studies in which to train his disciples, although there are several references in the gospels to his entering and leaving a residence (Mark 10:10; Matthew 13:1). Instead of students choosing him as their teacher, Jesus himself goes about and calls disciples to follow him.

His disciples are, for the most part, common folk, women and men of limited learning, and hardly the scholarly types who would pore over manuscripts. Jesus teaches them mostly through homey stories and apparently does not require them to commit these to memory. One has only to note the freedom that the Christian oral tradition developed and the liberty that gospel writers took with the sources to realize that Jesus taught a message that was substantial and unique, but which could be interpreted and developed by his later followers. In the Jesus "school," the focus was not on the master, but on the reign of a loving God. In fact, Jesus said little about himself in his teaching. As for imitation, the disciples seemed to have been called to imitate their master through a way of life, rather than through ritual gestures.

There are other notable contrasts between the scribal schools and the small band who accompanied Jesus. One of the most important is that Jesus looked upon the women and men who followed him as friends, not as servants. Striking also was Jesus' service to his own disciples. In the academies it would have been unheard of for the master to wash the feet of his students. Moreover, it would seem that the sense of urgency and immediacy of Jesus' mission moved both master and servant to put aside their jobs and trades during Jesus' public life. In addition, the disciples of Jesus seem to have been collaborators with him from the beginning, not merely passive students. And instead of being centered in a building or academy, Jesus' teachings took place in the open fields, on the lakesides, and often at table. When out in public, Jesus taught the crowds at large and did not let them passively stand by watching him teach his own disciples. Though there does seem to be a distinction between the intimate instruction he gave his disciples and the message he proclaimed to the masses, ultimately the good news was for all to hear.

The Secrecy Element

There are some elements of secrecy in the gospels. In Mark there is the account of some people coming in private to hear of the kingdom, while those "on the outside" hear only in parables (Mark 10:10, 34). Matthew recounts a similar incident when Jesus gives the secrets of the kingdom to his disciples, but uses parables for those who "do not hear or understand" (Matthew 13:13). In addition there seems to be a reluctance on Jesus' part to be known as messiah or to allow some of his miracles to be known. This, however, does not imply esoteric teaching as much as a concern on Jesus' part that his teachings and miracles not misrepresent him as being a political messiah. Much of the other secret elements in the gospels might well be from the minds of the early Christians, who were concerned about being discovered and persecuted.

For the most part, the parables seem to be a means of communicating Jesus' message; the Great Commission in Matthew would indicate that he wanted this message spread to all nations (Matthew 28:19). While there is a minor missionary theme in Judaism, there is nothing comparable to this thrust for missionary zeal in spreading the gospel.[12] While it is true that Jesus comes mainly for "the lost sheep of Israel," his message of the universal love of God and Jesus' love of all creation lays the foundation for spreading his word far and wide. Jesus did not establish an esoteric academy open only the elite. Rather he opened his discipleship to all of God's people, especially to sinners, outcasts, and the oppressed.

Fulfilling or Flouting the Torah?

Because Christianity did eventually move away from the Torah, and Paul declared Christ to be "the end of the law," there have always been questions about Jesus' actual attitude toward the Torah. Was Jesus attempting to reform Judaism and to bring it back to its genuine roots? Or did he have designs on starting a new religion? There can be no doubt at all that Judaism and Christianity did split irrevocably and become two separate religions in time, but was this Jesus' intent in his teaching mission?

Matthew's statement seems to have significance here: "Then Jesus spoke to the crowds and his disciples. 'The teachers of the Law and the Pharisees are the authorized interpreters of Moses' Law. So you must obey and follow everything they tell you to do; do not, however, imitate their actions, because they do not practice what they preach" (Matthew 23:1–3). Another key passage in Matthew is Jesus' statement, "Do not think that I have come to do away with the Law of Moses and the teachings of the prophets. I have not come to do away with them, but to make their teachings come true" (Matthew 5:17). Granted, Jesus did offend many of the traditional Jewish leaders with his attitudes toward Sabbath observance and ritual purity, and with his teachings on oaths and divorce. But it seems as though he was disagreeing with legalistic and unjust applications of the law, and not flouting the Law itself.[13] Rather than trying to abolish the Jewish Law, Jesus was trying to restore its radical foundations.

Even though Jesus did not seem to be intent on starting a new religion, he most certainly became a source of division among his own people. Other contemporary teachers would not have been greatly disturbed by Jesus' controversial interpretations—they were used to that in their own debates. What would have bothered them, however, was that Jesus did not argue within the boundaries of the expert opinions by the elders. He seemed free to bypass these expert opinions of the academy of scholars and to teach what he felt were true interpretations of the law. In addition, he radically moved the question of Jewish teaching away from legal observance and toward living in a radically new way. He vehemently opposed the legalism and hypocrisy of his day and in its place preached a message of love, compassion, and service.

Perhaps most important, Jesus proclaimed an image of God that was loving, forgiving, and intimately present. Such a God was simply not acceptable to many of the religious leaders of his time. His enemies thus concluded that he was a false teacher who led people astray. Later in the Talmud he is even denounced as a sorcerer.[14]

Unique as a Teacher

From what we have said, it seems clear that there was a "teacher" dimension to Jesus' identity and mission, and that, in many ways, he can be compared to other teachers of the time. As a teacher, however, Jesus was distinct. He avoided the zeal for violence and militancy that so often appears in the charismatic teachers within the Zealot and Essene movements. There was a newness and freshness in his teaching that seemed to astonish and amaze his listeners. He challenged his audiences to think thoughts that they had never considered before. He called people to live a way of life that had never before been thought possible.

Jesus spoke with an immediacy and directness that seemed to come from the depths of divine Mystery, and not merely from the expert interpreters of the time. He could speak as a Pharisee, as an apocalyptic prophet, or as a wandering charismatic story teller.[15] At times he sounds like the Socratic teacher, challenging his students to ask new questions and to think anew. At other times he seems to be the wandering Greek Cynic preacher, suffering for his teachings and standing up against the corrupt authorities of his time.[16] Many parallels can be drawn, but, in fact, Jesus of Nazareth stands alone as a unique religious teacher who was beyond comparison.

The Prophetic Dimension

Among the many unique aspects of Jesus' teaching activity, perhaps the most distinctive feature is the prophetic dimension. Jesus was a teacher who seemed to have a mission to speak for God. He brought a ringing prophetic message about the present and proclaimed the future plans that God had for all of creation. Similar to the prophets of old, Jesus brought a sharp critique to the abuses of his day and called his people to a conversion to a new vision of life now and in the time to come. Going beyond the wisdom and holiness expected of the other teachers of his time, Jesus spoke and acted as though his mission marked a decisive moment, a turning point in religious history. Something significant was breaking through in his words and deeds. Combining the insight of a sage and the vision of a prophet, Jesus was able to stir people to take part in this breakthrough.

Recognized as Prophet

There are a number of instances in the gospels where others recognize the prophetic role of Jesus. Mark's gospel points out that Jesus' reputation had spread widely, even to the court of Herod, and that some thought he was Elijah or John the Baptist, while others said: "He is a prophet, like one of the prophets of long ago" (Mark 6:15). When Jesus asks his own disciples how he is perceived by others, they tell Jesus that he is thought of as one of the prophets (Mark 8:27–29). Simon the Pharisee seems to assume that Jesus is a prophet, but then questions this assumption when Jesus does not appear to recognize the sinfulness of the woman crying at his feet during a meal at Simon's house (Luke 7:39).

The gospel stories indicate that Jesus recognized himself in this role of prophet. In the synagogue in Nazareth he seems to identify his mission of liberation with that of Isaiah the prophet (Luke 4:21). When his authority is challenged in Nazareth, Jesus makes the well-known remark: "A prophet is respected everywhere except in his own home town and by relatives and his family" (Mark 6:4). In other stories Jesus is portrayed as being aware that he shares with some of the prophets the fate of those killed by people who will not accept such messengers of God. Moreover, in the tradition of the ancient prophets, Jesus performs many symbolic actions to indicate the divine source of his message.

Prophets of Old

The prophets had played a key role in the religious history of Israel. They served as its visionaries and conscience. It had been a long time since such stirring figures had shown themselves among the Jews and there was in many a deep longing to once again hear from such charismatic figures. The scribes, who claimed to be the successors of the prophets, did not have the passion or the capacity to stir the people that the prophets of old possessed. Many Jews waited in hope that one of the ancient prophets like Elijah or Jeremiah would return and help to once again restore the glory of Israel.

The ancient prophets served as the conscience of Israel, constantly bringing its people back to the truth of their tradition, pointing out the ways they had strayed from that truth, and warning them of the dire future consequences such behavior could bring. The prophets often portray an angry and vengeful God, who vents wrath upon those who are evil, and who directs apocalyptic destruction upon those who are unfaithful.

Contrary to popular understanding, the prophets were not predictors of the future, nor were they mere microphones of God. They were human beings who could look at the human situation from God's perspective. They were a combination of "poet, preacher, patriot, statesman, social critic, moralist."[17] They were individuals who spoke out against the waywardness and injustice of the societies in which they lived, men and women who spoke out passionately against abuses to freedom. They expressed dread at the moral situation and outrage at the apathy that people displayed toward such scandals. At the same time, they showed a love and a pathos toward their people, offering them a hopeful future if they would but change their ways.

The prophets stood in the presence of God and counseled their brothers and sisters to return to the ways of God. Their driving force was to call their people back to God's plan for justice and peace—to reconcile people with their God. The prophets criticized and challenged the conventional wisdom of their times and, in contrast, offered new perspectives and alternatives.

Walter Brueggemann describes the work of the prophet in these terms: "The task of prophetic ministry is to nurture, nourish, and evoke a consciousness and perception alternative to the consciousness and perception of the dominant culture around us."[18] For example, Moses challenged the Egyptian perspective of domination and slavery and offered his people a vision of freedom and justice. In our own time, Gandhi condemned the British perspective of imperial domination and exploitation and offered his people a future of self-determination and liberation. Harriet Tubman condemned slavery and risked her life to liberate many of her fellow slaves. Dorothy Day protested her country's penchant for war, as well as its consistent neglect of the poor. Martin Luther King confronted his nation's racial prejudice and discrimination and offered his people a dream of civil rights and freedom. More currently, Nelson Mandela, Bishop Desmond Tutu, and other leaders in South Africa have challenged the consciousness that supports apartheid, and have demanded equality and justice for the Black majority in that country.

The prophets of old not only critiqued the immorality and oppression they experienced, they also were able to appeal to the imagination of the people and energize them to confront these abuses and move toward a new future. They portrayed a God "ahead of the people," drawing them to a new and exhilarating future. Using powerful symbols and dramatic language, the prophets stirred people out of apathy, and called them to conversion and change. With a deep sense of compassion, the prophets could both identify with the suffering of their people and, at the same time, move them to transform their lives and their society.[19] Since their critique was so stinging and their vision so radical, these prophets were usually rejected and sometimes killed by those whose power and wealth were threatened by this vision of goodness and freedom.

John the Baptist

In many ways the gospel writers portray John the Baptist in this role of ancient prophet. John came as an outraged critic of the immorality of the royalty and of the hypocrisy and evil of his time. John came from the desert wilderness, where one goes to meet Yahweh, and he brought a message of doom for the sinners of his society. He was a "fire and brimstone" preacher warning anyone who would listen of the wrathful vengeance that God would soon bring to those judged to be evil. He reminded the Jews that being among God's chosen people will not exempt them from the punishing hand of God.

John's message was designed to strike fear into the hearts of his listeners and drive them into the river for the baptism of repentance. He was an effective preacher and his message apparently was a serious threat to the powers of his day. Josephus points out that the reason Herod had John executed was that his following posed a threat to Herod's control over his people. John was indeed a prophet in his own right, and it is likely that Jesus began as a follower of this great, prophetic preacher. John's portrayal in the gospels as a mere forerunner of Jesus and herald of his coming seems to be a later Christian effort to align John's mission with that of Jesus and to put the two into continuity with each other.[20]

Jesus as Prophet

Even though Jesus apparently spoke of himself and was recognized by others as a prophet, he is distinctive in this role. He did not attempt to give credentials with phrases such as "Thus says the Lord," as did other prophets. Nor did he claim to have ecstatic states, visions, or some personal call in the manner of the ancient prophets.[21] Jesus also spoke with much more of a personal authority than did the prophets that went before him. Instead of bringing a message from God, Jesus seemed to set out to describe his experience of intimacy with God, one that he felt was graciously available to all.

At times Jesus speaks of judgment and calls people to conversion, just as the prophets of old did, yet he usually does not follow the traditional prophetic portrayal of God as vengeful. Instead, Jesus reminds his people of the best of their traditions, where God's love is described as "constant" and "eternal." He comes not to warn his people of the wrathful vengeance of God, but to call them to an awareness of the gracious mercy and love of God that is extended to all, most especially to outcasts and sinners. He does not usually threaten wrath, and yet he warns that destruction, indeed self-destruction, comes from rejecting this gratuitous mercy and love. It is here that Jesus departs from the warnings of the prophets, of their self-declared successors the scribes, and even from his own mentor, John the Baptist.

Jesus brings "news," the good news that the forgiving and saving power of God is in the midst of God's people, waiting for recognition, reception, and celebration. And it was this good news that generated such amazement and astonishment on the part of those who heard him. They had heard that God was loving and forgiving, but never had they heard or seen this so vividly dramatized as they did in the words and actions of Jesus. He proclaimed that God was in their midst, caring deeply for all, even those who had not yet repented. They had heard messages of judgment and calls to conversion in their Scriptures and in the teaching of their scribes and sages, but in Jesus they were hearing a prophetic teacher who spoke primarily from his own personal experience, taught with a unique authority of his own, and validated the divine origin of these teachings with his own distinctive symbols.

Jesus' own gifts, power, and message called for a radical decision. A person had to either accept his message or declare him a false prophet and an agent of the devil. Most of the religious leaders of the time apparently chose the latter, lest they have to drastically change their own perspectives and behavior.[22] Jesus prophetically challenged the prevailing consciousness of his time, offered salvation to those who had heretofore little hope of it, and predicted dire consequences for those who righteously thought of themselves as "the saved." He was a harsh critic of the oppression and injustice that he observed around him, and was a courageous advocate for the poor and the outcast.

As a prophetic teacher, Jesus was declaring a "crisis," a moment of truth, a turning point in history. In this sense, he has been described as the "eschatological prophet," that is, the prophet of the end-time and indeed the last prophet.[23]

Many Jews of the time were apparently looking for the return of one of the great prophets to end their domination by foreign powers and restore the glory of Israel. Others were anticipating the "end-time," the destruction of the world as they knew it, and the beginning of the "messianic era," wherein Israel would be restored and draw all nations to itself.

Jesus came in the midst of these varied interpretations of how the end-time would be fulfilled, and he took his own authoritative position. This was indeed the end-time: the end of the pessimistic doomsday predictions of the apocalyptic writers, of scribal legalism as a means of salvation, of the withdrawn and exclusive "holier than thou" mentality of the Essenes, of "salvation by Temple sacrifice" of the Jewish priesthood, and the end of liberation through violent zealotry. Against the backdrop of these false interpretations of the kingdom, Jesus initiated a new era of recognition of God's compassion, love, and saving grace freely offered to all.

For Jesus, this rule of God's salvation was not the distant promise of earlier prophets. The happiness and joy of being in the presence of a loving God were present now. The fulfillment that had been foretold by the prophets and that had been anticipated for so many centuries by the Jews was now here. There was no need any longer to promise or anticipate, for Jesus was announcing God's power as present in the *now*.[24]

This God did not come to destroy the wicked, but rather to be as the father of prodigal children, gathering them into his arms. This "nowness" gave a new urgency and immediacy to Jesus' message. It was not the urgency brought on by fear or dread, but the urgency of love that rushes out to meet and be at one with the beloved. It was the immediacy of God's will to identify with the anguish and suffering of God's people and to draw them into atonement with God and with each other. Now was the time to bring oppression and injustice to an end.

Jesus' prophetic symbols for the coming of this end of anguish and the beginning of a new era were usually not apocalyptic signs of God's destruction of the world. His symbols were expressed in healing miracles, meals at table with outcasts, feasts given to the masses, and a purification of the Temple from its collaboration with political oppression, empty ritualism, and greedy materialism. His final sign was his refusal to back down on his stand even though it meant going to his death on a cross. These were his prophetic symbols of sharing, wholeness, self-sacrifice, and hope in face of sin, suffering, and death.

Yes, Jesus anticipated an end. But this is not to say, as so many have, that he was a mistaken apocalypticist who wrongly expected the end-time. He did not deal in predictions. He admitted that he did not know how or when the end would come. What he did know from his experience of the Father's love was that something new and exciting was breaking into the world. Jesus' prophetic role was to announce the good news of this breakthrough. It spelled the end of despair, the end of the notion of a vengeful God, and the beginning of a new era of hope for the poor and the marginalized. There would be no further need for prophets, for Jesus had spoken and indeed lived the last Word of prophecy.

In the tradition of the great prophets and of his own former mentor, John the Baptist, Jesus recognized the moral depravity of his time and the need to return to the purity of God's word. Yet he had his own way of speaking out. Rather than speak for God, Jesus often sounded like Yahweh. He did not speak from visions or ecstasies on mountaintops, but from the experience of God's love, as Abba, that he felt in his heart. He uttered predictions, but usually of the self-destruction of those who refused the gift of God's love. He set his own personal teaching down as though it were God's and refused to withdraw it even if it were to cost him his life. He was driven by a mission to his own people and ultimately to all nations. In carrying out this mission, Jesus not only revived the prophecies of the past, he brought them all to fulfillment in his new presentation of the kingdom of God.

The Message of the Kingdom

The central message in Jesus' prophetic teaching was about "the kingdom of God." The phrase is used over a hundred times in the synoptic gospels, and is the core message behind most of the parables. Unfortunately, the language of "kingdom" is easily associated with monarchy and male domination, so the words "reign" and "rule" arc often substituted. But because these words often carry the same notion of domination, it might be just as useful to keep the term "kingdom" and explain what it meant in Jesus' teaching. We will see that his interpretation of the kingdom does not imply domination of any kind.

A Hebrew Tradition

The notion of the kingdom of God is deep within the Hebrew tradition and seems to be derived from God's function as Creator and sustainer of all reality.[25] The prophet Isaiah proclaimed the good news of the peace and salvation that flows from God's powerful reign over the world: "How wonderful it is to see a messenger coming across the mountains, bringing good news, the news of peace! He announces victory and says to Sion, 'Your God is king!'" (Isaiah 52:7).

Martin Buber, the well-known Jewish philosopher, maintains that this realization of God's all-embracing reign is "the Alpha and Omega of Israel."[26] Yahweh is thought of as a guide to the people, the provident and protecting Lord who leads and strengthens Judah. This is not a political domination, but a guidance through the power of love.

God's "constant love" and "eternal love" are common themes throughout the Psalms and other books of the Hebrew Scriptures. The Psalmist proclaims: "Your constant love is my guide" (Psalm 26:3). And this loving care and leadership is extended especially to the poor: "He does not neglect the poor or ignore their suffering" (Psalm 22:24).

In its purist meaning, the "kingdom of God" seems to refer to a process or course of events whereby God manifests God's will to save all humankind. The ruling or dominant power in this plan is God's reconciling graciousness, which stands in strong opposition to the power of evil, suffering, and injustice. It was this power that liberated the Hebrew people from the bondage they experienced under the many nations that subjugated them. This power revealed that God's will was one of love, compassion, and peace. Ultimately, it was Israel's mission to reveal this will to all nations.[27]

Unfortunately, this ruling power of God often was translated into military and political language. A common Jewish vision was that Yahweh would help the people to rise up against their enemies, destroy their enemies, and then restore the glory days of Israel. The nation once again would be independent. Jerusalem would become the center of the world and would gather all those dispersed by pagan tyranny. The hopes were most often expressed for a worldly kingdom, brought about by a God-ordained revolution. This kingdom would ultimately draw all nations to itself in a rule of peace and harmony.[28]

This political, military vision seems to have been common among many of the Jews of Jesus' time. The Essenes, the Zealot movement, and the various "parties" that prevailed in Palestine all had their own versions as to how this vision would come about. The Essenes withdrew and awaited their vindication as the true remnant. Those with the Zealot mentality held that this kingdom could only come about by violently crushing the pagan occupiers and restoring the sovereignty of God. The pharisaic movement, as well as those who dominated the Temple, prepared for the end-time more individualistically through proper legal practice and ritualistic sacrifices. John the Baptist called for repentance from sin before the vengeance of an angry God comes in the fiery destruction of God's enemies.

In one fashion or another, the Jews always had expectation and hope for liberation, restoration, and the ultimate dominance of a peaceful and just world. Much of the proclamation of the Hebrew prophets carried these expectations, although the prophets generally did not use "kingdom" metaphors because of many tyrannical experiences the Jews had with "kings," both Jewish and pagan. For the most part, their vision was of a just ruler who would protect the helpless and the poor. And the common view was that such peace and justice could not be brought about through human efforts. Only the power of God could liberate their people, and indeed the world, from the power of evil. The divine ruler of creation would also rule history and deliver his people in the end-time. This was a common theme in Near East myths, and it settled deep into the Jewish consciousness during times of exile and domination by foreign powers.[29]

Jesus' Version of the Kingdom
Jesus' teaching about the kingdom was a combination of the best of the Jewish tradition along with his own original insights. First of all, Jesus

proclaimed that the kingdom of God, or "of heaven," as Matthew prefers to call it, is not a remote ruling from somewhere beyond or some sort of political domination. It is neither a political theocracy nor any other form of government.[30] It is neither God's avenging judgment in favor of some elite remnant nor is it some ideal type of community constructed through moral behavior. The kingdom is "not of this world," for it is not concerned with the power of worldly domination.

The "Now" Factor

Jesus insisted that the kingdom of God, that is, the prevailing presence of God's loving power, is "at hand," here and now. He taught that this creative presence governs all of creation and history and is best experienced in everyday life. He believed that it is often most evident to the oppressed and the marginal, to the "poor in spirit" who depend on God for their survival. This kingdom is transcendent and yet it is within. It is intangible and yet somehow deeply felt as being nearby. The kingdom is a dynamic presence and power that will prevail over evil and suffering in the very present *now*.[31] Immediacy, urgency, and nearness are at the very heart of Jesus' teachings on the kingdom of God.

Future Factor

Along with the proximate dimension of the kingdom of God in Jesus' teaching, there is also a future orientation. The present is in tension with a future fulfillment, for Yahweh is also a "God ahead of us," drawing all reality toward completion. God's rule certainly includes the best of human experience in happiness and peace now, but there is a time to come when the limitations to this experience will be done away with. There is a "not yet" and "still to come" aspect of this kingdom.

Jesus' powerful images of a future banquet or a wedding feast indicate that the present experience of God's protection and love also serve as an invitation to the even better times ahead—thus the elements of "be ready" in Jesus' teachings. What we experience now is only a taste of what is ahead, and there is a need to be prepared for its coming.

In Jesus' teaching, both the present and the future aspects of the kingdom are kept in tension. If the kingdom is reduced only to the future, then the present is reduced to a mere waiting period without meaning in itself. Then the old Marxist charge that religion stoically bears injustice and awaits for "pie in the sky" takes on a certain validity. By the same token, if the kingdom is limited only to the present, then it is easy to live in the delusions that the kingdom can somehow be brought about by simply improving society. In reality, Jesus' disciples live "in between times," struggling for peace and justice now, and trusting that ultimately God's gifted future will somehow be brought to completion.[32]

The Plans of Others

Jesus taught that the kingdom of God, or God's loving and saving presence, is pure gift and cannot be brought to bear through human efforts. Apparently, one of the main ways that Jesus irritated his contemporaries was by being unwilling to accept any of their formulations on how the kingdom of God was to be brought about. There were, as was indicated earlier, many opinions on how God's kingdom would come. A dominant version of messianism was that an extraordinary person from the house of David would defeat Israel's enemies and establish the messianic kingdom of Israel. This, of course, was nothing other than another version of the ideology of the Romans—domination through military victory. In both versions the kingdom is spelled out in terms of political boundaries and power.

Other plans called for withdrawal and exclusivity while waiting for the in-breaking of the kingdom. The Essenes withdrew to their monastery near the Dead Sea and to their closed communities in the towns, refused to take part in mainstream Judaism, and prepared for salvation to come to them alone. The Pharisees and scribes, while not withdrawing from society, formed exclusive fellowships and prepared for the kingdom's coming through meticulous observance of the law. The Sadducees seemed to limit the kingdom to the here and now, and many of them interpreted it in terms of material possessions and pleasure: signs of God's blessings. To protect their "kingdom," the Sadducees chose to collaborate with the Romans.

All of these groups kept themselves ritually clean by avoiding undesirables and outcasts. The members of each group no doubt felt that they were "the saved," the ones whom Yahweh would gather into the future messianic kingdom.

Ultimately God's Gift

Against the background of all these plans and schemes of others to usher in the kingdom, Jesus stood apart with a unique vision and authority. When Jesus stated his case, the reactions were often extreme and varied. On the one hand, many were amazed and astonished at his teachings. On the other hand, many of the leaders were angered and shocked that an unknown and untrained workman from Galilee, followed by a motley group of uneducated and often disreputable women and men, would dare expound about a new age and the presence of the kingdom here and now.[33]

It must have enraged Jesus' enemies even further when Jesus challenged their "expert" plans for the kingdom. In so many words, he told them that the kingdom was right under their noses and that they were blind to it. Moreover, he was rooting the kingdom in an experience of intimacy with God and a way of life characterized by compassion, love, and service, not in exclusivity, ritual observance, or violent revolution.

Jesus seemed convinced that no human plan or performance could effectively open the way for the kingdom, for the kingdom was pure gift. God, Creator and Savior, offered loving care graciously to all, especially the marginal. The kingdom was not a political or religious plan to crush enemies with vengeance or violence. Rather, it was a gratuitous offer to empower people to love their enemies and to overcome evil with love and compassion. This was the divine power that would prevail (or "reign"). Now, and ultimately in the future, oppression, suffering, and, indeed, death would not be able to stand up to the overwhelming power of love and forgiveness.

Rooted in the Abba Experience

In the deepest layers of gospel tradition is Jesus' own unique and incomparable experience of intimate loving union with God, an experience expressed in Jesus referring to God as "Abba."[34] In the stories of Jesus' baptism and transfiguration, incidents highly stylized in view of later resurrection faith, Jesus receives direct and explicit approval as the Son of God. In both stories God is portrayed as a loving parent, showing enormous care for God's Son: "This is my own dear Son, with whom I am pleased—listen to him" (Matthew 3:17; 17:5).

Previous to Jesus, there is no tradition that would allow one to address Yahweh as familiarly as "Abba." Jesus had an experience of God that had simply never before been equaled in Judaism, and he was eager not only to share this good news with others, but to encourage them to freely share a similar closeness with God. The God whom Jesus knows and shares with his followers accepts and loves all people unconditionally. This is a Father who is ultimately trustworthy now, in everyday life, as well as in the future. This is a God who will never let God's people down, and whose enduring love is expressed in the image of "kingdom."

Jesus' mission was to preach about this experience rather than preach about himself. His role was to selflessly embody this divine graciousness. As Karl Rahner put it: "This man Jesus is the perfect man in an absolute sense precisely because he forgot himself for the sake of God and his fellow man who was in need of salvation...."[35] Jesus' uniqueness was that he extended the invitation to participate in this kingdom of love and selflessness to all, in particular to those who had been pushed out to the fringes of life in rejection and judgment by the self-righteous.

Call to Conversion

Jesus' message about the kingdom is summed up in the opening statement of his public ministry: "The right time has come...and the kingdom of God is near! Turn away from your sins and believe the good news" (Mark 1:15). This dynamic and prevailing power of God's love and forgiveness is not some distant event to be brought about through observance, sacrifice, or violent revolution. It is already here and freely offered. All that is needed is openness and acceptance on the part of anyone who will hear the good news.

This is not the conversion called for by John the Baptist, done in fear of an avenging God. Nor is it the mere external conversion through observance or orthodox belief called for by so many of the religious leaders contemporary with Jesus. It is a radical change of heart that recognizes in Jesus' words and deeds that "Abba" is at hand, awaiting with forgiveness and unconditional love. Jesus radically calls for a new imaging of God, self, and neighbor, based on this exciting and liberating news of the kingdom.[36] He invites his disciples to a new freedom from fear of God, self-hatred, and alienation from others. He summons them to a new freedom of intimacy with God, self-esteem, and friendship with others. And he promises that such freedom in this "kingdom" will perdure: "So if the Son sets you free, you will indeed be free" (John 8:36).[37]

Jesus Spoke in Parables

We have seen how Jesus differed considerably from the other teachers of his time: He did not meticulously quote the scribal interpretations of the law, but spoke with unprecedented personal authority. In many ways, Jesus was poetic rather than academic in his teaching. He used the folk wisdom and story forms of his day to convey his original insights into God's plans for God's people.

The word "parable" refers to a broad field of teaching models of the time, ranging from one-line wisdom statements to riddles, allegories, and longer stories with a lesson.[38] Jesus used many of these forms in his teaching. His "one-liners" have been recited in many cultures throughout the centuries. Many of them are familiar to us: "The Sabbath was made for the good of man; man was not made for the Sabbath" (Mark 2:27); "Whichever one of you has committed no sin may throw the first stone at her" (John 8:7); "For everyone who makes himself great will be humbled, and everyone who humbles himself will be made great" (Luke 18:14); "Let the little children come to me and do not stop them, because the kingdom of God belongs to such as these" (Luke 18:17).

A second technique that Jesus commonly used was the paradox, a statement that seems contrary to common sense, but which, in fact, contains a truth. For example, we have the expression "poor little rich child," referring to the paradoxical situation of a child who has many material things and yet is poor because he or she does not have love. Jesus is paradoxical when he says: "Unless you change and become like children, you will never enter the kingdom of heaven" (Matthew 18:3). On the surface, it would seem that Jesus is encouraging regression, but, in fact, he is recommending the necessity of being open and forgiving, and of trustfully accepting the powerful presence of God in one's life.

Jesus also made effective use of hyperbole, an extreme exaggeration that is not to be taken literally, but which dramatically brings home a point. For instance, you might remark to a friend that you really broke your neck getting over to her house to help her. Obviously, the statement is not to be taken literally, but it does reveal how much you hurried to her aid. Likewise, Jesus said: "If your right eye causes you to sin, take it out and throw it away!" (Matthew 5:29). Jesus is not recommending self-mutilation; he is strongly urging that his listeners avoid abusing their God-given capacities.

Teaching in Parables

Even though all the teaching devices mentioned so far might be considered to be "parables" in the broad sense, we more commonly think of parables as stories that ancient cultures used to teach a lesson. Such stories were frequently used by teachers in Jesus' time, but, as one would expect, Jesus often puts a different "spin" on them and conveys original insights. His followers felt free to alter these stories to fit their times and audiences, but dozens of these parables seem to originate from Jesus himself. Many scholars have concluded that it is in the parables that we truly meet up with the historical personality of Jesus and with his original teachings.[39]

Jesus seems to have been original in his use of parables. First of all, other teachers of Jesus' time tended to use parables as pedagogical tools to explain the Scriptures. The parables were thus given more as examples to back up academic scribal teachings. Jesus used the parables themselves to convey his own teaching and did not link them to some scribal teaching or even to Scripture. For Jesus, the medium was the message, and it was up to the listener to grapple with the story and discover the meaning that was being disclosed.[40] In this sense, Jesus was more of a poet in his presentations, offering parables as extended metaphors designed to reveal truths that could not be taught in the didactic prose of the scribes.

The gospel parables are fictitious short stories used to poetically explore religious mystery. The word "parable" means "placing one thing beside another" for the purpose of comparison. The teacher puts the message alongside the story and invites the listener to come to deeper understanding of the issue at hand through the story. For instance, on one occasion some chief priests and elders challenged the authority of Jesus. Jesus responded with a parable about a father who asked one of his sons to help him work in the vineyard. The son at first refused, but then had a change of heart and helped his father. The father then asked his other son to help him. This son said he would be glad to help, but never lifted a hand. Those challenging Jesus were to compare themselves to the two sons and realize that they were like the second—all talk, but no action (Matthew 21:28–31).

The parables of Jesus are earthy stories about everyday experience and it is this concrete reality that is to be put alongside the kingdom of God. The purpose is to bring the listener to an awareness that the kingdom of God is indeed at hand and can be encountered in all life experience. Thus parables might be described as "poetry that seeks to establish God's rule in our lives."[41] They are not stories containing some secret information from a hidden God, as many of the Gnostics implied in their gospels. On the contrary, they are stories that disclose the true meaning of God's plan and reveal how God is active in life situations, even the most ordinary events.[42] Jesus' parables are thus usually down-to-earth stories that put us in touch with the deeper and more sacred dimensions of life. For Jesus, they were an extremely effective method of revealing his message that a loving and saving God was actively involved in everyday experiences. The people could see themselves as the sheep lovingly sought after by their shepherd God, or as the prodigal son returning to the open arms of a loving father.

Those listening to Jesus could be challenged to a more inclusive notion of neighbor and moved to self-sacrifice by the good Samaritan. Or they could see the need to put aside all else in order to acquire this kingdom, this pearl of great price. The bad and the good in their lives could be accepted if they came to understand the parable of the wheat and the weeds. The hidden, nearly imperceptible movement of God in their lives was perceived in the image of yeast, while the enormous possibilities in the small things of life are disclosed in the story of the mustard seed. The stories in themselves have a certain incompleteness; the listeners are invited to enter into the story (and thus into the world of the kingdom) and then add an ending particular to their situations.[43]

There is also the element of surprise as the reader listens to these parables: surprise at the excessive kindness on the part of the supposedly heretical Samaritan; amazement at the unconditional love and forgiveness of the father of the prodigal son; bewilderment at the generosity of the foreman of the vineyard. All of this, of course, discloses the astounding gratuity and generosity of the God of the kingdom.[44]

The many surprising reversals and turns in the stories reveal the unpredictability of God's hidden power that can break through in the least expected moments of life. Cherished old beliefs and old assumptions are usually challenged by these stories, and new horizons of understanding open for the careful listener.

In many ways, Jesus himself is the main parable.[45] His person and his life are portrayed in the gospels as fraught with paradox and surprises. Indeed he embodies the message of the kingdom as the dynamic loving and saving presence of God in our lives. His own compassion, love, and self-sacrifice serve to "story" the kingdom of God in our world. His concern for those who lived hidden and difficult lives disclosed the powerful presence of God in the midst of the "little ones."

Summary

The historical Jesus is always difficult to discover, but even a glimpse makes the tediousness of the search worthwhile. Underneath the Christian stories and theology, we meet a great teacher whose lessons have enlightened and led the way for countless people over thousands of years. Although not formally educated or ordained, Jesus, the craftsman from Nazareth, was able to speak eloquently about his Jewish faith and his unparalleled experience of love and acceptance from his Abba. He never started his own rabbinic "school," but chose a rather motley group to follow him as disciples. He gave them and many others the "good news" that God's loving and saving presence was in their very midst, and he prepared them for the awesome task of taking this message to the world.

There was a prophetic edge to Jesus' teaching that challenged the leaders of his day to tear hypocrisy and oppression of others out of their lives. He courageously pointed out how much of the religious practice of his time was inconsistent with Yahweh's vision of justice and peace. With an authority all his own, he spoke of the kingdom of the loving and merciful God who was accessible for all, especially for those cast aside by society.

Along with his "good news" for the now, this prophetic teacher had even better news for the future: the coming of a time when there would be no more suffering or death. And he offered all this as "gift" to anyone who had the openness to receive it. Then he took a common teaching device, the parable, and made it into an art form through which many today still meet him and hear his message.

Questions for Reflection and Discussion

1. Compare and contrast Jesus with some of those who would be recognized as official teachers in his day.

2. In what ways was Jesus unique in the manner in which he selected and trained his disciples?

3. What aspects of Jesus' life have moved many to look upon him as a prophet?

4. The message of the "kingdom of God" was deep in the Hebrew tradition. What did Jesus contribute to this tradition?

5. Select one of the parables on the kingdom and point out its insights on the kingdom.

CHAPTER FOUR

Miracle Worker

A baby's heart suddenly and inexplicably repairs it-
self, and a doctor explains to the media, "It really seems to be a miracle." Parents hold their newborn and whisper to each other, "It's a miracle!" A young woman is cured of colon cancer after a healing service
at church, and she knows in her heart that she has experienced a miracle within her body. A team that has been given little chance to win the
championship comes from behind and wins, and the fans see the victory as a miracle. In each of these instances, the word "miracle" seems to
have a different meaning. Given such ambiguity, one can see why it is
necessary to proceed cautiously in discussing Jesus' role as a miracle
worker.

The *Oxford English Dictionary* has two definitions of the word "miracle." The first is from religion: "a remarkable and welcome event that
seems impossible to explain by means of the known laws of nature and
is therefore attributed to a supernatural agency." The second is the
more common understanding of the word: "a remarkable example or
specimen."

We often use the word in this second meaning when we speak about
the miracles of modern science or a miraculous escape from a crash or
even an amazing upset victory for a team. The religious connotation of
"miracle" is more problematic. While some believers accept the biblical
accounts of miracles as historical, for others miracles are simply impos-

sible, and these stories are mere myths from an ancient and primitive past.

This chapter hopes to take a middle position by arguing that there is a historical basis for miracles, but that many of the accounts are indeed highly stylized and shaped by past beliefs. We will begin by looking at how one's worldview affects attitudes toward miracles, and then discuss Jesus' miracles in the context of the "wonders" of his time among Jews, Greeks, and Romans.

We have placed a great deal of importance on discovering the historical Jesus. So here we must also deal with some important questions that surround these miracle stories that are so prominent in the gospels. For example, in what sense are the gospel miracles to be understood as being historical? What do these stories reveal about the kingdom? What is the role of faith with regard to miracles? How do these events fit into the overall mission of Jesus?

Differing World Views

As the dictionary definitions show, it is still common to define a miracle as an event that is somehow against the laws of nature. One of the difficulties with this perspective, however, is that it is not one that the biblical world would recognize. The ancient Hebrews did not use the word "nature," because they saw all reality as "creation." All reality came from the creative hand of God and, therefore, all events, whether they be sunsets, floods, or even plagues sent to the enemies of God's people, came from God. Yahweh was viewed as a God of both creation and history, a God who intervened in the world in such everyday events as storms, and in historical events whereby God saved God's people. In fact, the Exodus was viewed as the most significant "miracle" in Israel's history, and the other wondrous phenomena that surrounded that event, such as the plagues, the parting of the Red Sea, and the sending of water and manna in the desert, were wonders connected to this central miracle.[1]

The ancient Hebrew interpretation of the world around them was very different from our scientific understanding. They saw the world as three-layered, consisting of the upper world, the earth, and the underworld. The earth was a solid disc, arched over by the heavens, which were supported by huge pillars. The vault of heaven contained the "lights" (sun, moon, and stars) and had openings through which the rain poured. God resided in the upper world above the heavens. The underworld was the realm of chaos, death, and evil powers. God was up above and Satan was below. This perspective prevailed in the ancient and medieval world, and still exists in the minds of many people today.[2] It is curious how many contemporary insurance policies still refer to natural disasters as "acts of God."

The ancient Hebrews had no "laws of nature," as we understand them today from our scientific point of view. Events were brought about either by God or by evil spirits, and there was little understanding of natural causality. Yahweh was sovereign over all of the world and intervened as a matter of course. We see in the Psalms how the Hebrews were able to perceive God's power and glory in the world about them. The Psalmist writes: "How clearly the sky reveals God's glory! How plainly it shows what he has done! Each day announces it to the following day; each night repeats it to the next" (Psalm 19:1–2).

Jesus reflects this same sensitivity when he speaks of God's care and concern revealed in the birds of the air, flowers, sun, rain, and wind. Jesus was a Jew of his times and shared with his contemporaries their understanding of the world about them. For him, therefore, miracles were not viewed as actions that opposed the laws of nature, but as examples of God's power at work. As we shall see later, he did have an extraordinary and unique interpretation of how God's power was being manifested in the world.

Beginnings of Modern Science

From the ancient biblical perspective, as well as from the point of view of the great Greek minds like Aristotle and Ptolemy, the earth was the center of the universe. Understanding just how the earth operated was left to philosophy or to the myth-makers.

It was only in 1514 that this point of view was challenged by a Polish priest named Nicholas Copernicus, who proposed the revolutionary theory that the earth was not the center of the universe, but was rather a planet that, along with many others, moved in circular orbits around the sun. Later, two other astronomers, Kepler (d. 1630) and Galileo (d. 1642) confirmed this theory with the newly-developed telescope.

These early seventeenth-century scientific discoveries brought an end to the ancient notions of the earth and its relations to the heavens. A new method was born for understanding our world, the method of careful scientific investigation rather than reliance on philosophy or religious myth.

Another major breakthrough in the understanding of the "laws of nature" came in 1687 when Sir Isaac Newton put forth his theory of how bodies move in space and time. He postulated a law of universal gravitation to explain the movement of the earth and other planets. He also provided the mathematics to analyze these motions. From then on this approach to explaining reality would prevail.

There were many other significant breakthroughs that are familiar to us. In 1859 Charles Darwin published his *Origin of Species* wherein he described the evolution of all species as probably descending from one primordial form. In 1929 Edwin Hubble proposed that the universe as we know it is the result of a "Big Bang," a massive explosion of a infinitesimally small and infinitely dense mass. In 1905 Albert Einstein postulated his "theory of relativity." His theory revolutionized the way we think about the structure of the universe and led us into the nuclear age. In the 1920s the theory of quantum mechanics was put forth, based on the work of Max Planck, Werner Heisenberg, and others, a theory that led us into the world of microelectronics.[3]

These and many other advances, most notably the historic moon landing and other space achievements, have brought us into an age that often looks at miracles as an archaic leftover from another age. Formulas, scientific theories, and rational explanations have become the dominant method for interpreting the world in which we live. The modern mind seeking explanations for things often looks to science, not to the spirit world or the world of myth. Natural happenings are seen from the point of view of causes, known as laws of physics, and are no longer viewed as interventions of God or evil spirits.

Since the dawning of this modern scientific approach to reality, people have reacted to miracles in various ways. Fundamentalists, who hold that the Scriptures are a literal and historical description of miracles, have either denied the findings of science and forbidden believers to hold such theories (the rejections of great thinkers like Galileo in the seventeenth century and Teilhard de Chardin in the twentieth century); or they have turned to the Scriptures for scientific information (the modern-day Scientific Creationists).

Rationalists and materialists in the nineteenth century, on the other hand, maintained that miracles are, in fact, impossible because they interrupt the laws of nature.[4] The miracle stories, they conclude, must therefore be myths or fairy tales designed to make a religious point, but with no basis in history or reality.

Some nineteenth-century rationalists looked for natural explanations of the gospel miracle stories. They would argue, for example, that Jesus was simply walking in a shallow area and not on the surface of the water at all. In the story of the multiplication of the loaves, Jesus was simply able to persuade a young man to share his lunch, and that got a whole multitude to share their lunches with each other. And the so-called healings are explained by Jesus' ability to persuade people who had psychosomatic symptoms to change within them what was causing the illness.[5]

There are also those who accept scientific answers for most happenings but then interpose their God into the "gaps" that cannot be explained by science. The proponents of this approach have come to find less and less room for God, because as science advances there are fewer and fewer "gaps" within which to fit their God.

Even among those who believe in God and in Jesus, there are those who cannot accept the historicity of miracles. Many would agree with biblical scholar Rudolph Bultmann that miracles are simply impossible because they are incompatible with the findings of modern science. They conclude, therefore, that Jesus was portrayed much like a pagan wonder worker in the miracle stories in order to make him more acceptable to Gentiles. From this perspective, the miracle stories have no basis in history, and at best should be viewed as myths with a religious message.[6]

There is still another attitude toward miracles that is becoming more common among those who accept science and yet still hold for the possibility of miracles. Many are willing to set aside the ancient notions of the origin and workings of the world and accept the findings of modern science. At the same time, they are disillusioned with the road on which modern science has taken us, a road fraught with the dangers of nuclear and environmental destruction. They also perceive a new humility among scientists as it becomes more and more apparent that reality is much more mysterious and inscrutable than was ever suspected when science began so confidently. We have learned a great deal about our external world, but have neglected study of the origin and purpose of our world. As the renowned astrophysicist Stephen Hawking points out, we have been occupied for hundreds of years with the development of new theories about "what" the universe is; we have little knowledge about the *why*.[7]

Hawking is one of those scientists who is pursuing the Why, and his insights have many implications for our understanding of miracles. One does have to be wary, however, of Hawking's optimism in assuming that once scientists have answered the question of why we and the universe exist, "then we would know the mind of God."[8] Discovering the purposes and workings of God is simply not that easy, as we shall see as we examine the context and historicity of the gospel miracles.

Miracles in Judaism

That Jesus is portrayed as a worker of many miracles is unusual in

Judaism, for miracles are not as common among the Jews as some scholars have led us to believe. In the thousands of years of the Hebrew tradition, the only significant accounts of miracles are associated with Moses during the time of the Exodus, with the Elijah and Elisha cycle in the book of Kings, and with accounts in the book of Daniel.[9] Most of the stories are concerned with signs and wonders, such as the parting of the Red Sea in Exodus 14, the saving of the faithful from the fiery furnace and the lion's den in Daniel 3:1–25, and the feeding of five hundred men with twenty barley loaves in 2 Kings 4:42–44. Stories of healing are relatively rare, and they include the healing of Abimelech and his household in Genesis 20:18, Saul's being healed of an evil spirit in 1 Samuel 16, Elijah's healing of the widow's son in 1 Kings 4, and the restoration of the widow's son in 1 Kings 5. With regard to the number or significance of the miracles, however, nowhere in the Hebrew Scriptures do we find anyone who is comparable to Jesus.[10] Moreover, there is no precedent for the curing of the blind, lame, and mute as Jesus does in his ministry.[11]

Sources tell us that there were some miracle workers among the rabbis of the time of Jesus. Hanina ben Dosa and Honi the Circle Drawer were known as rainmakers. Both seemed to bring about results through intense prayer, and they gained a great deal of personal authority through their amazing feats.[12] Later rabbinic writings tell of some healings done through prayers, but there is no one person with an actual healing ministry comparable to that of Jesus. The rabbinic tradition looked upon these miracles as a way of confirming a teacher's authority to interpret the law. Again, such confirmation was not at issue in the case of Jesus' miracles.

The rabbinic tradition was suspicious of miracles. Sickness was often associated with the power of demons or with evil on the part of the person or his or her parents; therefore, anyone involved with the sick could well be suspected of conspiring with the devil. We see that to be the case in the gospels where Jesus is accused of working miracles through the power of Satan. Thus later rabbinic sources refer to Jesus as a sorcerer.[13]

There was a tradition in the Hebrew Scriptures that Yahweh was the sender of sickness as well as being a healer. In Exodus, Yahweh is depicted as saying: "I kill and I make alive; I wound and I heal; And there is none can deliver out of my hand." The power, then, belongs to Yahweh, and the rabbinic tradition seems rarely to grant that this power comes through the hands of a human healer. Thus many disabled and sick Jews at the time of Jesus felt hopeless in the face of the demonic. It is easy to understand why Jesus' healings and exorcisms, which so dramatically revealed the utter defeat of Satan, came to the sick and disabled as such marvelous good news.[14]

We can see, then, that the gospel portrayal of Jesus as a powerful and frequent worker of miracles is unique in the Jewish tradition. His curing of those with physical and mental disabilities is unprecedented among those of his time. He does not resemble the rainmakers, nor does he use miracles to gain personal authority or to demonstrate that he has the credentials to interpret the law. He reaches out with compassion to those rejected by society because of their disabilities, and, with incredible courage, he confronts what is perceived in his time as the power of Satan. But his actions are not to dazzle others or to get a personal following for himself. His primary motive, as we shall see in more detail later, is to reveal the healing presence of a parent God who brings wholeness and reunion to God's people. Jesus reveals in his miracles a God who is not a killer or a sender of plagues, but a God who loves and cares for the sick and the disabled. Good news indeed!

Roman and Greek Miracle Stories

There does not appear to be a strong miracle tradition among the Romans. Tacitus and Suetonius recount some stories of wondrous events, but these are rather rare. Tacitus reports that the Emperor Vespasian was able to perform cures of the blind and the crippled. The Romans were usually more concerned with stories of portents, omens, and dreams than they were with tales of personal healing.

Miracles appear to have been more common among the Greeks. The city of Epidaurus was the Lourdes of the ancient world, and excavated pillars from this area record many cures. Some of these records are of standard healings, while others are of rather incredible displays.[15] The miracles are not attributed to personal healers, but rather to the healer-god Asclepius who, from the time of Homer in eighth century B.C.E. to the time of Constantine in the fourth century C.E., was associated with healing and was looked upon as the founder of the ancient medical profession.[16]

Other documents from the ancient world give examples of persons walking on water and raising the dead, but these are not associated with the mission of one individual, nor is there any unique message attached to these actions. They are simply isolated events, and not integral to the ministry of an individual, as they are in the gospel stories.

Some have tried to compare the portrait of the "divine man" Apollonius (d. 100 C.E.), drawn by his biographer Philostratus, to the gospel portrait of Jesus. Apollonius was a contemporary of Paul of Tarsus and was widely known as a holy man and miracle worker. Apollonius, however, seems to perform his cures more by natural therapy and special insight, whereas Jesus seems to be set on revealing the healing powers of a merciful God. Nor does Jesus come across as one who is concerned with displaying his own divinity in the fashion of Apollonius.

It is also worth noting that most of these ancient miracle stories are described in documents written long after the gospels, and it is doubtful, therefore, that these stories had much influence on the gospel writers. On the other hand, it does seem to be true that the Greek literary model for telling a miracle story—with the description of the illness, the account of the cure, and the recognition of the success of the healing—was often used by the gospel writers.[17] It is difficult, however, to build a strong case that the gospel writers were simply borrowing from the content of these ancient stories and recreating Jesus as an ancient charismatic healer. If anything, the gospel miracle stories are told in the context of the Jewish belief in the healing power of Yahweh, rather than in the framework of Greek mythology or magic. In the miracle stories the gospel writers reflect the conviction of the early Christians that the saving power of God was experienced both in the life of the earthly Jesus and in the continuing work of the Christ.

Magicians of the Time

Some scholars have attempted to show the parallels between the actions of Jesus and the magicians of the time.[18] Using accounts of these magicians (which were written much later than the gospels), these scholars suggest that Jesus somehow fits into this category of ancient wizardry.

There apparently were magicians who worked secretly and privately, claiming to possess mysterious and arcane knowledge and power. These individuals made use of magical formulas and were known for sensational actions that gained them a following. They claimed to be adept at manipulating spirits and were even known to use evil spirits to achieve evil ends. These magicians were also known to claim divinity and have access to divine power. In performing their magic, they would often get results by overpowering the will of the person upon whom they were working their enchantment.[19]

From what we seem to know about ancient magicians and what we know about the historical Jesus, the comparison between them limps badly. Jesus does not work in secret as though to preserve arcane knowledge and powers. Many of his miracles are done publicly, and they proclaim the loving, healing powers of God. If Jesus does, at times, ask those healed to be secretive, it doesn't seem to be because he wanted to hide his methods from the public; instead he asked them to be secretive because he was concerned about being proclaimed a messiah-king.

Jesus also does not use magical formulas or incantations. Generally, his miracles are performed simply by a simple word or gesture. And these actions are not to draw a following to himself; rather they are performed to reveal the power of the Father.

Jesus makes no claim to divinity, nor does he manipulate evil spirits or work for evil purposes. Instead his healings and exorcisms proclaim God's sovereign power over evil. Nor are Jesus' miracles done in any spectacular or sensational fashion. They are generally performed with remarkable restraint and sensitivity. And, finally, in the miracle stories of Jesus we find no evidence of him overpowering the other person's will. Instead they come to him, and all that he usually asks is an openness on their part to the power of God. He calls them to faith and freedom, not manipulation and submission.

If all this be true, then one has to ask why he was considered to be a sorcerer by some of his contemporaries and even by later rabbinic writers. A. E. Harvey has made an interesting observation in this regard. He points out that Jesus' own unique style of performing miracles ran the risk of being interpreted as sorcery. Had Jesus followed the procedures of many of the charismatic healers, wonder workers, and magicians of his time, he most likely would not have stood out as very dangerous or have made so many enemies. Had he used magical formulas, prayers, or medicines, he would have been perceived as a recognizable figure of his day, would have gained a certain recognition, and might today be indeed classified as a typical healer of his time.[20] But Jesus chose to "follow his own bliss," to use the words of Joseph Campbell. He carried out his own unique and incomparable mission, and the Jewish leaders had no category for him. So they condemned him as a sorcerer and a false prophet. Otherwise they would have been faced with the very threatening prospect of following his call to conversion. They simply had too much to lose by following that course.

Apocryphal Miracles

There is also a tradition of miracle stories in the apocryphal gospels. While some of the apocryphal stories resemble those in the gospels, others are rather outlandish and beyond credibility. In fact, when compared to some of these stories, the gospel miracles are models of moderation and restraint.

In the Infancy Gospel of Thomas, for example, the young Jesus is challenged for shaping some pigeons on the Sabbath, and so, in response to the challenge, he simply claps his hands and the birds come to life and fly away. In the same document some of Jesus' playmates spoil the pools of water he is making, so in revenge he denounces them and causes one of his taunters to fall down dead.

In the Acts of Peter, the daughter of Peter has contracted an infirmity to prevent her from being too attractive and seductive to the neighboring lads, but she is eventually healed of this infirmity. In the same document Peter competes with Simon Magus and the stories that ensue include a dog that is made to talk, the restoration of a broken statue of Caesar, and the bringing back to life of a fish that is hanging in the local market.[21]

These stories come more from the tradition of magic; they are out of character for Jesus and his disciples. The sensationalism and the vindictiveness on the part of God and Jesus, as well as the demonstrative nature of these stories, are not in continuity with the nature of Jesus' person or message.

Historicity of the Miracles
So far we have seen that the gospel miracle stories, while bearing some similarities to the stories of other traditions, are unique and do not relate in any clear fashion either to the accounts in Jewish, Roman, or Greek stories, or to the magical or apocryphal tales. The question still remains: Are these stories historical or do they simply represent another literary genre that was invented by the gospel writers, much the way they invented the "gospel genre" itself?

Perhaps the most convincing argument for the historicity of the miracle stories is the central role they play in the gospels themselves. About one fifth of the literary units in the synoptics allude to miracles of healing and exorcism, and a large portion of the Johannine gospel is concerned with miraculous "signs."[22] Much of this material is in the earliest strata of the gospel sources and is even linked to the earliest "sayings of Jesus."[23] Without these miracle stories the synoptic gospels would simply not hold together as authentic testimonies of the significance of Jesus' words and deeds. They are simply too integral to the gospel message. Moreover, because they are attested to by all of the synoptic gospels, and are on the whole congruous with the character of the historical Jesus as he is portrayed in the gospels, one may safely conclude that these stories have historical foundation. And we have already noted that the later rabbinic descriptions of Jesus do not deny that he performed miracles; they simply attribute his activities in this regard to sorcery.

To say that the miracle stories have a historical base, however, is not to deny that these stories have been reworked, edited, and theologized in both the oral and written traditions. We now know enough of the nature of biblical writing to know that these are not eyewitness accounts or an attempt at writing factual history. These are "faith accounts" and their primary purpose is to proclaim the risen and glorified Lord as he is experienced and understood by the early communities.

The main issue for these communities was not "what happened," but the meaning of the events of Jesus' life in the light of resurrection faith. The "what happened?" question is ours. It belongs to our post-Enlightenment generation's deep concern for the facts and for a historical perspective that was unknown in the ancient world. They had little access to exact facts of the past, nor did they see the continuity of history as we do. For them the past was wrapped in myth and story, and the religious past was only relevant if it could be brought to bear on the present.[24]

The Jews had preserved the great event of Exodus, which they certainly maintained was historical—not so much in its facts as in its meaning to them. It was in the past, but at each Passover they brought this event into the present to restore their faith and to give them hope for the future. Likewise, the Christian communities looked back at the memories they had of Jesus as miracle worker and reinterpreted these memories in terms of their present beliefs and struggles.

In examining the historicity of gospel miracles, it is important to distinguish between miracle events and miracle stories. That there were miraculous events in Jesus' life there can be no doubt. Otherwise, the later miracle stories have little purpose or meaning.[25] At the same time, we have little means for ascertaining what exactly happened when these events took place. The stories have become too stylized and filled out with faith insights for us to be able to peel all that away and restore some sort of original painting of the event.

It is widely accepted by biblical scholars that Jesus did perform healings and exorcisms (the so-called nature miracles are another matter), and it would seem that many biblical scholars are willing to grant that these stories are more theological than they are historical. Yet what we seem to have in the formulation of the gospel miracle tradition is an author or community taking "the kinds of things" that Jesus did and using these as the basis for creating a miracle story that proclaims him to be the Christ.[26]

In other words, miraculous events did happen during Jesus' earthly life, and later served as a reliable tradition of memories about what Jesus did. It is these memories that are the basis for the creation of the miracle stories after the resurrection. It was the historical Jesus himself who gave a uniquely new meaning to the phenomena of miracles. This certainly must have amazed and attracted people to him, perhaps without their really understanding what he or his deeds really meant. Later, the early Christian communities extended both the description and the meaning of these actions in order that the gospel stories might proclaim Jesus as the risen and glorified Christ.

Miracles as Proofs

Traditionalists have often viewed the miracles as proof of Jesus' divinity. Those who do not make the distinction between the Jesus of history and the Christ of faith assume that Jesus as the Christ walked about Galilee performing miracles to give proof that he was indeed God. As we saw in chapter two, the recognition of Jesus as the Christ came after the resurrection. The earthly Jesus did not claim to be divine and thus did not perform miracles for the purpose of proving such to be true. He made it quite clear that he was not performing these miracles on his own authority, but through the power of the Father who sent him. He said: "truly the son can do nothing of his own accord....Bear witness that the Father has sent me" (John 5:30, 36).

The gospel language itself leads us away from any notion of the miracles being performed as demonstrations or displays. The Greek word for miracle, *thauma*, is not used in the gospels, and even the word for wonder, *teras*, is generally avoided by the gospel writers. These are words used in pagan literature for sensational acts, and this simply was not what Jesus was about. The most common word used in the synoptics for the events is *dunameis* (the root of our word for "dynamic" and "dynamite"), which means acts of power, specifically acts of God's power.[27] The language indicates that Jesus was not inclined to do the sensational or wondrous in his miracles. His resistance to such displays is evident in the temptation stories, where he refuses to do stunts such as turn stones into bread or miraculously be saved from a jump from a great height. Jesus' low-key approach to miracles is also evident in the warnings about secrecy he sometimes gives to those who have been healed. Recall also the testiness that Jesus shows in the story where the government official requests that his son be cured. Jesus tersely remarks: "None of you will ever believe unless you see miracles and wonders" (John 4:48).

Neither will Jesus respond with proof of his credentials when challenged by his enemies. In the story of his trial before Herod, he deprives the ruler of some hoped-for miracle (Luke 23:8). Mark relates the story of the Pharisees who ask Jesus to perform a miracle to show that God approved him. In response Jesus groans and says: "Why do the people of this day ask for a miracle? No I tell you! No such proof will be given to these people!" (Mark 8:11–12). Jesus' ministry was not carried out to prove anything so much as to reveal the presence and power of the living God. His miracles were to meet human needs and to show that all, especially outcasts, had access to the power of God.

That neither the letters of Paul nor the other books beyond the gospels discuss the miracles of Jesus might be another indication that miracles were not used by Jesus for apologetic purposes. Apparently some of the early Christians found it quite possible to spread the good news without reference to the miracle stories. Had these events been used by Jesus to prove the validity of his identity and mission, it would seem that these stories would be used throughout all of the Christian Scriptures, not only in the gospels.[28]

It should be evident that the miracle stories in their context are not effective proofs of anything. Many of the miracles are public, viewed by all kinds of people who have diverse reactions. Many persons reacted negatively; some thought that Jesus was out of his mind; others that it was quite presumptuous for a simple Galilean to be doing such works. There were even those who believed that he was working through the devil. Others reacted positively, filled with gratitude and admiration. Many seemed to experience the power of God in Jesus' actions, and their faith in God and hope for the future were deepened. It is quite possible that many of those whom Jesus cured later became his disciples.

Miracles as Signs of the Kingdom

The kingdom of God was at the very center of Jesus' message. The purpose of his miracles was to complement this message with actions that dramatically revealed the presence of the kingdom.

Jesus taught that God's reign of love and salvation was near at hand, and miracles concretely manifested the presence of God's loving care and healing. The "Good News" of Jesus was that God was not simply a past figure in the glory days of Israel. Nor was God in some remote place in the firmament sending sickness and disabilities as punishment for sin. Rather, God's reigning power was present in the midst of God's people. In the midst of their sufferings, sickness, and death God was presént as Consoler, Healer, and Restorer. Jesus' miracles served as dynamic signs that pointed to and revealed the presence of this prevailing power of God.

Jesus did not perform miracles to prove anything about himself, and here he differs significantly from the other wonder workers and magicians of the time whose personal reputations were often the focus of their actions. Jesus' miracles were a proclamation of Abba's presence, the same parent-God who had sent him to bring this good news to the world.

There is, in Jesus' miraculous actions, a continuity with God's saving actions in the past. At the very beginning of his public ministry, Jesus linked the work he would do with the saving power of Yahweh described by Isaiah. Luke portrays Jesus' reading of Isaiah in the synagogue in Nazareth and then reports Jesus as identifying himself with the prophecy: "The Spirit of the Lord is upon me, because he has chosen me to bring good news to the poor. He has sent me to proclaim liberty to the captives and recovery of sight to the blind, to set free the oppressed..." (Luke 4:18–19).

Matthew uses this Isaiah reference as the answer Jesus gives to the followers of John the Baptist when they ask him if he is the one who is to come. Jesus answers: "Go back and tell John what you are hearing and seeing: the blind see, the lame can walk, those who suffer from dreaded skin diseases are made clean, the deaf hear, the dead are brought back to life, and the Good News is preached to the poor" (Matthew 11:4–6). The miracles are clearly signs of the good news of God's healing and saving presence among God's people.

Most notable in this passage is the preferential attention given to the poor and the rejected. In his teaching and his miraculous actions, Jesus is radically opposing the conventional wisdom that the disabled and sick should be avoided as ones who obviously are somehow involved in evil. Jesus' miracles stand as a contradiction to these beliefs and reveal that the will of his Father is wholeness and reconciliation within the human community. Disease and disability are not punishments from God or signs of complicity with the demonic. They are physical evils that can be overcome by the power of God, and this power is here now and available to those who are open to it.

Jesus links his present mission with the past, but he also reveals a promising future. He came as the "eschatological prophet," teaching that although the ruling and healing power of God was present, the time of fulfillment of this kingdom was still to be realized in the future. He made no attempt to heal all disease and disabilities; he knew these would remain with the human community. The miracles revealed,

however, that in the midst of suffering and death there is always reason for hope for a future of wholeness and intimacy with God. The
powers of evil have been overcome by God, and goodness will ultimately prevail for those who believe in the reign of God. The Father's
will, therefore, is not in complicity with sickness and death as a punishment for sin. Rather the divine will is for the end of brokenness, oppression, and rejection.

The miracles not only point to these truths, they make them experi-
ential for those who have suffered and been rejected because of their
disabilities. One scene that brings this out dramatically is drawn by
Matthew. The Pharisees in the scene are critical of Jesus' followers for
picking grain to eat on the Sabbath. Jesus remarks that in his work
there is something greater than the Sabbath laws, or even than the Temple sacrifice itself: the experience of God's power. To reveal this, Jesus
goes to the synagogue and heals the man with the paralyzed hand on
the Sabbath.

Matthew tells us that Jesus' confrontation with the Pharisees' legalistic and oppressive notion of God's reign was totally unacceptable to
these Jewish leaders. When Jesus healed the man, the Pharisees "left
and made plans to kill Jesus" (Matthew 12:14). Here, the miracles are
given central significance in Jesus' ministry. They are, therefore, more
than actions of compassion. Miracles are at the heart of Jesus' message
and are done at the very risk of his own life.

Matthew also links healing miracles with the so-called "cleansing of
the Temple" scene. Scholars have increasingly come to place a great
deal of significance on this action as pivotal in Jesus' mission, and as
the key to explaining why Jesus was killed. In the gospel of Luke, immediately after this scene, Jesus' enemies are described as plotting to
kill Jesus (Luke 19:45–48). Matthew tells us that immediately after Jesus
drove out the buyers and sellers, the blind and the lame came into the
Temple (where Jewish law forbade them to come) and Jesus healed
them. Here, Jesus brings his good news of a loving and healing God to
Jerusalem and into the Temple itself. Those who have been excluded
from the Jewish community and from Temple worship are able to experience the healing power of God in their own place of worship.

The power of God, according to Jesus, transcends laws and even religious beliefs, and comes into the hearts of the excluded.[29] Jesus would
eventually have to pay with his life for revealing this in his miracles.
His message of liberation was too much for those who had wealth and
power to lose if such a message should prevail among the poor and the
oppressed.

The purpose of miracles, then, goes far beyond physical healing or freeing people from whatever "demons" control their lives. Jesus, of course, is concerned about freeing people from the pain and anguish of physical suffering. But his approach is also holistic in that he is attentive to people's spiritual and social needs as well. The miracles not only restore physical wholeness, they offer those healed an experience of God that changes their lives. Moreover, for the sick and disabled who had been for so long excluded from the Temple and from social gatherings, and who had experienced the anguish of personal rejection, Jesus offers acceptability and reunion.

The miracles reveal that God's reign is sovereign in all aspects of life. For those who are open to this power a new and exhilarating freedom is accessible. Jesus' miracles are not designed to prove anything or to demonstrate some secret magical tricks. Rather, his miracles empower and restore the recipients to authentic human experience, characterized by love, forgiveness, and wholeness.[30]

With the miracles, the kingdom penetrates the physical with healing, but it also enters into the areas of human prejudice that exclude lepers, centurions, women, and many others. As each of these people experience God's power in miracles, the lesson of God's universal love is revealed to them as well as to those who are open to what they see.

Miracles and Faith

The element of faith is often introduced into the gospel miracle stories. Sometimes the accounts themselves seem to be struggling with the question of belief. Often it seems that faith is integral, almost necessary, before the miracle can take place. At times it is the faith of the person that brings about the healing. In the curious story of the woman who had hemorrhaged for many years, for example, the woman reaches out in desperation to touch the cloak of Jesus and is cured. Mark says that "Jesus knew power had gone out of him" and he asks who touched his cloak. Jesus then tells the woman: "Your faith has made you whole" (Mark 5:25-34). It appears as though the woman is almost looking for magic in the touching of Jesus' cloak, yet somehow she has genuine enough faith to experience the healing power of God.

On another occasion, it is the faith of the client's friends that seems to be crucial in the miracle. In the story of four friends of a paralyzed man going to all the trouble to carry him up to the roof and lower him through the ceiling for a cure, Jesus recognized *their* faith and thus forgave and healed their friend (Luke 5:19–27).

At other times it would seem that faith on the part of the healer is required for the miracle. Matthew tells a story about Jesus' disciples not being able to cure a boy with epilepsy. Jesus is frustrated with his followers in the scene and tells them that they could not cure the boy "because you do not have enough faith" (Matthew 17:20). John tells us that, before the miracle of Lazarus being brought back from the dead, Martha was asked if she believed that Jesus was the resurrection and the life (John 11:25).

Faith does not seem to be at issue in other miracle stories. Peter's mother-in-law did not express faith, nor did she asked to be healed. (Matthew 8:14–15). In Gennesaret many came to Jesus and were healed simply by touching his cloak. And a leper was cleansed by Jesus for simply saying: "If you want to, you can make me clean" (Mark 1:40). In this instance, Jesus seems to be moved out of pity for the man, and there is no explicit mention of faith. In short, the picture varies from one story to another, and it makes it all the more difficult to ascertain what faith actually is in these instances and how it is connected with miracles.

It would seem certain that we are not talking here about the kind of "faith-healing" that involves some kind of power of suggestion exerted by a charismatic figure. Nor is the faith associated with the miracle stories the kind of faith that would somehow "earn" a miracle for self or others. This is the common misinterpretation of Jesus' statement: "Your faith has made you well" (Mark 5:34).[31] Neither Jesus nor his disciples claimed to have miraculous powers, nor did they demand that others recognize such powers before a miracle could be performed.

What Is This Faith?

The faith at question here seems to be an openness to the power of God in one's life or in the life of another. Without such openness both the healers and the healed block the experience of the power of God. Apparently such openness is not self-achieved. It is pure gift, and the contribution that the candidate makes is one of response and receptivity. Such faith is an amazing gift that itself is a "miracle" and even brings about astonishment on the part of Jesus.[32] Matthew tells the story of Jesus being surprised at the faith of the Roman officer and proclaiming: "I have never found anyone in Israel with faith like this" (Matthew 8:10).

Karl Rahner maintained that a miracle presupposes that a faithful person is willing to enter into the depths of his or her existence and be open to the element of the truly "wonderful." He pointed out that, as materialists, we are too often locked into a one-dimensional reality and neglect to recognize reality's spiritual and mystical dimensions. Miracles have something to do with these dimensions, and to experience them it is necessary to have a certain "inner-expansiveness," a willingness to go beyond the observable and the measurable to the transcendent.[33]

Such faith is indeed gift insofar as it is offered freely to all who wish to receive and nurture it. Once received, it offers new vision and new perspective whereby one may be receptive to the power of God working among people and in the world. Such faith is not interested in magic, nor is such faith looking for evidence or proof. Faith in this context is the willingness to recognize the power of God in operation. This recognition is what seems to be operative in miracles. It presupposes not only belief in God, but trust and confidence in God's power.

So many of the miracle stories, whether it be the calming of the storm, the walking on the water, or the feeding of the multitude, are attempting to teach this notion of faith. Each story in its own way dramatizes the action of God in everyday life and the need of an openness to be able to recognize it. Whether this faith be on the part of friends seeking healing for another, on the part of an individual seeking a cure, or on the part of the healer, such openness seems to be an integral part of dealing with miracles.

Resurrection Faith and Miracles

As was said earlier, the miracle stories were not composed orally or in writing until after the resurrection. It should also be remembered that the early Christians saw the resurrection as the supreme miracle.[34] When Jesus' followers experienced him as having been raised from the dead, they then believed that he had been raised up to be their Christ and Lord.

It was here in these post-resurrection days that Christian faith was born. The experiences that many had during Jesus' ministry were now looked back on, reinterpreted, and retold in the light of this Easter faith. The faith that once was openness to the experience of the power of God now became an openness to the messiahship and divine sonship of Jesus.

As Edward Schillebeeckx points out, it was the task of the earthly Jesus to arouse unconditional faith in God, but after Easter the focus of faith was on Jesus himself.[35] This has to be remembered when reading the miracle stories, for in them we are often hearing more about the struggle of the early Christian faith communities than we are about historical details of miracles during Jesus' earthly life. Indeed, during his life he did work many signs to point to the power of God, but after the resurrection these signs also become proclamations of Jesus the Savior. The faith that once was an openness to God's power now was transformed into a receptivity to Jesus as the Son of God.[36] But the original signs performed by Jesus remained treasured memories for the early communities. They were now not only signs of God's power but comforting signs that the risen Lord was in their midst, unseen and yet experienced in faith.

There is a contrast between the miracles as signs of the kingdom and as symbols of Jesus' identity as the Christ. This contrast is evident if we compare the miracles in the synoptics with those in John. In the synoptic gospels, Jesus seems to perform miracles to point to the establishment of the kingdom of God through destruction of Satan's power. This is especially apparent in the exorcism stories where the miracle is an act of power that demonstrates the presence of God's reign. Jesus says to those who accuse him of healing through the devil: "If it is by the Spirit of God that I cast out demons, then the kingdom of God has come upon you" (Matthew 12:28). The miracles here are not focused on Jesus, but on the power of God revealed through him.

There is a different approach to miracles in the gospel of John. John views miracles as signs (semeia) or, more appropriately, symbols of Jesus as the Christ. The miracles begin at Cana, where Jesus "revealed his glory," and then John goes on to depict Jesus as the resurrection in the raising of Lazarus, and as the "light of the world" in healing the blind man. Throughout the gospel John develops seven signs that he apparently has taken from a larger "signs source." Each of these in its own way reveals the identity of the risen and glorified Lord.

Doubts and Faith

The stories not only carried the faith convictions of the early Christians, they also conveyed their struggle with doubt. Undoubtedly, there were still those who demanded signs, just as the Pharisees had done earlier.

There were those who were not open to Jesus as the Christ because they needed evidence. The fascinating story of blind Bartimaeus depicts the struggle of the early Christians to see the Lord in faith. The blind beggar calls out in his darkness and asks mercy of Jesus. When Jesus summons him he jumps up and says: "Teacher, I want to see again." Jesus restores his sight, and Mark writes: "At once he was able to see and followed Jesus down the road" (Mark 10:46–52). For the early Christians, faith was the power to see Jesus, and it was not possible to follow him without it. But faith always includes darkness and struggle.[37]

Miracles as Mission

Monika Hellwig has pointed out that each of the four categories of miracles (healing, exorcisms, raising of the dead, and the nature miracles) is a "representative expression of the whole redemptive mission of Jesus."[38] In the healing miracles, Jesus reveals a God who is all-inclusive in caring for God's world and God's creatures. This God is the healing Yahweh of the Hebrew Scriptures, but without the shadow side of vengeance and punishment through sickness or oppression. Faith, openness to God's power, is the way to healing and wholeness. In the exorcism stories a contemporary person would have to translate the message into the availability of God's power to help those who have psychological problems, or erratic behavior patterns, or who have allowed evil to dominate their lives. Moreover, the evil forces behind racism, injustice, and oppression can and will be overcome by the sovereign power of God. Those "possessed" by such forces need to be liberated by the healing of the Lord.[39]

The stories wherein people are raised from the dead proclaim that the risen Jesus is Lord. Traumatic, tragic, and death-dealing events in life can find hope and new life in the Christ. Death, both spiritual and physical, was overcome when Jesus of Nazareth was raised from the dead and glorified as Son of God and Savior. He indeed is the source of life here and in the life to come.

The nature miracles are often put in a category of their own because of their apparent lack of historicity. The distinction would have been lost on the gospel writers because all the miracles were primarily written to proclaim faith rather than to describe history. The well-known walking on the water story, the calming of the sea, and the others reveal God as sovereign over all creation. Creation is sacred, and we are called to be stewards over the earth and partners in the creative process. This is a valuable revelation for our times when the environment around us is in such perilous danger of being destroyed.

Summary

Jesus was indeed a worker of miracles. There seems to be good reason to believe that the earthly Jesus performed healings, exorcisms, and other actions that amazed some and scandalized others among his contemporaries. These events are unique in both number and significance when compared to similar accounts in Jewish and pagan literature.

In spite of the historical character of these miraculous events, however, it should be recognized that the early Christian communities and the gospel writers often enlarged on and transformed these events in order to express the faith of the time. As a result, the miracle stories are often designed to reveal the Christian faith in Jesus as the Christ, explain his teaching, reflect on the nature of faith, and comment on the meaning of his mission.

These events would have been understood differently in the pre-scientific period than they are today. Still, even in this era of advanced scientific knowledge and technology, these stories have something important to say about the mysteries beyond analysis and about the saving power of God that is still experienced by those with faith in Jesus Christ.

Questions for Reflection and Discussion

1. Compare the Hebrew notion of the cosmos with the modern scientific view.

2. Contrast Jesus' views on sickness and disability with some of the other views of his day.

3. Name ways in which Jesus was unique among other wonder-workers of the time.

4. What are your views on the "historicity" of the miracle stories?

5. What are some of the teachings about the need for faith in the miracle stories?

CHAPTER FIVE

Advocate for Women

Christianity, like the many cultures into which it has spread, has been largely male-dominated. There have been numerous outstanding women among its saints and pastoral leaders, but, for the most part, the hierarchy, clergy, and scholars have been men. In recent times, however, there are signs of major shifts toward equality in the Christian churches and denominations. Many Protestant groups have extended ordination and official leadership positions to women, and there is a vigorous movement among Catholics to achieve equality between the sexes. Among both Protestants and Catholics, women scholars are beginning to gain prominence in the areas of theology and biblical studies.

In this historic shift toward equality in Christianity, one of the key questions has been: "Where did Jesus stand on sexual equality?" Many Christians do not want to proceed with developments toward equality unless they can be assured that such movement would be faithful to Jesus' own words and deeds and to the practices of the early communities as they are reflected in the gospels.

Approaches to Jesus' views vary widely. Some would portray Jesus as a radical feminist. They would point to how he uniquely departed from the sexist customs of his day. Others disagree and argue that those who see Jesus as a radical feminist are anachronistically projecting a contemporary perspective back into the time of Jesus.

In fact, as he is portrayed in the gospels, Jesus has little to say explicitly about sexual discrimination or equality in ministry. Those who believe that there is little hope of discovering the historical Jesus (because the gospels reflect a much later theology and faith) also feel that it is not possible to discover Jesus' views on matters of gender equality. Even among those who believe that it is possible to discover the historical Jesus and his teachings, there is disagreement about his perspective on the role of the feminine in Christianity.

Some radical feminists challenge whether Jesus can be a savior figure for women: As a male, he does not offer appropriate modeling or inspiration for a feminine spirituality or liberation.[1] On the other end of the spectrum, many conservatives hold that Jesus followed the patriarchal structures established by God and that this structure must therefore be continued in today's churches. Among these traditionalists, there are those who are willing to grant that although Jesus did, in fact, depart from the patriarchal and sexist patterns of his own religion, he still insisted on appointing only male apostles. This male apostleship, they believe, is the basis for the modern hierarchical structure, and this structure, therefore, must be maintained.

Some scholars today, especially women scholars, would depart from both these radical and traditional views. They would argue that Jesus' teaching and actions regarding women were indeed a remarkable departure from the prevailing religious and cultural views of his time. He treated women with respect as persons, included them equally in the reign of God, and invited them to be his followers and disciples.

Those who argue from this position point out that Jesus' attitude toward women was carried forth and developed in the early communities, and then was dramatically reflected in the gospels. These egalitarian views were lost, however, as the patriarchal system gradually regained prominence and as male exegetes and theologians imposed a masculine interpretation on the gospel sources. Those who hold this point of view hope to retrieve the original gospel views about the dignity and equality of the sexes and their role in ministry and to restore these views to present-day Christianity.

In this chapter we are going to explore this extremely complex question of Jesus' views on women. We will begin by discussing some of the attitudes toward women that prevailed in the cultures surrounding Jesus, especially in his own Jewish culture. Then, using the gospels as our primary resource, we will examine a number of significant ways in which Jesus seems to have challenged the oppression of women. We will also review how Jesus gave women their rightful place in the kingdom, and how he chose them to be his own disciples.

Ancient Attitudes Toward Women

The contemporary women's movement, which, in this century, gained significant impetus in France after World War II and in the United States in the 1960s, is not an isolated movement. It is part of a recurring cycle of efforts on the part of women throughout history to claim their rightful place in society as dignified and equal persons. There are numerous instances in history where women began a rise toward equality, gained a certain degree of prominence, and then once again receded to the background of social, political, and religious life.

This cycle of women's efforts for liberation is notable even in ancient cultures. Our knowledge of these cultures is, of course, limited. The sources are fragmentary, and they generally reflect what was going on in the more educated and affluent groups. We know little about the struggles among the common women, but we can assume that many of them experienced considerable oppression and had to struggle for their rights just as women often do today. We must remember, therefore, that whatever observations we can make about the progress of women in these cultures are only tentative and open to debate among scholars.

The struggle on the part of women to liberate themselves had both high and low points in ancient cultures. In most Near Eastern cultures the social and religious structures were patriarchal, but there are examples where struggles to overcome male domination were successful, at least for a time. Several thousands of years before the birth of Jesus, women in the ancient culture of Sumer (to the east of Palestine) seem to have been in an extraordinary position. Some of them had more than one husband, owned huge tracts of land, received equal pay for their work, and were rated among the top-ranked intellectual leaders of their time. The conquest of Sumer, first by Babylonia and later by Assyria, seemed to put an end to all this, and in the centuries to follow the women of this area lost many of their rights in a legal system that was markedly favorable toward men.[2]

Egypt, Greece, and Rome

A similar cycle occurred in Egypt around the year 2500 B.C.E. At this time women were able to choose their own husbands on the basis of love, were considered equal to their husbands, had a right of inheritance not known in other cultures, and for the most part had a place in society equal to men. Here, too, these rights for women soon went into serious decline when Egypt was conquered by Greece and later by Rome.[3]

Women's rights in Grecian culture also went through various phases of freedom and repression. In Greece from 3000–1000 B.C.E., women seemed to enjoy a high status in society but, in the so-called Golden Age of Greece (fifth and fourth centuries B.C.E.), their status went into decline, particularly in Athens.

Plato and Aristotle, both of whom had a great deal of influence on later cultures and eventually on Christianity, had deep prejudices against women. Plato maintained that women should be obedient to men and remain at home. Aristotle held that women were by nature far inferior to men and should allow their fathers and husbands to rule over them.[4]

In the Hellenistic period, which followed the conquests of Alexander the Great and lasted until the rise of Rome in the first century B.C.E., women once again began to gain freedom. Although not considered equal to men, Hellenistic women had extensive rights in the family and in the economic and social spheres. Spartan women participated in the Olympics, and there are records of excellent women athletes in the foot and chariot races just forty years before the time of Jesus. Women also distinguished themselves in music, medicine, arts, crafts, and professions.

Women during this Hellenistic period were also recognized as writers and philosophers, especially among the Stoics, Cynics, and Epicureans. In addition, women played an active and even priestly role in many of the Hellenistic cults and mystery religions.[5] None of this means, however, that women had achieved rights equal to men.

Roman culture had been much influenced by the liberal Hellenistic views toward women. By the third century B.C.E., Rome had somewhat improved its own laws for women, and yet the family structures remained largely patriarchal. Marriage and divorce laws almost always favored men and there was a decidedly double standard with regard to sexual practice.

At the same time, however, some Roman women seem to have been actively involved in business, social life, traveling, and even politics. Women from the upper classes had considerable access to education, and there is evidence that some women distinguished themselves in literature, art, and medicine.[6] In other instances, Roman women were permitted official positions in religion. They were allowed to act as vestal virgins who tended the sacred hearth-fire of the state. They also acted as priestesses in some of the cults. There is little evidence, however, that Roman women gained access to the highest positions of religious authority.

At the time of Jesus, the structures in the Near East were patriarchal, and women generally found themselves oppressed. As this brief survey has shown, however, the cultures that surrounded and possibly influenced Jesus contained some precedents for allowing women to have active and even prominent roles in both society and in religion. Jesus no doubt knew women who were struggling for freedom and equality. It is possible that some of his own women disciples were influential in helping him develop what seems to be an enlightened view on the dignity of women.

Women in Early Judaism

The Hebrew Scriptures were a thousand years in the making and they reflect a wide variety of attitudes toward women. There are two accounts of the creation of woman in the Genesis creation stories. The earlier Yahwist account tells of women being created after man and from the body of man as kind of an appendage. This account is followed by the story of the fall, where Eve is led into evil by the serpent and, in turn, persuades the man to sin.

This story has often been interpreted to mean that women are inferior to men and often seduce men into evil. A later Genesis story, however, composed by priestly editors, tells of how both woman and man were created in the image of God and how both were blessed and commissioned by God, but this account has never received as much attention as the first. Jesus, of course, would have been well aware of both traditions from his Torah training and from engaging in the spirited religious debates that were so commonplace among his Jewish associates.

The Hebrew Scriptures tend to take a mixed attitude toward women. Generally, Yahweh is described in male images: as a warrior defending his people, as a father extending love and care to his children, or as a husband displeased with the infidelity of his people. On the other hand, in a more minor key, God is also portrayed in feminine images: as a seamstress clothing her people, as a nurse caring for her children, or as a mistress, a midwife, and a loving mother. For a time during the exile in Babylon, the Hebrews seem to have incorporated into their rituals a devotion to the Goddess as well as to the God.[7] Such worship was roundly condemned by the prophets Isaiah and Jeremiah. This practice was stopped after the return from Babylon, and the feminine beliefs were translated into the Wisdom tradition, which is often feminine in character.

The social structures of Israel were generally patriarchal. In these structures women were often viewed as disposable property and as servants to be ordered about. The divorce laws and laws for multiple spouses were in favor of the male. Women had few rights in the court.

At the same time, however, the great women of the Scriptures, Sarah and Rebecca, were honored as mothers of Israel. Miriam, the sister of Moses, was described as a prophet and one of the leaders of the Exodus. Deborah is described as both a prophet and a judge who brought God's word and justice to her people. Moreover, at different times women served as queens of Israel. Most notable was Alexandra, whose rule was one of peace and prosperity seventy years before Jesus was born. It is possible that stories about this amazing woman were still circulating in Jesus' day.

All these women, of course, were rare exceptions, and they were usually not from the lower classes where oppression and marked inequality were usually the norm. Although Jewish women could function as prophets, sages, and even queens, they were never permitted to be priests, or even to prepare the sacrifices in the Temple. In the Temple itself, women were generally confined to the Court of Women, and there is also evidence that they were segregated in the synagogues and generally not permitted to read at services.

The main reason for this religious discrimination toward women was the "uncleanness" that women contracted from menstruation and pregnancy. The Book of Leviticus (11–17) taught that issue from sexual organs was one of the causes of ritual impurity. Because women were considered to be "regularly unclean," they could not be permitted to function officially in the Jewish religion.

Women in Jesus' Time

It is difficult to ascertain precisely what the lot of women was during the time of Jesus. First of all, we cannot really speak of the Judaism of the time, for now scholars know that there were many "Judaisms" during the time of Jesus. Indeed, during his life, he would have experienced all kinds of legal, mystical, theological, ritualistic, and prophetic elements swirling about him.

We also have problems with the sources used to ascertain the social and religious trends among the Jews of the time. Philo and Josephus are the common Jewish authors consulted, but both wrote from their own unique perspectives and with their own personal prejudices and agenda. The Talmud and Mishna are also useful sources, but these are much later documents (second century C.E. and later) and we cannot be sure that what they describe really reflects conditions at the time of Jesus. These rabbinic sources contain many extremely offensive statements about women, but we don't know if ordinary husbands shared these opinions. Moreover, one would expect to find more enlightened views toward women among the Jews of the diaspora, who were often influenced by liberal Hellenism.[8] Even the gospels cannot be considered to be accurately portraying the situation as Jesus experienced it, because these too are later documents that, for the most part, were written after the split between Christianity and Judaism.

Those who accept the gospel views as those of Jesus can easily portray him as a crusader for women in defiance of the Jewish injustices of his time. In point of fact, Jesus was a Jew working within his own religion and attempting to reform it with the best of his own traditions. Consequently, it would be a distortion to oversimplify the situation by portraying Jesus as one who offered a "Christian" position regarding women over and against the Jewish injustices toward them.[9]

The situation regarding women at the time of Jesus was complex. As one rabbi commented recently: "Where you have four Jews, you have five opinions." The same was true in the time of Jesus. Jews were constantly engaged in controversy over the role of women in their society and religion, and there was a wide divergence of views. Jesus probably engaged in these controversies with his own interpretations of Jewish tradition. Unique and radical as his positions might be, they came from his experience and from interpretations of his own tradition. Jesus' own personal teachings with regard to the dignity of women probably served as a seed for the more fully developed notions that we encounter in the gospels.

With all these complications and limitations in mind, we will now attempt to offer, at least tentatively, some notion of what Jesus might have encountered with regard to the role of women in his time and how he dealt with these issues. We will look at the areas of marriage, family, and religion, and then move on to discuss other ways in which Jesus recognized the dignity of women and called them to a central position in his following.

Patriarchal Structure

During the time of Jesus, a woman's identity was generally derived from her role in the family as wife and mother. Women were expected to marry young, and marriages were usually arranged by the father. Success for women was largely dependent on how well they carried out their duties in the home. A girl was thought to "come of age" at twelve and a half. Prior to that she had few if any rights, even to possess anything of her own or to keep payment for work done. As a result, though fathers often lamented having daughters rather than sons, they viewed the daughters as cheap labor and as property they could sell for a large sum of money in a marriage arrangement. In some cases, when fathers were financially desperate, they would even sell their daughters into slavery.[10]

In the patriarchal system that was so common to the East, the wife was often revered in the home as a source of happiness for the husband and a means of inspiration for the children. Her primary responsibilities were to maintain the household, do all the chores, dutifully care for all the needs of the children, and take special care to provide the husband with services, such as bringing him his cup and washing his face, hands, and feet when he returned home.

In return for her obedience and service, the wife could rightfully expect food, shelter, sex, care when ill, and a decent burial. She was not expected to receive the same respect from the children as the father could expect. If her husband could afford it, she might have to share him with one or more other wives. (Polygamy, though allowed, was exceptional because of the expense of "purchasing" other wives, sustaining them, and running the risk of having to support them after a divorce.)

Because the home was the place for women, they were seldom to be seen in public. If they did have the occasion to appear in public, their faces were to be veiled and they were not permitted to speak to anyone, most especially men. A woman caught conversing in the street could be divorced without the usual financial settlement.[11] (This may sound extreme, but today we still see examples of such customs in such countries as Iran and India.) The Jews did, of course, allow for exceptions. While husbands were away, women were permitted to run family businesses. In the rural areas (with which Jesus would be more familiar) women were permitted to work in the fields, but were not permitted to ever be alone with a man in such a situation.

This strict segregation of women seems to have come from several sources. First of all, Judaism viewed itself as a "chosen people," a tribal nation. According to this view, in order to keep this people intact and to preserve bloodlines and lines of inheritance among the men, the women had to be carefully monitored.[12] Women were thought to be weak and prone to seduction. Careful safeguards were taken to prevent infidelity, and a double standard of sexual behavior was maintained.

Divorce was largely the privilege of men in patriarchal societies. In Judaism there were some extreme cases where a woman could obtain a divorce, but it was usually done on the initiative of the husband. Opinions varied as to the grounds for divorce. The school of Rabbi Shammai allowed a man to divorce his wife for infidelity, while the more liberal school of Rabbi Hillel permitted men to divorce their wives for a more attractive woman or even because the wife had ruined the supper.[13] Even though divorce was permitted, it does not seem to have been common, largely because there was a public stigma connected with it, and because men often had to provide support for the wife set aside.[14]

Women who lost their husbands in death were especially vulnerable. Generally women were not allowed to inherit, so if the widow did not have a son who gained the inheritance and cared for her, she could be penniless. Moreover, the widow's destiny lay largely in the hands of her husband's brothers, who were free to take her or not into a levirate marriage. Until they decided, the widow could not remarry and get on with her life. Whether or not she would be taken in to serve, or cast aside to live in destitution was entirely up to them.

Jewish Women and Religion

During the time of Jesus, Jewish women were also given a secondary position in the area of religion. The sacred sign of the covenant itself, circumcision, was a rite in which only a male could participate. While the religion of the mother was significant in the life of the children (one had to have a Jewish mother to be considered a Jew), it was the men who often carried out serious family instruction in the Torah.

Torah was the heart of Jewish religion, and yet women were usually exempt from studying it. For the most part they were also forbidden to be official teachers. (There were exceptions. In the second century C.E., Beruria, whose father and husband were both rabbis, was a recognized scholar of the Torah and could hold her own with the best of the men teachers.[15] She, of course, lived after the destruction of the Temple, and it does seem that in times of crises women were given more prominence in religion.) Women were not obligated to make pilgrimages to Jerusalem for the feasts, as men were. In the Temple they could not go beyond the lower Court of Women.

Women could not belong to the priesthood. They were often segregated in the synagogue, generally limited in their participation in public prayer, and had to defer to the men for leading the Sabbath observance.

Again, most of what we know of the religious role of women is filtered through the eyes of male authors who were mostly negative toward women. Moreover, the literature seems to portray the picture more harshly than it might have been experienced in daily living.[16] We can assume that many women in Judaism struggled against the odds to be well-informed and devout Jews. Most likely such women helped form the progressive views of Jesus, helped implement his liberating perspective, and assisted in carrying these views to fruition in the early Christian communities.[17]

Jesus' Perspective

Jesus grew up in a Jewish home and seems to have been respectful of its customs. Most of his life was probably centered at home where he worked as a craftsman, following in the footsteps of his father, Joseph. If Joseph did die early in Jesus' life, as tradition has it, then Jesus as the son would have been the benefactor, and we might assume that he used what little he gained, as well as what he made as a craftsman, to support his mother. It is possible that this "single parent" experience with his mother may have had some influence on his views on women.

Though Jesus never explicitly criticized the patriarchal system, he apparently did subvert many of the premises of this system by refusing to view women either as property or as servants. He seemed to challenge patriarchy by telling all people that they are "somebody" and that God loves them. He revealed a kingdom where people relate as friends, brothers, and sisters, not masters and slaves.[18]

In the gospel stories Jesus is portrayed as regarding women with the same respect and love that he extended to all persons. There is no evidence that he talked down to women, considered them to be inferior, seductive, or in any way less worthy of human rights and freedom than men. From what we can learn from the gospels, Jesus apparently viewed all persons as created by God, as equal "brothers and sisters," and as members of the family of God. For Jesus, it was not so much a matter of being female or male, but of being a person: All persons, young or old, married, single, or widowed, healthy or disabled, sinner or innocent, were sacred. Women received their identity and meaning in life primarily from being human persons, not from their roles of wife or mother.[19]

There are a number of stories in the gospels that would indicate that Jesus' followers remembered him as one who treated women with the same respect and love he gave to men. There is the well-known story of the woman taken in adultery in the gospel of John (8:1–11). The woman in the story is publicly humiliated and threatened with death for her actions. (In line with the double standard of the day, no mention is made of the man involved.) Jesus turns the tables on her accusers by saying "Whichever one of you has committed no sin throw the first stone at her." After her accusers slink away, Jesus speaks to the woman with tremendous compassion and respect, and sets her free without judgment or rebuke, simply telling her to sin no more. Though the story is late (perhaps inserted into the gospel in the third century), it reflects a tradition common to Luke, that Jesus reached out to women who were oppressed by the laws of his time.[20]

Another well-known example is that of the woman who comes to Jesus while he is at table at the house of Simon the Pharisee (Luke 7:36–50). The woman is, perhaps, a prostitute, and the others in the house consider her to be unclean and an outcast. (Prostitutes then, as today, were generally victims of social conditions and male oppression.) She comes to Jesus in the role of servant and beggar, washing and kissing his feet and drying them with her hair. But Jesus does not allow her any of these traditional female roles. Instead, he speaks of her as one who offers him the hospitality that Simon the host has overlooked. Jesus praises her publicly as a woman filled with love and faith. He seems to treat her with great dignity and respect because she is a human person, and not because she is a woman.

In this story and in others, Jesus sets aside the taboos that decreed that he could not touch or be touched by women or speak to them in public. With courage and openness he reaches out to women who are marginal, diseased, even disgraced, and offers them freedom and wholeness. From his own Abba experience of a God of tenderness and love, Jesus learned that each person is sacred, deserves to be included, and belongs to the solidarity of the human family. When dealing with women, he neither idealizes them nor treats them as an inferior species. Rather he sees women, as he does men, as persons worthy of love and respect.

Mothers and Children

Jesus further challenges the abuses of the patriarchal system by reminding the teachers of the law that God commands: "Respect your father *and* your mother" (Matthew 15:4). In this statement Jesus challenges the traditional view of his people that gives the father preference; the mother is due equal respect.

Jesus is also portrayed as honoring the dignity of all children, female as well as male. In Jesus' time children had few rights and were shown little regard outside their home and family. Inside the home, female children were not given the same value as the males. On one occasion, his own disciples display this disregard for children and try to get them out of Jesus' way. Jesus rebukes them and asks that the children (along with their mothers) be brought to him. He then says that these children, in their innocence and simplicity, should be a model for gospel living

(Mark 10:13–16). Luke tells the story of a time when Jesus took a child to his side and proclaimed: "Whoever receives this child in my name receives me..." (Luke 9:48). There could be no more profound statement on the dignity of all children, without regard to whether they be female and male.

"Pairing" of Gospel Stories

Scripture scholars have called attention to how the "pairing" of gospel stories might be reflective of Jesus' teaching on sexual equality. Such "pairing" is noticeable in Luke's gospel, where the author links Mary and Joseph, Zechariah and Elizabeth, Anna and Simeon, and others to show how women and men have stood in partnership before God throughout the Hebrew tradition.[21] Miracle stories are also paired to proclaim that the power of God worked through Jesus on women and men without partiality. Some examples are the cure of the demoniac and the cure of Peter's mother-in law (Luke 4:31–41), the cure of the Gerasene and the woman who had hemorrhaged for twelve years (Luke 8:26–48), and the curing of the centurion's servant and the raising of the son of a widow (Luke 7:1–17). In all of these stories Jesus reaches out to men and women without partiality, revealing that the power of God is not one of domination or oppression, but a power of healing and enabling, a power that frees from oppression and discrimination.[22]

Challenging Abuse in Divorce

Jesus' opposition to divorce further challenges abuses within the patriarchal system (Mark 10:1–12; Matthew 5:31–32). Although the text in Mark and the exception in Matthew are extremely problematic and have led to continuing debates about their meaning, it is widely accepted that Jesus did oppose the liberal divorce interpretations of both the Hillel and Shammai schools. The teaching, which seems to find its source in the earthly Jesus, advocates a return to what Jesus considered to be the ideal of the Torah, a partnership that is permanent. His insistence on monogamy and his opposition to divorce were in conflict with legal interpretations of the law that brought a great deal of oppression and injustice to women. In addition, his insistence that lust comes from within men's hearts (Matthew 5:28) seems to have been directed against the stereotypic notion that women are seducers, a common belief among Jesus' contemporaries. Positions such as this, as well as his stand against divorce, were indeed "dangerous" views for that time, and probably contributed to the fierce opposition that Jesus eventually met.

Defender of Widows

The gospels also reveal a "Jesus tradition" that defended another group oppressed by the patriarchal system. Widows were often impoverished and marginalized by the death of their husbands, the very men they served and upon whom they had become totally dependent. Jesus often mentions widows favorably in his teachings. In Mark, Jesus says that the two copper coins that the widow dropped into the Temple treasury are worth more than the large offerings of the rich because she is such an example of self-sacrifice (Mark 12:42–43). Just previous to that passage Jesus is attacking the teachers of the law for their oppression of widows (Mark 12:38ff).[23] In Luke, Jesus speaks of the power of prayer in the story of the widow who persistently pursues the judge until he agrees to help her (Luke 18:1–8). Luke also tells the touching story of how Jesus was moved to pity when he saw a widow taking her only son to be buried. Jesus reached out to her, consoled her, and returned to her the son who was her only means of support (Luke 7:11–17).

Ignoring the "Unclean" Taboo

Judging by the gospels stories, which we can assume are generally true to his memory, Jesus seemed to be intent in offering women equal opportunities for taking part in religion. First of all, he seemed not only to ignore but even to challenge the religious taboos concerning how women are "unclean" and therefore not worthy to fully participate in the authority or rituals of their religion.

Mark's gospel weaves together two stories that bring this out. One story begins with Jairus, a Jewish official coming to Jesus to plead with him to lay hands upon his sick daughter. As Jesus follows him home, he encounters a woman who would be considered "constantly unclean" because she has been hemorrhaging for twelve years. She wants to touch Jesus' cloak, apparently hoping to be magically cured and then slip back into the isolation and anonymity she had known for so long. Jesus will not allow her the magic, nor accept her rejected role as a woman who is permanently unclean. Moreover, he is not in the least concerned about being rendered unclean himself by being touched by such a woman. Jesus calls her forth, praises her faith publicly, makes her whole, and restores her to the human dignity that should have been hers all along (Mark 5:25–34). Then Jesus proceeds on to Jairus's home only to find that the daughter had died. Jesus pays no attention to the taboo of touching the dead girl. He takes her by the hand and speaks to her: "Little girl, I tell you to get up!" Life is restored to the youngster, and Jesus in the midst of all the amazement simply gives the very practical order to give her something to eat (Mark 5:21–42).

Jesus' respect, recognition, and compassion for females both old and young are dramatically revealed in these two intertwining stories. Jesus gives no indication here or anywhere else in the gospels that he considers women to be "unclean." He freely converses with them and instructs and heals them in public. These stories, as well as others, point to a strong tradition of Jesus confronting the taboos of his day regarding women. They speak of his determination to treat women inclusively with respect and honor.

It is perhaps out of this "memory" of Jesus that Paul was later able to write: "So there is little difference between Jews and Gentiles, between slaves and free men, between men and women; you are all one in union with Christ Jesus" (Galatians 3:28). Jesus reached deeply into his tradition and shed a new light on values and truths that had long been forgotten by many of his Jewish contemporaries. New patterns of behavior in society and religion would dominate the early communities that were to follow.[24]

Kingdom for All

As we saw in chapter three, the kingdom of God is central to the message of Jesus. Women and men alike are incorporated into this reality in many of the gospel stories, giving further indication that Jesus' teaching was inclusive of both sexes. It is remarkable how many feminine images are associated with the kingdom of God in the gospels. In some stories a mutuality among the sexes is represented. John's description of the wedding feast at Cana, viewed by many scholars as a symbol of the kingdom, is a gathering of both women and men (John 2:1–12). Likewise, the Judgment scene in Matthew portrays both sexes coming together in the days of fulfillment for reward or punishment (Matthew 25:31–46). In the parable of the virgins, the wedding feast (again a symbol of the kingdom) is once again an occasion where both sexes gather for celebration, and where the women who act wisely enjoy the celebration with the bridegroom (Matthew 25:1–13).

The gospels also use "parallel stories" to show that, in the Jesus tradition, both sexes participate in the kingdom and carry forth the mission. In the parable of the sower a man sows the seed, symbolizing spreading the Word of God (Matthew 13:1–17), while in the parable of the yeast a woman is portrayed as the one who helps in the spread of the kingdom (Luke 13:20–21). Luke's pairing of the parables on the lost coin and the good shepherd is particularly striking.[25] In the first story God is imaged as a shepherd rejoicing in the finding of his lost sheep. In the second story God is strikingly portrayed as a woman celebrating the recovery of her silver coin (Luke 15:1–10).

Also notable is the gospel account of Jesus' own willingness to use feminine imagery for himself as he weeps over Jerusalem. "How many times I wanted to put my arms around all your people, just as a hen gathers her chicks under her wings, but you would not let me" (Matthew 23:37). The passage not only reflects Jesus' value for the feminine image, it also reveals the inclusivity of his own personal embrace.

Although Jesus' mission seems to have been largely to his own people, there are indications in the gospels that he gave his followers precedents for also inviting Gentiles, both women and men, into the kingdom. A most striking example of such inclusivity is the story of the Syro–Phonecian woman. Many scholars think the story is authentic for no other reason than it shows a rather embarrassing side of Jesus, one that could well have been passed over in later writing.

As the story is told in Mark, Jesus was in seclusion in a house in the city of Tyre. A Gentile woman sought him out and begged Jesus to cure her daughter. Jesus was not inclined to cooperate, apparently thinking that such an action would not be relevant to his mission. His statement as it is written in the gospels is sharp: "Let us feed the children. It isn't right to take the children's food and throw it to the dogs" (Mark 17:27). But the woman is not easily discouraged and smartly retorts, "Sir, even the dogs under the table eat the children's leftovers." She apparently made her point, because Jesus commends her for her insight and concedes to her wishes by healing her daughter.

This is an extraordinary story. It probably reflects the difficult time later Judaic Christians were having with the question of spreading the gospel to non-Jews. The story seems to reveal Jesus' own gradual awareness that God's reign and power transcend both nationality and sexuality. In Matthew's version Jesus praises her as a "woman of great faith" (Matthew 15:26–27). Here in Mark the woman seems to be a symbol of the many persistent Gentile women who became leaders and examples of great faith as the early communities spread beyond Judaism.

Call of Women Disciples

Traditionalists have made much of Jesus' choice of only male apostles. They have used this as a justification for an all-male hierarchy and ministry. According to Mark (3:14–15), Jesus chose the Twelve to be with him, to preach, and to cast out demons. The twelve men seem to have symbolic value in that they stand for the twelve heads of the tribes of Israel. They were also the key witnesses, although not exclusively, to the person and teachings of Jesus, as well as to the resurrection.

Their apostolic witness was of enormous value in forming the early communities, but it is doubtful whether the rapid spread of Christianity could have come about through their efforts alone. Moreover, the apostles were not replaced when they died. Judas was replaced by Matthias, but after that the role of apostle died with the men who held the title. It is true that Paul uses the title of himself, and the title is used of others in the Christian Scriptures, but in these cases the word "apostle" seems to have had a broader meaning than it did in the gospels.

It would seem that Jesus' mission to bring the gospel "to all nations" was carried out not only by apostles, but also by disciples, both women and men. Some of these disciples apparently were chosen by Jesus himself to be his intimate followers during his life. Others joined the community after the resurrection of Jesus and played key roles in the early church.[26] The "disciple" model, consisting of both sexes, seems to be the one followed in the early communities; this is reflected in the gospels stories as they were told orally and later put down in written form. This sending forth of women disciples to teach had no precedent in Jesus' time. Jesus choice of women followers was indeed one of the most radical moves that he made in his career.

In making such a choice, Jesus was challenging some of the fundamental positions of many of his rabbinic peers. First of all, Jesus was challenging the position that the home is the only place for the Jewish woman and that she must derive her identity only from being mother and wife. While Jesus did not attack the home or family, he did take the position that taking part in the kingdom and carrying on his mission should have priority over family ties.

In John's account of the wedding feast at Cana, Jesus seems to make it clear that the call of God supersedes a mother's request of her son for a favor. His answer to his mother is sharp: "You must not tell me what to do. My time has not yet come" (John 2: 4). The mission of God would take precedence over maternal roles for women.[27] Similarly, in the story of Mary and Joseph finding Jesus in the Temple, the mission of "his father's business" takes precedence over family concerns. "Why did you have to look for me? Didn't you know that I must be in my Father's house?" (Luke 2:49). And though the story says that the boy returned home and was obedient for years to come, the point has been made. The mature disciple, though honoring family life, must give discipleship and mission first priority.

Some of Jesus' strongest statements involve this theme of the priority of spiritual bonds over blood bonds and familial ties. All three synoptic gospels tell the story of Jesus' mother and brothers, who apparently think he has gone mad and are attempting to get through the crowds surrounding him. When they finally get a message to him, they receive a strong reply. His answer, which is by no means a rebuke to his family (provided they are faithful to God) states his position: "Who is my mother? Who are my brothers?"; "Look! Here are my mother and my brothers!"; "Whoever does what God wants him to do is my brother, my sister, my mother" (Mark 3:31–35; Matthew 12:46–50; Luke 8:19–21).

Other stories indicate that Jesus advocates autonomy and independence for his mature followers. When the rich young man goes away sad because he is not able to detach himself and follow the Master, Jesus says: "...I tell you, he who leaves home or brothers or sisters or mother or father or children or fields for me and the gospel will receive much more in this present age...and in the age to come will receive eternal life" (Mark 10:29–30).

Discipleship and mission take precedence over ties to patriarchal structures and roles. This radical message gives the women in the Christian communities an opportunity to identify themselves in roles other than traditional family ones. Women like Joanna, Mary Magdalene, Martha, and Mary, and indeed his own mother, Mary, were able to choose to move beyond the patriarchal structures that often made them property and servants. They could freely engage in Christian service. Jesus was opening the way for a new identity for women in his own Judaism and in the Christian communities that would develop this perspective even further.

Jesus also attacked the traditional notion that women were weak and seductive. As we saw earlier, these attitudes led to laws that kept women sequestered in the home, and that required that they be veiled and silent in public. Apparently, Jesus does not subscribe to such attitudes. He shows no fears of being seduced and seems comfortable with women both in public as well as in domestic situations. He thus felt free to call them to follow him and to break tradition by having them travel with him and his male disciples.

Besides giving women the possibility of finding identity other than in a patriarchal home, and freeing them from the image of seducer, Jesus also seems to indicate that women should be free to participate in their religion unimpeded by the taboos of inferiority and uncleanness. We have already seen that he did not concern himself with the "unclean" myth. He felt free to converse with women in public and to accept them as friends and followers. The gospels give examples that would indicate that Jesus made deliberate efforts to free women from the obstacles that prevented them from fully participating in prayer and worship in the Temple and synagogue. It is significant that the woman taken in adultery is freed from male oppression while Jesus is teaching in the Temple (John 8). For many women of the time, the Temple must have been a symbol of male dominance and exclusivity; thus freeing a woman in this environment is most meaningful.

Similarly, Luke describes Jesus teaching in the synagogue on the Sabbath when he suddenly spots a woman who had been crippled and bent over for eighteen years. With no request on her part, Jesus simply calls out to her: "Woman, you are free from your sickness!" Then, with no concern for Sabbath prohibitions or fear of being rendered unclean from touching this woman, he places his hands on her. She straightens up and praises God. The leaders of the synagogue are angry with his action, but he declares them hypocrites and makes them "ashamed of themselves" (Luke 13:10–17). This is indeed a richly crafted story that seems to proclaim Jesus' liberation of women from religious laws that oppress them and keep them from fully participating in their society and their religion.

One other significant example here is the story of the Samaritan woman. As a Samaritan, she belongs to "renegade Jews," who had purportedly intermarried, fouled their bloodlines, and been cut off from the Temple in Jerusalem. Because she is a woman, and a much-married one at that, she also is also cut off from her own Temple in Gerizim. In the story, which is late and apparently comes from the Johannine community's mission to Samaria, Jesus offers her the living water for new life and promises her that "by the power of God's Spirit people will worship the Father as he really is, offering him the true worship that he wants" (John 4:23).

The story seems to confront the discrimination that many women in Jesus' time had experienced with regard to Temple worship. Recognizing this oppression, Jesus offers women free access to worship as children of God. Women are to be freed from the taboos of uncleanness and the stereotype of being weak seducers. They, like men, are persons who image God in their very being, are equally called to be friends of God, true worshipers, and, indeed, disciples of Jesus. Jesus frees women from the taboos and interpretations of the law that support an oppressive patriarchal system so that they can join him along with men in an intimate and loving community to spread the good news of the kingdom.

Leading Women Disciples

One of the most innovative actions Jesus did was to call women to be his disciples. There is simply no precedent in the Judaism of his time for a rabbi to call women to learn from him, follow him, and share in his teaching mission. As we noted earlier, women in these times were not given formal instruction in the Torah, could not attend the rabbinic schools, and certainly would not leave their homes and families to travel with their master and his male students on mission.[28] From the very nature of the gospels as we understand them, we know that they often tell us more about what was going on in the early Christian communities than about the time of Jesus. Yet, it would seem that the development of inclusive ministry in these stories is built on and reflects the ministry that Jesus established. Let us now examine some of the gospel portrayals of leading disciples of Jesus and see what this might reveal to us about Jesus' call of women to follow him.

The Mother of Jesus   The nature of Mary's discipleship comes through in a number of gospel stories. In Luke's account of the nativity, the incarnation itself seems to wait for the word of consent of this young maiden (Luke 1:26–38). From the beginning she proclaims that she is the "Lord's servant," the central image of discipleship in the early communities. Her prayer of the Magnificat is not one of private domesticity; it is a free and open proclamation of her share in God's mission to overcome the oppression of the lowly at the hands of the rich and mighty (Luke 1:46–56). It is, indeed, the statement of a prophet and teacher, and today it has inspired many women in the liberation movement in the Third World.[29]

In the story of finding Jesus in the Temple, the maternal role that was so central for the women of the time gives way to the importance of God's work (Luke 2:42–52). The traditional role of women in the patriarchal system is also challenged in the story of the wedding feast at Cana. In this story, Mary is portrayed as one among the servants who ministers to others in what might be considered a "sacramental role," as seems to be symbolized by Mary's request to the servants to "Do whatever he tells you." This story might well be an indication of the key liturgical roles that were played by women in the Johannine community.[30]

In the gospels, Mary stands with other women who are described in the role of ministerial service. Along with Peter's mother-in-law after her cure, and with Martha, who serves Jesus in her home, the mother of Jesus may symbolize the diaconal services that women were exercising in the early communities. In John's Calvary scene, Jesus joins his mother with the beloved disciple in what might well be interpreted as an inclusive partnership in ministry (John 19:26–27). In the upper room she becomes part of the pentecostal community that will carry on the mission of the risen Lord. From the gospel stories, especially those of the Johannine community, Mary becomes a model for women taking their place along with their "brothers" in Christian discipleship.[31]

Mary Magdalene   Mary Magdalene, who seems to have been one of the key disciples of Jesus and another important model for the later communities, has been seriously misunderstood. Tradition has often looked at her as a former prostitute on the periphery of Jesus' group, and "pop" culture has even portrayed her as a woman who had fallen in love with Jesus. The musical *Jesus Christ Superstar* and the novel and film *The Last Temptation of Christ* portray her in this way, but there is no basis in Scripture for either of these fantasies. Most likely she has been thought of a prostitute because the gospels note that she was cured of seven demons. Male exegesis has been quick to interpret this in terms of sexual sins, when in fact "demons" in this context means some serious illness. (It is curious that when men were cured of demons in Scripture it was not viewed as a reference to sexual sin.) Once it was assumed that Mary was a public sinner, it was then concluded that she was the woman of ill-repute who came to Jesus while he was at table at the house of Simon the Pharisee. Perhaps Jesus' comment that this woman has loved much then led to the popular interpretation that Mary Magdalene was in love with Jesus. In fact, there is no indication in the gospels that Mary was either a sinner or that she was in love with Jesus.

Fantasies about Mary Magdalene's dark past and her relationship with Jesus have trivialized her and diverted our attention from realizing that: "Mary Magdalene is, without doubt, the disciple whose place in the paschal mystery is most certainly attested by all four gospels."[32] Three gospels (Mark, Matthew, and John) name the women who were present at Calvary, and though the lists differ, Mary Magdalene is always included and is mentioned first by both Mark and John. Since these accounts are highly theological interpretations rather than pictorial accounts of the crucifixion, Mary's presence with Jesus at the cross seems to have special significance for the discipleship of women.

Mary is also prominent in the resurrection accounts. In the six resurrection narratives, Mary Magdalene is mentioned in five of them and is always the first person named.[33] She is the first witness to the risen Lord and is commissioned by him to spread the word to others. Jesus told her: "Go to my brothers and sisters and say to them: I ascend to my Father who is now your Father; to my God who is now your God" (John 20:17). In the early church writings she was referred to as an "apostle to the apostles."[34] Indeed, being a disciple from Galilee who followed Jesus in his mission and who was a witness to the resurrection, Mary does indeed qualify as an apostle. The prominence given her in the Johannine community would indicate that she was a significant role model for Christian discipleship.[35]

The Samaritan Woman The story of the Samaritan woman, which, as we noted before, seems to have come out of the missionary activities of the Johannine community rather than those of Jesus, is another example of a woman commissioned to apostolic ministry. In the story, Jesus ignores the taboos that forbade women to talk in public—especially a "heretical" woman of questionable morals—and that would not allow Jesus to ask her for a service. Jesus accepts her as a person even though he apparently does not approve of her lifestyle. (Her many marriages may well be a result of patriarchal oppression rather than immorality, since divorce was nearly always initiated by the man.)

In the story, Jesus reveals to her his identity as messiah, and she accepts his work without a sign (which is the mark of an authentic disciple).[36] As a model disciple, the Samaritan woman leaves her things behind and bears witness about Jesus to her townfolk (John 4:5–42). Her listeners come to full faith in Jesus as Savior on the authority of her witness. This is the kind of discipleship Jesus prayed for at the last supper when he said, "I pray not only for them, but also for those who believe in me because of their message" (John 17:20).

Once again, an "outcast" woman is given center stage as an authentic disciple of Jesus, and her story is told to reveal the inclusive character of ministry carried out in the early communities. In the story we are even able to see the shock of the males at such a radical move on the part of Jesus, a reaction probably felt by many in the early communities, and still felt today by those who resist equal participation in ministry.

Other Models of Feminine Discipleship

The gospel stories present us with still other ample evidence of the apostolic roles played by women in Jesus' time and in the early communities. There is Martha, who is reminded that domestic roles for women are not as important as listening to the Word. In John's gospel it is Martha who "serves" at the dinner at Bethany and who is the central figure in the resuscitation of Lazarus. Jesus reveals himself to her as the resurrection and the life, and, in return, Martha makes a confession comparable to that attributed to Peter: "Yes Lord!...I do believe that you are the messiah, the Son of God, who has come into the world" (John 11:27). This story indeed reveals an advanced feminine ministry in the

Johannine community, a ministry prefigured by a close friend and disciple of Jesus.

Martha's sister, Mary, is also a model of ministry. Breaking with tradition, Jesus comes to her home and teaches her, and she becomes an authentic "hearer of the Word." Just before his death Jesus is once again at her home, and in what Matthew seems to describe as a miniature "last supper," Mary anoints his feet as if for burial with an abundance of her best perfume and dries them with her hair (John 12:1–8). At the final meal before his death Jesus would use this same symbol and wash the feet of his disciples, proclaiming that this gesture would be a sign of discipleship. Mary is, therefore, another striking symbol of women who seemed to have performed sacramental ministry and carried on the memory of the Master in the Johannine community.

Finally, there is Joanna, who apparently felt called by Jesus to leave the luxury and courtesan's role in the corrupt court of Herod, where her husband was the minister of finance. She stands as a model of women disciples who are drawn even from royal security to have the independence to follow Jesus.[37] Luke portrays her as one of the women who were the original witnesses to the resurrection and as one who brought the news to the apostles.

The portrayal of Joanna would indicate that the Lucan community also had, in their ministry, courageous women of independent means who left everything to follow Jesus. And we find many more examples of such women in Acts and in the letters of Paul, where women seem to serve as "missionaries, preachers, teachers, prophets, apostles, healers, speakers in tongues, leaders of house churches."[38]

Summary

Renewal has brought Christianity back to the very roots of its tradition, and there the treasures of freedom and equality are being recovered. A careful rereading of the Scriptures has revealed a Jesus who accepted people as beloved creatures of God, a Jesus who significantly confronted the oppression that patriarchal structures were imposing upon the women of his day.

In the new community structure that Jesus would introduce, men and women were not to relate as master-servant, or even as father-daughter, but as brother and sister. He challenged the stereotypes, traditional roles, unjust laws, and taboos that had for so long impeded women from their rightful dignity and equality. And then, in an unprecedented move, he called women to follow him as his disciples and to share in the continuation of his mission. We have seen that many of the gospel stories convey this "memory" of Jesus as an advocate of women. They reflect how the early communities carried forth this tradition of liberation. It is clear that those who wish to deny women equality in the home, the culture, or in the church will not find justification in the gospels for their wishes.

Questions for Reflection and Discussion

1. Name significant ways in which Jesus departed from ancient attitudes toward women.

2. Cite several specific gospel stories that seem to reflect memories of Jesus' unique attitudes toward women.

3. Do the gospels offer us sufficient grounds for providing women today with equal opportunities in ministry?

4. What do the portraits of Jesus' mother, Mary, the Samaritan women, and Mary Magdalene in the gospels tell us about the role of women in the early Christian communities.

CHAPTER SIX

Man of the Earth

The litany of damages to the earth's environment is both familiar and frightening. The world's oceans, waterways, and aquifers are being polluted. Toxic chemicals, nuclear waste, and garbage are fouling the land. The rain forests are being rapidly destroyed, and many species of plants and animals there and elsewhere are being rendered extinct. Poisonous chemicals are frequently sprayed on foodstuffs, endangering the health of workers and consumers. Acid rain brings death to lakes and forests. Strip mining tears at land that was once beautiful. The oceans and lakes are rapidly being overfished. Severe damage seems to have already been done to the protective ozone layer, while a building "greenhouse effect" from exhausts is seriously affecting weather patterns. The list grows each year, and although there seem to be some serious efforts to slow down the deterioration of our environment, one gets the feeling that many of these efforts are simply too little and too late.

Christians could be effective voices in the ecological movement if they could better integrate their Christian beliefs with their environmental concerns. Jesus' teachings, as well as the Christian tradition that has developed over two thousand years, offer values and insights that can move Jesus' disciples to join those who want to face the present ecological crisis with conviction and productive action.

The Christian tradition has always been in the process of evolving and adapting to each age in which Jesus' followers live. The gospels reflect how Jesus' teachings were reinterpreted by the early Christians, enabling them to face challenges and crises during the first century. Likewise, through subsequent periods of history, the gospel teachings were reinterpreted to face the pressing issues of those periods. If Christians hope to deal effectively with the crucial environmental issues that press us today, then the tradition must be once again reinterpreted.

In this chapter we are going to consider how the person and teachings of Jesus Christ might relate to the environmental issues of today. We will first look at how the understanding of creation has changed over time and how these shifts in understanding have affected our attitudes toward the environment. Then we will look at how the scientific perspective has moved Christian thinkers to reinterpret some of their beliefs about Jesus Christ and his teachings. Finally, we will look at how some gospels and Christian traditions are being understood and applied in ways that better empower disciples of Jesus to become active in the ecological movement.

Creation Reinterpreted

In much of Christian theology, creation has become detached from Christology. Creation is traditionally understood as an event in the distant past, connected to redemption only in that Jesus came to restore the pristine harmony of creation that was lost in original sin. In this section we will contrast traditional models of creation and world with those that have emerged in our times in order to see how these models have affected our attitudes toward our environment.

Static Model

The cosmology that has served as a backdrop for the Hebrew as well as much of the Christian tradition on creation thinks of the world as being a fixed or static reality. In the Genesis stories, the world was created by God at some time in the distant past. Created as an ideal world at first, the world has become corrupted by sin and death.

The philosophical explanation of the structure of this world was worked out by Aristotle and put into schematic form by Ptolemy. It prevailed in the West until the sixteenth century. It views the universe as a unchanging reality with the earth at the center, surrounded by spheres that orbit the earth in circular orbits. Above the earth existed the heavens, which medieval Christians assumed to be the dwelling place of God, as well as the place from which Jesus came when he descended to earth and to which he returned in the ascension. The heavens were also thought to be the abode of the good angels, who are given the power to determine the motion of the spheres of heaven. Below was the underworld, which medieval thinkers thought of as the abode of evil spirits. This universe was a finished product, created about five thousand years before the birth of Jesus. It was thought to have been directly created by God, who guided it with divine will and power according to predetermined laws of nature.

The fixed model of the universe was hierarchical and patriarchal, with God viewed as the Supreme Being at the top of the pyramid. Then the pyramid proceeded downward to angels, heavenly bodies, humans (with men given superiority over women), and then the other creatures of earth. This pyramid was extended to other institutions as God's creative will. The church was established in a hierarchy with the pope as the head. The state was established as a monarchy and the divine right of kings was derived from God's "plan." The family was designed in the same pyramidal structure, with the father as the head, and the wife and children placed in their descending order of importance.[1]

This fixed model of creation, which is still a backdrop for many traditional theologians, has profound ecological implications. First of all, this view perceives creation solely as God's activity in the distant past, and often ignores the need for human stewardship in the present. From this perspective, the environment and its resources have simply been placed here for use and consumption. Moreover, the resources are seen as unlimited, managed by a bountiful and provident God, and little concern is given to their conservation or replacement.

Although one of the two Genesis stories of creation calls on humans to be the cultivators and caretakers of the earth (Genesis 2), the other creation story, in which humans are called to be the "masters" of the earth (Genesis 1), has prevailed throughout history. Think of the plunder that took place when the New World was discovered; little or no thought was given to conservation and replacement of resources. The Native American attitude of the sacredness of the environment and its resources was scoffed at and even condemned as pagan nature worship by "God-fearing" Christians. Think of how belief in "manifest destiny" was used to overrun this land and its native peoples. It is only recently that we have begun to appreciate the wisdom of Chief Seattle's answer to the United States government's attempt to purchase land from his people: "The earth does not belong to man, man belongs to the earth. All things are connected like the blood that unites us all. Man did not weave the web of life, he is merely a strand of it. Whatever he does to the web, he does to himself."[2]

The static model of creation also seems to reflect the dualisms of

Greek and Gnostic thinking, where materiality is viewed as evil, and where exaggerated views on original sin see the world as fallen and corrupted by the sin of Adam and Eve. As a result, there has always been a certain "world-denying" mentality in Christianity, which appeared in its extremes among the Gnostics, in much of the thinking of Augustine (d. 430), the medieval Cathars, Luther (d. 1546), Calvin (d. 1564), and in the theology of Jansen (d. 1638). Many think that this negative approach toward materiality contributed enormously to the Western loss of the sacredness of nature, as well as to its tendency to abuse nature and its resources.

The hierarchical nature of this understanding of creation has also been used to justify those on the top of the pyramid having an abundance of the earth's resources, while those on the bottom languish in deprivation. A pyramid of people can be used as a justification for a pyramid of socioeconomic conditions and even for oppression. The feudal structure is a good example of a justification of haves and have-nots, and an unrestrained use of resources that were thought to be bountiful and unlimited.

Few Christian voices were heard in opposition to such social inequality and abuse of the environment. St. Francis of Assisi was a notable exception. He was an ardent advocate for the poor, and had a deep appreciation for the sacredness of all creation. Perhaps this is why some environmentalists look to Francis of Assisi as a patron saint for environmental concerns. Who better embodies Jesus' simplicity, solidarity with nature, and outreach to the poor?

Beginnings of a Modern Perspective

The first major step toward a new cosmology was taken in 1514 when a Polish priest, Nicholas Copernicus, proposed a radically new theory: The sun, not the earth, was the center of the universe, and the earth and its planets were in motion around the sun. This revolutionary new theory was supported by Galileo Galilei (d. 1642), a scientist who further confirmed the theory with the use of a new invention, the telescope.

Galileo was condemned by the church because its officials believed that this new theory was incompatible with Scripture. He spent a good deal of the rest of his life under house arrest. Science, however, was not to be deterred by such ecclesiastical sanctions. John Kepler (d. 1630) made a major contribution by demonstrating mathematically that the orbits of planets are elliptical rather than circular, and Sir Isaac Newton (d. 1727) discovered the gravitational forces that held the planets together.

Science gradually moved off on its own as the Enlightenment challenged religious views of the world and opted for intellectual and scientific freedom, independent from ecclesiastical control. An unfortunate division between scientific and religious thinking was initiated that still prevails today. Science often proceeds from a secularistic point of view devoid of any religious perspective. And religion often proceeds with a kind of naïve scriptural fundamentalism and with little understanding of, or, in some cases, even acceptance of the findings of science. On the one hand, Jesus and his teachings are seen to have little relevance to science. On the other hand, science is seen to have little to teach Christian theology. With such division, one can see how industry and technology might eventually proceed without an ethic, and how religion can become a private matter with little awareness of how faith connects with action on behalf of the environment.

The Enlightenment

Two orientations came out of the period of the Enlightenment that have greatly affected thinking about creation and the environment. First, the Newtonian model of the universe as a machine became a dominant image and was instrumental in our thinking in terms of controlling and manipulating the environment. Gibson Winter has pointed out how this model has influenced us to develop an approach to our world and even to people that attempts to dominate by "systems," accenting calculations and production quotas. The earth, its resources, and, indeed, its people are all conceived of as "parts" of the production machine that ultimately is in motion for profit. Winter maintains that this mechanistic approach to reality is at the heart of our contemporary experience of oppression, ecological destruction, and potential nuclear holocaust.[3]

Another significant outlook from the Enlightenment that affected attitudes toward the environment might be traced back to the English philosopher Sir Francis Bacon (d. 1626). While many have attempted to blame our manipulative approach to the environment on the Judeo-Christian tradition in Genesis, it seems to be more Bacon's and other Enlightenment thinkers' *interpretation* of Genesis, coupled with their conviction that "knowledge is power," that led us to our dominative attitude toward nature.

Bacon and another "father of the Enlightenment," René Descartes (d. 1650), both held that science could restore divinity to humanity and once again give humans the sovereignty they once had over the earth.[4] This introduced a new hierarchy into Western thinking that would replace the older views of hierarchy. Here, intelligence was seen as uniquely characteristic of humans. Through the use of this power, humans could now dominate the earth through science. Through its new creative powers, science could now "bring good things to light," and dominate the earth and its resources for human ends.

Once industrialization was put in place, the Western world had not only the knowledge but also the means to "harness" energy and ride as masters of the world.[5] The Genesis tradition of "subdue the earth and have dominion over it" was used by many as a religious justification for such domination of the earth and its resources. The hierarchical and patriarchal model, of course, offered a kind of pecking order and model for absolute authority that was needed to sustain such a system. The kingdom of God could easily be translated into human progress through science, and the rulers of the systems often assumed the monarchical power of God.[6]

Alfred North Whitehead once observed that the Judeo-Christian tradition did, in fact, beneficially de-sacralize the earth and material things in its constant opposition to nature religions, and in so doing opened the way for modern inductive thinking and scientific investigation of reality.[7] Unfortunately, science pushed the distinction between material and spiritual into a dichotomy and often abandoned the spiritual as irrelevant to reality. Once the spiritual dimension of reality was ignored, the earth was reduced to being a thing to be used, a commodity for exchange. It was no longer seen as a sacred gift to be shared. Christianity could then be limited to a private relationship with God and Jesus Christ, with little connection to such larger public issues.

Contemporary Perspective

Our contemporary view of the universe and, therefore, of creation has been shaped in recent centuries by a number of discoveries. In the nineteenth century, Darwin proposed a theory that would shake the Judeo-Christian view of creation to its foundations: the evolution of species through the process of natural selection. The theory of evolution, which proposes that all life has evolved from simple cellular life in the sea, challenges the traditional notion of direct creation of living creatures by God. It has radically changed the notions of Creator and creature, and demanded that Christian theology reinterpret its understanding of how creation came to be. At the same time, evolution has challenged the historical existence of pristine nature as portrayed in Genesis, the original justice of the first humans, and the historicity of original sin. It has also forced Christians to consider how evolution relates to the coming of Jesus of Nazareth and the nature of his mission.

Another crucial breakthrough that has forced Christians to rethink their notions of the cosmos was made by a German Jew, Albert Einstein, at the beginning of the twentieth century. Einstein was able to propose his theory of relativity through mathematical calculations as well as through ingenious intuitions. Using the speed of light as a constant, he was able to give us a means of calculating distances between the planets and a way of coming to a clearer understanding of the structure of the universe. His theories also led others to discover how to split the atom and release nuclear energy. These theories have led to an understanding of the universe as limitless in its scope and incomprehensible as to its very structure and meaning.

Another crucial scientific breakthrough that would force Christians to further rethink their understanding of the universe was the Big Bang Theory proposed by Edwin Hubble in 1929. After observing that distant galaxies were moving away from us, Hubble concluded that the universe was indeed expanding. This expansion was a stage in a process that began with a massive explosion of a small and dense mass about 15 billion years ago. The universe as we know it, with its millions of galaxies, is the result of this massive explosion.

As for our planet earth, it is now known that it is a relatively tiny planet among hundreds of billions of stars in the Milky Way, just one galaxy among millions of others. Some scientists now maintain that this universe never really had what we might call a beginning, and that its end might well be what could be called "the Big Crunch," or the collapse of the universe in upon itself. Others maintain that before this comes about, our earth will end through a process of entropy whereby our sun will burn out and thus end the possibility of life on this planet.

Theological Implications

The dynamic, evolutionary, relative, and infinitely expansive notion of the cosmos now prevails in the contemporary consciousness. Most people no longer view the universe and earth as fixed realities that were created by God somewhere in the past. Instead the earth is considered to be in process, with its own laws and its own forces of destruction and repair. We are not sure of either its origins or its ultimate goal. Further advances in science have for the first time in human history given humanity the power to enter into the creative process and even to intervene and possibly end life on this planet through nuclear or environmental destruction.

These major shifts in the understanding of the universe, the earth, and life have compelled Christians to develop a new theology of creation as well as a new Christology that is compatible with these new perspectives. Questions are now being asked of the Christian tradition that were simply never even thought of in the past: "Was there a beginning to creation?" "Will there be an end?" "What do the terms 'incarnation' and 'salvation' mean today?" and "What role can humans play in the whole creative process?" Christian thinkers have also begun to ask where Jesus Christ and his teachings fit into these more recent views on creation.

Out of this questioning, new perspectives are emerging in Christology that link Jesus Christ with the contemporary scientific point of view as well as with current environmental crises and the socioeconomic issues arising out of these crises. In the following section, we will examine some of the directions this new thinking has been taking.

Contribution of Teilhard de Chardin
Any attempt to link Jesus Christ with our ecological challenges today should use as a benchmark the work of the great Jesuit scientist and religious thinker, Pierre Teilhard de Chardin (1881–1955). Teilhard was the first Christian thinker to integrate Christian theology with the scientific view of evolution, the first to link Jesus Christ with the contemporary cosmic perspective. True, his synthesis has its limitations, but as Teilhard scholar Christopher Mooney has said, one is not surprised that Teilhard's vision is not completely successful; what is surprising is that it was ever thought of at all.[8]

Teilhard often expressed his concern that Christology was still understood in the old medieval framework of a static universe. He feared that Christianity would become ineffective because it had not brought Jesus' message into the modern world. Teilhard saw Christian doctrine evolving over the centuries—through the gospel period, the early councils, and throughout subsequent periods of the church's history. In the same way, he believed, the needs of the contemporary world called for a new formulation of Christology. Just as the gospel of John had linked Jesus to the Logos and the Council of Nicea had explained how God was related to the human in Jesus Christ, Teilhard believed that our age was called to link Christ to evolution and to the cosmos.[9] In many ways Teilhard did for our age what Aquinas had done for the thirteenth century. He reinterpreted Christian thought in new categories. For Aquinas, the categories were Aristotelian and Scholastic; for Teilhard, they were evolutionary and cosmological.[10]

Christ and Evolution
Teilhard perceived a certain "withinness" in all things, which ultimately

culminated in human consciousness. In this sense, humans depend upon matter historically. There is an organic and genetic interdependence among all things in creation.[11] It is from this genetic pool, this evolution of matter toward spirit, that Jesus of Nazareth comes. Jesus represents the peak of human consciousness, the fullness of human life in the image of God.

Teilhard believed that Jesus Christ represents concretely what God had in mind in creation; Jesus comes to personify this plan and to provide the energy to bring it about. Jesus Christ reveals the plan of creation, both as it was in its inception and as it should be in its culmination. Teilhard found this best expressed in the epistle to the Colossians, where the author says of Jesus Christ: "He is the image of the unseen God and the first-born of creation, for in him were created all things in heaven and on earth" (Colossians 1:15–16). Another key text for Teilhard in this regard was from Ephesians: "He has made known to us the mystery of his will in accord with his favor that he set forth in him as a plan for the fullness of time, to sum all things in Christ in heaven and earth" (Ephesians 1: 9–11). Linking the person of Jesus to evolution and the origin of the universe, Teilhard gave Christians a whole new understanding of the words "God became man."

The Cosmic Christ

Teilhard took this Pauline theology, which was thought out in the fixed notion of the first-century world, and made it speak to the evolving earth and expanding universe of today. Teilhard first encountered the term "Cosmic Christ" from his theology professors in 1916. (The term was first used in 1894 by John Denney and then adopted by other Pauline scholars at the turn of the century.) Teilhard used this interpretation of Christ as a unifying factor throughout his writing. For him, the Cosmic Christ was a third dimension of Jesus Christ and linked Christ with both the beginning and the goal of Creation.

The term Cosmic Christ goes beyond viewing Christ as a legal and personal Savior and sees him as a creative and sustaining energy within the cosmos. The Cosmic Christ, while linked to the humanity of the historical Jesus, now exercises divine power within the universe, bringing it to a positive fulfillment.[11] The Cosmic Christ provides the energy that can bond people together to bring evolution to its intended completion.[12]

Teilhard's vision of evolution was one of ascent and convergence. Throughout his writings, he traces the movement upward from the birth of the cosmos, the bursting forth of life, the emergence of spirit, and ultimately the convergence of all things in what he called the "Cosmic Christ," the fullness of Jesus Christ with all creation transformed and brought to completion. The ultimate converging of all reality is brought about by the power of love. Teilhard hoped that humanity would now move to a greater social unity—what he called "planetization." Indeed, Teilhard foresaw the coming of the "global village" long before others did. Yet he was increasingly distressed by what he perceived to be false and destructive attempts at such unity in Communism, Fascism, and Nazism. These ideologies, he maintained, made humans more into ant colonies and not into the communities of solidarity that God's creative purposes intend. For Teilhard, such unity could only be brought about by the Cosmic Christ, a powerful presence in the world that can bring the world to unity through the power of love and progress.

Teilhard thought that Christians of his time were too concerned with the "world beyond" and not sufficiently concerned about the progress of this world. His life's work was dedicated to bringing the work of modern science and Christian vision into dialogue and integration. He believed that at this point in evolution it was our responsibility to advance this process through modern technology. Christians, he maintained, should be in the vanguard of leadership in such progress with their vision of the Cosmic Christ.[13]

Teilhard's vision has helped us enormously to integrate the person of Jesus Christ, as well as the Christian tradition, with the findings of science. He was also instrumental in moving the church to find its role in participating in (as well as critiquing) progress in the modern world. Indeed, Vatican II's perspective on the church's role in modern society as significantly influenced by Teilhard's thought.

Calling for a vision of unity in creation, Teilhard attempted to show how withinness links all things in an interdependence of all things, culminating in an interdependence of all reality on Christ. Teilhard offered Christians a sweeping vision that enables them to better understand how to link faith with the need for progress and world unity. His vision gave Jesus Christ and the power of love a central role in the upward movement of the earth and universe and in the evolution of human life.

Beyond Teilhard

We have said that the work of Teilhard is a benchmark in the effort to integrate the Christian tradition with the modern consciousness. This implies that Christian thinkers have moved beyond this vision, and indeed they have. The nuclear threat, environmental crises, and devastating hunger and poverty throughout the world have helped to disillusion many about scientific advances and industrial and technological progress.

Today there is more concern for "down to earth" solutions to pressing problems than there is for sweeping visions. There is new criticism of how modern progress has often been made at the expense of the poor. In looking for solutions to world problems, Christian thinkers have moved beyond their own tradition to examine the perspectives of other religions. At the same time, they have reexamined their own tradition for ways of confronting oppression and injustice.

More Earth-Centered

Teilhard spoke of the conscious human as the peak of evolution. Our focus, however, somehow needs to be more earth-centered than human-centered. Teilhard's emphasis is on how humans have come from materiality and how they have transcended it to become spirit. Today's emphasis should be more on our interdependence with nature, than on our superiority to it.

Thomas Berry sees human history as now moving into what he calls "The Third Mediation." In the first mediation, religions and many human activities were concerned with the divine-human mediation. Then, through the centuries of industrialism, class struggle, and nationalism, the emphasis was on inter-human mediation. Berry maintains that in the future both mediations will heavily depend on how well we carry out the next stage, a third mediation between humans and the earth.

In this perspective, the earth becomes the context for survival, and our future will hinge on how successfully we integrate all the human activities within this earth context.[14] For some this may mean moving away from being human-centered and becoming more earth-centered. This view includes a stronger sense of solidarity among all created things, a new awareness of how all things in the environment are linked and depend upon each other for nurturing and indeed for survival, and a deeper understanding of nature not so much as a stage on the way to spirit, but as a reality that is in serious danger of being destroyed. We are now not so much concerned with the goal of evolution as we are with it being disrupted, perhaps beyond repair, through nuclear or environmental disasters.

Critique of Progress

The Teilhardian vision seems to turn evolution over to humanity and expresses a great deal of hope that progress and technology can bring the earth to fulfillment. Granting all the advantages that modern progress has brought, there is a dark side to modern development. Advances on the part of the First and Second Worlds often have been made at the expense of the Third and Fourth Worlds. For instance, the United States has six percent of the world's population, but uses forty percent of the world's resources. Furthermore, the poverty and shortages of resources in the poorer countries have often moved them to do serious harm to their own environment just so they can participate in world trade, or even simply survive.

Love and Justice

Teilhard maintained that love was the basic energy that made all things one. He wrote: "Love is the only power that makes things one without destroying them."[15] And, of course, love of God, neighbor, and self is at the heart of Jesus' teaching and is essential for world unity and cooperation. But the liberation theologians of the Third World have made us aware of the importance of justice in the message of Jesus. They point to his teachings on the dignity of all, the equality of all, and to his special compassion and courageous stands for the outcasts of his time.

The ecological crisis today demands more than a love of nature. It also calls for a just sharing of nature's resources and the end of oppression of whole peoples whose natural resources have been stolen or destroyed. Ecology is thus a religious, political, and economic issue. Much of the destruction of our environment has come from greed and the drive for power over others, as well as from an indifference to natural conservation. Thus, liberation theologians say that the only thing that will save us from environmental disaster is a return to Jesus' teaching on the need for mutuality and human partnership in love and justice. Only a recognition of the gospel teaching that sin comes from the heart can bring us to an awareness of how human greed and injustice are leading us to environmental disaster. Love will not be enough to save us. A critique of "progress" and a commitment to social justice are needed as well.[16]

Not Unity by Dominance

It is obvious that technology and industrial and economic linkage are bringing a certain kind of unity to our planet. Yet, the "unity" of communication, commerce, and a world economy are often sustained by the economic domination and oppression of whole continents of peoples. This is not the oneness that Jesus proclaimed and prayed for. It is not the oneness brought about by love and service of others, the oneness maintained through equality and freedom. More often our unity is brought about by a singleness of purpose as both the capitalistic and communist systems struggle to dominate and manipulate others, and as they build and sustain enormous weapons systems to compete for this domination.[17]

Much of the ecological crisis today arises from this drive for dominance. Meeting the crisis, therefore, calls for a dismantling of the war systems that can utterly destroy the environment. Dealing with environmental problems requires putting aside national sovereignty so that we can form a new global interdependence and cooperation. For the Christian, this is described in terms of a sense of community with peoples of the world and of following Jesus' teaching on the dignity of human life, detachment from material things, and concern for the oppressed and the poor.

Appreciation for Other Religions

The notion of the Cosmic Christ can help Christians move toward a more global perspective. At the same time, however, it can be understood in an exclusive manner that can lead us to miss the insights other religions can bring to global issues. Many of the ancient religions hold treasured beliefs about the connectedness of creation and the sacredness of life. A spirituality of ecology might well include the sacredness of the earth of the Native American religions, the deep regard for all living things in the Hindu tradition, the spirit of detachment in the Buddhist tradition, as well as the respect for the dignity of human life in the Jewish, Muslim, and Christian traditions. Moreover, other images of God from ancient religions can help the contemporary religious person overcome some of the insensitivities toward living things that has built up in Western religion.[18]

The Whole Jesus Christ

The image of the Cosmic Christ can be extremely helpful in keeping in touch with the goals of creation. It is important, though, that the Cosmic Christ not become some "galactic Christ" somewhere in outer space or be reduced to some abstraction. If the Cosmic Christ is to be viewed as integral and supportive in the environmental struggle, Christ must be identical with the historical Jesus who was and continues to be friend and companion in everyday life. The incarnation continues, beginning with a birth in Bethlehem and a life in Galilee, and now in "a perpetual Cosmic and personal process. It is an everlasting bringing forth in the universe and also in the individual ascending soul, of the divine and perfect Life, the pure character of God, of which the one historical life dramatized the essential constituents."[19] This is the Jesus Christ who offers his followers the vision and the energy to prevent ecological disaster.

An Ecological Perspective

It would be an anachronism to portray Jesus of Nazareth as an ecologist; our notions about the environment and the severe threats to its survival were not part of Jesus' world. In fact, Jesus did not use the word "nature" in his teachings—that was a Greek rather than a Hebrew term. Neither did Jesus develop a theology of creation as such. At the same time, the gospels depict Jesus as one who was devoted to the Hebrew tradition of creation as a good gift from God, a person deeply sensitive to the presence of God in the world about him. He grew up among people who prayed: "The heavens proclaim the glory of God, and the firmament shows forth the work of his hands" (Psalm 18:1–2).

Jesus was a man of the earth who lived most of his life in a rural area known for its natural beauty. His teachings, as they are recreated for us in the gospels, reveal a person who was more enchanted with the beauty of the wildflowers than he was with the magnificence of the royal courts. He was one who experienced the protective and loving care of God in everything from the birds of the air to the disabled person along the roadside. As a teacher, he had the gift of sharing these experiences and making creation "speak and preach about God."[20] While we should not read our ecological interpretations back into biblical times, we might well begin to reinterpret the gospels for our own needs and apply this "living Word" to the environmental crises we face today.

Jesus' teachings are filled with images from the picturesque area of Galilee where he seems to have been raised and where he worked for most of his life as a craftsman. In his messages he speaks of flowers, fruit, mustard seeds, salt, harvests, the sun, lightning, rain, wind, fish, sheep, birds, and other images from nature. Jesus is not simply using these images as teaching aids that would effectively get his message across to a rural audience. Rather, he is sharing his experience of a loving God dynamically present in the world. He is encouraging his listeners to have eyes that see and ears that hear the movement of God in the world. Jesus was passing on to his listeners what he had discovered about God's reign in the natural things around him.

In the following section, we will examine some of the themes that come through in Jesus' teachings that might be applied to our ecological concerns today. We will look at some of the individual images from nature, the parables, miracles, and the natural imagery surrounding key events of his life.

God as Protecter and Provider

In the Sermon on the Mount as it is created by Matthew, Jesus points to both wildflowers and birds as examples of how God's love and care are extended to creation. Jesus thus proclaims that God's covenant is extended to all creatures, not only to humans, and that all are provided for by a benevolent Creator. Here Jesus reclaims the teachings of Genesis where, after the flood, God tells Noah that the covenant is being established with "everything that lives on the earth" (Genesis 9:10). Jesus reveals "Abba's embrace" of the earth and all its creatures from the tiniest sparrow to all the children of God. In Jesus' teachings, all of nature bears witness to this universal care of the parent-God.[21]

Jesus also points out that the Father-Creator provides resources for the needs of creatures. In Matthew's account, Jesus admonishes his listeners: "…I am telling you not to worry about your life and what you are to eat, nor about your body and how you are to clothe it" (Matthew 6:25). Initially this text might strike us as rather naïve and unrealistic. After all, all people, especially the millions who live in poverty and deprivation, are concerned about the basic necessities of life. The millions who die every year of starvation throughout the world preclude that kind of simplistic interpretation of Jesus' injunction "not to worry."

The key word in this passage is *merimnate*; rather than meaning "worried," it more accurately conveys the sense of being "preoccupied with" or "absorbed by." Jesus seems to be telling his followers that in being concerned about their needs, they should not be so anxiety-ridden that they lose hope and trust in God. Possibly he is warning the poor about the kind of obsession for things that leads to bitterness, apathy, and even violence. Jesus might also be telling those who are well-off that being obsessed with material things leads them to greed and to insensitivity to the needs of the less fortunate—thus the earlier injunction: "Do not store up treasures for yourselves on earth" (Matthew 6:19). It would seem that Jesus is teaching that God's creation provides us with ample resources and that equitable sharing and concern for each other will bring us to a peaceful and hopeful relationship with one another and with the Creator.

The Jesus tradition calls upon people to shift the focus away from their anxieties and toward God's love for all. God is the shepherd who protects and provides for the flock (Matthew 18:12–14). The resources of God's creation are to be shared in a caring manner, a manner wherein people best reflect the caring Creator in whose image they have been made.

God's Love as Model

We saw earlier that one of Jesus' most radical teachings was that God's love embraces sinners, even those who have not yet repented. Jesus spoke of this unconditional acceptance by noting that sunshine and rain come to both the good and the bad, and that weeds and fruitful plants grow side by side. Jesus put aside the law of revenge and turned instead to the Golden Rule: "So always treat others as you would have them treat you"(Matthew 7:12). But Jesus even went far beyond this in his unique and shocking injunction: "Love your enemies, and pray for those who persecute you, so that you become the children of your Father in heaven. For he makes his sun to shine on bad and good people alike, and gives rain to those who do good and to those who do evil" (Matthew 5:43–46).

Here Jesus proclaims the accepting, forgiving, and non-violent atmosphere wherein environmental issues must be faced. Environmental issues are explosive. Already we have seen signs of violence. Already people have lost their lives for protesting the destruction of the environment. At the same time, there have been incidents of dangerous sabotage on the part of protesters. A Christian approach to ecology rules out an atmosphere of hatred, revenge, or violence in the struggle to deal with environmental issues.

Nature as Parable

Earlier, we saw how Jesus often made use of parables to teach his followers about the loving and forgiving reign of God in their midst. These parables, many of which are derived from those used by Jesus himself, reveal his "sacramental sensitivity" to the revelation of God's saving power in the sowing of seeds, in harvests, in the vineyards, with flocks of sheep in the fields, and in fish being drawn from the sea. While the gospel presentations of these parables often take on nuances from conflicts and controversies in the later Christian communities, the stories still carry the pristine insights from nature that were common in Jesus' teaching. Here we will examine a few of the creation themes that underlie some of the parables.

God's World   One of Jesus' most significant parables describes the kingdom as a vineyard (Matthew 21:33–43). The owner has leased the vineyard to others. At harvest time, he sends his servants to get his share of the grapes. The tenants beat up and stone both the first and second groups of servants that are sent on the mission. Finally the owner sends his own son. The tenants kill him also, hoping that they will now be able to take possession of the vineyard. Their plans are overthrown when the owner has them killed and leases the vineyard to others who will share the harvest.

This parable has various levels of meaning and has been traditionally interpreted in terms of God's turning the kingdom (vineyard) over to the Gentiles after God's Son, Jesus, was crucified by some of the Jewish leaders. On another level, however, the parable seems to reveal that creation is the kingdom of God and that its resources are here to be shared. The "vineyard earth" is God's creation and is pure gift, "leased" for stewardship and for mutual sharing. Abuse of this gift through greed and wanton destruction brings death upon others and ultimately upon ourselves.

Creation as Gift   Two other parables in which Jesus proclaims the graciousness of the Creator are the parable of the sower and the story about the wage dispute in the vineyard. In the first story, God is described as a sower generously spreading the seed of the Word in all directions (Mark 4:1–20). Unfortunately, because of poor understanding, shallowness, too much concern about other matters, or love of riches, many of these Words never take root. There are many levels of meanings in this parable as well, but one cannot help but see its environmental application: We are destroying the earth through these very same failings to perceive the sacredness of our environment and its resources.[22]

In the parables of the workers in the vineyard, Jesus also teaches that this is God's world and that all its resources are pure gift (Matthew 20:1–16). Those who worked all day complain that they received the same pay as those who came on the job later. The employer makes it clear that this is his vineyard and his money, and that he has a right to be as generous as he wishes. As liberation theologian Juan Luís Segundo has observed, God has planned the kingdom so that all have equal rights to its resources. The reign of this generous God calls us to give the shirts off our backs and walk the extra mile to make sure that all have what they need and deserve. It is not meant to be a kingdom of haves and have-nots, of the privileged and the marginalized. God's gifts are to be shared freely in equality and justice.[23]

Value of Simplicity   In the parable of the mustard seed, Jesus teaches that the reign of God is manifested in the small, the hidden, the simple things (Mark 4:30–32). The reign is a power that is generally imperceivable, and yet it can break forth with tremendous energy and authority. So often Jesus stresses that God is best experienced in humble folk, the apparently insignificant, and the outcasts.

Jesus' own life was one of simplicity and detachment, but it was also filled with a zest for all of creation. It was a life that continues to grow in its significance and power even today. Jesus proclaims a new perception of earth and creation that is recognized by "the little ones," those with a sensitivity for the hand of God in creation and who live simply with a willingness both to conserve and to share the earth's resources. The "mustard seed" also demonstrates the ultimate importance of what might seem like "small gestures" of recycling, clean-up efforts, and conservation of energy.

Miracle Stories and God's Power

Some of the miracle stories in the gospels also reveal the power of God over creation. Think, for example, of the story of the calming of the storm. The sea, which in the Near East was a common symbol for the powers of evil and chaos, rages about the disciples threatening their lives. Jesus is sleeping in the back of the boat, symbolic, perhaps, of his enduring confidence in God's protection. With a simple word, Jesus reveals the power of God over nature, a theme reminiscent of Psalm 107. Suddenly, the sea is calmed and the disciples are saved.

The story might indicate to us today that, ultimately, enduring environmental disasters, both natural and human-made, calls for a strong faith in God's power as the Creator and sustainer of life. For the Christian, this power is experienced in Jesus Christ. As Paul wrote to the Colossians: "Through him God chose to reconcile the universe to himself" (1:20).[24]

In another nature miracle, Jesus is described as walking on water (Mark 6:45–52). In Mark's version, Jesus has just fed the five thousand and goes to a hill to pray. The disciples are fishing in the darkness and straining at the oars against strong winds when Jesus comes to them and tells them to have courage. In Matthew's version, Peter impetuously jumps into the water to join the Lord, but his doubts "sink him," and the master has to help him back into the boat. The winds subside and the disciples recognize Jesus as the Son of God. Again, there are many levels of meaning at work here, including the trials and doubts of the early church. The story might also be to the helplessness so often experienced in feeling engulfed by the pollution of the land, air, and water.

The story reveals the saving power of God that can turn despair into hopeful efforts toward dealing with environmental crisis.[25]

Miracle Stories and Providence

Some of the miracle stories also reveal that God provides ample resources to sustain people, implying that it is only greed and waste of resources that cause many people to go wanting. The so-called social, or feeding, miracles are stories wherein Jesus provides people with food and drink. In Mark's account of the miracle of the loaves, when it is reported to Jesus that the people are hungry, Jesus tells his disciples not to merely stand by, but to take the initiative and provide the hungry with food (Mark 6:30–44). Jesus gives the disciples loaves and fish to distribute. The people are satisfied, and twelve baskets of food are left over. While the story has obvious eucharistic meaning, it is also a statement about how plentiful the resources are for God's people, provided there is effective leadership and sharing.[26]

Likewise, at the wedding feast, Jesus takes an enormous amount of water and changes it into wine for those celebrating. This miracle is described in John's gospel as Jesus' first miracle. It is one of John's "signs" that proclaims the glory of Jesus and leads his disciples to believe in him. The story is another revelation of the extreme generosity of the Creator in providing resources for people. Shortages are not to be attributed to God, but to human oversights, misplanning, or greed. Leadership and effort coupled with faith in God's power can move us to share resources. Ten million children die of malnutrition throughout the world each year, while tons upon tons of food are wasted in this country. It is toward this kind of horrible human injustice and tragedy that this and the other "feeding" miracles might be addressed.

Healing Miracles

Throughout the gospels, there are many miracles concerned with healing people of blindness, deafness, disability, and disease. The persistent theme is that the natural evils are not punishments from God. Revealed in these stories is a God who wants creation and people to be whole. God's power is a healing and saving power, not one of magisterial domination or vengeance.

Many of the illnesses and disabilities from which people suffer are the direct result of human irresponsibility. Consider the many veterans of Vietnam as well as the countless Vietnamese who have been seriously harmed through the spraying of Agent Orange on the jungles during the war. Think of the victims of Love Canal driven from their homes and carrying the destruction of toxic waste in their bodies. Remember the thousands who died in 1984 in Bhopal from toxic gas from a Union Carbide factory, as well as of the countless who have suffered from the Chernobyl nuclear power plant disaster. Think of the thousands of migrant workers whose lives have been blighted by the spraying of toxic chemicals or those whose lives have been diseased through the pollution and toxic waste at the Fernald Nuclear Plant in Ohio. "I brought you into a plentiful land to enjoy its fruits and good things," God says in Jeremiah. "But when you came you defiled my land" (Jeremiah 2:7–8).

In the healing stories Christians meet the compassion and power of a God who wants people to be whole. Jesus' healing miracles reveal that these afflictions are not the "will of God," and that the blindness, deafness, greed, and irresponsibility that causes so much suffering must be confronted prophetically by the disciples of Jesus Christ.

Nature and Jesus Events
It is notable how the gospel writers link the life of Jesus with all of creation by surrounding the main events of his life with symbols from nature. They link his life with creation. As one begins to notice the many connections, it becomes evident that there may be more awareness of the sacredness of creation in the Judeo-Christian tradition than it has ever been given credit for. The following are some examples of the use of nature as symbol in the gospels.

Matthew's description of the birth of Jesus gives prominence to a star and links the meaning of this birth to the heavens (Matthew 2:9–10). Luke's account of the nativity features shepherds with their flocks, and has a great army of angels sing "Glory to God in the highest heaven, and peace on earth to those with whom he is pleased"(Luke 2:8).

In Mark's account of the baptism of Jesus, the Lord stands in the Jordan (a highly symbolic river for the Hebrews). The heavens open and the Spirit of God descends, dovelike, reminding us of the creation scene when the Spirit of God hovered over the waters. A voice from heaven recognizes and affirms Jesus and his mission: "You are my beloved Son, in you I am pleased" (Mark 1:9ff). Indeed creation serves as the backdrop for the baptism, as Jesus prepares for his mission to usher in the new heaven and the new earth.[27] A similar theophany is described at Jesus' transfiguration. Matthew tells of a cloud, which in the Hebrew Scriptures represents the presence of God, and the same affirming and loving voice of Abba.[28]

Natural phenomena are also part of the gospel descriptions of the death of Jesus. In Mark's gospel the earth is plunged into darkness, and it is in this darkness that Jesus' cry of abandonment is heard (Mark 15:34). Matthew reports an earthquake at the death, and Luke reports a solar eclipse, in the midst of which are heard Jesus' confident words, "Father, into your hands I commend my spirit" (Luke 23:34).[29]

The resurrection stories also incorporated natural imagery with the use of the sunrise, an earthquake, and a garden. In Luke's account of the ascension, Jesus leads his disciples to Bethany, blesses them, and is taken into heaven. The pentecostal community of women and men come together in wind and fire to experience the power of the Spirit of the Lord and begin their mission of spreading his Word.

In all these stories the events are linked to creation, perhaps to reveal that all of Jesus' life and saving acts are for all of creation, and that his mission was to bring light and wholeness to the cosmos. He is indeed portrayed as the "Savior of the world," a title which, in light of today's environmental crises, can take on new levels of meaning.

New Interpretation of Jesus Events

Contemporary theologians are also shifting away from some of the more traditional interpretations of the beliefs of the Christian tradition and are moving toward approaches more relevant to contemporary concerns. For example, the traditional understanding of incarnation was often based on a transcendent or "outside" God sending his Son to a fallen earth to save humankind from sin. Here the stress was on God becoming human in order to open the gates of heaven and offer eternal life after death.

This approach often stressed the divinity of Jesus, but it neglected his human personality, the development of that personality, and his solidarity with the human family and the earth. Thus the incarnation has often been understood as a "coming down for the world," rather than as a "coming forth from the world." The accent on the transcendence of God, the fallen earth and humanity, and the eternal life of the Spirit often led us away from seeing the goodness of creation, and did not seem to provide us adequately with reasons for "building the earth."[30]

An incarnational theology more appropriate to today's ecological awareness would stress immanence and an "inside" God who communicates self continually through creation. Just as our bodies express who we are, so creation might well be thought of as "God's body," a God who is revealed definitely and fully in Jesus.[31] Jesus, then, is viewed as the personal and human embodiment of God.[32]

In Jesus, God comes as a caring and creative God, revealing that the divine has been with us all along in all of the cosmos in beauty and creativity, and now in human freedom and love. In Jesus is revealed a God who relates intimately with creation, not as subject to object, but as I to Thou in a relationship as intimate as parent to child, life-giver to living person. Since Jesus comes from creation, from the evolution of our earth and our species, then we know that the earth and humankind must be sacred. He reveals that the earth is worth caring for. The earth, its resources, and its people are not "things" to be used. They are, rather, gifts to be cherished, nurtured, and shared.

Jesus Christ embodies a God who is inclusive, loving, and caring for all of creation, from the birds of the air to the harvests, to the outcasts and sinners. He enfleshes a God who has, from the beginning, urged creation toward a consciousness and freedom whereby love could be expressed personally. In Jesus, God proclaims this love in the most personal manner possible: love that is selflessly given to all of creation, love that demands justice among people. Jesus Christ thus establishes love as the basis of a solidarity that is needed among people and their world as they face the possibility of self-destruction.

Jesus "incorporates" a God of power, but not the power of domination or manipulation. The kind of godly power revealed in Jesus is the power of healing, of recovery after destruction, of giving, of freeing and enabling. It is the power that brings new life, the power that sustains that life with hope and meaning. Jesus, raised and glorified as the Christ, now offers his followers the support and power to confront the greed, apathy, and ignorance that are causing the relentless destruction of the earth and its resources.

Jesus Christ re-presents a God who is compassionate and empathic toward creation. Some theologians view Jesus as the revelation of a "suffering" God who became part of our anguish and even our death to show us that the divine is always with us even in tragedy and loss, always offering new life and victory over the destructive forces in creation.[33] Jesus is the incarnation of a "God of pathos," who, throughout history, has been involved in human events and has, in a way, suffered with humanity.[34] Jesus reveals a God who is friend and companion, a God who has entered the "stuff" of life, the very bloodstream of creation in order to accompany humans in their struggles.

This is a God who indeed is affected by the disturbance of the creative process through environmental irresponsibility, by the rapid destruction of species that took millions of years to evolve, and by the disease and death that humans are sowing in their bodies and the bodies of future generations through pollution and contamination. The smell of death, ecological death, is in the air throughout the world. In

Jesus Christ, God gives God's people the hope and courage needed to restore life to the earth, the atmosphere, the oceans, and to those oppressed by pollution.

The incarnation, then, is not an afterthought "decided" by God after the Fall in order to repair a fallen world. The incarnation is integral to God's creative plan whereby God continually communicates self to creation and brings this communion to its climax in the incarnation.[35] In Jesus Christ, God says: "This is what I had in mind all along; to produce loving and sacrificing people who would be at one with each other and with their world." Jesus is the revelation of God's plan for the fulfillment of creation, not its destruction.

Redemption Reinterpreted

Traditional interpretations of redemption have emphasized the elements of reparation for original sin, pardon, and expiation through the sacrifice of the cross. When Jesus is called "Savior of the world," it traditionally refers to his making amends for the sins of the first humans and winning forgiveness for all. Little is said in this traditional interpretation of saving the world or cosmos as such. Those who interpret redemption narrowly often apply salvation only to people, sometimes only to Christian people, and at times even more exclusively to those within one ecclesial body of Christians. This is hardly the universal and cosmic notion of salvation that we find in the Christian Scriptures.

The cross is revelatory for the Christian environmentalist. It teaches the destructive power of evil, a force that appeared to end the life and work of Jesus of Nazareth at Calvary. At the same time, the cross reveals that the power of this destructive evil cannot vanquish love, forgiveness, and hope for a future amidst apparent devastation. We learn from the cross that there are destructive forces surrounding us, but that those forces can be ultimately overcome with courage and determination.

This is the lesson that has been learned by many Eastern Europeans as they watched the beauty of their environment destroyed by the reckless and irresponsible industrial policies of the Communist regimes. Now, with the collapse of these regimes, environmental groups are emerging with renewed hopes for overcoming the death that has been brought to their environment. Elements such as reparation and forgiveness for sin are certainly part of the redemptive tradition.

Christ's redemption extends beyond the cross to include his whole life. Jesus of Nazareth was a person who brought freedom and salvation to people through a life of simplicity, detachment, self-sacrifice, and service. He "saved" people from low self-esteem, personal sin, hopelessness, estrangement, and alienation. His passion and death were a culmination of this life and, in a sense, were brought on by his determined commitment to justice and integrity. His life was indeed a "compensating correction" to the entire process of creation, because it momentarily pulled back the veil from God's plan for harmony and peace in the world. In knowing Jesus Christ, we now know the "why" of creation and "how" it can come to fulfillment.

Loving service and a commitment to justice, not consumerism and waste, were shown to be the way to live a life of meaning and purpose. In Jesus, his early followers had discovered God in their midst as Creator and redeemer. This was the "good news," and in the gospel stories we see them searching their Scriptures and the images of other religious traditions around them for images and titles that would somehow describe this experience and share it with posterity.[36] They perceived that Jesus had initiated a new earth and a new creation.

Teilhard points out that, for Jesus' early followers, redemption was primarily a transformation of all of creation. For Teilhard, the Christian symbols speak more of this transformation than they do of reparation. In his vision, Christian baptism symbolizes a raising up of the world more that it does a purification. The cross stands more for the ascent of creation than it does for expiation of an original offense. The blood of Jesus represents life and vitality for the earth more than it does reparation for sin. Without denying the traditional aspects of redemption, Teilhard makes them secondary to the elements of fulfillment, transformation, and progression in evolution. For him, the redemption of Jesus Christ is ongoing, a dynamic force within the very process of evolution.[37]

To carry such thinking a step further, we might say that Christ's redemption includes our present-day efforts to save our world from ecological destruction. Not only is there a need to be "saved" from the "sins" of our environmental destruction, there is also a need to "raise up" our earth and its resources to the dignity it has in God's creative plan. In this scheme of things, we act as images of our God when we protect and cultivate, but not when we dominate and destroy.

The Resurrection and Ecology

The traditional interpretation of the resurrection was often limited to understanding it as a proof of Jesus' identity. In recent times we have come to see the resurrection with more of the richness that it held for the early Christians. Today, many see the resurrection as the very foundation of faith in Jesus, as well as the basis for hope in life eternal.

The resurrection is not an isolated action, but one in continuity with creation, incarnation, and redemption. It is the climactic approval of all Jesus' earthly work, vindication of all his teaching and miracles, and the designation of Jesus as the Christ. It is integral to the whole process of creation and evolution. It reveals the ultimate goal of God's plan for the cosmos.

There are a number of ecological implications in the resurrection of Jesus Christ. First of all, the resurrection affirms the sacredness of the physical, of materiality. In the resurrection appearances, Jesus does not come to the faithful as disembodied spirit, but as a risen person. He is described as embracing, accompanying friends, forgiving those who let him down, and sharing meals. The appearance stories seem to be telling us that, in resurrection, materiality will not be destroyed but transformed. In resurrection, the physical is no longer subject to time or space and can no longer suffer and die; at the same time, however, it somehow is in continuity with life as we know it. The resurrection reveals that the physical and the material are sacred and are drawn toward ultimate fulfillment.

The resurrection also discloses God's power over death and destruction. What was an apparently hopeless situation of abandonment and despair on one day was altered to triumphant new life on another. Jesus' conquering of death offers hope and courage to those who may feel helpless in the face of the many overwhelming environmental crises. The creative and life-giving power of God is indeed operative in the world, and death can be overcome through this power.

Finally, the resurrection experiences portray a solidarity among Jesus and his followers, a bonding in the Spirit that seems to transform them from fearful, on-the-run persons into an inspired and dauntless community of disciples. The same Spirit that hovered over the waters to bring creation out of chaos hovered over the disciples and began the new creation of Pentecost. This same empowerment is available to those struggling with timidity and hesitation over getting involved in the environmental movement. The power of the risen Lord, along with the energy of his community, can make a formidable impact on the critical ecological problems of today.

Summary

On the whole, Christians do not have a good history when it comes to caring for the environment. There has been a certain regard for nature, as well as an awareness of the presence of God in creation, but until recently little has been done to connect the Christian tradition with environmental concerns.

We have seen how ancient myths understood creation as a static and finished product, and a "fallen" reality. Such views could later be employed to justify the mere "use" of the environment and its resources.

We have pointed out how the Enlightenment came to a more accurate scientific comprehension of the universe, and added a mechanistic interpretation that promoted a "mastering" of the environment and its resources. In the ensuing secular mentality, a belief in the universe and world as "God's creation" and a commitment to Jesus' teachings about the sacredness of reality were often abandoned.

In the contemporary era, the optimism about the accomplishments of science and progress has been tempered with the realization that many of these so-called advancements could lead to the destruction of life as we know it. Led by thinkers like Teilhard de Chardin and others, Christians have begun to reinterpret their understanding of creation in the light of modern science. They have also searched for ways to apply the treasured teachings of the Judeo-Christian tradition to the environmental crises that face the world.

Christian theologians have begun to retrieve the role Jesus Christ, his gospel teachings, and the Christian tradition can play in saving the world from environmental destruction.

Questions for Reflection and Discussion

1. What contributions did Teilhard de Chardin make in the integration of Christianity with evolution?

2. In what areas have we had to move beyond Teilhard's views in order to deal with the contemporary environmental crises?

3. Cite several of Jesus' teachings that might be relevant to an "ecological spirituality."

4. Select and interpret several parables of Jesus that might be used to move Christians to become more active in the environmental movement.

5. Choose several miracle stories where the teaching might offer lessons on the sacredness of creation.

CHAPTER SEVEN

Born in Bethlehem

Christmas is an extraordinary time for followers of Jesus Christ, a time rich in church celebrations, traditional carols, and the familiar manger scene with a couple in a stable huddled around a newborn baby in a straw-filled manger and surrounded by shepherds, Magi, and angels singing "Gloria in excelsis." The season also denotes extensive decorating, trees glittering with lights and ornaments, family gatherings, and children anticipating the coming of Santa Claus. Although the season has for many become merely social and commercial, Christians struggle to remember that this feast is first and foremost the commemoration of the birth of Jesus of Nazareth.

In this chapter we are going to examine the two gospel stories of Jesus' birth. After some general observations, we will describe how the early Christians used the event of Jesus' birth, about which they knew little factually, to proclaim their post-resurrection faith in Jesus as Son of God and messiah. Then we will look at how Jesus is contrasted with the other rulers of his time, and how the nativity stories reveal the broad spectrum of people who had welcomed Jesus Christ's message of salvation.

Tale of Two Stories

The Christmas story familiar to all who celebrate this season is actually a blending of two stories, one attributed to Matthew and the other to Luke. These are the only two gospels that give an account of Jesus' birth. Mark, the earliest gospel, begins with Jesus' baptism. John begins with a highly stylized account of Christ's existence before creation. Both Matthew and Luke were written about eighty-five years after Jesus' birth and seem to be much more concerned with the theological significance than with the historical details of the birth. It seems as though the main question for people at the time was: "What does this birth mean for our faith?" They did not spend much time with the question that we might ask today: "What really happened?"[1]

Interest in the significance of Jesus' birth came rather late in the gospel communities. The crucifixion (which we will discuss in the next chapter) was a much more pressing event to deal with initially because of its tragic, indeed scandalous character. The other events upon which they reflected in light of their resurrection faith were largely from Jesus' public life. They seem to have had little concern about his first thirty years, and when they turn to look at his birth, they seem more concerned with apologetics and theology than with history as we understand it.

One of their practical concerns may have included charges made by enemies that Jesus was the illegitimate son of a poor country woman who had committed adultery with a Roman soldier by the name of Panthera.[2] In face of such slanderous attacks, the nativity stories established for all time the identity and unquestionable integrity of the parents, Mary and Joseph, and powerfully demonstrated that this birth was from God in a special and unique way. Another practical concern seems to have been the continuing existence of followers of John the Baptist. The Christian communities wanted to make it clear in the nativity stories that, while John was an outstanding and prophetic figure, he was not comparable to Jesus and should be viewed as one who came to prepare the way for the messiah and Son of God, Jesus Christ.

A number of theological concerns went into formulating the nativity stories, first orally, and then in the highly crafted versions of Matthew and Luke.[3] Both gospel writers are concerned with teaching a number of beliefs to the early communities. Among these beliefs were the Jewish roots of Jesus, his identity as the Son of God become human, and the "good news" of Jesus of Nazareth was for all: Jew and Gentile, rich and poor, young and old. As Raymond Brown observes, each of these distinctly different accounts of Jesus' conception and birth is, in fact, the "gospel in miniature," summarizing the faith of the early communities in the person and message of Jesus Christ.[4]

The broad diversity of details indicate that we are not dealing with eyewitness accounts of the birth of Jesus in these stories. It is true that there are some similarities in the two accounts: the names of the parents, Mary and Joseph, the account of the virginal conception (although not as explicit in Luke as in Matthew), the designation of the place and time as Bethlehem during the reign of Herod, the name designation by an angel, the Davidic line, and the eventual settling in Nazareth. Many notable differences exist in the stories, however, differences that are often overlooked in our traditional blending of the two stories into one. For example, the two genealogies are different. Matthew starts with Abraham and traces Jesus' forebears through the ruling Davidic line. Luke, who delays his genealogy until after Jesus' baptism, goes Matthew one better and traces Jesus all the way back to Adam.

Matthew's gospel, which seems to come out of a Syrian community of both Jews and Gentiles, focuses on Joseph, the plot of Herod to kill the child, the visit of the Magi, and on how Jesus is the fulfillment of many Hebrew prophecies. Luke's gospel, which seems to come out of Syrian Antioch, centers instead on the story of Mary, the miraculous birth of John the Baptist to Elizabeth and Zechariah, and the visit of the shepherds.

Even more noticeable are the accounts of the "hometown" of the parents, their marital status when the baby is born, and the logistics involved in the birth event. In Matthew's account the parents seem to be already married and living in Bethlehem, where Jesus is born. When Joseph discovers Herod's plot, the family moves to Egypt and then goes to settle in Nazareth when Herod dies and the danger is over. In Luke's account, the parents seem to live in Nazareth, go to Bethlehem for the Roman census, have the baby in a manger while apparently still engaged, and then return to Nazareth after they present their infant in the Temple for circumcision.

Obviously, the Christmas story familiar to most of us is really an amalgam of both stories. When we set up our crib scenes, we usually include the manger, star, Magi, the shepherds, and angels as though they are all part of the one story. The Scriptures, however, offer two diverse accounts of the theological significance of the birth of Jesus Christ. We might look at these narratives as two plays, the ingredients of which are some basic historical facts, a large amount of material from the Hebrew Scriptures, and the belief of the early Christian communities that Jesus of Nazareth is the Christ.

Jesus' Family Tree

Both gospel accounts of the birth of Jesus insist that he was born a Jew and, therefore, had genuine ethnic as well as authentically human roots. Matthew's account tells of Jesus' good "genes" going back through Joseph and some of the "big names" in the Bible, including Josiah, Amos, Solomon, Bathsheba, David, Jesse, Ruth, Tamar, Jacob, Isaac, and Abraham.

The family tree, as in most families, includes outstanding examples of character and fidelity, as well as some rogue "skeletons" in the family closet. The family heritage includes the adultery of David and Bathsheba, the deception of Jacob, the seductiveness of Tamar, the cowardice of Abraham, and the disobedience of Adam.[5] Jesus is portrayed as descending from a long line of people who had their weaknesses, but who were still able somehow to contribute to God's plan. In contrast to all of them, however, Joseph, Mary, and others are portrayed as individuals who are utterly faithful to God's will.[6]

Matthew puts Jesus' father at the center of his narrative. Apparently knowing little about Joseph, Matthew seems to rely on the Hebrew Scripture account of the patriarch Joseph for his material. Like the Joseph of old, Jesus' father is a dreamer and interpreter of dreams. In the story he learns the divine origin of his betrothed's pregnancy from a dream. Like his namesake, Joseph is also a man of compassion and forgiveness, and thus is willing to quietly divorce his betrothed, who seems to be carrying someone else's baby, rather than denounce her publicly. Joseph, like the patriarch of old, is also forced into exile into Egypt, and is faithful to God's word and dedicated to his family.[7]

The Egypt of the ancient Joseph story also offers Matthew the backdrop he needs for a mini-exile-Exodus theme. The story of the flight to save Jesus' life from Herod provides the basis for proclaiming that Jesus is the Moses figure who will lead his people out of exile. For the Jews of Jesus' community, what could be a more convincing argument of the authenticity of Jesus' life and mission than this parallel with the great Moses? Moreover, Matthew's selection of many Hebrew prophecies that are fulfilled by Jesus would convince the Jews of the Matthean community even further that Jesus was authentically the messiah for whom they longed.

Luke chooses to feature Mary as the central character of his story. It is to Mary, rather than to Joseph, that the angel comes to announce the nature of the conception of Jesus. Mary, the young Jewish girl who would be so key in shaping the character of Jesus' personality and life, is portrayed as feisty ("How can this be?") and yet faithful to God's challenge to her once she understands. She is shown as caring and other-centered in the story of her trip to assist her cousin Elizabeth. As a close reading of her "Magnificat" reveals, Mary is a deeply spiritual person, both prayerful and radical in her social concern for the poor. Mary is many of the things that we later see in the gospels as characteristic of her first-born, Jesus. Luke may have had to go to Hannah in the Hebrew Scriptures for the formal material of Mary's prayer, yet it seems to authentically capture the determination and courage that early Christians believed were characteristic of Jesus' mother.[8]

Luke further delineates Jesus' Jewish background by linking his bloodlines to those of John the Baptist. The first annunciation scene in Luke's gospel pictures the angel Gabriel revealing to Zechariah, a minor priest of the Temple, that he and his wife Elizabeth are about to have a son. Like Abraham and Sarah, from whom the portrait of John's parents is at least in part drawn, they are senior citizens long past their child-bearing years.

Thus John's conception is viewed as a miracle of God, but not comparable to the virginal conception of Jesus. John will be a prophet, but one whose role is to prepare the way for Jesus. The scenario, as Luke describes it, further portrays Jesus as related to other faithful Jews. At the same time, it portrays John as a distant relative whose future mission would be to prepare the way for Jesus. Historically, it is more likely that Jesus was at one time a follower of John the Baptist. That Jesus did not start his own mission until John had been executed by Herod, and then begins with a message similar to John's might be indications of their "master-disciple" relationship.[9] The gospels also link both John and Jesus in the prophetic tradition, for both come to challenge the religious and political abuses of their times.

So far, we have seen how some of the features of the nativity stories have shown that Jesus was indeed a Jew, a historical human being with forebears who go back to Abraham (Matthew) and even move universally to Adam (Luke), a person whose parents were devout Jews, and whose extended family also consisted of faithful Jews. Jesus' Hebrew background is further established by naming his birthplace as Bethlehem, the small town just five miles south of Jerusalem, which was the ancestral town of David and where David was anointed king of Israel by Samuel. There can be no doubt that both the early communities of Matthew and Luke, and the communities where these stories originated, all knew Jesus to be an authentically Jewish and human person whose birth was indeed real and historical. Now let us look at some of the key faith statements made about Jesus in these nativity stories.

Jesus as Son of God
Further details from these narratives reveal other aspects of early Chris-

tian beliefs about Jesus. Most important, the early Christians believed that Jesus was the Son of God. Son of God was originally a royal and messianic title that gradually came to indicate divinity. Paul's theology represents this development in his statement to the Romans: Jesus may have descended in the flesh from David, but he was "established as Son of God in power according to the spirit of holiness through resurrection from the dead, Jesus Christ our Lord" (Romans 1:3–4).[10]

Many features of the nativity stories seem designed to establish that Jesus' origins are uniquely from God. Matthew's vignette of the annunciation to Joseph seems to be patterned after annunciations to Sarah and Daniel in the Hebrew Scriptures. It is designed, at least in part, to dramatize Christian belief in Jesus' divine sonship. The message is given by the angel Gabriel, one of the "angels of the face," who in the Hebrew Scriptures stands before God and is the bearer of divine messages.[11] For the Hebrews, the angel denotes the very presence of God and thus symbolically confirms that this message is indeed the very Word of God. In Luke's shepherd scene a multitude of angels sing "Glory to God in the highest" (apparently a later liturgical hymn) to celebrate the birth of Jesus, indicating the divine nature of this event.

In Matthew's version, Joseph is an engaged man with a terrible dilemma: His betrothed is pregnant and it is not his child. He has to decide whether to have her punished or to simply and quietly end the engagement. Joseph apparently had decided to divorce Mary quietly, which would still mean that although he might provide some initial financial support, she would live in disgrace and probably would be forced to raise the child by herself. Legally, she could later marry an Israelite commoner, if he would have her, but she could never marry into a priestly family.[12]

After deciding for compassion, Joseph had his revelation that the conception was "through the Holy Spirit," and he was asked to now follow through with the second stage of betrothal and take Mary into his house as his wife. The baby would be a son by the name of Jesus, fulfilling the prophecy of the coming of Emmanuel (God with us). The story clearly reflects the early Christian belief that Jesus was indeed born of God and that he was the Savior for whom the Jews had been waiting.

Luke's annunciation story is different in approach from Matthew's, but it also reveals an early Christian belief in Jesus as the Son of God and Savior. Luke's annunciation to Mary follows the one made to Zechariah, who, as a minor priest, is about to take advantage of his yearly privilege to offer incense in the inner sanctuary of the Temple. This annunciation of John the Baptist's birth sets the scene for a whole series of divine interventions, culminating in the birth of God's own Son. Here an elderly couple are told that they are about to miraculously have a son, John. Then in the sixth month of Elizabeth's pregnancy, the angel Gabriel now comes to Mary, a virgin betrothed to Joseph, and announces that she too will conceive a son. When Mary questions the possibility of this, the angel informs her: "The holy Spirit will come upon you, and the power of the Most High will overshadow you. Therefore the child to be born with be called holy, the Son of God" (Luke 1:36). The phrase seems to echo the creation in Genesis, where the Spirit hovers creatively over the waters. Again, the narrative reflects the belief of the earliest communities that Jesus was both born miraculously of a virgin and that he is indeed the Son of God. The early Christians had perceived the true identity of Jesus Christ in his resurrection. In this gospel, this identity is read back into many of the events of his life, even back into his very conception.

What happened historically with regard to this virginal conception is extremely difficult to resolve. It is difficult to simply put the virginal conception in the category of a myth similar to those that surrounded the birth of other great heroes.[13] This story is unique and there are no exact parallels either in the Hebrew Scriptures or in the literature of other religions. Although the virginal conception has never been formally defined as a dogma, it appears in the early creeds and has been commonly held among the Christian traditions. The Roman Catholic church as well as some of the mainline Protestant churches are quite sensitive in this area of belief. There are some exegetes, however, who maintain that the virginal conception is primarily a proclamation of belief in the divine origin and nature of Jesus Christ. Whatever one's conclusions about the factuality of the virginal conception, the import of the passage seems to be fundamentally one of faith.

Jesus as Messiah

We have already seen how the genealogies and the designation of Bethlehem as the birthplace underscore Jesus' lineage with David, and thus confirm him as the messiah who is to come from that line. The early communities accept Jesus as the new king of the Jews, as is indicated in Luke's inscription over the cross: "This is the king of the Jews" (Luke 23:38).

This same theme appears in the story of the Magi in Matthew's nativity narrative. These mysterious men from the East come to Jerusalem following a star and asking: "Where is the newborn king of the

Jews?" (Matthew 2:2). When the reigning king of the Jews, Herod, hears of this, he is threatened and assembles all the chief priests and scribes to search the sacred texts and discover where this king will be born. When they report that he will be born in Bethlehem, Herod sends the Magi off to find the king so that he might be killed. The Magi then continue to follow the star to the place where the newborn messiah lies, and there they pay royal homage to the infant, offering him gifts fit only for a king: gold, frankincense, and myrrh.[14]

The so-called flight into Egypt in Matthew's narrative also brings out the messianic dimension of Jesus. The "exile" of Jesus and his parents parallels the original exile of the Jews in Egypt. Most likely playing to the Jewish members of his community, Matthew portrays Jesus as fulfilling the Moses figure whose life is threatened by Herod, just as Moses' life was endangered by Pharaoh, and who, as an adult, will lead his people in a new exodus.[15] These incidents clearly align Jesus with the greatest leader of the Jews as well as with the central event of their saving history. The early Christians proclaim that Jesus is indeed the messiah to the new "chosen people."

Luke's shepherd episode further demonstrates the early Christian acceptance of Jesus as the messiah.[16] The shepherds receive the "good news" of Jesus' birth, as so many others in these narratives have, from an "angel of the Lord" who tells them: "I proclaim you good news of great joy that will be for all the people. For today in the city of David a savior has been born for you who is messiah and the Lord" (Luke 2:10–12). Here Luke explicitly reflects the joy and excitement, especially among the Gentiles of his community ("for all the people"), with which the gospel ("good news") of Jesus' messiahship is accepted.

Luke's depiction of the presentation in the Temple is another indication of early faith among both Jewish and Gentile Christians that Jesus is indeed the messiah. In the narrative, Simeon is a devout Spirit-filled Jew to whom it has been revealed that he will see the messiah before he dies. In a touching scene, Simeon takes the infant Jesus in his arms, sees that his life is now fulfilled, and praises God: "Now, Master, you may let your servant go in peace, according to your word, for my eyes have seen your salvation, which you prepared in the sight of all the peoples, a light for the revelation to the Gentiles, and glory for your people Israel" (Luke 2:29–32).

Simeon then tells Mary how this child will be a sign of contradiction for Israel. Here Luke seems to use Simeon as an instrument to show the deep divisions in the early church between Jews and Christians over Jesus' messiahship.

A number of allusions to the Temple in Luke's gospel cast even more light on Jesus' messiahship. By the time this gospel was written, the Temple in Jerusalem had been destroyed by the Romans in the 60–70 C.E. war, and Jews and Christians had become separated, with the latter no longer permitted in the synagogues. In this context, the Temple seems to have stood as a symbol of the deep division among Jews and Christians.

Ironically, the Temple is dealt with positively in these Christmas narratives. It is in the midst of prayer in the inner sanctuary of the Temple that Zechariah receives the angelic annunciation about the conception of his son. As we have just seen, the presentation scene depicts both Mary and Joseph, as well as Simeon and Anna, as Jews who are devoted both to fulfilling the laws and reverencing the Temple. Luke also adds the episode of Mary and Joseph finding Jesus in the Temple, further demonstrating how Jesus and his family observed the pilgrimages to the Temple in Jerusalem for the great feasts, and how well received Jesus was among the elders. All this might reflect the position of Luke's community that Jesus indeed came as messiah to reform Judaism and the Temple, not to destroy them. These Christians seem to take a stand against their opponents by saying that they are in no way responsible for the destruction of the Temple or the division in Judaism.[17]

Study in Contrasts

One way the gospel writers seem to fill out the portrait of Jesus Christ, as he is understood by the early communities, is to set him in contrast to some of the major figures of his time. For instance, the comparison between the corrupt and vicious Herod and the innocent infant Jesus is striking. Some background might make it easier for us to see how those who knew of Herod would have looked at this contrast.

Herod had conquered Galilee with the help of the occupying Romans about thirty years before Jesus was born. This merited him being promoted from being a kind of sheriff of the area to being crowned as a puppet king by the Romans. Herod took his monarchical title seriously. He dutifully collected the heavy tribute demanded of the area by Rome, and, if anyone objected to the tribute or to any other aspect of Roman rule, he would see to it that that person was sought by his secret police and either imprisoned or killed. He was known for the vicious slaughter of great numbers of people who got in the way of his or Roman authority. On one occasion a number of Torah scholars and their students objected to Herod's putting the golden eagle of Rome over the gate of the Temple, and they eventually cut down the eagle in protest. Herod had the offenders burned alive.[18] On another occasion, he caught some persons who were conspiring against him. He had them chopped up and thrown to the dogs. He was so fearful of losing his power that he had his wife and some of his sons murdered because he thought them a danger to his throne.

Besides the tribute for Rome, Herod also extorted enormous taxes from his people for his own use. As we saw in an earlier chapter, Herod carried out enormous building programs, erecting entire cities, temples, monuments, and amphitheaters, many of which he dedicated to Caesar. One can well imagine the resentment toward him from his own people. Not only was he corrupt and vicious, and only a "half-breed" in his Jewish background, but he paid homage to Caesar and even had statues dedicated to himself—two activities that devout Jews would have considered horrendous evils.

Herod was especially hated for the massacres he had inflicted on his people. It is said that Herod knew that he was detested and, as he approached death, feared no one would mourn him. As he lay dying, Herod ordered that thousands of his underlings from all parts of the country be locked in the hippodrome at Jericho and killed when he died so that there would be mourning after his death. (Fortunately, they were all released when Herod did die.)[19] If one wanted to make comparison to ruthless dictators of modern times, one might compare Herod to Stalin, Pol Pot, or Idi Amin, all savage men who massacred millions of their own people in order to silence dissent and prevent any opposition to their corruption and depravity.

Compare this monster to the carpenter from Nazareth whose birth is commemorated in these narratives. The communities that formulated these stories knew that they were commemorating the birth of a man who was a full-blooded Jew, loyal to his people, and concerned about the oppression that he saw about him as he grew up in Galilee under similar oppression from Herod's son. Jesus was not a hateful or violent man. He was dedicated to healing, compassion, and forgiveness. He did not plot to kill his enemies; he forgave and loved them. Even from the cross, where he had so unjustly been hung as a criminal, he forgave those who had betrayed him and those who had condemned him. His was not a power of domination that had to be protected by the slaughter of those who opposed him. His was a power that freed, healed, forgave, enlivened, and enabled. Unlike Herod, Jesus did not do the bidding of Rome. In fact, he was sentenced to death by Roman authorities as a danger to the realm.

While there is no evidence that Jesus ever advocated the overthrow

of Rome, neither is there any indication that he encouraged cooperation. The famous passage "Give to Caesar what is Caesar's and to God
what is God's" does not seem to indicate any separation of civil and religious duties. The Jews of his time did not so easily separate the political from the religious. The statement by Jesus might well mean that
Caesar should be given nothing but the coin of tribute, and that this
should be done unwillingly and only because of fear of severe punishment. Beyond the coin, Caesar deserves nothing, neither the homage
and obedience that Herod offers, nor even the cooperation that was advocated by the Sadducees in order to protect their vested interests.[20] It
is easy to see why in the nativity story this newborn "king of the Jews"
would strike terror into the heart of the tyrant Herod, and it is understandable why, later in the real history, Herod's son was willing to be
an accomplice to the crucifixion of Jesus.

Augustus and the Prince of Peace

Luke's birth narrative provides us with another important historical
figure who stands in contrast to Jesus of Nazareth. Traditional readings
of Luke's account have seen the mention of Caesar Augustus and his
call for worldwide census as a mere occasion to demonstrate how compliant Joseph and Mary (as well as later Christians) were to the bidding
of the Romans. More recently some scholars have pointed out that giv-
en the Roman oppression at the time of Jesus' birth, as well as during
the time the gospels were written, there is more to the census of Augustus than was previously noticed.[21]

It is important to remember the events involving the Romans previous to the writing of Luke's gospel. About fifty years had passed since
the followers of Jesus had experienced the brutal beating and public
crucifixion of their master under the authority of the Roman government. Much more recently, perhaps ten years or so before, they had
lived through a long and bloody rebellion against the Romans. The Romans had been true to their reputation for brutality: They carried out a
"scorched earth" policy in the areas of rebellion, slaughtering anyone
involved in resistance. At the war's end, the Romans had destroyed the
Temple, leveled the city of Jerusalem, and massacred many of its inhabitants.

It is with these and many other experiences of domination and oppression from the Romans that the Christian communities in and about
Palestine would hear the account of Augustus's census. Caesar Augustus was indeed the Roman emperor during the time when Jesus was
born. It is unlikely that a census of these proportions was really carried

out.[22] However, Luke's use of the "worldwide" census, which forced an engaged and expecting couple to leave their home and take an arduous and dangerous trip to an overcrowded Bethlehem, does dramatize the uncompromising and universal force of Roman authority.

The census was, of course, for taxation purposes. For many years the Jews had strained under the heavy burden of having to pay the Roman tribute, Herod's taxes, the tithes to the Temple, and the mortgages on the farm land. Nearly ninety percent of the population of Palestine had been reduced to peasantry as a result of this oppressive system.[23] Many had been driven to impoverishment because of their debts. These people were often imprisoned or sold into slavery. Many fled to the hills to live as bandits. Some fathers actually sold their daughters into slavery in order to be able to pay their debts. Some women were forced into prostitution as a result of poverty, or because they had been victims of rape by Roman soldiers and could never again regain respectability.

Caesar Augustus had a reputation among the Romans for being a great peacemaker, the "divine one" and "savior" who established the well-known Pax Romana. His renown has been enduring. (We still name one of our summer months after him; the word "august" in English means dignified and illustrious.) It is true that Augustus did bring a great deal of the internal strife in Rome to a close and stopped the civil wars that had been tearing the empire apart. At the same time, however, the so-called peace he established throughout the empire was gained through conquest and subjugation. It was a peace enforced through rigid control, reprisals, and punishment through crucifixion. The peace of Augustus was the kind of peace that prevailed in Western Europe under Nazi occupation, or in Eastern Europe under Communist domination.

With all this as a background, Luke's picture of Mary and Joseph traveling from Nazareth to Bethlehem for the census may be more an account of helplessness in the face of oppression than a portrait of compliant obedience. And the birth of Jesus on that trip places the significance of his life and his message in glaring contrast to what Caesar Augustus and imperial Rome stood for. Jesus would grow up to be the authentic "Prince of Peace" for whom Isaiah longed. He would be the authentic leader of his people. Rather than rule through conquest, subjugation, or fear, Jesus would reign in a kingdom where love, compassion, recognition of human dignity, and freedom prevail.

The "Way" that Jesus proposed and lived was one that reached out to the poor and the outcasts to give them dignity and hope, not degradation and punishment. His was a call to love enemies, not to destroy them. His gospel was one of forgiveness, not reprisal. He would weep over Jerusalem and the Temple and call his people to conversion, not to violence. The savage destruction by Rome and the slaughter of its people would be a contradiction to Jesus' message, "Peace be with you."

Shadow of the Cross

The early Christian communities not only believed that Jesus was the Son of God and the messiah, they also saw him as a man of simplicity, compassion, and love, who stood as a threat to the other kings that ruled over them. They had either been present at or heard of his crucifixion, and many of them had known persecution and martyrdom in their own times. During the period when Matthew's gospel was written, Christian preachers were being dragged before the Sanhedrin and other hostile leaders and were often flogged or executed. Christians were well aware of the dangers inherent in Jesus' message and way of life.

A number of features in the birth narratives reflect the early Christian awareness of how Jesus was a marked man throughout his life and how he shared this destiny with many who would take a stand with him. The episode with Herod in Matthew sets Jesus in stark contrast to the corruption, violence, and luxury of Herod and his court. Jesus is from the common masses. His parents are simple and faithful Jews displaced from their home in Bethlehem, forced into exile, and then made to settle in Galilee. The kind of creative and loving power symbolized in this miraculous birth is a threat to Herod, so he orders the toddlers and infants in the area to be murdered in order to make sure that Jesus is eliminated.

The story of the "slaughter of the innocents" has been part of the Christian myth and has grown substantially in the telling. In the Byzantine liturgy the number of infants is 14,000 and in other calendars of saints one sees numbers as high as 64,000 and 144,000. Population studies of the times would put the number more realistically at about twenty-five.[24] In fact, the incident itself might well not be historical at all. The various lives of Herod make no mention of it, although that would not be conclusive proof that it did not happen: Compared to Herod's other atrocities, this incident could have been passed over as minor.[25]

The main problem with holding that this story is historical is the accompanying presupposition that Jesus' birth and identity as "king of the Jews" was known by Herod, the chief priests and scribes, the Magi, and, indeed, "all of Jerusalem." As the gospels unfold and describe his public ministry, however, there is no sign that his birth was widely known. Furthermore, as has been noted, if we are dealing with history here, why is the event not mentioned in Luke's account? Might it not be more probable that Jesus' birth was a private family event that happened at home, only later becoming significant more for theological than for historical reasons? The story might well be merely a reconstruction of the Hebrew story wherein the infant Moses escaped a similar murderous plot by Pharaoh. As such, it is integral to Matthew's theme of Jesus as the fulfillment of the type of Moses.

Whatever the case may be historically, the story does dramatize the danger that Jesus was in from the beginning. Those who could not understand why a man like Jesus could be condemned as a criminal, tortured, and crucified, now came to realize that he was a marked man from the time he took his stand on freedom, goodness, and love for all. Concomitantly, the resurrection and their belief in eternal life had taught them that evil and death cannot ultimately triumph over goodness and the life-giving Spirit of God. Just as God has saved God's servant Moses from death, God also raised God's Son from the dead and glorified him as Son of God and Savior.

The Herod of Matthew's birth narrative also foreshadows Herod's son who humiliated and mocked Jesus and sent him off to Pilate to be condemned. In the chief priests and scribes who act as accomplices to Herod's plot to kill the infant, we see the prefiguring of the chief priests and scribes who conspire to have Jesus executed in the passion stories. The shadow of Caesar will fall on Jesus in the person of the Roman procurator, Pontius Pilate. For as Simeon had prophesied in Luke's narrative: "This child is destined for the fall and rise of many in Israel, and to be a sign that will be contradicted..." (Luke 2:34).

Receivers of the Word

So far we have seen some of the basic beliefs about the person of Jesus that were proclaimed in the infancy narratives: that he is the Son of God, the messiah, a leader who stands in contrast to despots like Herod and the Roman emperor. In the story where the child is saved from the murderous Herod, Jesus is shown as marked for suffering from the beginning, and yet as one who was raised and glorified by God. In this next section we will examine how these narratives also are a commentary on the broad spectrum of people who were offered the good news of Jesus Christ.

Entrusted to the Jews

Matthew's community seems to have been made up of both Jews and Gentiles. In composing the birth narratives, Matthew seems particularly concerned about demonstrating that Jesus is indeed the messiah who has fulfilled the prophecies of old.[26] As we have seen, Matthew's genealogy traces Jesus' lineage from Abraham through David to Joseph. Throughout his dramatization, Matthew points out how each event is a fulfillment of "what has been written by the prophet." Even the massacre of the infants somehow fits into the vision of the prophets.

In the incident with the Magi, Matthew seems to be commenting on an ironic situation in the early church: Many of Jesus' people, the Jews, were rejecting Jesus and persecuting Christians while, at the same time, Gentiles were coming to Jesus as Savior in great numbers. This irony is dramatized in Herod's rejection and attempt to murder the infant Jesus, and in the assistance given him by "all the chief priests and scribes," while the pagan Magi come to pay the new king homage. The priests and scribes are portrayed as knowing the place through the prophecies, yet they stood by while Herod's death squads went out to murder infants and toddlers. For Matthew, the chief priests and scribes are the forebears of Jewish leaders who would hand Jesus over to be crucified, and who would later throw Christians out of the synagogues and persecute them.

In Matthew's narrative it is the faithful Joseph and Mary who represent Hebrews who heard the Word of God and kept it. They seem to also stand for those of the peasantry among the Jews, the "little ones" to whom the message was both revealed and received. ("Little ones responding to Jesus" seems to be carried to the extreme in Luke's account of the yet unborn infant John the Baptist leaping for joy in the womb when he hears Mary's greeting to Elizabeth.)

Jesus' unique call to the lowly and the outcasts among the Jews is brought out in Luke's use of shepherds. It has, perhaps, been exaggerated in the past that shepherds were hated for their dishonesty in using the land of others for grazing, and for not observing Jewish purity customs. This "despised image" of shepherds seems to be from an era later than that in which these birth narratives emerged.[27] On the other hand, the idealized version given the shepherds in so many Christmas pageants and manger scenes is not realistic either.

In reality, it seems as though the shepherds of the time were marginal people, peasants who grazed sheep in the Bethlehem area that was too rocky for farming.[28] They wandered with their sheep and gave little attention to the customs and proprieties of the towns and cities or to the technicalities of Jewish observance. In the nativity story they seem to stand for the Jewish peasantry, the simple poor for whom Jesus had such a preference. They, as well as the animal feeding trough in which the infant was placed, express the simplicity of Jesus' background as well as his unique mission to the poor and disenfranchised.

It is to people like the lowly shepherds that God's word is revealed. And it is folk like these who respond and "go in haste" to pay homage to Jesus, the Christ. As Mary's Magnificat puts it: "He has thrown down the rulers from their thrones but lifted up the lowly. The hungry he has filled with good things; the rich he has sent away empty"(Luke 1:52–54).[29] At the same time, the shepherd image of Luke connects Jesus with the earlier Hebrew images of God and of David as shepherd, and prepares the way for the later description of Jesus as "the Good Shepherd."

Luke also indicates that Jesus' message had been responded to by a wide spectrum of Jews. Mary, the young Jewish maiden, is asked to accept the overshadowing of the creative Spirit of God in her womb and be the mother of Jesus. Joseph, her espoused, is asked to accept his beloved as prematurely pregnant and to parent a child that is not from his own seed. There is also Zechariah, the father of John the Baptist and a minor Jewish priest, who eventually responds to God's word—only, however, after being rendered speechless as a punishment for his stubborn resistance. Elizabeth, his wife, faithfully accepts God's miracle in her life. Simeon, the official of the Temple to whom the infant is presented, seems to stand for some among the Jewish leadership itself who have accepted Jesus as their Savior. And Anna, the elderly prophetess and devoted worshiper in the Temple, also seems to represent the many devout Jews who had become Christians. All four of these characters in Luke's play may also dramatize how uniquely God's word comes to and is received by the elderly.[30]

The Message to the Gentiles
Gentile Christians seem to have been in Matthew's community and were predominant in Luke's community. There are some elements in these nativity narratives that deal with these Gentile members. Matthew's inclusion of Abraham and other "Gentiles" in the genealogy may be construed as indicating the universality of the Christian message. Luke's linking Jesus to Adam in his genealogy might also be interpreted in this manner.

The most significant reference to Gentiles in the infancy narratives is Matthew's account of the visit of the Magi. A great deal of tradition has been built up around these men over the centuries. They have been known as the "three kings," although the gospel neither designates them as kings nor even says there were three of them. There have been many attempts to prove the historicity of their visit and of the "star" phenomenon of the time.[31] It seems more likely that the visit of the Magi is a religious myth that very effectively emphasizes the paradox of Gentile conversions to Jesus while he is being rejected by his own Jewish people.

The Magi are certainly the most exotic figures in these narratives. Historically, the word *magos* has been applied to a number of different kinds of people. The Greek historian Herodotus wrote of certain Medes called Magi, existing six hundred years before Christ. He says that they were men known for their special power to interpret dreams. Apparently, when the Persians conquered the Medes, the Magi became part of the Persian priestly caste, subsequently appear in literature as Zoroastrian priests, and are later characterized as those privy to secret lore and magic.[32] The term, then, can refer to a number of exotic figures, including priests, fortune tellers, and astrologers. Matthew seems to draw his figures from the latter group, men who could read the stars and who would make key decisions in their lives by virtue of what they read in the heavens.

The visit of the Magi effectively brings out the irony of Gentile acceptance, as opposed to Jewish rejection, of Jesus. These Magi seem to know nothing of the Jewish Scriptures and prophecies. The text for finding their God seems to be the stars. The paradox is that these pagan star gazers are more prepared to find Jesus than are the great sages among the chief priests or Herod, the powerful king of the Jews. Moreover, these Gentiles are more open to receiving Jesus as their king, and better disposed to paying him royal homage with magnificent gifts. Their homage and generosity stand in vivid contrast to the hatefulness and violence that characterized Herod and his entourage. The contrast would not have been lost on the gospel communities who were experiencing these same ironies and conflicts in their own day.

Role of Women

It is only recently, and largely because the gospels are now being interpreted by women exegetes, that we have noticed the important role given to women in the nativity narratives. Since these stories reflect the early communities' beliefs about Jesus and his teaching, we can assume that these narratives authentically reflect the important role that women had among Jesus' disciples and in the early communities. This topic was discussed in some detail in chapter five, and what is to follow only serves to further corroborate the observations that were made there about Jesus' advocacy for women.[33]

Mary, the Mother of Jesus

Matthew's birth narrative centers on Joseph and is, therefore, perhaps more realistic than Luke's when it comes to reflecting the patriarchal structure of Jesus' time. In Matthew's version, Mary is typically situated in this patriarchal system as a young maiden whose marriage was presumably arranged by her father when she was twelve or thirteen.

In the story, Mary's pregnancy is from God, yet she lives within a system of laws that are much in the favor of males. According to Deuteronomy (22:12ff), if a bridegroom, in having relations with his bride, discovered that she was not a virgin, he could bring charges against her publicly. To do this he would have to bring the marriage sheets before the elders of the city and make formal charges. But Joseph did not have this option because she was found with child "before they lived together." He could, however, bring her to the courts and have her guilt ascertained.

According to Deuteronomy (22:25ff), if Joseph could show that she had relations with someone in a place where she could have cried out for help, but did not, she and the man (if they could identify him) could both be stoned to death. (During Jesus' times, divorce without financial support, rather than stoning, seems to have been the accepted punishment for the woman.) If it could be shown that she was attacked in the open fields, where crying for help would be of no avail, she would not be held guilty of a capital offense, while the man would be liable to death.

Joseph, however, chose to avoid having recourse to public authority and was going to divorce her quietly, probably on less serious grounds than infidelity, and hence give her a sum of money to support herself and the child. Even so, Mary would still have gone off in disgrace and would probably have had to raise the child herself. As was pointed out earlier, it would be possible for her to marry a commoner, if one would have her, but she would never be permitted to marry into the priestly caste.

The entire situation as described by Matthew reveals the vulnerability of women in ancient cultures, an inequality before the law that still is common today. In Eastern cultures, such as in Pakistan, the legal situation is still such that should a young woman claim rape, the charges are often easily turned upon her for seduction or adultery. Once violated, the young woman usually faces a lifetime of disgrace, even in the eyes of her parents and family.

The story of Joseph's dilemma in Matthew contrasts the plan of God for compassion and justice over against the patriarchal laws. Moreover,

Mary's virginal conception of Jesus might also be viewed as a dramatic confrontation with the patriarchal system, where the man's seed and the role of father is central. Joseph, the patriarch, must concede to the power of God and the independence of Mary in conceiving. He must assume an accepting and supportive role. Even though it is up to him to "normalize" the situation and take Mary into "his house," patriarchy has been challenged.[34] Like many women (symbolized by Tamar, Rahab, Ruth, and Bathsheba), Mary triumphs in an irregular situation and cooperates to carry out God's plan.[35]

In Luke's account, Mary and, in turn, the feminine, is given much more significance. Here the miraculous conception does not throw a shadow over her reputation. Rather, it is announced to Mary by a messenger of God, with little or no consideration given to Joseph. In addition, Mary is challenging and questioning about the "good news," and accepts it only when it is explained. And, most significantly, the actual overshadowing of the Most High, the coming of the messiah, awaits her decision, her "May it be done to me according to your word" (Luke 1:38). It is Mary who sings the Magnificat and ponders in her heart the message of the angels to the shepherds and the prophetic message of Simeon. Her faithful acceptance of the good news contrasts with the punishable hesitation of Zechariah the priest. Her extraordinary conception of her son is much more remarkable than that of John the Baptist.[36]

Mary here seems to symbolize the thoughtful and yet challenging reception with which the gospel was being received by women disciples, as well as the central role they must have played in the pre-Lukan groups where these stories first evolved. Mary, as well as the women disciples who would view her as a model of gospel fidelity, are obviously still within a patriarchal structure. But something "new" and "good" is bursting forth from Jesus' message of human dignity, freedom, and concern for the disenfranchised.

It is in her "Magnificat" that Mary reveals her dedication to the liberation of the oppressed. Like Mary's forebear, Hannah, from whose song this canticle seems to be in large part derived, Mary is a favored one of God and identifies with the "poor ones" of Israel.[37] The "might of God" is not the dominating and oppressive might of patriarchy, but the power that will empower women and men with the pentecostal Spirit and send them forth in dignity and equality.[38] In this song that parallels the beatitudes of her son, Mary proclaims God's option for the poor and the downtrodden. Great things have been done for her and for other women who join with Jesus as those who hear the Word and keep it. She joyfully sings of a gospel that teaches the triumph of humility and service to the hungry over the arrogance and greed of the "rich and famous."

In her haste to assist Elizabeth in her pregnancy, Mary exemplifies the service that is at the heart of the gospel that will make her and others "most blessed among women." In Luke's gospel, Mary stands with Elizabeth and Anna the prophetess as the models for women who will accept the power of God in their lives, joyfully receive the good news of Jesus, and join in carrying out the mission of Jesus Christ.

Summary

The nativity stories of Matthew and Luke have been told and celebrated for almost two thousand years and, no doubt, will continue to be passed on. The beautifully crafted tales are early proclamations of the faith of the early Christian communities. In these narratives the early disciples reflect on the meaning of the birth of Jesus of Nazareth and, in so doing, proclaim their faith that he was an authentic human person, a Jew from Galilee, who is indeed the Son of God and messiah. He was born to lead his people in a new Exodus from the "slavery" of sin and death into a new creation of peace and justice on earth and eternal life after death. Through these stories, the early communities reach out over the centuries to share the good news that Jesus Christ was sent to Jew and Gentile, rich and poor, female and male. He was a new kind of king who, in contrast to the Herods and the Caesars of the world, reigns not through force and domination but through love and compassion. He was their Lord and their God.

Questions for Reflection and Discussion

1. "The infancy narratives are worthy vehicles of the gospel message: indeed each is the essential gospel in miniature." Comment on this quotation, pointing out specific gospel teachings that seem to appear in these narratives.

2. What parallels do you see between Joseph of the Hebrew Scriptures and Joseph the husband of Mary?

3. What are some of the aspects of Jesus' adult life that seem to be reflected in the two nativity stories?

4. Name some of the elements in these stories that seem to indicate that Jesus was believed to be the Son of God.

5. Cite some of the "types" among early Christians that might be portrayed through some of the characters in these birth stories.

CHAPTER EIGHT

Crucified at Golgotha

The event in Jesus' life that was the most difficult for his early followers to grasp was his horrible execution on Calvary. After Jesus' resurrection his disciples came to believe that the man whom they had grown to love and admire was indeed their messiah, Lord, and God. And yet a burning question remained: How could it be that such a magnificent person, whose short ministry was filled with healings and a message of love, was scourged and nailed to a cross as a criminal? In the deepest layers of the gospels we find the disciples struggling with this question and attempting to develop a theological interpretation of Jesus' death.

Most of what we know about Jesus' crucifixion comes from the four gospel accounts, although there is some evidence outside of the Christian Scriptures to verify that it actually happened. The Roman author Tacitus mentions "Chrestus" with disdain as one who was put to death as a criminal by Pilate. The Babylonian Talmud admits that he was hanged for seducing Israel. The evangelists make obvious efforts to show the historicity of the crucifixion, even though they differ considerably in significant details.

The gospel accounts might be best described as four "historical plays." Most certainly these dramas have a basis in fact, but the authors are more concerned with theological interpretations than they are with historical details. Along with theological reflection, the gospel writers also seem to be concerned with the current issues facing the early Christian communities. For example, in the development of the "characters" in the narratives, one can find the authors portraying the different ways that people are responding to Jesus in the early communities. In these communities there were those like Judas, who despaired in their betrayal of Jesus, or those, in the manner of Thomas, who had to see in order to believe. There were also followers like Peter, who repented and experienced the mercy of God.

In this chapter we are going to examine the suffering and death of Jesus. We will start by looking at the four differing gospel accounts, and then we will consider the "why," "who," and "how" of this profoundly significant event. Under the "why" we will examine the extremely controversial question regarding the motives for putting Jesus to death as a criminal. We will also discuss Jesus' own personal awareness as he faced such a horrible end. In considering the "who," we will be looking at the *dramatis personae* of the four passion plays, from both a historical and symbolic perspective. It is here that we will be looking especially at the crucial "trial" scenes. Finally, under "how," we will look at the crucifixion itself and focus on the historical background of this form of execution and the methods used at the time of Jesus.

Gospel Passion Stories

The gospel writers make great efforts to stress the historicity of Jesus' death on the cross. Each gospel gives extensive treatment to the events surrounding the crucifixion.[1] At the same time, the gospel writers give few details on Jesus' personal experience of suffering and death. The scriptural accounts differ considerably with regard to details and the sequence of events. The evangelists characteristically seem to be more concerned with the religious meaning of the events than they are with giving details of what really happened.

Each of the four gospels sheds a different light on the event of the crucifixion, revealing different facets of Jesus' experience. This is not to say that anyone had access to Jesus' inner feelings during the ordeal. It is quite possible, however, that some of these traditions were drawn from personal witnesses to the events. Other impressions may have been developed by those who knew Jesus and were familiar with how he faced difficult situations. Whatever the historical core may be, these accounts are primarily literary creations, and a good deal of the material used in them is actually adapted from the Hebrew Scriptures.

Four Portraits

Mark In the gospel of Mark, Jesus knowingly enters the ordeal of the passion. He acknowledges that the woman who anoints him at the dinner at Bethany is indeed preparing him for burial, and he predicts that his own will betray and deny him. In this drama, it appears that Jesus is resigned to his death as something that he must do to fulfill the Scriptures and bring about the kingdom of his Father. Here Jesus is alone and abandoned by his followers, who repeatedly fall asleep in the garden and run away when he needs them.

In Mark's drama, Jesus silently accepts his fate. During the two night sessions before the Sanhedrin he has little to say other than to admit that he is the messiah. He stands resolutely as he is mocked, spat upon, and beaten. In death he seems even to be abandoned by the God whom he preached so eloquently. At the end he cries out: "My God, my God, why have you forsaken me?" and dies (Mark 15:34).

Matthew   Matthew's portrait of Jesus' suffering and death is similar to the one in Mark. Jesus is abandoned by his disciples and denied by Peter. This is even more shocking in this account because they had earlier recognized that he was the Son of God. In this account Jesus is also abandoned, sorrowful, and yet accepting of the will of his Father. He stands totally innocent of the charges leveled against him, and silent before his accusers. In Matthew, as in Mark, Jesus is mocked as he suffers on the cross and dies with the same loud cry of agony.

Luke   Luke presents a different picture of Jesus undergoing the passion and death. Here Jesus is not isolated and deserted. His disciples sleep only once in the garden, and then out of sorrow rather than indifference. Moreover, they are present at the crucifixion itself. This is not so much a resigned and troubled Jesus as one who is peaceful and compassionate. He heals the ear of the high priest's slave in the garden, and he looks at Peter after the denials in such a way that Peter is moved to repentance. Jesus clearly is recognized as innocent by both Herod and Pilate, and is even instrumental in healing the enmity that has existed between them.

In Luke's drama, there is no brutal mocking by the soldiers. Instead, the soldiers seem to follow along with the crowds, actually lamenting the suffering of Jesus. The women of Jerusalem also weep for Jesus, and he expresses concern for their children. Jesus does not cry out in on the cross, but asks his Father to forgive his ignorant executioners. Jesus promises the criminal on his right "paradise" this very day, an indication of his intense hope for the immediate coming of the kingdom after his death. For Luke, the cross means forgiveness, not atonement, and, in bringing healing to humanity, Jesus dies peacefully, saying: "Father, into thy hands I commend my spirit."

John John's account presents the divine dimension of Jesus that becomes so evident to his followers after Jesus was glorified in resurrection. Here Jesus is a strong, majestic figure who chooses death fully aware that he will live again. He is the all-knowing Son of God who goes through the passion completely in charge of every scene. When they come to arrest him in the garden, he is not prostrate in grief but standing proud. Those who come to arrest him are struck down in awe, and he seems to have to assist them in his own arrest. At the same time Jesus makes it clear that he does not want any harm to come to his followers and that they should be allowed to go free.

In John's scene of the interrogation before Annas, the high former priest is obviously out of his depth in trying to deal with Jesus. Likewise, in the Pilate scenes, the prefect seems at times to be quite deferential when addressing Jesus and, at one point, even asks for instruction on truth. After the scourging, Jesus still seems to stand majestically before the crowds as Pilate all but intones: "Behold the man." On the way to Calvary Jesus needs no Simon to help him carry the cross. While hanging in pain, Jesus seems to be reigning from the cross as an authentic king of the Jews. The sign on the cross proclaims this to the world in three languages.

Neither is Jesus deserted and alone on the cross, for a number of his followers are there with him. Before he dies, Jesus leaves behind a "family of faith" as he gives his mother and his beloved disciple to each other. Then Jesus decisively completes the mission his Father had given him by saying "It is finished." He then gives up his own spirit. Joseph of Arimathea, a member of the Sanhedrin and a secret disciple of Jesus, along with Nicodemus, the Pharisee who came to Jesus at night for instruction, take the body, anoint it in kingly fashion with an enormous amount of spices, and bury Jesus in a new tomb.

Why Was Jesus Crucified?

The question of why Jesus was crucified is central in most discussions of his passion and death. Biblical scholars have been divided on this question. Some scholars, following the lead of Bultmann, maintain that Jesus was killed by the Romans who mistook him for a rebel. Here the death is viewed as simply a tragic and senseless killing of an innocent man. This approach disconnects the death of Jesus from the rest of his life and ministry, evades Jesus' own intentionality and freedom, and robs the death of any significant meaning. It follows Bultmann's minimalist position with regard to what can be known about the historical Jesus. It reduces the gospel accounts to legend or theology.[2]

On the other side of the spectrum, fundamentalists often take the gospel accounts literally and hold that Jesus was condemned by the Jewish leadership and then handed over to Pilate to be executed as king of the Jews. This approach fails to deal with the many historical and textual difficulties that surround the gospel accounts of the passion of Jesus. As one moves from one gospel account to another, it is hard to be clear about what was a trial or a hearing, what charges were actually made against Jesus, or how Jesus responded to these accusations.

Fundamentalists also tend to accept the gospels' theological reasons for "why" Jesus was crucified: Jesus had to die to fulfill the divine plan or to ransom humanity from sin. While these are valued theological interpretations of Jesus' death, they were developed by later reflection and should not be projected back into the time in which Jesus lived and died. There must have been actual historical reasons why Jesus was put to death. Otherwise, it might well seem that Jesus had little free choice in facing his death, but simply accepted it passively as his fate, a fate long ago decreed by God as necessary to atone for sins.

Some few hold that Jesus was sympathetic toward, if not identified with the spirit of Zealotry and that he was arrested and executed as a seditionist.[3] This approach seems to presume that the gospel writers hid Jesus' support of violent revolution and blamed the execution on the Jewish authorities. This theory, which goes back as early as Reimarus, an eighteenth-century biblical scholar, greatly distorts the obvious non-violent teachings of Jesus and caricatures the gospel writers as deceivers. It also ignores the information in the gospels that Jesus' followers were not arrested with him, which most certainly would have been the case if Jesus was perceived to be a revolutionary.[4] This approach also disregards the fact that Jesus' early followers did not use either his teaching or example to advocate violence or insurrection.

Finally, there are those who challenge the basic historicity of the gospel accounts, claiming that these stories were written with a bias against Jews and are at least in part responsible for the anti-Semitism that has prevailed ever since. Those who take this position advocate abandoning the view that the Jews were in anyway responsible for the death of Jesus. The Sanhedrin trials or hearings are thus seen as fabrications of Christian communities who were alienated from Judaism and who were attempting to placate Rome. From this perspective, the condemnation and execution of Jesus was solely carried out by the Romans.[5]

This approach seems to ignore the threat that Jesus did in fact pose to the religious leaders of his time. It also gives scant attention to the radical edge of Jesus' teachings that alienated many leaders, Jewish or Roman. Jesus opposed those who used power to manipulate and dominate the underclasses and outcasts. Neither can we ignore the later rabbinic sources that recall that Jesus was executed by the Jews as a sorcerer and a seducer of his people.[6]

This approach also seems to be out of line with much of contemporary biblical studies, which indicate that Jesus was condemned by both his religious leaders and Roman authority. Religion and politics in those times were of a piece, with a great deal of collusion among the Romans and their appointees amidst the Jewish leadership. It would seem, then, that both the Jewish and Roman leaders of the time should be held responsible for the horrendous miscarriage of justice in condemning and crucifying Jesus of Nazareth.

At the same time, it does have to be stressed that such responsibility on the part of the Jewish leaders of the time does not in any way justify anti-Semitism. It would be absurd to hold descendants of the Romans responsible for the actions of Pilate and the soldiers who tortured and crucified Jesus. Neither can the young Germans of today be held answerable for the atrocities of Hitler and the Nazi party.

What Were the Real Reasons?

Jesus' death does not seem to have come about because he was a man of violence or even because he was mistaken for a rebel. Nor is his death an isolated event, cut off from the rest of who he was and what he stood for. His death is, in a sense, the culmination of his life. It came about because of what he stood for, as well as his relentless refusal to back off from his prophetic positions, even in the face of crucifixion. Jesus' death seems to have come about as a result of his teaching and ministry, both of which caused him to have many enemies, particularly among the Jewish and Roman elite. For whatever reasons, and there probably were a variety of them, those who hated Jesus were driven to scheme not only for Jesus' death, but for the most painful and humiliating death then known in the Roman empire: crucifixion.

Was Jesus' Teaching Dangerous?

What had Jesus taught that would generate such deep feelings of hatred toward him? As E.P. Sanders has noted, it is unreasonable to think that Jesus would have been executed simply because he taught mercy and forgiveness or because he debated on points of the law.[7] Contemporaries of Jesus proposed similar teachings, and they were not arrested and executed.[8] For Jesus to generate such animosity, there had to be something extremely threatening to the leaders of his time in what he taught, how he taught it, and in the way it affected his followers.

As we saw earlier, Jesus had unique views on the Jewish belief in the kingdom of God. For him, this kingdom stood for the dominance of love, justice, and forgiveness in the world. It meant the experience of the creative and freeing care of "Abba," the divine parent of all, the source, sustainer, and goal of all life. Jesus taught that his intimate and loving friendship with God was extended to all, most especially to those who were traditionally seen as inferior or outcasts in the Judaism of his day. Jesus showed a special concern for women, children, the sick and handicapped, and sinners. Jesus also proclaimed that this magnificent kingdom, this new creation, was breaking into the world and challenging the traditional laws of Judaism, the corruption in its leadership, even the Temple worship. Jesus also seems to have believed that the coming of this kingdom to the world was somehow connected with his own person and ministry, and that those who followed him were indeed going to be participants in this kingdom of God's love and justice.[9]

Jesus taught that the immediate breaking in of this kingdom called for a radical conversion and response (repentance or *metanoia*). It required a rooting out of old prejudices and legalisms, a rejection of the haughty domination and manipulation by leaders, and a condemnation of the prideful and hypocritical exclusion of others who were considered to be "unclean."

Jesus asked for a turning from the injustices inflicted upon the poor and the marginal, as well as a divesting of greedy attachments to material things. He demanded a universal recognition of human dignity, an inclusive acceptance of all people as God's children, a courageous commitment to justice for everyone, and a humility and simplicity that make one willing to share self and things with others. He pointed to the narrow and difficult way of self-sacrifice and service, rather than to the high road of luxury, oppressive power, and violence.

Central to Jesus' teaching was his message that every human being is "somebody," a person loved by God and called to intimacy with the Creator. He preached this to the self-righteous who had a false and exclusive image of themselves as the only ones "saved." He taught this to the "outcasts," for whom it was welcome good news. He declared "blessed" the masses who had been made to feel inferior, unclean, even unsaved because of their infidelity to religious law, their physical condition, or even their age or sex.

Jesus offered freedom to those who had been victimized by the injustice and oppression of the Roman occupiers and their own religious leaders. He extended the saving power of God to those who had been dominated through fear, superstition, and deprivation. Jesus said: "So if the Son frees you, then you will be truly free" (John 8:36). Jesus proclaimed that every person was a beloved child of God and completely and unconditionally accepted by God.

Like so many leaders who learned from him, such as Mohandas Gandhi, Martin Luther King, Jr., or Dorothy Day, Jesus taught people that they counted. He gave them self-esteem. He made them whole physically and spiritually, and thus empowered them to stand up for justice and equality. And perhaps most radically of all, he taught his message of love and mercy to sinners, proclaiming to them a loving God who accepted and loved them even before they accepted the repentance to which they were invited. This all, indeed, bespeaks revolution, but a non-violent revolution that starts in the heart. Jesus was not a violent subversive, and yet, in the long run, his brand of non-violent resistance could be more subversive than that of the terrorist.[10]

Jesus' Manner of Teaching
Jesus took his position on the kingdom with an authority that was unique in his day. As we saw earlier, he did not quote the scribal teachings of rabbinic scholars, nor did he even often quote the Hebrew Scriptures themselves. Instead he spoke with a personal authority that seemed to find its source in his own uniquely intimate experience of Abba and the kingdom. The primary requirement for being part of this kingdom was not adhering to the scribal laws, but simply following Jesus' way of love and self-sacrifice.

Enthusiastic Response
There are many indications throughout the gospels of the enthusiastic response that Jesus received because of his teachings. People were amazed at his teachings, some apparently thinking that he was one of the prophets returned to bring the message of the final time. There were even those who wanted to make him the new king of Israel. Even some of his disciples got caught up in this and argued about who would be first in the new kingdom. They were apparently willing to leave their jobs and even their families to follow him. Crowds were attracted to Jesus as he taught and healed, and the information that his enemies were reluctant to arrest him publicly in the daytime indicates that he must have had a great deal of popular support. His rousing reception when he entered Jerusalem, as well as the later willingness of his followers to

face death to preach his message after the resurrection, are other indications that the teachings of Jesus stirred many people deeply.

Those Alienated

Clearly such good news of a loving God, such inclusive vision of the dignity and freedom of each person, would be a threat to those who had for so long controlled and manipulated the masses with a God of fear and exclusivity. Certainly many leaders of Jesus' time would have been alienated, even frightened, by his empowerment of the poor and rejected, as well as his condemnation of those who oppressed them through legalism and intimidation. The religious and political leaders both had a great deal to lose if the masses suddenly realized that they were loved and called to freedom by Jesus. Such liberating good news would, no doubt, have been deeply resented by those in "legitimate" authority, those who expected the loyalty of the people to be toward them, and not toward some poorly educated rustic from Galilee.

The Leaders

The Jewish leaders knew full well that their tradition gave them but two choices when facing someone with the unique and prophetic message of Jesus. They either had to accept his teaching (and thereby give up the profitable and comfortable way of life that the domination of their people provided) or they had to show that he was a false prophet and have him killed in order to preserve the integrity of their tradition. Apparently many of the religious leaders of Jesus' time saw that there was too much at stake for them to accept Jesus.[11]

As for the Romans, their primary concern was subjugation with a minimum of resistance. Anyone who stirred the people with a message of affirmation and freedom would be highly suspect. A person with an enthusiastic following of people indignant over their unjust oppression would also be a threat to Rome's ultimate authority over the Jews. And, of course, anyone who was in direct confrontation with the Roman-appointed leadership of the Jews would be perceived as being seditious toward a well-established system of collaboration.

Controversial Actions

One can think of a number of actions on the part of Jesus that might have made him appear dangerous to both religious and secular authority. For instance, the gospels give significant space to stories of his healings. The way Jesus carried these out may well be one of the reasons that he generated so much hostility.

First of all, he performed these healings in the same fashion as he taught, that is, on his own authority and without invoking the name of God. As if calling on a unique power of his own, Jesus brought sight to the blind, sound to the deaf, and wholeness to the crippled and infirm. In addition, he sometimes performed these healings on the Sabbath, deliberately siding with the teachers who took a more liberal view toward the Jewish laws. Jesus forgave sin freely, audaciously, and as though the power to do so somehow resided within his own person. He also openly associated and befriended sinners, dined with them, and even called them to be his own disciples.

Reviewing the actions of Jesus makes it obvious that those among the elite who were self-righteous and haughty must have viewed Jesus as arrogant in his display of authority and power, disgusting in his lifestyle, and downright "blasphemous" in his actions of healing and forgiving. It is really no surprise that many came to despise him and wanted to see him destroyed.

Jesus' Entrance into Jerusalem

Jesus' entrance into the city of Jerusalem might also have made him even more enemies. Jesus had come to Jerusalem to celebrate the Passover, and he seems to have been greeted with considerable excitement by many of the people gathered for the feast. As described in the gospels, this was not the triumphant entry of a man seeking power, but the coming of a person of simplicity and compassion. Contrasted with the conquering heroes who had ridden into the city on horseback, Jesus came on a donkey. Yet there was a power in his coming that must have been threatening to those who were in authority.[12] In John's gospel this event is placed at the very beginning of Jesus' last week of life and is connected with the raising of Lazarus. The Pharisees appear extremely distraught at the acclaim given Jesus, and they say among themselves, "Look, the whole world has gone after him" (John 12:19).

Temple Scene

Scholars seem to be coming to more of a consensus on the crucial role that the so-called cleansing in the Temple played in bringing on Jesus' execution. Mark's gospel explicitly points out that it was after this event that the chief priests and scribes planned Jesus' death.[13]

The scene portrays Jesus reacting violently to what was the long-standing custom of selling sacrificial animals and exchanging foreign money in certain areas of the Temple grounds. This was not simply a spontaneous outburst of anger. Jesus' action carried with it a great deal of meaning and symbolism. First of all, it was a confrontational action against the Jewish elite who had made the Temple into a highly profitable industry. Taxes and sales of sacrificial animals provided a hefty income, particularly during the pilgrimage times for the three important feasts.[14] Jesus had spoken against these "heavy burdens" that the Jewish leaders had laid upon their people. His first-hand experience of the poverty and oppression throughout his land seemed to make him resent the great profits that the wealthy elite were making by taking hard-earned money from the poor people.

This action also carried a more directly religious symbolism, challenging the narrowness, corruption, and exclusivity of Temple worship at that time. Jesus had taught of a broader presence of God in nature and people, of a worship in the spirit, and of a Temple where all nations could gather to worship the God of all peoples. The Temple stood as the symbol of the Sanhedrin's autocratic authority over the people of Israel. Perhaps this action was a challenge to that authority. Like Jeremiah—another prophet who foretold the destruction of Jerusalem and its authority—Jesus was symbolically giving more emphasis to a message he had preached earlier. The corruption and hypocrisy of those in authority in Jerusalem would bring destruction down upon themselves and their people.

Because much of the gospel material was written after the destruction of Jerusalem, Jesus' initial warnings would take on even more profound meaning for the early Christian communities. The devastation by the Romans could now be interpreted in the light of Jesus' earlier warnings and could also be linked to the Jewish rejection of him as the messiah.

Hostility Developed

The gospels seem to indicate that there was some vicious opposition to Jesus from early in his ministry. As we saw earlier, it is quite possible that the story of Herod's attempt to kill the child was inserted into Matthew's nativity story to symbolize that the shadow of the cross hung over his life from the beginning. Mark's gospel points out that Jesus felt as though he was "without honor" in his own town of Nazareth and could work few miracles there because of people's lack of faith. Luke begins his account of Jesus' ministry in Galilee with the story of Jesus' own townfolk attempting to throw him off a cliff for applying a text of Isaiah to himself. The same gospel describes how, after a debate with Jesus on healing on the Sabbath, the scribes and Pharisees "became enraged and discussed together what they might do to Jesus" (Luke 6:11).

Early in Mark's gospel the Pharisees object to Jesus' curing the man with the withered hand on the Sabbath, and they immediately hold counsel with the Herodians to see how they might put Jesus to death.

All this hatred toward Jesus festered and finally came to a head during that last fateful week of his life. The enthusiastic reception he received upon entering the city must have hardened the resolve of his enemies to do away with him. Then his challenge to the Temple and the huge profits to be gained there would have been the last straw for Jesus' enemies. They began to look for an opportunity to eliminate this dangerous upstart from Galilee, and apparently it was Judas who provided them the needed opportunity to snatch him in the privacy of his prayers.

Did Jesus Have Foreknowledge of Calvary?

How one answers the question as to whether or not Jesus had foreknowledge of his crucifixion hinges on where one stands with regard to biblical interpretation and criticism. Fundamentalists, as we have remarked earlier, generally don't distinguish between the historical Jesus and the Christ of faith. From their perspective, the Jesus portrayed in the gospels is the historical Jesus who seems to be aware of his upcoming fate through his divine knowledge and who, in fact, accurately predicts his suffering and death during his public ministry.

A different approach is taken by those who accept historical criticism of the Scriptures and who recognize the genuine humanity of Jesus. There seems to be a common opinion among biblical scholars that Jesus' predictions of his passion and death are later formulations, written in the light of later resurrection faith. Historically, Jesus was indeed human, and as such did not have access to knowledge of the future. He had to make his decisions the way all people do: in uncertainty and risk.

At the same time, Jesus would have had plenty of reason to suspect the dangers that surrounded him. No doubt he saw the hatred in the eyes of his enemy, had experienced threats on his life, and knew of plots to get rid of him. Failure and rejection are always ominous signs, and Jesus was familiar with both. He had been rejected and threatened by his own townsfolk of Nazareth. Members of his own family thought he had gone mad. Even his own disciples did not seem to understand his teaching. Nor did his followers seem to be capable of standing up for him if he encountered danger. The gospels indicate that Jesus perceived serious weakness in several of them, especially in Judas and in Peter.[15]

Jesus also was well aware of the fate of his mentor John the Baptist, who was beheaded for confronting Herod and for having a following among the people. Jesus was no doubt aware of the dangers attached to his close association with the Baptist. He begins his mission with John's message of repentance to prepare for the kingdom. Jesus refers to Herod as "that fox, " and proclaims teachings on divorce, poverty, justice, and other moral questions that stood in contradiction to the licentious-ness of Herod's court. At one point, he hears from some of his friends among the Pharisees that Herod was actually seeking to kill him.

Jesus knew that death was often the the fate of prophets who challenged injustice and oppression. He would have had first-hand experience of the brutal stonings and crucifixions of those who were condemned by church or state. From human knowledge alone, Jesus would have been aware that the dangers around him were escalating and that continuing his mission could mean his death. Eventually, it must have become clear him that the only way to save himself would be to retract all that he stood for and return to the anonymity of a carpenter in Nazareth.

Jesus chose to go on. His entering into Jerusalem for Passover and the incident in the Temple (even though the gospels differ on when these incidents occurred), might well have been the events whereby Jesus indicated his resolve to pursue his mission to the very end, even if it meant death. Fully aware of the risks, Jesus made the crucial decision to take his mission to the very heart of Judaism.

The dramatic scenes of the last supper and the agony in the garden reveal a man determined to stay the course no matter what. Both scenes indicate that Jesus was aware of what was going to happen, and yet he adamantly refused to turn back. His statement in the garden, "thy will be done," is not a passive acquiescence to some pre-ordained divine plan to have him sacrificed. Instead, it is a resolve to carry through with his God-given mission, even if it has to end in an excruciating death. He had preached that the kingdom was coming; now it seemed that, somehow, his death would play a part in bringing this kingdom.

Jesus, therefore, was not a mere automaton moving in blind obedience toward a death decreed by God. Rather, Jesus freely chose to begin his mission, and of his own free will decided to continue on with it to the very end, even if it meant facing a terrible death on a cross.[16] He had promised his disciples that the mission for God's kingdom would bring a cup and a baptism of suffering and death. On Calvary he showed that this was not mere rhetoric.

Jesus had stood in friendship with the outcasts of society and confronted hypocrisy, greed, and violence. Now he had to pay for it with his life. His self-sacrifice has served as a model for those who would come after him. People like Oscar Romero, the Salvadoran archbishop who was murdered in 1980, and countless other martyrs throughout history have followed Jesus' example and have sacrificed their lives fighting oppression.

Who Was Responsible for Jesus' Death?

There has been much debate over the question of who should be held responsible for the execution of Christ. The distorted view that the Jewish people are "Christ-killers" has spawned a great deal of anti-Semitism over the centuries. Some have held that a so-called "blood-curse" came upon the Jewish people when people shouted to Pilate, "His blood be upon us and upon our children" (Matthew 27:25). This has been used to justify the frequent abuse and persecution of the Jewish people, culminating in the Holocaust in World War II.

Such anti-Semitism can in no way be justified by the gospel accounts of the passion and death of Jesus. The line "His blood be upon us ..." is a traditional Jewish statement of acceptance of responsibility at that time, and in no way carries the intention of cursing descendants. Moreover, the Jews of this or any time cannot be held responsible for the actions of a small number of Jewish leaders who at one time opposed Jesus.

It should also be remembered that even those who did hand him over were exonerated early on. Peter points out that the Jews acted out of ignorance of who Jesus was (Acts 3:17). Paul also says that the Jewish leaders did not understand who Jesus was (Acts 13:27). Jesus himself in portrayed in Luke as saying: "Father, forgive them for they know not what they do" (Luke 23:34). If there are strong feelings against Jews in the Scriptures, these would seem to come primarily from specific events of separation and persecution in the first century. They are aimed at specific individuals and events and not at Jews in general.

Role of the Pharisees

Traditionally, the Pharisees have been seen as the main enemies of Jesus, and thus viewed as having a significant role in his execution. We know that the Pharisees in the gospels seem to be drawn from the Pharisees of later times, who gained absolute power after the destruction of Jerusalem and who were often hostile toward Christians. At the same time, however, it seems reasonable to assume that Jesus did have his serious differences with conservative Pharisees on such issues as divorce, Sabbath observance, the laws of purity, and on associating with the "unclean."

The gospels tell us that some Pharisees plotted to do away with Jesus. It is likely that there were extremists among the Pharisees who wanted to get rid of Jesus, but they were not successful.[17] And even though some members of the Sanhedrin may have been scribal Pharisees, as we shall see, it is doubtful whether the Sanhedrin formally condemned Jesus. As the gospels describe the last days of Jesus, we see less and less involvement by the Pharisees (especially in the synoptic gospels). Most of the blame seems to be given to the high priests, scribes, and elders.

Other Enemies Among the Elite

Even though much of Jesus' ministry seems to have been carried on in the northern province of Galilee, it is possible that he often visited Jerusalem for the feasts and was known among the Jewish leaders there. It seems unlikely that the hatred and animosity that we see in the passion stories could have been generated in just a few days. It is more probable that this animosity had built up over a period of time and suddenly came to a head on one specific visit of Jesus to Jerusalem to celebrate Passover.

Some of the Sadducees would have had reason to want Jesus out of the way. The Sadducees, as we saw earlier, were the wealthy and aristocratic elite of Jerusalem. Many of the priests and elders in high positions, especially those who held positions on the Sanhedrin, were from the Sadducee group. These men were reputed to be conservative, exclusive, and very much concerned with maintaining the "status quo" with the Romans. The "arrangement" that they had with the Romans worked well for the Sadducees, politically, socially, and financially. They would not have been in favor of allowing some upstart preacher from Galilee to disrupt the people or to challenge the prevailing structures in any way. There simply was too much position and prestige at stake to allow for any possibility of unrest or upheaval.

Among this religious elite were also the high priests, men of extraordinary religious and political authority over their people. These men, of course, were designated by Rome, so there is little likelihood that these high priests were given to stirring the people with controversial views. Caiaphas, for instance, had an unusually long career from 18–37 C.E., and he had prospered and gained great power by knowing how to placate both his own people and the Romans. Neither he nor the other priests would have been open to a young Galilean teacher arousing the people by challenging the traditional ways that had worked so well for those in charge of the Jewish system of worship and observance.

If some Jews of the time are to be held responsible for Jesus' execution, it would seem that the blame should be given largely to these priestly leaders. It is unlikely that all the clashes that Jesus had with the Jewish leadership throughout the gospels can be attributed simply to later clashes between Christians and Jews. Jesus sided with some very radical positions within Judaism and added some unique insights of his own. His prophetic attacks on injustice and his defense of the marginal and oppressed seemed to alienate those in powerful and wealthy positions. He apparently had enemies who hated him, and hatred can and often does kill.

Roman Responsibility

There are some scholars, especially Jewish scholars, who maintain that Jesus was condemned and executed by the only authority that could carry out such a punishment at that time: the Romans.[18] Could it be, then, that the Romans did view Jesus as dangerous simply because he had a following and caused a commotion wherever he went with his healings, debates, and teachings? Or was he, perhaps, more of a revolutionary than we have thought in the past? Did he promote or at least approve of the violent overthrow of the Romans? Or could it be, as Bultmann would have it, that Jesus was simply mistaken for and executed as a rebel?[19]

None of these theories seems satisfactory for explaining who was responsible for Jesus' death. Jesus did not have an army, nor did he advocate violence. At his own arrest, he seems to have dissuaded his followers from violent resistance, and he gave none himself. Most important, he alone was arrested, and not his followers. The Romans did not have a reputation for being "selective" in their crucifixions of seditionists and their followers. Thousands associated with the Spartacus uprising were publicly crucified. On the other hand, a considerable amount of the responsibility for Jesus' death does have to be given the Romans. It was by Roman authority that the decree for execution was given and carried out.

Overlapping of Religion and Politics

In the search for who to blame for the execution of Jesus, it would be simplistic to make too sharp a distinction between politics and religion. To say that if the charges are political the Romans are guilty, and if the charges are religious the Jews are to blame, is to make a dichotomy that belongs more to our secular age than to the time of Jesus. When Jesus lived, religion and politics were generally intermeshed. Religious issues had political implications both for the Jewish system of rule and for dealing with the occupying Romans. Likewise, Rome knew that dealing with the Jews was always both a religious and political challenge.

Did the Jews Have the Authority to Execute?

A great deal of ambiguity surrounds the question of whether the Jews really could have condemned and executed Jesus. Herod's order to have John the Baptist executed indicates that the Jews did have what was called "the right of the sword." The Christian Scriptures speak of stonings (the woman caught in adultery, and the martyrdom of Stephen), but both of these are late stories and do not necessarily reflect the legal situation at the time of Jesus. John's gospel, which, ironically, is the gospel that tells of the attempted stoning of the adulteress, maintains that the Jews did not have the authority to execute and, therefore, had to go to Pilate for the decree for capital punishment (John 18:31). But given the absolute control that the Romans exerted over legal matters, it is unlikely that they would allow any serious juridical decisions to be made without their permission.

If the Jewish authorities decided to execute in any fashion, the final decision would most likely be made by Rome.[20] If the enemies of Jesus wanted him to be publicly humiliated and to suffer the excruciating death of the cross, they would have to bring their case to Pilate and ask that Jesus be crucified. Only the Romans had the authority to crucify. In seeking a Roman decision, the Jewish leaders also may have been hoping to forestall any negative reaction against themselves from their people.

Was There a Trial Before the Sanhedrin?

Mark, the earliest gospel account, and Matthew, who follows Mark's version, tell us that Jesus was tried before the Sanhedrin at night. At this trial an attempt to bring witnesses against Jesus misfires, so he is questioned directly, condemned as a blasphemer, and pronounced worthy of death. The next morning, at another session, the Sanhedrin consults again and then sends Jesus away to Pilate to be handed over for crucifixion. In Luke's version there is merely an interrogation before the Sanhedrin, with no witnesses or condemnation. In John's account there is an interrogation before the high priest Annas, who after being seriously out-pointed in an exchange with Jesus, sends him off bound to his son-in-law Caiaphas. He, in turn, apparently charges Jesus with claiming to be king of the Jews, and hands Jesus over to Pilate.

It is doubtful whether these accounts accurately reflect how Jesus was actually charged. What we have in the gospels seems to be largely a literary creation written later to establish Jesus' innocence, reveal his enemies, and, most important, reflect on the religious significance of his passion and death.

In spite of the many theories about the supposed trial, it is really impossible to accurately reconstruct the events preceding Jesus' crucifixion. Whatever sessions were held were secret and the followers of Jesus had no access to them. In fact, we are not sure if there really was a trial or what the charges were.[21] It is unlikely that the Sanhedrin would have met the night before Passover. It is more probable that there was some sort of hearing in order to prepare the charges that could brought to Pilate with the request that Jesus be executed by crucifixion.

There does seem to be a historical core to the passion accounts that the gospels give us. It seems probable that Jesus was arrested in the garden of Gethsemane, where he had gone to pray. It is plausible that the Jewish leaders, their alienation toward Jesus having peaked after the recent incident in the Temple, wanted to apprehend Jesus but were fearful of causing a reaction from those who had sided with him.

It was Judas who gave them the opening they needed. He apparently offered to reveal Jesus' place of prayer, and a time when they could secretly arrest him. He even offered to signal who Jesus was with a kiss of greeting. We know little of Judas's motivation for such a betrayal. It might have been greed, jealousy, even self-preservation. The gospels indicate a frantic and futile attempt to return the money and then despair ending in suicide (although in Acts 1:18–19 Judas buys a field with the money and then dies in some sort of violent accident).

The passion dramas also differ in recounting who made the arrest. In the synoptics, it is an armed mob sent by the chief priests, scribes, and elders. In John, the arresting party consists of Roman soldiers and Jewish guards sent by the chief priests and Pharisees. Jesus will not allow violent resistance, and, as he is taken off, his followers apparently flee. (Luke plays this down, and John says that Jesus asked that they be let go.)

Trial Scenes

Mark's version of the trial scene seems to be designed mainly to show the innocence of Jesus. The trial is constructed as a travesty of justice. False witnesses who cannot agree are brought to testify. Although it is required by Jewish law, no witnesses are called upon to defend Jesus. Then, almost out of desperation for a conviction, the high priest asks Jesus directly if he is the Christ and the Son of God. Jesus' answer in Mark's version is a clear acknowledgment, and for this Jesus is condemned for blasphemy.

Jewish readers would know that blasphemy is the sacrilegious use of the divine name, and that claiming to be the messiah or the Son of God is not blasphemous. The high priest, however, seems unconcerned with any such details and maintains that there is now a crime deserving of death. The scene becomes even more ludicrous as we observe the Jewish leaders cavalierly changing the charge from blasphemy to one of claiming to be the king of the Jews. (Luke mentions the other charges of misleading the people and opposing the payment of taxes to Caesar.) It would appear that the Jewish leaders realized that their religious motives for getting rid of Jesus would have to be politicized in order to persuade Pilate that crucifixion was called for. The Romans would hardly be willing to crucify someone for claiming to be the messiah, unless this implied inciting the people to some sort of revolt against Roman authority.

Trial Before Pilate

The Romans did not hold jury trials. The legal procedure consisted in the pronouncement by legitimate authority (in this case the Jewish officials) of formal charges along with a request for punishment. The Roman procurator had absolute authority to then make a judgment on matters of guilt and appropriate punishment.[22]

In the gospel passion dramas, Pilate appears weak and easily intimidated by the Jews. He seems inclined to believe that Jesus is actually innocent, and he even makes efforts to get Jesus released. This all makes good drama to demonstrate the guilt of the Jewish leaders and, perhaps, to put a better face on the Romans (with whom the early Christians are now trying to live in peace).

The portrait of Pontius Pilate that we get from other sources, however, is not as favorable as what we get in the passion accounts. Philo, the Jewish historian, portrays him as a corrupt and arrogant official, well-known for his savagery.[23] In Luke, we read of his slaughter of a group of Galileans as they offer sacrifice. Josephus gives an account of his savage killing of a large number of Samaritans at Mt. Gerizim, which proved his undoing. Pilate was eventually recalled to Rome in dishonor, and there are stories that he was later executed or even committed suicide.[24] In actuality, it would seem that if the Jewish leaders could show that Jesus was dangerous, the procurator would have been most willing to issue the decree for execution.

Role of the Dramatis Personae

The characters in these "passion plays" seem to be based on historical figures, but often they are symbolic of what the early Christians themselves were experiencing in their own struggle to remain faithful to Jesus. It is generally accepted that Judas did betray Jesus, but at the same time he is also symbolic of those in the later communities who turned on Jesus and ended in despair because they were not open to God's forgiveness.

There is also good reason to believe that Peter also denied Jesus, for it is difficult to accept that the early Christians would circulate such an embarrassing story about the leader of the apostles unless it had some basis in fact. But Peter might also symbolize those who were not faithful to Christ and yet were later moved to repent.

In the biblical stories, the disciples are afraid and flee to avoid the "dangers" connected with being a follower of Jesus. The early Christians also knew such apostasy in their midst and, in these stories, they dramatize their deep faith in God's unlimited mercy. In their own day there were the Herods, the chief priests, elders, and Pharisees who often persecuted them in the same way as their counterparts had oppressed Jesus. But there were also Gentiles who, like Pilate's wife, recognized Jesus to be a "righteous man" (Matthew 27:19). There were also disciples similar to the Roman centurion, who accepted that Jesus was "the Son of God" (Matthew 27:54) There were wealthy and powerful Jews who, like Joseph of Arimathea, courageously spoke up for Jesus and were willing to divest themselves of material things in order to serve him.

The early Christians experienced the cross in their own lives in personal sacrifices, persecution, and even martyrdom. The question of why they must suffer for following Jesus and his teachings seems to have been often before them. The answer lay in the story of their Master's own passion and death, which carried the same irony and mystery. The gospel stories dramatize these searching questions and invite even contemporary readers to enter the play and reflect on where they themselves might fit.

How Jesus Was Killed

Death on a cross was the most horrible type of execution in the ancient world. It was such an unspeakable subject that we find very little mention of it in the ancient authors.[25] Actually, the most detailed descriptions of crucifixion seem to be in the gospels. The historical accuracy of the scriptural description of crucifixion has been verified by excavations of ancient cemeteries, where the skeletal remains reveal the methods that were used in this form of execution.[26]

Crucifixion did not originate with the Romans; its use was widespread in antiquity. The Hebrews used this form of capital punishment for treachery and sorcery in some of the older kingdoms. The Mishna mentions the crucifixion of 800 Pharisees in the Hasmonean Kingdom.[27] But the Jews dropped this form of execution at the beginning of the Roman occupation, possibly because it had become too closely associated with the brutality of the Roman occupiers.

The Romans used the cross often, usually to punish rebellious slaves, dangerous criminals, and any others who were involved in insurrection against the Roman state. In the famous rebellion of the slave Spartacus, seven thousand of the rebels were crucified along the public highways. The sight of men writhing in agony and being picked apart by birds of prey and wild animals was to be an effective deterrent against rebellion.[28] So loathsome was this form of torture and death that the Romans would not permit any of its citizens to be subjected to it, no matter how heinous the crime.

Physical Description

Crucifixion was designed to humiliate, torture, and kill in a manner that would satisfy vengeance against the criminal. This method of execution also appealed to the blood lust of both the soldiers and the spectators. To describe how this was actually done brings us to a more realistic picture of what Jesus experienced. Too often the crucifixion becomes so idealized and so subject to theological interpretation that it is easy to lose sight of what a horrifying experience it was.

An integral part of Roman crucifixion was the flogging or scourging of the victim. This brutal beating debilitated the condemned person and thus insured that there would be no later resistance to the execution. The process of killing began with this flogging. First, the prisoner was stripped of his clothing, then his hands were stretched out and bound to the top of a post that was upright in the ground. This position exposed the back, buttocks, and legs for the whipping. The instrument used was a short whip with a number of braided thongs of varied length. These thongs contained small iron balls and sharp pieces of sheep bone. Two soldiers, one on the right and the other on the left, would flog the victim with alternating blows. As the beating progressed, the iron balls would inflict deep contusions, and the leather thongs and sheep bones would cut deep in the skin. Eventually the lacerations would tear through the skin into the muscles, causing tremendous pain, loss of blood, and usually shock.

After the scourging, the victim was in a severely weakened, even critical condition. Now he would give his executioners no trouble or resistance when they marched him on toward the place of crucifixion.[29] Before the arduous march to the place of execution began, the cross-beam, weighing about one hundred pounds, was placed along the shoulders of the prisoner. Then the difficult walk began, accompanied by soldiers who roughly prodded the victim along. One soldier carried a sign, bearing the prisoner's name and his crime. This sign would later be affixed to the cross for all to see. John tells us that Jesus' sign read "Jesus of Nazareth, King of the Jews."

Once the group arrived at the place of execution outside the city, the crossbeam would be placed on the ground and the prisoner would be thrown down on it face up and nailed to it through the forearms with six-inch nails. Four soldiers would then lift up the crossbeam and fix it to the upright beam in the ground. Then the feet would be nailed to the upright beam. The discovery of a crucifixion victim in an ancient bone-yard reveals that the feet were joined together, one over the other, and a large nail was driven through the heel bones.[30] In order to prolong the agony, a crude seat was provided on the upright beam, on which the victim could rest between gasps for breath.

The dying process was usually one of slow asphyxiation. The hanging position itself severely constricted breathing, and the person would have to repeatedly rise up and strain to get air in the lungs. As the victim pulled himself up on the nailed forearms in order to breathe, he would experience excruciating pain from the severed nerves in the hands and feet. Eventually the victim would be too weakened to continue the process of struggling for breath, and would then collapse and die. Before being taken off the cross, the legs were usually broken to assure that the victim could no longer pull himself up for another breath. At times a spear would be pushed through the heart to guarantee that the person was truly dead.

Summary

The cross has been a central symbol for Christianity. It has been worn around the neck as a sign of discipleship, as a talisman, or perhaps merely as a piece of decorative jewelry. It has been hung in churches, carried into battle, and mounted on hillsides along the highway. For many the cross symbolizes redemption, the involvement of God in suffering, and the struggle that humans go through to find meaning in their own suffering and death. The cross points back to an event that for Jesus' followers has always been difficult to understand. Why did their Lord and Savior have to undergo such a humiliating and painful execution?

We have seen how all four gospel writers, with whatever sketchy facts that were available, take this horrible event of Jesus' crucifixion and reflect on the event through the light of faith. Each author constructs a drama that depicts various sides of Jesus' own experience of the execution. Each explores the reasons why such an unjust and cruel killing took place at all.

While there is no simple resolution to the question of why Jesus was executed, it would seem that Jesus' teachings and actions in the areas of religious reform and empowerment of the poor alienated a good many of the religious and political leaders of his time. His prophetic confrontations with hypocrisy and injustice, along with his refusal to back off when under threat, resulted in his death by crucifixion. Throughout, the gospel writers also attempt to get to the ultimate meaning that this event has for the faith of Jesus' disciples. They find in this crucifixion a verification of God's love and forgiveness, of God's longing to save people from sin and death. They see it as a prelude to God's vindication and glorification of Jesus Christ in resurrection.

Questions for Reflection and Discussion

1. What do you think were the main motives of those who conspired to kill Jesus?

2. "The gospels are all influenced by the desire to incriminate the Jews and exculpate the Romans." Do you think that this is an accurate assessment of the influences behind the passion stories?

3. Cite specific teachings and actions of Jesus that you think might have alienated people toward him.

4. Compare and contrast how Jesus' final moments are described in the four gospel accounts.

5. Name some of the "types" among early Christians that seem to come through in the individuals described in these passion dramas.

Chapter Nine

Raised from the Dead

Paul warned the Corinthians that their faith was in vain if Jesus Christ had not been raised from the dead. Yet, until recent times, Christian theologians have neglected this central mystery of the faith. At times the church fathers of the first centuries of Christianity seem to be more concerned with the incarnation of Jesus Christ. The early councils follow this direction as they concentrate on the nature of Jesus and the issues of his divinity and humanity. Little or nothing was said by the councils of Nicea (325) or Chalcedon (451) on either the crucifixion or resurrection.[1]

In the medieval period the emphasis was on redemption. Anselm (d. 1109), who dominated this area of theology, stressed the importance of the crucifixion, but generally ignored the role of the resurrection in the salvation process. Both Bernard of Clairvaux (d. 1153) and Thomas Aquinas (d. 1274), who were two of the most influential thinkers of the medieval period, gave the resurrection serious consideration, but, unfortunately, their emphasis did not prevail.[2] To see this neglect, one has only to examine the theological clergy training manuals that were used in the past centuries. In these texts the resurrection is usually mentioned only in passing as a proof of the divinity of Christ.

It was only through the efforts of scholars such as F.X. Durrwell and D. M. Stanley that the importance of the resurrection began to be restored.[3] Vatican II, which ended in 1965, was also an important milestone for regaining the significance of the resurrection to Christian faith. In our own era, there have been numerous biblical and theological studies of the resurrection, and they have helped to restore a great depth of meaning to this mystery.

In this chapter, we are going to study the resurrection of Jesus. We will begin by looking at the Jewish and pagan background on afterlife. Then we will examine the early Christian formulas, and the various interpretations of the appearance narratives and the Easter event. Finally, we will discuss the stories of the empty tomb.

The Jews and Resurrection

The uniqueness of the resurrection of Jesus Christ is best understood in the context of the beliefs in an afterlife current at that time. The resurrection of the dead was not unfamiliar to the Jews of the first century C.E. The foundation for such a belief was laid with accounts of Enoch and Elijah being whisked into heaven, by the Psalmists' reflections on union with God after death, and by the early images of Sheol, a holding place where the dead waited for the final judgment.[4]

In the book of Daniel (c. 538 B.C.E.) there is a suggestion of the heavenly exaltation of one "like a son of man," with the subsequent powerful testimony that "Many of those who sleep in the dust of the earth shall awake; some shall live forever, others shall be an everlasting horror and disgrace" (Daniel 7:13; 12:2). The book of Wisdom speaks of the souls of the just who have been persecuted being "in the hand of God" (Wisdom 3:1–8). The belief in afterlife also emerges explicitly in the Maccabean period (c. 170 B.C.E.). As a young son dies in the presence of his mother, he says to the king who has had him tortured: "You accursed fiend, you are depriving us of this present life, but the King of the world will raise us up to live again forever" (2 Maccabees 7:9).

This tradition on afterlife often appears in an apocalyptic context, wherein the Jews express hope for survival during times of crisis. This tradition proclaims that God will dramatically intervene to save God's people and that they will transcend death and enjoy some heavenly sphere of reality.[5] Divine vindication of God's people as well as the transformation and exaltation of creation also seem to be integral to this tradition. In later rabbinic writings, the Mishna Sanhedrin, there is a statement that "All Israelites have a share in the world to come." As for the wicked, God has created Gehenna, a place of fiery torture for them. There the wicked would wait for the Great Judgment in the future. The righteous, in contrast, will go to paradise and await the future Messianic Banquet.[6]

These traditions continued into the time of Jesus. The Pharisees held firmly to a belief in the resurrection of the body in the end-time. The same tradition of immortality exists in the writings of Philo, the Jewish historian contemporary with Jesus.[7] The Sadducees, however, were noted for their refusal to believe in such resurrection.

Pagan Beliefs

There also seems to be some semblance of belief in afterlife among the pagans at the time of Jesus. Greek thought still was influenced by Homer's notions of the survival of the soul after death and the notion of immortality among the stars, as well as punishment for evil in Hades. There are also traditions of the rising of divine figures like Isis, Asclepius, and Adonis. The conventional wisdom among the masses, however, seemed to view death as an annihilation.[8]

The Roman authors have some accounts of emperors being seen borne aloft into the heavens by eagles or by a chariot during the cremation ceremony. These and other vague references to afterlife among the Romans did not, however, seem to affect the popular belief. The Roman cemetery markings reveal little hope for life after death, and some pagan critics mocked the Christians when the new belief in resurrection surfaced.[9]

Earliest Christian Formulas

The earliest Christian testimony on resurrection appears in brief teaching and liturgical formulas. (The appearance accounts seem to have been developed later than these formulas.) A brief statement, such as Paul's to the Corinthians, typifies the earliest Christian tradition on resurrection: "For indeed he was crucified out of weakness, but he lives by the power of God" (2 Corinthians 13:4).

The classic and perhaps most foundational statement in Paul's writing is in 1 Corinthians 15:3-9: "For I handed on to you as of first importance what I also received: that Christ died for our sins in accordance with the Scriptures; that he was buried; that he was raised on the third day in accordance with the Scriptures; that he appeared to Kephas, then to the Twelve. After that, he appeared to more than five hundred brothers at once, most of whom are still living, though some have fallen asleep. After that he appeared to James, then to all the apostles. Last of all, as to one born abnormally, he appeared to me." This was written about the year 50, and apparently was learned by Paul at the time of his conversion, five or six years after the death of Jesus. This could place the tradition in the oldest missionary community, sometime during the 30s.[10]

In what might be an even earlier formula, Paul wrote the Thessalonians: "... you turned from idols to serve the living and true God and to await his Son from heaven, whom he raised from the dead, Jesus, who delivers us from the coming wrath" (1 Thessalonians 1:9–10). The prominence of Jesus' resurrection is also featured in Paul's proclamation to the Romans with regard to "the gospel about his son, descended from David according to the flesh, but established as Son of God in power according to the spirit of holiness through resurrection from the dead, Jesus Christ our Lord" (Romans 1:3–4).

It is interesting to note that in this early Pauline tradition the emphasis is on the power of God raising Jesus from the dead and establishing Jesus as Son of God by that very act of vindication and glorification. It is also notable that although the appearances are mentioned there is no effort to narrate them. Nor is there any mention of the empty tomb.

For the most part, the manifestation of Jesus' resurrection is proclaimed as a powerful experience that happened to Paul, the importance of which he must share with others. No attempt is made to describe this resurrection itself and it is clear from these early formulas that Jesus now exists in an entirely new mode of existence, offering all those who encounter him an experience of the "kingdom come," a glimpse into the end-time. As Paul tells the Colossians: "He is the image of the invisible God, the firstborn of all creation" (1:15).[11]

Appearance Stories

Much controversy has surrounded the so-called appearance stories of the gospels. These stories have sparked hotly contested debates. Are they historical accounts? Fabrications by an ambitious group of Jesus' early followers? Figments of the overactive imaginations of Jesus' disciples? Literary forms used to describe inner conversion? Or do they fit with any number of other possible explanations?

The gospel accounts contain a number of discrepancies. In what appears to be the most authentic ending of his gospel, Mark does not give a narration of appearances. He simply says that very early on the first day of the week three women came to anoint the body of Jesus, only to find the tomb empty and to hear a young man inside tell them that Jesus is raised. They are told to carry the message to the disciples that Jesus is going to Galilee, but instead they leave filled with fear and tell no one.

In Matthew's account the scene occurs at dawn on the first day, with only two women—and they come to see the tomb rather than to anoint the body. They experience an earthquake and then see an angel sitting outside the tomb. The angel tells them that Jesus is raised and that they are to tell the disciples that Jesus is going to Galilee. On the way, presumably to tell the disciples, the women meet Jesus. They grasp his feet and worship him. Subsequently, on a mountain in Galilee, the Eleven encounter the risen Lord.

Luke narrates a different account. Here three women, one of whom is different from the ones named in the other stories, bring oils to the tomb and find it empty. There are two men inside and they tell the women that Jesus is raised as he had predicted in Galilee. The women tell the disciples this news, but the disciples do not believe it. Peter then runs to the tomb to see for himself, finds the burial cloths, and goes home amazed. Later, the risen Lord appears to Peter, accompanies two disciples on the road to Emmaus, and appears at a meal with the disciples in Jerusalem.

John's narrative is different yet. This story opens in the darkness, before first light. Mary Magdalene and possibly one other woman find the tomb empty. Mary thinks the body has been stolen and goes to tell Peter and another disciple. The two men run to the tomb, find that it is empty and then return home. Later Mary Magdalene looks into the tomb and sees two angels sitting there. They ask her why she is weeping and she tells them that people have moved the body of her Lord. Jesus then appears to her, and she eventually recognizes him when he calls her by name. Her embrace is forestalled by Jesus because he has not yet ascended, and she is then told to tell the disciples that he is going to the Father. Jesus later appears to the disciples (except Thomas) at a meal, then to the disciples with Thomas, and finally to seven disciples at the Sea of Tiberias.

Categorizing the Stories

It is very difficult to categorize these appearance stories. We have seen that there are marked discrepancies with regard to time, the women present, the message announced, the sequence of events, and the details of what actually happened. These discrepancies might well indicate that what we have here are not so much historical accounts, as they are literary narratives that are pointing to some other set of events or experiences.

Of course, the basic question here is: "What really happened in the Easter event?" By Easter event, we do not mean the actual resurrection of Jesus. Not even the gospels make any attempts at describing the actual raising of Jesus. What has been at the center of this inquiry is the very character of the disciples' experience of Jesus as risen.

Hostile Explanations

Early on, those hostile to Christians and their beliefs offered explanations for the resurrection stories. One of the earliest attacks was that the disciples simply stole the body and made up the story of the appearances. Justin Martyr (d. 165), perhaps the most important of the early apologists who defended Christianity against its attackers, tells of a humorous, but incredible version of this. It seems that the gardener in the area where Jesus was buried moved the body to another tomb to prevent visitors to the tomb from trampling his vegetables.[12] It might well be that Matthew's account of the posting of a guard at the tomb to prevent such skullduggery came out of Christian attempts to counteract accusations that the body had been moved.[13]

Celsus, who wrote one of the most venomous attacks on Christianity in 180 C.E., maintained that the appearances can be explained by hallucinations or hysteria. He adamantly denied the reality of the resurrection and at one point observed that, if the appearances had been true, they would have been experienced by everyone. It was Origen (d. 254), one of the most brilliant of the early Greek fathers, who effectively answered the attacks of Celsus.

In modern times, H. E. G. Paulus, a nineteenth-century writer, proposed the so-called swoon theory as an explanation for the resurrection stories. This view maintains that Jesus was not really dead when taken down from the cross. He was, in fact, buried alive and then revived in the tomb. He then came forth to be experienced "as raised."

Such a theory would have to hold that the Romans were careless in their executions, and there is no evidence that Roman executioners bore such a reputation. The "swoon theory" also seems to be based on the assumption that either the disciples were stupid enough to mistake a beaten and half-dead man as their glorious messiah, or that both Jesus and his disciples were involved in a massive deception in producing the gospel tradition.[14]

Finally, there is a more modern version of the old hallucination theory. Ian Wilson proposed that Jesus prepared his disciples for a new awareness of him by a kind of hypnosis. After the death of Jesus, the disciples entered a kind of post-hypnotic state wherein they gained a new perspective on Jesus. The appearance stories are attempts to describe this experience.[15] This theory, as well as the others above, are not taken seriously by many contemporary scholars.

Solely Subjective Experiences

There also seems to be a school of thought on the Easter event that would explain it purely from the subjective side. In other words, it would seem that the Easter event is an event of faith for the disciples and not necessarily an event happening to Jesus. From this perspective, which was held by Bultmann and his followers, faith is faith in the cross as an act of salvation, and this faith is expressed in the early church through resurrection myths.[16] Others would say that the real event was the disciples finally grasping the significance of Jesus' message after his death and then continuing on with his cause. The resurrection stories dramatize this new awareness on their part; they announce that the "cause of Jesus" lives on, but not Jesus Christ himself.[17]

At the root of this approach is the notion that the resurrection tradition is a myth used in the gospels to proclaim a new awareness, a conversion, or new insight on the part of the disciples. From this point of view, the resurrection was not an objective event and it did not in any way actually affect Jesus himself. Such conclusions would, of course, then preclude the real and personal presence of the risen Lord in sacraments, in Scripture, in people, and in the world, a fundamental belief in Catholic and many other Christian circles.

Significant Conversion
In coming to any understanding of the nature of the Easter event, we must keep in mind that it brought about a radical change in the original disciples and touched off one of the most significant religious movements in history. A group of demoralized fearful men and women were in hiding. They had only been with Jesus for a short time, perhaps a year, when their just-budding hopes for him were shattered by a horrible crucifixion that brought humiliation to both Jesus and his followers. Suddenly, in the midst of all the devastation and confusion, these followers of Jesus were transformed into enthusiastic witnesses for Jesus, into people who were willing to risk everything: loss of their Judaic identity, financial insecurity, even death, in order to spread the good news. Moreover, their testimony was believed by the faithful at that time and is still accepted by countless followers of Jesus today.[18]

A similar transformation came over Paul when he experienced the risen Lord. In the past, he had stood by approvingly as Christians like Stephen were stoned. As a Pharisee, he had been convinced that the followers of Jesus were unfaithful to the covenant and therefore should be hunted down and turned over to the authorities for punishment. Paul's experience of resurrection on the road to Damascus was the beginning of a deep conversion to Christian discipleship that culminated in his becoming an authentic apostle and a tireless missionary to the Gentiles.[19]

Commensurate Event
It is difficult to accept that such major conversions would take place in

people or that such a phenomenon as Christianity could have been ignited by fraud, hallucinations, visions, hysteria, or even by a merely subjective conversion to a new insight into the meaning of Jesus' crucifixion. The more obvious reason for such profound conversions and the spread of Christianity would seem to be one given by the disciples themselves: They had encountered the risen Jesus, the Lord.

Resurrection Faith

The unique and profound manifestation of Jesus as raised from the dead seems to have been experienced exclusively by the faithful, bringing them to a new level of "resurrection faith." This faith seems to have come from a profound experience of Jesus in a new mode of existence. It was not simply a case of something happening to them; it was also a profound experience for Jesus himself. They met a Jesus raised to a new level of existence beyond time and space. They encountered Jesus as no longer subject to suffering and death. They could now "see" that Jesus was indeed the Son of God, the messiah, the Lord and Savior. This resurrection faith enabled the early disciples to now look back on their memories of what Jesus of Nazareth said and did and to see them in an entirely new light. With this resurrection faith, the early communities could now confidently apply the treasured titles of their Hebrew faith to Jesus, see him as the fulfillment of so many of the prophecies of old, and give to him the worship and devotion that had previously been reserved for God alone.

Was There Faith Before Easter?

If the Easter event was only experienced by the faithful, some kind of foundational faith had to exist in the disciples, through which others could respond to the risen Lord. The following question arises, however: Was this foundational faith also brought about by the resurrection, or did the disciples have some level of faith in Jesus even before the resurrection? In other words, was resurrection the beginning of faith or was it the continuation of a faith that had been placed in the historical Jesus?[20]

It is reasonable to assume that the original disciples of Jesus were moved in their religious faith when they witnessed the healing and forgiving power of God working through Jesus. Similarly, as they listened to his teaching, they must have come to some level of understanding that Jesus was indeed a unique instrument of God's revelation. Perhaps it is this "faith" that provided the foundation through which they could accept the ultimate realization of God's power in raising Jesus from the dead. In Jesus' life they had both heard of and felt the Abba experience, at least in its beginnings. In the resurrection they encountered the ultimate Abba experience for Jesus and for themselves. In the raising of Jesus, they were given the promise of eternal life for themselves.

Authentic faith, however, is always a divine invitation freely given and freely received. The historical Jesus invited his disciples to follow him, trust him, and be faithful to him. He held out to them the promise of healing, forgiveness, and new life. The invitation to Easter faith specifically offered forgiveness to Peter and to others who had been unfaithful. They were invited to accept a new faith that would transform them and, indeed, the whole of creation. It was in the acceptance of this invitation that we see the commencement of resurrection faith.

Unique Encounter

This unique encounter with the risen Lord was very different from the experiences the disciples had of him before his death. Jesus was not "back in town." Although for them the encounter was indeed real, it was experienced only by the faithful and not by the public at large. The Sanhedrin would not be able to bring him to trial again; Pilate could no longer have Jesus marched off to be crucified. Jesus was not once again walking along the dusty roads of Galilee, speaking on the shores of the Sea of Tiberias, or teaching in the Temple courtyards. Those days were over forever. The disciples could not produce the visible evidence of his being alive again, much as they may have wanted to in order to verify their belief in Jesus' resurrection.

Vividly Real Experience

The early disciples most likely developed the appearance stories in an attempt to somehow convey the nature of their extraordinary experience of Jesus as raised from the dead. On one level, these appearance stories dramatize that this raised person was really Jesus of Nazareth. Thus, in the stories, he comes among them as the same forgiving, peaceful, and compassionate person that they knew before. There is a definite element of recognition in the stories. In John's gospel, Mary Magdalene eventually recognizes him in the garden and embraces him. The disciples see him and talk with him, and Thomas is invited to touch the wounds and recognizes him as Lord and God. The women in Matthew's account grasp his feet and worship him, and, in the same gospel, the Eleven see Jesus on a mountain in Galilee and worship him, even though they still seem to be plagued with doubts. In Luke's account, Jesus comes to the disciples insisting that he is not a ghost but is truly "flesh and bones." He shows them his hands and his feet and then sits down for a fish dinner with them.

Luke seems to go a bit overboard in his efforts to convince his readers that the risen Lord was real, but, nonetheless, he does make his point in the story he tells.[21] The gospels may emphasize the physical nature of the risen Jesus in order to distinguish the disciples' experience of his resurrection from the reappearance of prophets. Recall that when Jesus asked his disciples who others thought he was, they said that some thought he was Jeremiah or Elijah or one of the prophets. Herod thought that Jesus might be John the Baptist reappearing. And, in the transfiguration story, Jesus seems to be conversing with Moses and Elijah. In none of these cases is it implied that these figures have risen from the dead.[22] The physical and realistic descriptions of the risen Jesus sharply distinguish him from such visions.

The realistic portrayal also might have been directed toward the Gnostics, who detached the risen Jesus from the historical Jesus and reduced resurrection to a kind of ethereal exaltation.[23] It also set the resurrection experiences apart from the pagan dream-like "sightings" of mythical figures such as Isis and Asclepius.[24]

Not Jesus as Before

Although the gospel writers use their stories to confirm the reality of the resurrection experience, they also use these stories to demonstrate that the risen Jesus was in a transformed state. Here the element of "non-recognition" is effective. Mary Magdalene thinks Jesus is the gardener. The disciples on the road to Emmaus spend an afternoon with Jesus and have a meal with him without recognizing him. At one point, the disciples think that he is a ghost. Jesus is clearly not in the same form of existence that he was in before the resurrection.

The distinctiveness of Jesus' transformation is also brought out in the appearance stories by describing Jesus as no longer being limited to time and space. Jesus will simply appear in a locked room and then just as suddenly disappear. He is with the disciples, and then suddenly he is assumed into the heavens. The ascension story might also be a way of indicating that the appearances did, in fact, come to an end. The only subsequent appearance is that which uniquely came to Paul, and which Paul uses to lay claim to an authentic apostolic mission.

Jesus Transformed

The appearance stories seem to indicate that Jesus had been physically transformed. His materiality now had a new and glorified mode of existence, one that defied description. Even though the gospel writers at times seem to stress the physical by having Jesus eat and by having people touch him, it is obvious in the narratives that Jesus now is in an entirely new mode of existence.

Paul also indicates that a transformation came over Jesus in resurrection, but he does not approach this with the physical emphasis that we find in the gospels. Instead, he stresses that Christ's risen body is not flesh and blood, but lives with a spiritual existence whereby the corruptible is raised incorruptible, the weak is raised to power, and the natural body is raised to be a spiritual body (1 Corinthians 15:42–43). From this perspective, resurrection is a revelation that all of creation has somehow been transformed. The resurrection reveals a "new creation," whereby the entire world has been radically changed and given a new relationship with the Creator. That seems to be what Paul had in mind when he wrote to the Corinthians that the resurrection is so that all things might be subjected to God through Christ so that "God may be all in all" (1 Corinthians 15:28).[25]

In being raised from the dead, Jesus now also seems to take on a cosmic existence. He exists in the world with a unique presence. There is now a new creative force or energy within the cosmos that is driving creation to its fulfillment in God. In the vision of Teilhard de Chardin, the goal of the evolution of the cosmos is revealed first in the incarnation, and then in the resurrection of Jesus. Jesus Christ now becomes not only the goal of creation, but the very source of power to move others to become part of the movement toward that goal.[26]

Was the Resurrection Historical?

There has been great deal of debate among scholars about the historicity of the resurrection. The term history, of course, is ambiguous, especially when we are dealing with faith events. If we look at history in terms of recordable and concrete events that are witnessed by impartial witnesses, the resurrection does not fit into normal historical categories. Apparently, no one witnessed the actual raising of Jesus from the dead, and only the faithful seemed to encounter him as risen. At the same time, both his resurrection and the encounters with him occurred during a certain period of history, involved specific historical figures, and ignited a movement that was and is observable.

Yet even admitting these historical dimensions of the resurrection event, the raising of Jesus and the encounters with him were spiritual events that were impossible to record and unverifiable by means of concrete evidence. Jesus did not set out to prove that he had risen; he invited his followers to accept it in faith. Neither did his disciples attempt to give concrete proof that he had risen. Instead, they proclaimed that he was raised and invited people to accept Jesus Christ as their Lord and God. Their recognition of Jesus was in faith and they invited others to share this faith with them.

What Did the Disciples See?

"Seeing" and "hearing" seem to be a part of the gospel descriptions of the appearances. Are we to conclude, then, that these were indeed sensible experiences of sights and sounds? The Greek word commonly used in the stories for the visual is *ophthe*. It is the passive of the verb "to see" and might be translated as "appeared to." In meaning, it can range from the encounters with God and angels to actual physical sight.[27] In the case of the resurrection experiences, one might suspect that we are using the word analogously here. This seems to be Aquinas' interpretation, for he pointed out that the disciples saw with the "eyes of faith." The most acceptable approach seems to be to explain the seeing and hearing in terms of insight into the new meaning of Jesus' life and death. As Kasper puts it, this was a "believing seeing," and not physical sight.[28] If these experiences were actually of the senses, as some maintain, then why wouldn't they be experienced by disinterested observers as well as by believers? Whatever the nature of the "seeing," however, it seems to have been brought about by a real experience of the risen Lord.

To say that the Easter event was somehow outside of history and sensible experience is not to deny its reality or authenticity. Neither is it to overlook how the risen Lord was perceived to be in continuity with Jesus of Nazareth. It is true that the disciples do not say that they have seen Jesus; instead, they say that they have seen the Lord. Still, there is recognition, and their acceptance of the risen Lord is based on the memories they had of him before his death and the commitment they made to him during his public life.

Traditionalists have often pointed out that the disciples were able to recognize Jesus because he had predicted his resurrection and they were thus prepared to experience him again. It is widely held by biblical critics, however, that Jesus' predictions of resurrection and other references to his rising are post-Easter statements that have been read back into the life of Jesus. After the death of Jesus, the disciples had no such expectations. If they did expect Jesus to rise, why would they tell the story of the women going to anoint the body, and why would those who heard of the resurrection be either amazed or incredulous? The resurrection seems to have been a surprising and new event, and the discrepancies of the gospel accounts might well indicate the extreme difficulty that the early disciples had in finding some storied fashion to share their experience with others.

Unique as they were, the encounters with the risen Lord did tie in to the memories and experiences the disciples had of the earthly Jesus. As Schillebeeckx has observed, the resurrection made it clear to them who Jesus was and who he had now become. The life, death, and resurrection are all of a piece and come together with resurrection faith in a new revelation.[29] For the disciples, the resurrection sheds a new light on the life of Jesus of Nazareth. They can recognize that he was their Savior all along and now is revealed in that role. They had perceived God acting in him before; now they could see that there was such a close identification between Jesus and Abba that they could indeed worship Jesus as their Lord and God.

Is the Resurrection Event Still Going On?

Were the original resurrection encounters the same as subsequent believers have had of the risen Lord in Word, sacrament, and in the world about them? This question has been asked many times. While the two kinds of experiences seem to be similar, they are more analogous than identical.[30]

The Christian faith had its beginning in those first experiences, and original witnesses were commissioned to begin the spread of the good news.[31] These original witnesses knew the historical Jesus and were thus uniquely able to see the meaning of Jesus' life and death in light of the resurrection.[32] Therefore, as Central American theologian Jon Sobrino has pointed out, these original experiences are in a category of their own and are not repeatable. Subsequent acts of faith were based on these original witnesses and are made by those who have neither experienced the historical Jesus nor been commissioned to be original witnesses and initiators of a new movement of faith. We might say, then, that the experience that the faithful today have of the risen Lord is as authentic and real as the original experiences, but it is not identical to them.[33]

Experience of the End-Time

Theologians often refer to the resurrection experiences as eschatological, that is, as occurrences that reveal the end-time that God has in store for creation. The kingdom that Jesus had announced as near has been made present in a new and dramatic way.

From this perspective, the risen Lord is seen as proclaiming that creation is to be transformed and not destroyed, and that life and love prevail over violence and destruction. The raising of Jesus from the dead discloses the end-time of divine vindication of those who have suffered unjustly.[34] It is a first glimpse of how the power of God will be poured out in the end-time.[35] The resurrection, then, is perceived as a unique breaking in of divine power, power that contradicts the apparent failure of Jesus' mission and ignites a new age of the kingdom.[36]

Jewish Resurrection Revised

We have already seen how the resurrection of the body was part of the Jewish tradition during the time of Jesus. If that be true, then why did the resurrection of Jesus cause such a stir? The reason is that the type of resurrection that the disciples of Jesus proclaimed was unprecedented in Jewish tradition.

The Pharisees believed in the general resurrection and judgment at the end-time. But, as Raymond Brown points out, "There was no expectation of the resurrection of a single man from the dead, separate from and preliminary to the general resurrection."[37] The disciples of Jesus were laying claim to something unforeseen and, for some, unacceptable in the Jewish tradition—that Jesus awoke from the dead before the end-time.[38] To add to the apparent absurdity, the man raised was one who had been tried, convicted, and executed as a criminal.

To those who maintain that the disciples simply made up the story of the resurrection, Brown replies that if the disciples had wished to deceive others, they most certainly could have chosen an easier story to sell. They could have proclaimed that Jesus was a prophet or even the messiah and that they had seen him assumed, like Elijah, into heaven. Or they could have used the Wisdom tradition and declared that Jesus was now in the hand of God as one of the souls who had been unjustly persecuted.[39]

Empty Tomb Narratives

The traditional approach to the tomb narratives is a familiar one, still commonly held in many Christian communities. The view holds that Easter faith came from the discovery of the tomb by the women, their reception of the announcement by the angel, their passing on the message to the disciples, and then the many appearances of Jesus to his followers. In the traditional view the empty tomb and the angelic announcement stand as "proofs" that Jesus rose from the dead; they verify faith in him as Lord and God. Modern scholarship has seriously challenged the traditional approach to the tomb stories, pointing out that the tomb stories are not part of the ancient kerygmatic teaching of Paul, and seem even at times to be constructed by writers who are not conversant with Jewish burial customs. Some maintain that these stories should not be viewed as integrally connected with resurrection faith.[40]

Earlier we noted the many discrepancies in the tomb narratives. These inconsistencies have led some to hold that the tomb narratives are legends used, perhaps, to dispel the notion that Jesus' body was stolen by the disciples or to explain the apparent lack of worship at the tomb after the Christians fled Jerusalem.[41] Others would say that these legends or myths were created as a means for the early Christians to demonstrate the reality of some inner conversion that they experienced.[42]

One problem with the story is connected with the burial itself. The normal practice after a crucifixion was to dump the corpse unceremoniously into a common grave used for malefactors.[43] It was possible, however, for relatives to get permission from the Roman authorities to give the body a decent burial. In this case, all four gospels point out that Joseph of Arimathea took the body and placed it in a tomb. In Acts 13:29 there is a different version, which says that the Jewish rulers took him from the "tree" and laid him in a tomb. One might say that since Joseph of Arimathea was a member of the Sanhedrin he could be considered to be one of the Jewish rulers in question, but the passage in Acts creates difficulties nonetheless.

The coming of the women to anoint the body is another problem in the narratives as we have them. Given the hot Palestinian climate and the fact that Jesus' corpse was supposed to be already in the tomb for two days, it seems rather farfetched to think that women would come to anoint the body. In addition, there is the conflicting story in John that Jesus' body was anointed with a hundred pounds of oil before burial. If this be true, there was hardly need for further anointing.

In addition, the announcement of the young man, or angel, seems to be a typical literary form used in Scripture to indicate a revelation of some sort from God. This might be even more reason to believe that the tomb stories are indeed literary constructs rather than historical accounts.

There are, however, a growing number of scholars who hold that the tomb narratives are historical and that they played some role in the early Christian verification of the resurrection. The narratives seem to be very early, bear little influence from the Hebrew Scriptures, and do go back to a real discovery of the empty tomb by some women disciples.[44]

One of the most cogent arguments for the historicity of the empty tomb is that there has never been any tradition about the discovery of Jesus' body. Even the Jews who were hostile to Jesus and to the Christians maintained that the body had been stolen from the tomb, not that it still existed somewhere. Nor has there ever been any mention of the disciples of Jesus following the usual Jewish custom and going to the grave after some time to gather the bones and put them in a ossuary so that they might be ready for the general resurrection.[45] There is no evidence that there was originally any veneration of the tomb of Jesus, as was so often the case at the tombs of prophets and other holy men.[46]

Finally, if the tomb had not been empty, one might assume that those not accepting resurrection could have disproven the disciples by merely going to the grave and displaying the body. Even though the Jews of the time were uncomfortable disturbing graves, Jesus enemies' would have had strong motivation—discrediting Jesus—for enduring such discomfort. It is also possible, however, that the opponents would have interpreted the reappearances as being similar to that which they expected from Elijah, and thus would have given no thought to examining the grave.

Whatever the case, there is no evidence whatsoever that anyone thought that the body was in the tomb. It seems that we must conclude that either no one knew where the grave was (and that is highly improbable), or that the tomb was indeed empty.[47]

The consistent use of the women as witnesses in the empty tomb narratives also argues for historicity. In the culture of the time, the testimony of women was of little value. If the early disciples had wished to put together convincing proof that Jesus had been raised from the dead, proposing that women were the initial witnesses would not have been an effective way to do it. Some of the details are, in fact, rather embarrassing, and they could have easily been passed over if persuasion were the issue.

In Mark's gospel, the women run away frightened instead of carrying out their charge to tell Peter and the others about the resurrection. In several accounts, Peter has to go see for himself rather than take the word of the women. In John's gospel the disciples view the story of the women as "idle tales" and go to see for themselves. On the one hand, the early writers seem bound to the history of the women witnesses, and on the other they reveal the typical biases of the time. Fabricated stories would most likely be smoother and more consistent in their details.

Even granting the historicity of the tomb narratives, the empty tomb experience does not seem to play a role in bringing about resurrection faith. If anything, the discovery of the empty tomb seems to have brought about fear and confusion. Only when coupled with the resurrection experiences would the empty tomb stories make sense to the disciples.

Scholars thus propose this scenario.[48] After the crucifixion the disciples returned home to Galilee, perhaps already hearing about the discovery of the empty tomb by the women, but not knowing what to make of it. In Galilee, Peter and then other disciples encounter the risen Lord and come to resurrection faith. Integral to the resurrection experience was a commissioning to spread the good news of salvation. The disciples thus return to Jerusalem for the Jewish feast of Pentecost, and the church of Jesus Christ is born in a magnificent manifestation of the Spirit of the Lord. The appearance stories are then composed as means for attempting to describe their indescribable experiences. When the tomb narratives are constructed, the empty tomb story is now told in light of the resurrection experiences. Thus the announcement of the angel is in fact the gospel message of resurrection that is already being preached by the disciples. Faith, then, is not in the empty tomb, but in the Lord as risen. The appearances describe this encounter, and the significance of the empty tomb becomes clarified.

Summary

The resurrection of Jesus as the Christ is at the very heart of the Christian tradition. It was an experience on the part of Jesus' disciples that their Master had been raised from the dead and glorified as their Christ.

This experience of the early followers goes far beyond other traditions of "afterlife" found in the Hebrew Scriptures or in the literature of other civilizations. Here a young man, executed in the prime of life just a few days before, is now experienced in faith as alive, present, and transformed into a new kind of existence.

We have seen how the gospels attempt in varying ways to narrate this experience and describe an experience that is, in effect, beyond description. A Jesus "somewhat similar, but somewhat different" is with them again, not in some hallucination, illusion, or other form of trickery, but in reality. The resurrection was an event that not only transformed Jesus, but brought a deep conversion of faith to his disciples, giving impetus to the beginnings of the Christian movement.

Frightened, guilty, and confused people, many of whom were uneducated and poor, were now filled with faith in Jesus as the Christ. They too were transformed and became empowered to courageously follow Jesus' ways and proclaim his good news to the world. With this experience of the risen Lord, there commenced for his followers a "new creation" where there was hope for peace and justice in the world, and for eternal life beyond it.

Questions for Reflection and Discussion

1. "What is unquestionably unique about Jesus is the *result* of his life and work. This culminates in the resurrection and the foundation of a movement which endured." Comment on whether or not you think this quotation accurately evaluates Jesus' accomplishments.

2. Do you think that the resurrection should hold a central position in the Christian tradition? If so, develop your reasons.

3. What are the appearance stories trying to tell listeners about the experience that Jesus' followers had of him as risen?

4. In what ways did the experience of the risen Lord affect the disciples' understanding of Jesus?

5. What importance would you give to the empty tomb stories? Do you think they are historical? What are the reasons for your answers?

CHAPTER TEN

Early Doctrines

Christian doctrines are the official teachings of the church. These teachings are generally defined by formal councils of bishops gathered for the purpose of officially stating the church's teaching in some area of belief. There is a certain development of doctrine because beliefs undergo revision and reinterpretation as time passes and historical changes take place. The church's official teachings about Jesus Christ were defined in early councils in the fourth and fifth centuries. These beliefs began in the oral stories of the early disciples who looked back on the person of Jesus of Nazareth and interpreted his teachings and his actions in the light of resurrection faith. These interpretations took on new imagery, meaning, and theological depth as they were written down in the form of Scripture. New stimulation and direction were given to this development as controversies and heresies arose that demanded response. Then solemn ecclesiastic councils gathered to officially formulate the community's position clearly and in such a way as to preserve the integrity of the tradition.

In this chapter we are going to look at some of the main stages in this development. We will begin with a brief overview of the early beliefs about Jesus' humanity and divinity. Then we will look at the first stirrings of controversy and how these were addressed by the early apologists and church fathers, who were the influential theologians of the early centuries of the church. The great challenge to Jesus Christ's divinity by Arianism will then be discussed, along with the doctrinal response of the Council of Nicea in 325. Finally, we will look at the post-Nicean controversies about Jesus' humanity and divinity and see how the Council of Chalcedon in 451 attempted to settle these doctrinal conflicts.

Early Proclamations of Faith

There can be little doubt that the early believers understood that Jesus of Nazareth was truly human. The apostles and disciples, the primary witnesses, knew Jesus in person. They had seen him laugh and cry. They watched him grappling with some of the same questions they had. They saw him learn and grow in the understanding of himself and others. They observed that, like themselves, Jesus had to struggle with the question of what he was supposed to do with his life. Those who knew Jesus saw him experience the human emotions of love, anger, fear, expectation, and abandonment. They ate and drank with him daily and were aware that he had the same appetites as they did. They knew his astounding gifts and his limitations. No doubt none of them could forget the time he was arrested, spat upon, mocked, scourged, and nailed to a cross. Nor could they forget the forgiveness he offered to all those who had either deserted or persecuted him.

The gospels are filled with such stories of Jesus' humanity. We see him hugging children, crying over the death of a friend, indignant with those who try to entrap him with trick questions, outraged over hypocrisy, and tenderly compassionate toward someone disabled or hurting. He can admit ignorance of the end-time and show amazement at the faith of the centurion. Both deep excitement and sorrow come over him at his last meal with his friends, and he anguishes over his fate in the garden. The gospel stories, even with all their flourishes of theology and imagery, leave no doubt that Jesus walked a human path.

Belief in Jesus' Divinity

The early Christian communities seemed to have no difficulty in accepting Jesus as their Lord and God. The gospel stories reflect this post-resurrection faith in Jesus as the Son of God. Mark, the earliest gospel, opens with the story of Jesus' baptism and proclaims this pristine Christian faith in the words from the heavens: "You are my beloved Son; with you I am well pleased" (Mark 1:11). In Matthew's account of Peter's confession about Jesus, Peter is depicted as saying: "You are the messiah, the Son of the living God" (Matthew 16:16). The same gospel's passion story portrays the centurion and others who witness the crucifixion as proclaiming: "Truly, this was the Son of God" (Matthew 27:54). In Luke's nativity story, Gabriel announces to Mary: "He will be great and he will be called the Son of the Most High" (Luke 1:32).

In John's gospel, the last gospel to be written, the divinity of Jesus is proclaimed more clearly and explicitly than in the synoptic gospels. In John's prologue, Jesus is acclaimed as having "the glory as of the Father's only Son." (John 1:14) In the opposition story involving Thomas, the "doubting apostle" confesses to Jesus: "My Lord and my God" (John 20:28). These and many other passages in John indicate that early on there was a strong belief in Jesus' divinity in the first Christian communities.

The letters of Paul also reflect the early communities' view of Jesus as God's Son. Paul writes to the Galatians that, "God sent the spirit of his Son into our hearts, crying out, 'Abba, Father!'" (Galatians 4:4). And, in a magnificent passage, Paul tells the Colossians that Jesus "is the image of the invisible God, the firstborn of all creation" (Colossians 1:15). In this and in so many other passages, Paul witnesses to the early faith that Jesus is indeed the Lord and God, the Christ.[1]

Post-Scriptural Testimony

Early post-scriptural writers also bear witness to early Christian faith that Jesus is the Lord of heaven and earth, the redeemer, indeed, God. Like the scriptural witnesses, these writers are concerned with professing their beliefs, not with a philosophical discussion of them.[2] In the oldest surviving sermon of the Christian church, which is attributed to Clement of Rome at the end of the first century, the community is told that "We ought to think of Jesus Christ as of God."[3] In one of the oldest surviving stories of someone being martyred for the faith we read: "It will be impossible for us to forsake Christ or to worship any other. For him, being the Son of God, we adore...." And in an ancient Christian liturgical prayer the early Christians cry out to Jesus Christ, *Maranatha* or "Lord, come."[4]

From early in the second century we have an account of Ignatius of Antioch (d. 112) writing to the local churches as he travels under guard to his death in Rome. He describes Jesus as the presence of the Father, God in a human being, and as Lord. In the *Didache*, a second-century disciplinary manual, Jesus is spoken of as Lord and as Son of God. Even the Romans seemed to be aware of this remarkable Christian belief. Pliny the Younger writes about how these "Christians" gathered before sunrise to sing "a hymn to Christ as though to a god."[5] This early Christian testimony to their faith in Jesus as God is straightforward proclamation, with little consideration given to *how* this might be. Considerations about the nature of Jesus would begin later with the early Christian apologists as they attempted to defend Christian beliefs against a growing body of "heretical" positions.

Divergent Views

Divergent views on the divinity of Jesus arose while Christianity was separating from Judaism and, at the same time, attempting to remain faithful to its Jewish heritage from Jesus and the original disciples. The struggle is highlighted in that early conflict with the Ebionites, Jews who accepted Jesus but insisted on the continuation of Jewish laws and customs. For them, Jesus was the elect of God and a true prophet, but they denied the virginal birth and the pre-existence of the Son. For them, the Son was created as an archangel who, in time, descended upon Jesus the man. Jesus' main mission was to end the Old Testament priesthood and to show people how salvation could be attained through proper fulfillment of the law.[6] Jesus, then, was no more than a man endowed with special powers who served as a good example for others.

Christians also struggled in the early centuries to remain faithful to the monotheism of Judaism as well as to the absoluteness and unchangeableness of God in Hellenistic thought. This struggle is evident in such heresies as Monarchianism and Adoptionism. The former stressed the "monarchy" of the Godhead and denied any distinction between Father and Son. As a result, the individuality and humanity of Jesus was given little consideration. The Adoptionists, on the other hand, attempted to preserve the oneness and unchangeableness of God by maintaining that Jesus was the adopted son of God and not truly the divine Son.[7] We see two extremes here in the effort to protect the oneness and absoluteness of God: The Monarchists denied Jesus' humanity, while the Adoptionists denied his divinity.

Gnosticism

Gnosticism was one of the most significant movements that orthodox Christianity had to struggle against. It has been described as a "vast and amorphous movement" that existed both outside and inside the church. The name given to this movement by later scholars is derived from the Greek word *gnosis*, which means "knowledge." It is applied to this group because of its claim to have secret knowledge that is available only to the elect. Gnostics were also dualistic, maintaining that matter is evil, or at best unreal. The material world, therefore, is not a divine creation, but an erroneous production by a "spiritual being" other than God. The material body is nothing more than a prison for the eternal human spirit, and, as such, leads the spirit away from its true destiny. Salvation for the Gnostics means escaping the material world and being united to the true world of the spirit.[8]

From what has been said about the Gnostic movement, it should be clear why Christian Gnostics found traditional views of incarnation unacceptable. Since materiality and the flesh were evil and illusionary, it seemed to them repugnant that God would become enfleshed and genuinely take on physical existence. Christ's salvific role was to save us from materiality and the flesh, so it was not logical that he would take on such fleshy "imprisonment" himself.

For some Gnostics, this meant that the human Christ was really a shadowy figure accompanied by the true Christ. The true Christ was, in fact, exempt from birth, suffering, and death. For other Gnostics, the human Christ was simply a phantom and had the same illusionary quality as any other "flesh." Christ only seemed to have a human body, and he only appeared to suffer and die.[9]

This view was central among the Docetists, who argued that Jesus merely appeared to be human and, therefore, that his suffering and death were mere illusions.[10] Jesus' humanity was simply a costume that was worn to give the impression of being human. This attitude toward Jesus has perdured in one version or another throughout the history of the church. The mentality is, in fact, still prevalent today among those who resist viewing Jesus as being genuinely human in all aspects.

Notion of "Logos"

In order to answer these early "heresies" about Jesus Christ, the early church turned to the notion of the Logos, a notion found in both Jewish and Greek sources. For the Jews, the Logos was the Word or that reality through which God was active in history. The Word was the creative agent in Genesis, the prophetic agent given to the prophets, and the source of Wisdom in the Jewish literature of the same name. The Word of God was the means for God to be operative in history and to exercise divine power and presence.[11] We also see this notion operative in the beginning of the gospel of John where the Word is given pre-existence, has the character of the divinity, and becomes flesh.[12] In the writings of the early fathers, the notion of Logos seems to have been derived more from Proverbs 8:22–31 than from the gospel of John, and the term came to mean a "timeless and therefore eternal substance in God."[13]

Whereas the Hebrew notion of Logos is more functional, the Greek notion is metaphysical. The Greek notion goes back five hundred years before the time of Jesus to Heraclitus, and was developed through Platonism and Stoicism. It is better translated as "reason" than as "word." For the Greeks, Logos was the principle of order and rationality in the universe.[14] This principle of rationality was in God and was the link between God and rational creatures.[15]

In these early centuries, the philosophical tools to get at Christological questions were often taken from various versions of Greek Platonism. Unfortunately, that system of thought had its own built-in dualism, distinguishing between the visible phenomena of the physical world and the eternal essences that were behind them. These eternal essences had the highest value and reality.[16] In addition, Greek thought on the whole was committed to maintaining a God who was immutable and absolute.

Logos Theology

The early apologists were concerned with preserving both the humanity and divinity of Jesus Christ. Central was the concern that if Jesus were not divine he could not perform the task of being savior. Conversely, if he were not divine, then we could not be united to God, or "divinized," as the Eastern mind liked to put it. For these early Christian thinkers, Jesus Christ was held to be the mediator between God and the human. To function in this role, he had to be truly human and truly divine.

The early fathers used this notion of Logos to link the Son of God with the human in Christ. The Son becomes identified with the Logos and then is somehow joined with Jesus. The Jewish and Greek notions of Logos are often blended here, so that the divine principle of creativity, revelation, and reason becomes incarnated in the man Jesus. The notion of Logos can link the Hebrew Scriptures with the Christian Scriptures and both can be linked with classical philosophy.[17] Precisely *how* the Logos was the Son and in what manner the Logos was linked with Jesus would be a matter of heated debate for centuries. The notion that somehow the Logos was "created" would constantly haunt the discussion and would be the crux of the question in the classical debate with Arianism.

Early Apologists

In the last three quarters of the second century, a group of Greek apologists defended Christianity against various movements of magic, Gnosticism, and heresy. By then, Christianity had broken from Judaism and had begun to spread throughout the Roman Empire. As a movement, Christianity was now predominantly Gentile, and that meant that Jesus

Christ had to be explained in new language and concepts. The Greek philosophy predominant at the time would prevail in the Christological debates to follow.

Justin the Martyr   Justin was a outstanding teacher in Rome in the middle of the second century. He spent his career attempting to harmonize Christianity with the Hellenic culture and was eventually martyred for the very beliefs he so well defended. Justin had a strong background in Greek philosophy, especially Platonism. In his Christology he made broad use of the "Logos," identifying the Logos with the Son of God. For Justin, the Logos seems to be a derivative of God, but is not the first and ultimate deity. Thus the Logos seems to be somewhere in between the divinity of God and the non-divinity of creatures. In Jesus, the Logos becomes incarnate as the principle of reason that overcomes the demonic forces of "unreason."

This point of view would cause later reactions from various sides of the debate. Those devoted to seeing God as one (e.g., the Monarchians) would see this as proposing a plurality in God. Gnostics and Docetists would argue that the Logos of God could never be degraded by being incarnated in evil flesh. The "creaturely" character of the Logos would serve later Arians in their argument that the Logos was, in fact, of creation and not divine. The seemingly inferior position given to the Logos in the divinity would be useful for the Subordinationists as well as Adoptionists, who both played down the humanity of Jesus.[18] Still others were led to view Jesus as merely a divine messenger. From this perspective, little value is given to Jesus' human life and ministry, and he is described in philosophical terms rather than in the personal terms used in the Scriptures.

Irenaeus   Irenaeus (d. 200) was the bishop of Lyon in the latter half of the second century. He was a contemporary of Justin, but he approached Christological questions more biblically than Justin and resisted Justin's subordinationist tendencies. Irenaeus's teaching and writing took aim mainly at Gnostics and Docetists who viewed Jesus' humanity as a mere phantom or apparition. He also vigorously opposed Marcion, who repudiated the God of the Hebrew Scriptures for being responsible for the creation of the evil world and humanity. Marcion only accepted the God of love of the Christian Scriptures, claiming that this was the God made known by Christ. Marcion's dualism had, in effect, produced two Gods (evil and good) as well as two Christs (heavenly and earthly) in his system of thought.[19]

Irenaeus's main contribution is his integrated and holistic approach to Christian belief. For him, creation and redemption, matter and spirit are in continuity. He prefers the integrated perspective of the Scriptures to the dualism of Greek Logos theology. As a result, when Irenaeus does speak of the Logos it is more in the Hebrew sense of the self-communication of God. For Irenaeus, God is a God of history who, from the beginning, created in order to share divinity with the world and humanity. The incarnation of the Word with the human is the climax of this creation, for it sums up or "recapitulates" what God had willed from the beginning: the union of the divine and human.[20]

The incarnation, then, does not come about so much because of sin, but because of God's intention to unite self with the human. Because sin did enter the world, however, Jesus comes as a Second Adam to reveal what God has planned for creation. In Christ, a new humanity is created and sin is overcome. God's goal of creation, the union of the divine with the human, thus becomes personified in Jesus Christ. This would not be possible unless the Word were truly human and truly divine, the true union that God had intended from the beginning of creation.

Irenaeus effectively refutes the dualism of the Gnostics and Marcion, and he challenges those who would see the Logos in Jesus Christ as belonging to creation. Some maintain that Irenaeus did not satisfactorily establish an equality between the Father and the Son, but he does have to be credited for establishing some of the foundations for later doctrine on the true divinity and humanity of Jesus Christ. In addition, he provided Christianity with a positive view of creation and an integral view of both incarnation and salvation history. Today's "incarnational theology" might well be traced back to Irenaeus. In this perspective, the world is not viewed as a place to be avoided, but as God's world where concern for justice, the environment, and peace are integral to Christian faith. This approach to the world has been dealt with in some detail in chapter six, and will be discussed again in chapter twelve.

Tertullian   Tertullian (d. 220) was a North African theologian whose center of activity was Carthage. His background was in law and rhetoric. Because his powerful theology was written in Latin it had far-reaching effects in the Roman church of the West. Some of this thinking seems to have been most influential on Pope Leo (d. 461), and consequently on the Council of Chalcedon in the mid-fifth century. It was Tertullian who wrote of Jesus being one person and two substances, a formulation that in some ways anticipated the classical formulation of "two natures" at Chalcedon.

In opposition to those who maintained that Jesus was a semi-god, subordinate to the absolute God, Tertullian maintained that Jesus was one person with two substances (divine and human) that are conjoined without being confused. For Tertullian, "substance" was the "stuff" that something is made of, and in his thought this "stuff" almost seems to have a material quality about it. Tertullian's outlook is also more legalistic than speculative, and his notion of substance seems to be related to the notion of *ousia*, or "essence," that was later used at the Council of Nicea. The Father and the Son are of the same substance. The Son is, therefore, divine, yet Tertullian did not see the Son as equal to the Father. The Son was somehow derived from the Father and, therefore, subordinate to him within the hierarchy of the Trinity.[21] So, while Tertullian supplied language that would be useful at Chalcedon, he also developed notions that would be used by the opposing Arians as well.

Tertullian also made efforts to defend the true humanity of Jesus against the Gnostics and Marcion. Even though Tertullian did not have a positive view of flesh, he wanted to include it somehow in his understanding of Jesus and in the scheme of redemption. He maintained that although the flesh is weak and ugly it can still be used as a means for God's presence and saving activity.[22] Therefore, Jesus is indeed one person but with two "substances," the flesh and the spirit. Tertullian's negative view of the flesh ultimately led him to join the extreme, rigorist Montanists, a second-century group that rejected the world and lived austere lives as they waited for the end of the world.

Early Theologians

Clement Clement (d. 215) was one of the earliest Christian theologians. He was a Greek philosopher who had converted to Christianity and became the main instructor at a great center for Christian scholarship, the catechetical school in cosmopolitan Alexandria, Egypt.

Clement believed that God is revealed to the philosophers as well as to the prophets. Revelation came through the Logos, which in time became incarnate in Jesus Christ. It is this Word, "clothed in human flesh," that reveals God to humans and leads them to God. Clement seems to have believed in the true humanity of Jesus, but his Platonism renders the humanity vague and places emphasis on the teaching of the Word rather than on the concrete life and death of Jesus. Clement's thoughts might sound rather enigmatic today. He is significant, however, because he was one of the first to apply Greek philosophy to Christian beliefs and is credited with laying the foundations for the later School of Alexandria.[23]

Origen   Origen (c. 253) succeeded Clement in the catechetical school at Alexandria and was renowned for being a remarkable teacher and scholar. For reasons that are not clear to us, he got in trouble with the ecclesiastical authorities in Alexandria. His theological views were considered to be "unorthodox" by some church authorities, and some of his views were eventually condemned as heretical. Like so many others at that time, Origen applied Platonism to the questions about Jesus Christ, and used the Logos as mediator between human beings and the God who is completely transcendent. In Origen's Platonic thought, the divine never gets very close to the flesh, but must be mediated through the soul. He believed that the human soul is higher than the flesh and is the only human element that can attain divinity. Thus the point of contact for the Logos with the human is in the soul and not in the flesh.[24]

For Origen, the Word is the image of God, but not God; therefore, it is subordinate to the Father. As one sees so often in this Greek theology, there is a willingness to see the Logos as divine. At the same time, however, there are different degrees of divinity and the Logos is often considered to be lower than the Father.

Summary of Pre-Nicene Era

We have seen so far that belief in Jesus' divinity began as a proclamation of faith. Most of the theology that eventually began to surround this proclamation was philosophical and concentrated more on the roles that Jesus Christ performed. (Some refer to this as a "functional theology.") There was a marked shift in theology as heresies about the nature of Christ began to develop. A gradual need developed for an apologetic, a manner of defending the "true" position. At this point, a speculative approach to the understanding of Jesus began to predominate. The integration of Christianity with the Hellenistic world accelerated the need for a philosophical approach to Jesus. With tools of Greek philosophy available, questions could be asked that were never before considered. Christians not only asked "if" Jesus was divine, but now they speculated on "how" this could be possible.

The early theologians commonly used the notion of "Logos," both in its Jewish and Greek connotations, to explain how the incarnation was possible. The "Logos" best served as a needed intermediary between the divine and the human. The Logos was often identified with the Son of God, and it was the Logos that was united with humanity. Quite often, as we have seen, these writers fell short of viewing this Logos as equal to God. For Justin, the Logos was derivative of God. For Irenaeus, the Son was not quite equal to the Father. For Tertullian, the Father and the Son are of the same substance, but not equal. And for Origen, the Logos is indeed an image of God, but is clearly not God.

In actuality, the true divinity of Jesus was being challenged in many of these teachings, and yet, somehow, the approach was kept on such a metaphysical and Platonic level that it did not present a problem for orthodoxy. It was only when Arius (d. 336) came on the scene that a major Christological upheaval ensued, for Arius set aside the metaphysical language that had kept the controversy esoteric, and baldly declared that Jesus was a creature.

Arius

Arius was a tall, austere priest of Alexandria. He was extremely popular among the people of that city and he had many followers, especially among the many "virgins" who had consecrated themselves to the church. Arius apparently was deeply influenced by Origen's teaching of the subordination of the Son to the Father, but what more directly led him astray was his literal interpretation of Scripture. Some feel that his roots also lay in the earlier notion that Jesus was some sort of angelic mediator.

It is not certain that Arius was original in his views. In addition, much of what later developed as Arianism came from the thought of other individuals, many of whom disagreed with Arius.[25] Moreover, the term "Arian" was often used later to brand someone considered to be heretical, and does not necessarily apply to Arius's views.[26] What is certain, however, is that Arius became the focal point of a very large debate.

In many ways, Arius was what we today would call a "Bible fundamentalist." Although many others at that time read the Scriptures metaphorically and mystically, Arius took them to be literally true. Following Genesis, he held that God created all things out of nothing. He applied this also to the Logos, and thus considered that the Logos had to be considered in the realm of the creature. Arius was true to the Greek philosophical position that God was completely transcendent, absolute, and indivisible. As such, God could be the creative source of all reality, but could not impart his substance to anything. To do so would render God divisible and changeable, and might even produce a duality in God. Whatever exists outside of God, therefore, is created, including the Logos.

Arius's main proof text from Scripture was Proverbs 8:22–31, which describes the birth of Wisdom, beginning with the words: "The Lord begot me, the first-born of his ways."[27] From this, Arius concluded that the Logos is some sort of demi-God interceding between God and the world. Even though the Logos is a superior creature, even one worthy of worship, it is nonetheless a creature. It was through this Logos that God made the Son as well as the Christ. Therefore, Jesus Christ was himself a creature, a demi-God suspended between God and man, identical with neither and related to both.[28] Neither was this Logos eternal, for, in the phrase of Arius, "There was [a time] when he was not."[29]

Reaction to Arius's views came swiftly from Alexander, the bishop of Alexandria. He called a meeting of the priests, and Arius was asked to recant. When Arius refused, a meeting of the bishops of Egypt and Libya was called in 320, and they voted to condemn and exile Arius. He fled to his friend Eusebius (d. 340), the bishop of Caesarea in Palestine, and from there continued to make converts to his teaching in parts of Asia Minor.

When Constantine, the Roman emperor who gave legal status to Christians in 313, conquered his rival, Licinius, and became the ruler of the entire Roman world, he included among his efforts to establish peace a call for Arius and Alexander to settle their differences. Constantine did not seem to think that this controversy over the Logos was of much significance, yet he realized that it was greatly dividing his people and causing massive demonstrations of opposing sides in the streets of Alexandria. A reconciliation could not be worked out, and Constantine took further action. To prevent any further dissension, Constantine insisted that these controversies regarding Jesus be settled as soon as possible, and he called for an official council to handle the matter.[30] He had given the church a free hand, partially because he wanted a means of unifying the empire. Instead, he found that Christianity was becoming a source of division.

Council of Nicea

In 325, Constantine decreed that a solemn council be held in Nicea, what is now the insignificant village of Isnik in Turkey. Apparently the emperor hoped that such a council, the first of its kind in Christianity's history, would act much like the Roman Senate and solve the controversies that were in the air. Viewing himself as representing the divinity on earth and having God-given power over both material and spiritual matters, the emperor felt it his right to participate in the debates and to confirm the decisions made by the council.[31]

About 250 bishops gathered for the opening of the council in the imperial summer palace near Nicea. Most of the bishops were from Eastern Sees, with only a small number from the West. There was great enthusiasm in the air as the emperor delivered the opening address. After all, this was the first time that the bishops could observe and experience just how far Christianity had spread and what great diversity it now included. The irony of the Roman emperor paying their travel expenses and hosting them was certainly not lost on those who had been tortured and maimed by previous emperors for this same Christian faith, now proclaimed as the religion of the empire.[32]

The agenda for the council included a number of legal matters, but the main question to be addressed was the position of Arius. After much heated debate, the teachings of Arius regarding the created nature of Jesus were condemned. A creed was formulated that is still recited today: "We believe in one God the Father Almighty, Maker of all things visible and invisible; and in one Lord Jesus Christ, the only Son of God, begotten of the Father, God from God, Light from Light, True God from True God, Begotten, not made, of one substance with the Father, through Whom all things were made." It was made clear that Jesus was not created and that he was of the same "substance of the Father." The word used for "same substance" was the Greek word *homoousios*, a slippery term that can be translated as "one in essence," "one in being," or even "same materiality." The first two meanings seem closer to what the council meant, but, for many, the ambiguity remained and the controversy was not closed. The decision by the council fathers to go beyond the Scriptures and to settle the Arian controversy through Greek philosophy was a crucial one. It represented a major adaptation of Christian belief to a perspective and culture other than that of the Scriptures.

The decree was signed by all but three bishops, and these were quickly deposed and banished from their cities by the emperor. For the time, the Christian belief in Jesus' divinity, which had been so evident in the Scriptures and the worship of the early church, had been saved from Arian distortions. Still, the ambiguity of the term *homoousios* would allow the controversy to continue on for centuries. Moreover, the council had also established a "high Christology" that would for centuries accent the divinity of Jesus to an extent that would push his humanity into the background. This emphasis on divinity would also affect liturgy, shifting the emphasis from the celebration of a communal meal to that of a service of worship.[33] And, unfortunately, the biblical understanding of Jesus Christ would now often be replaced by Hellenistic philosophy.

Antioch and Alexandria Schools

After Nicea, two major schools of thought about Jesus developed, one in the city of Antioch in Syria, and the other in Alexandria in Egypt. Sorting out how these schools differed is no easy matter, because the thought on each side was mixed and complex. Fundamentally, the differences seemed to spring from two conflicting theological approaches to God: One held that God was a single reality; the other school took the position that there was a double reality in the one God. The theological lines seem to be drawn in these terms more than on the basis of which city one lived in. The tension between the cities, however, did localize much of the opposition in this dispute.

One area where the two cities were generally divided was in their understanding of the nature of Jesus Christ. While both schools were concerned with preserving both the divinity and humanity of Jesus, it seems that one of Antioch's chief tendencies was the insistence that, if Jesus was to be the Savior, he had to be fully human. Therefore, they made great efforts to stress that the indwelling of the Logos in Jesus in no way diminished his humanity.

To safeguard the humanity of Jesus, the Antiochenes developed a "Word-man" Christology that stressed that the Logos dwelled in the man Jesus as in a Temple. This "indwelling" approach tended to set up a duality in Jesus and, as a result, came dangerously close to losing touch with the true divinity of the person of Jesus.[34] Yet Antioch's approach often appeals to theologians today because it favored a "low Christology" that starts with the life of Jesus of Nazareth rather than with the pre-existing Logos, and that sees his life as a gradual ascent to the Father. Following from this, salvation is seen more in terms of the imitation of the life and ministry of Jesus than in terms of becoming divinized through the incarnation.[35]

One of the influential Antiochene theologians was Theodore of Mopsuestia (d. 428). In opposition to Arius and Apollinarius he proposed that Jesus was both God and man. Yet when he came to explain how this union took place, Theodore used language like "assume," "adopt," and "indwelling," which seemed to be simply a return to dualism. Though he seems to see Jesus as a unity, he also seems to view Jesus as merely appearing to be one individual.[36]

In contrast to the Antiochenes, the theologians of the Alexandrian School developed a "high theology" and stressed the descending of the Logos. Its roots were in the earlier theology of Clement of Alexandria and Origen. Their stress was on the divinity of the Logos and of Jesus, but they often neglected Jesus' humanity. A "Word-flesh" approach to the incarnation developed in Alexandria, and here the stress was on the oneness of the union. In Jesus, the divine was fully revealed in the union of Logos with flesh. In the extreme, this view seems to eliminate a human soul in Jesus.[37]

Athanasius

The Arian controversy continued on after the Council of Nicea. The most effective champion of the council during this period was Athanasius (d. 373). Athanasius has been described as a short, dark man, who was raised among a lower class Coptic family in Egypt. Some called him "the Black Dwarf," and he was known to have the ascetic endurance of a monk and the brilliance of a learned theologian. Athanasius had been a deacon at the Council of Nicea. After the conciliar gathering, he reluctantly accepted the position of bishop of Alexandria.

Constantine revoked the banishing of Arius in 328, and there was a strong revival of Arianism. Eusebius of Nicomedia spread rumors to the emperor that Athanasius was a tyrant and a magician, so Athanasius was brought before the emperor and eventually banished. This was the first of five banishments for Athanasius, yet he kept returning and never let up his attack on Arianism until his death in 373.

Athanasius was a loyal Alexandrian in his theology. He stressed the full divinity of the Logos as well as the reality of the flesh to which it was united. For him, divinization of humankind was the purpose of the incarnation, and that could only come about if Jesus was truly divine and human. Salvation is the restoration of fallen humanity and the true selfhood made in the image of God.

God became human so that we might become divine. To achieve this, the Logos had to be divine. But that reopened the perennial question in the debate as to whether God suffered. Athanasius tried to answer this by distinguishing between the Logos in himself, where there is no suffering, and the Logos in the body, where there is suffering. Yet, in saying that, Athanasius seemed to have the Logos replace the human soul or conscious selfhood of Jesus. His answer as to how Jesus is truly human has, therefore, never been completely acceptable. Apollinarius (d. 390) brought the Alexandrian position to a further extreme, teaching that the union between the Logos and that flesh was such that Jesus was a "heavenly man" and did not in fact have a human soul.[38]

Climax of the Conflict

The dispute between Alexandria and Antioch climaxed in the conflict between Cyril, the Patriarch of Alexandria (d. 444), and Nestorius, the Patriarch of Constantinople (d. 451). Nestorius was an Antiochene and a student of Theodore's. He insisted that the two natures in Christ remain distinct and unchanged. Otherwise, he pointed out, the Logos would undergo change, which is impossible in God. Thus the two natures in Jesus are so distinct that they seem to be two persons, the man Jesus and the Son of God.

Where Nestorius created a storm was in his position that Mary was the Mother of Jesus but not the "Mother of God," a title used of her in a treasured liturgical hymn that originated in Alexandria. According to Nestorius, Jesus as a human being was born of Mary, but the Logos was not born of her. He held that the fusion of natures in the Alexandrian position would indicate that the Logos suffered. It would also raise a question as to whether Jesus underwent real suffering.[39]

Cyril's Reaction

Cyril of Alexandria responded to Nestorius' position swiftly and vehemently. There can be little doubt that politics as well as doctrine played an important role in the response. The Patriarch of Constantinople was attempting to gain in the East the equivalent of the power that the Bishop of Rome had in the West. As a result, the churches of both Alexandria and Antioch vied to have their men in control of Constantinople. Nestorius, who now ruled as Patriarch of Constantinople, was an Antiochene. So when Nestorius stated his controversial position on Mary, Cyril was ready to strike a blow for Alexandria. He wrote several letters to Nestorius, pointing out to him that his teachings reduced Christ to an inspired man who was awarded divine status. He asked Nestorius to give up his position and accept the teaching that the Logos became the subject of a human life, in a union which Cyril called "hypostatic." When Nestorius refused to recant, Cyril wrote to the emperor and had a council called to deal with Nestorius.

The council met in 431 in Ephesus, a city in Asia Minor. The followers of Nestorius were delayed in arriving, but Cyril deliberately went on without them, condemned Nestorius as a heretic, and deposed him. When Nestorius's supporters, along with John of Antioch, finally did arrive (Nestorius himself did not opt to appear), John proceeded to call a rival council, declared Cyril a heretic, and reinstated Nestorius. Amid a great deal of confusion and shouting, the emperor intervened and had both Cyril and John arrested. Eventually a formula of agreement was arranged, but, in fact, Cyril's council prevailed. Nestorius was exiled and died a broken and abandoned man in Petra, a desolate area of Palestine. The council's decrees confirmed the "hypostatic union" approach of Cyril, defined that Mary can be called the Mother of God, and rejected Nestorius's notion of the "indwelling" of the Logos.

Ephesus by no means settled the controversy. It flared up again in 449 when Flavian, the Patriarch of Constantinople, called a synod to condemn Eutyches, a monk who maintained that Jesus had but one nature, a divine nature. Eutyches was undaunted by the condemnation. He appealed to the emperor and to Dioscorus, Cyril's successor as Patriarch of Alexandria. Dioscorus got Emperor Theodosius II to call another council in 449 at Ephesus. The entire council was rigged by Dioscorus so that Eutyches would be exonerated and Flavian condemned. Pope Leo's men were not allowed to have the floor, and when Flavian objected, Dioscorus feigned being attacked and called for the police and some local toughs who were waiting outside. They charged in and beat up Flavian so badly that he subsequently died of his injuries.

The council condemned those who taught that there were two natures in Christ, and some of the bishops chanted: "Cut him in two who divides Christ."[40] Later, the pope called this council a band of robbers and asked the emperor to ban it. Theodosius refused to cooperate, but died soon afterward in a riding accident. The way for a more orthodox council was soon opened by the emperor's sister Pulcheria, who seized power along with her husband Marcian, the new emperor. In the meantime, Eutyches was imprisoned in a monastery, and most of the bishops who attended the "robber council" recanted their positions. If nothing else, one has to admit that these were colorful times in the history of the doctrinal development of the church.

Council of Chalcedon

A new council was called by the emperor to meet at Nicea in 451, and hundreds of bishops gathered to attempt to settle these doctrinal controversies. Dioscorus, backed by many monks and bishops who supported him, tried to disrupt the council, and, although he failed, the council had to move to Chalcedon.

In October 451, the Council of Chalcedon opened with hundreds of bishops, including Dioscorus and his followers, dozens of court patricians, and a number of papal legates in attendance. Amidst shouting matches and even occasional fist fights, it soon became obvious that Dioscorus and his followers were losing ground. Eventually most of the bishops of the robber council of Ephesus recanted, and Dioscorus and his closest associates were condemned. Several days later, the Creeds of Nicea and Constantinople, along with Cyril's second letter to Nestorius and Leo's Tome were read to the gathering. The bishops shouted their approval and proclaimed the famous statement: "Peter has spoken through Leo."[41]

It was in the fifth session, after much heated debate, that the council fathers decided to side against Nestorius, Apollinarius, and Eutyches. They took aim at any theories that taught a double sonship, a mixture or confusion of the two natures, or that viewed Jesus' humanity as being a mere pretense. In a doctrinal statement going beyond the creedal position of Nicea, the fathers declared:

> Wherefore, following the holy Fathers, we all with one voice confess our Lord Jesus Christ one and the same Son, the same perfect in Godhead, the same perfect in manhood, truly God and truly man, the same consisting of a reasonable soul and a body, of one substance with the Father as touching the Godhead, that same of one substance with us as touching the manhood, like us in all things apart from sin; begotten of the Father before the ages as touching the Godhead, the same in the last days, for us and for our salvation, born from the Virgin Mary, the Theotokos; as touching the manhood, one and the same Christ, Son, Lord, Only-begotten, to be acknowledged in two natures, without confusion, without change, without division, without separation; the distinction of natures being in no way abolished because of the union but rather the characteristic property of each nature being preserved, and concurring into one Person and one subsistence, not as if Christ were parted or divided into two persons, but one and the same Son and only begotten God, Word, Lord, Jesus Christ; Even as the prophets from the beginning spoke concerning him, and our Lord Jesus Christ instructed us, and the Creed of the Fathers has handed down to us.

As one reads this definition, now over fifteen centuries old, it is easy to see what an impact it has had on Christian thinking. First of all, it became definitely established in the church of the West that Jesus Christ was indeed Son of God. We also hear in the statement many echoes of controversies of the past that either distorted the divine or the human in Jesus.

This was a historic effort to deal with these controversies as best as the fathers could, using the Greek philosophical terms that they had at hand. Jesus was perfectly human and perfectly divine, with a human soul and body, and was of the divine essence and also of the human essence. The Christ was not created in time, but was, from all time, of God. And the crucial question as to how these two natures are united was dealt with in terms of Jesus being one person, one center of unity.

Not a Complete Answer

It was not a complete answer, and many areas were left for later discussion. Many problems were glossed over, including the problem of how God can suffer and die, and how humanity can be united to divinity without being changed. The word *ousia* is used to describe the nature of God and the nature of the human, and yet it was never made clear how one and the same notion can be applied to such totally different realities. In fact, one wonders in what sense the notion of "substance" can be applied to the mystery of God at all.

The blurring of Jesus' human personhood is also problematic today.[42] The notion of person that was used in the definition views personhood metaphysically, as the center of unity. Today we describe the person, in psychological terms, as a center of human consciousness and action. Given the contemporary understanding of person, the doctrine of Chalcedon seems to make the human personhood of Jesus problematic, and can thus put him out of the range of personal experience as we understand it.

The definition also has Scriptural limitations. Those who framed this formula in the fifth century were interpreting Scripture either literally or allegorically. In our own time, the enormous amount of biblical scholarship that has been done since the beginning of the historical-critical approach has offered significantly new understandings of the nature and interpretation of Scripture. As part of these biblical advances, contemporary scholars have reclaimed the Christian understanding of the historical Jesus, the humanity (as well as the divinity) of Jesus, the deeds and teachings of Jesus, the centrality of Jesus' death and resurrection, and the importance of the "saving" aspect of Jesus' mission. Such findings would seem to call for re-interpretations of these early conciliar statements.

Summary

After the resurrection, Jesus' early disciples recognized that the man they had known and loved in Galilee was indeed their Lord and God. Jesus, the Christ, was both human and divine. In the early centuries, the profession of this belief gradually turned into an analysis of "how this could be." The philosophical tools available from Greek philosophy were used in an attempt to explain how God could become man. Some so stressed Jesus' humanity that they lost touch with the divinity. Others placed so much emphasis on the divinity that Jesus was no longer viewed as a human being. Ultimately, two general councils, Nicea and Chalcedon, were called to officially declare that Jesus was indeed divine, and to offer an explanation of how his two "natures" could be united in one "persona."

These early councils of Nicea and Chalcedon served to protect Christian tradition on Jesus' divinity and humanity, but there were many other facets of Jesus Christ that they did not address. We might say, then, that these early councils represent a beginning stage in the development of the Christian tradition. But Christians have moved on and will continue to move on beyond this very early stage of doctrinal development. Each era, with its own unique philosophical tools, its own scriptural insights, and its unrepeatable historical context, has built upon this foundation and has developed new understandings of both the person and the work of Jesus Christ.

Christians came to understand Christ as Savior and victor over Satan during the centuries following these councils. In the Middle Ages they came to know Christ as the suffering redeemer who satisfied a just God for their offenses. Jesus has been known as "Christ the Monk" in the days when medieval monasticism flourished, the "Bridegroom of the Soul" in Christian mysticism, the "Universal Man" in the Renaissance, and as the "Prince of Peace" during the Reformation. In contemporary times Christ is understood in many images and is increasingly being recognized by the oppressed of the world as "Liberator."[43] The images of Savior and Liberator will be dealt with in detail in chapters eleven and twelve.

Questions for Reflection and Discussion

1. Cite examples from the gospels that might indicate that Jesus' early disciples perceived Jesus to be human.

2. Why did many Jews find it so difficult to accept that Jesus was really divine?

3. What is your understanding of "logos"? Indicate some of the ways in which this notion was used to explain the union of the divine and human in Jesus Christ.

4. What was it about Arius's position that caused such divisions among the Christians of that time?

5. What specific contributions to Christian doctrine were made by the Councils of Nicea and Chalcedon?

CHAPTER ELEVEN

Savior

"Are you saved, brothers and sisters?" In the past, this was the question of the circuit-rider preacher on the first night of the tent meeting. Today it might be the query of some well-meaning missionary who comes to your door. The question sounds rather archaic in today's fast-moving society. In our modern world with all its material comforts and personal independence, the answer to the question "Are you saved?" might well be, "saved from what?" Many people seem satisfied with their way of life and are not particularly looking to be "saved" from anything. Millions of others who suffer deprivation are perhaps looking more for being saved from hunger, homelessness, or even the danger of being killed. The kinds of "salvation" offered to them by evangelical preachers often do not seem to really meet their more pressing personal needs.

The message of salvation has always been central to the Christian tradition. From the beginning, the Christian church's mission has been to proclaim Christ's message of salvation and to invite all who heard to turn their lives around and accept Jesus as their Savior. If this be true, however, then why is it that the church's message of salvation raises so little interest for many people today? Why is the message too often associated with some slick TV preacher who is, perhaps, more interested in the collection than in bringing salvation to others? Could it be that Christians have lost touch with one of the central beliefs of their tradition?

In this chapter, we will attempt to retrieve some of the richness that has surrounded the Christian belief in salvation as it has developed over

229

the centuries. One thing will be most noticeable: The belief in salvation has had many different meanings over time. The official church has never formulated a doctrine of salvation; it has been left to theologians to interpret salvation in many ways to meet the varying needs of different times and places.[1] We will begin by examining a number of these interpretations as they appear in the Scriptures, in the patristic writings, and in medieval thinking. We will give special attention to the Anselmian theory, which has held sway in many ways until recent times. Then we will look at some of the more contemporary questions about salvation and examine some of the more recent efforts to address these questions.

Biblical Themes

Very early on, the first Christians apparently recognized that God had saved them in and through Christ, and they seemed to be anticipating that he would soon come again to bring this salvation to its fulfillment. The resurrection experience had convinced them that Jesus was the messiah, the anointed one of God. As the Christian Scriptures unfold, we see these early disciples using many images and themes from their Jewish tradition to explain these beliefs. The notions of salvation, redemption, justification, ransom, atonement, sacrifice, reconciliation, and liberation are all used to indicate the many nuances and the great depth of their initial experience. These notions would serve as the bases for future development in the community's understanding of Jesus as Savior. In the following section we will discuss these major themes as they appear in the early tradition.

Salvation

A notion of salvation seems to be common in most religions, and it is most certainly at the heart of the Judeo-Christian religion. This belief seems, at least in part, to arise from the experience of being safe and well in the protection of God, or of being rescued in times of danger or need. For the Jews, the central event of salvation was the Exodus, the event wherein they were "saved" from slavery in Egypt. Yahweh then continued to be the rescuer of the "chosen people" throughout their long history of exile and persecution. No matter what the difficulty or suffering, even the horrible Holocaust of recent times, many Jews have placed their trust in God for the strength to survive and for the hope and courage to begin again.

In ancient times, the trust that built up from repeated liberations produced a prophetic tradition that looked forward to a future time of complete salvation. It also produced a tradition of prayerful confidence in God for God's saving power, as well as a tradition of thanksgiving for God's many saving deeds. The Psalms, as well as the book of Daniel, carry many passages that express the belief that the just person, and most especially the poor and the meek person, will be saved by God. In Psalm 51, the believer prays to God for a clean heart, renewal of spirit, and "the joy of your salvation" (Psalm 51:11).

The Jewish tradition into which Jesus was born thus viewed salvation as a many-faceted experience and promise. Salvation was a covenanted relationship with God, a deliverance from evil and hostile powers, a rescue from personal and social sin, and a trust in an ever forgiving and faithful God. Jesus would restore the best of this tradition. In his own loving dedication to his people, he raised this tradition to a level never before acceptable. He would live and die in utter self-sacrifice and be raised in resurrection to stand as the personification of the best in the Jewish tradition of salvation.[2]

Gospel Salvation

The "salvation" theme is often present in the gospels as the stories of Jesus' life are retold in the light of Christian faith. Jesus saves the sick from the despair of their mental and physical illnesses. He saves the handicapped from isolation and degradation. He rescues sinners through his power of acceptance, compassion, and forgiveness. All those inklings of God's power manifested through Jesus of Nazareth are now recognized in their full meaning by the early community. This becomes clearly and universally proclaimed in John's tradition: "For God did not send his Son into the world to condemn the world, but that the world might be saved through him" (John 3:17).[3]

Other images in the stories of Jesus further indicate that the early communities who constructed these narratives held him to be their Savior. Jesus struggles with and overcomes Satan. Jesus comes to save the lost sheep and to call sinners to repentance. Jesus challenges his disciples to "lose" their lives so that their lives may be saved (Luke 9:24). In the Pentecost scene in Acts, Peter proclaims that God has made Jesus Lord and Messiah. Peter invites his listeners to repent and be baptized in the name of Jesus so that they may save themselves "from this corrupt generation" (Acts 2:40). These early disciples had experienced in the risen Lord a definitive rescue from sin, suffering, and death, and from God's judgment in the end-time. They received a promise of an everlasting future of peace and happiness.

The earliest tradition seems to anticipate an imminent return of Jesus when the faithful, in view of their gifted faith in Jesus, would become the elect of God.[4] It was only gradually that they came to realize that salvation was already accomplished in Christ. This carpenter from Nazareth, whose very name, "Jesus," meant "Yahweh saves," was experienced to be their Savior and God. Because of their personal experience with him during his earthly life, and now in their experience of him as exalted, they knew that they were accepted by God and forgiven for their infidelity. The saving power of God had saved them from despair and powerlessness in the face of evil. They now understood that Abba, whom they had experienced in Jesus, had indeed sent him to mediate the salvation that had been planned for people from the beginning of time.[5]

Redemption

The use of the redemption language in the Scriptures adds further nuances to the understanding of God's saving action in Jesus Christ. Even though the redemption theme does not seem to be in the oldest layers of the scriptural tradition, it developed rapidly once it appeared.[6] The notion seems to be derived from a Jewish family practice where the closest relative of someone who lost goods and property or was enslaved had the obligation of "buying back" what was lost and gaining freedom for the enslaved person. The notion is operative in the Exodus description of God redeeming the people from slavery in Egypt.[7] In addition, the prophets, especially Isaiah, Ezekiel, and Jeremiah, commonly refer to Yahweh as "Redeemer," the one who redeems Yahweh's people from sin and guilt.

Redemption and Christ

Arland Hultgren maintains that there are four main approaches to Christ as redeemer in the New Testament.[8] In the first two approaches, "redemption in Christ" and "redemption through Christ," God is more at the center of the redemptive process than Christ is. In the other two models, "redemption by Christ" and "Christ as mediator," the central role in redemption is given to Jesus Christ. The approaches that stress the centrality of Christ seem to come from later epistles and the Johannine tradition. It may well be, therefore, that the tradition of the early Christians gradually moved from identifying God as redeemer to recognition of Christ himself exercising that role.

Redemption in Christ   Redemption "in Christ" is found in Mark, the earliest gospel, and in the epistles of Paul. The emphasis here seems to be that redemption has been planned and promised by God, and was accomplished by God sending God's Son to redeem us. Here, Jesus seems to be passively obeying the divine decree. He takes on the "curse" of human sin, and obediently gives himself in the sacrifice of the cross. The death of Jesus is for all and manifests the saving power of God. Here the cross and resurrection mark the end of an era of sin and slavery and the commencement of a new age of oneness between the whole human family and God.[9]

Redemption through Christ   In the gospels of Matthew and Luke, and in Acts, the stress is placed on redemption "through Christ." Here, again, God is the initiator of salvation, and Jesus is the one carrying out the will of the Father, but, in this case, there is more of an identification of their wills and less stress on the role of Jesus' death in the redemptive process. Redemption seems to be brought by the Christ who is in an exalted state. Matthew's Christ, according to Hultgren, is a royal figure who has the resources to avoid suffering and death, but accepts them in order to fulfill the divine purpose.

Jesus' blood is poured out at Calvary, and his life is given as a ransom, yet he yields up his own spirit in the death scene, and, as the risen and exalted Lord, gives the benefits of his redemptive act to his followers. With "all authority" he then commissions his disciples to go forth and teach redemption to everyone, and he promises that he will be with them with his power until the end of time.[10]

In Luke's gospel and in Acts, the notion of redemption is fully developed: Jesus is portrayed as the one who buys us back from the slavery of sin and death and brings us into a new land that is safe and happy.[11] Here, again, this is all carried out according to a divine plan whereby Christ brings forgiveness to many during his life and must then suffer, die, and rise so that forgiveness might be extended to all people. Luke does not choose to use the "ransom image" of Mark and Matthew. Instead, he views redemption as an ongoing process. It had its beginning in the divine plan, was acted out in Jesus' ministry and death, and is now the benefits of forgiveness and the promise of final redemption extended to those who repent.[12]

Redemption by Christ   In the later Pauline epistles, which seem to have been written by authors other than Paul, as well as in the Johannine tradition and the pastoral epistles, Christ is portrayed as the redeemer in his own right. Christ is pre-existent and, rather than being sent, comes in his own power as a vigorous redeemer who dynamically sacrifices himself and draws all to himself so that they may be redeemed.

He loves his own, gives himself for them, and reconciles all to himself. Christ is not so much one who performs the act of redemption as he is the redeemer himself. He is the "image of the invisible God" (Colossians 2:9), the agent of creation (Hebrews 1:2; 2:10). It is not so much by deeds as by his very nature that Christ is the redeemer, the reconciler, the "victor" over the cosmic and demonic powers. Christ reigns from the right hand of God as a powerful source of salvation for all humanity and promises final victory over evil in the final coming.[13] This is the image of the redeemer that would be prominent in much of the patristic writings, as we shall see later. And, since the work of Aulén in the 1930s, it is this image that has been described by some scholars as the "classic" version of redemption.

In John's tradition, the role of mediator is also incorporated into the notion of redemption "by Christ." Jesus is sent by God to act as a mediator of the salvation of the world. Jesus comes from above with authority from the Father to give eternal life to those who accept him. In John, the cross is more of a throne from which the divine Jesus reigns as he establishes his community to follow him, finishes his mission, and hands over his spirit. As the exalted risen Lord, Jesus extends forgiveness, peace, and redemption to those who believe in him.[14] For the Johannine community, the God who is love has given the Son, who in turn lives and dies out of love for others.

Ransom

Sometimes connected to the "buying back" notion of redemption was the element of "ransom." Fuller suggests that it was the celebration of the paschal meal that moved Christians to turn to the language of the suffering servant in Isaiah 53 and the language of ransom.[15] It first appears in Mark: "For the Son of Man did not come to be served but to serve and to give his life as a ransom for many" (Mark 10:45). In the liturgical formula of the Lord's Supper, the notion comes through in terms of Jesus' blood, "which is to be shed for many" (Mark 14:25). The same notion is later repeated in Matthew's gospel, now in the context of Jesus asking his disciples to be servants of each other.

In the pastoral letters, the ransoming takes on a much more universal character. In 1 Timothy 2:6, the author reveals a well-developed redemptive theology: "There is also one mediator between God and the human race, Christ Jesus, himself human, who gave himself as a ransom for all." Using what appears to be a very early tradition, Paul employs a similar image in writing to the Corinthians: "For you have been purchased at a price" (1 Corinthians 6:20).

The Scriptures do not push this image any further to discuss who received the ransom. As we shall see when we discuss the patristic writers, the metaphor became distorted when Satan was brought into the transaction. Instead of God being the one who both gave and received ransom, suddenly the Devil became the one holding humanity in slavery and thus the one receiving the ransom.[16] This caricature of redemption prevailed for centuries until Anselm put it to rest in the Middle Ages.[17]

Atonement

The Hebrew word *kippur* (Yom Kippur) can be translated to mean "expiation," "propitiation," or even "atonement," each with a different nuance of meaning. The most common ancient religious meaning for expiation was to purify, or make pleasing to the gods, that which was sinful. For the Hebrews, it meant being purified of whatever sin divided one from God, and an effort to renew the covenant. This later restoration of a broken relationship is clearly brought out in the English word "at-one-ment," or the act of restoring oneness or unity. The final result is that both God and the people are once again propitious, or favorable, toward each other.

One of the purposes of sacrifice in ancient Israel was to expiate the sin of the people and make them once again pleasing before Yahweh. Blood, which was viewed as the source of life, was sprinkled upon them to signify their new propitiousness and regained at-one-ment with Yahweh. The sacrifice was an outward symbol that signified the inner conversion on the part of the people. It also served as intercession to God for forgiveness and reunion. It was not, as many have thought, an attempt to change God's disposition. It was meant to represent a radical change in the one participating in the sacrifice.[18]

The biblical writers commonly turned to this Hebrew tradition of atonement in attempting to develop a theology of redemption. Paul writes to the Romans about those who are justified: "They are justified freely by his grace through the redemption in Christ Jesus, whom God set forth as an expiation, through faith, by his blood..." (Romans 3:24). The author of Hebrews explicitly uses the Temple imagery and describes Jesus himself as a faithful and merciful "high priest," who expiates the sins of the people. In the Johannine tradition, God is described as sending his Son to be an expiation for sin (1 John 4:10).

It is important to note that expiation or atonement here does not mean that sinners are attempting to appease an angry God. Rather, a gracious and merciful God is here initiating and carrying out atonement for a people who could never bring about such forgiveness or reconciliation on their own.[19] God provides the gift of God's own Son, and then accepts that gift as having the power to bring all people home to their God. This is not some isolated Temple event, but an event symbolic of God's saving power and process in creation, in history, in the life of Jesus of Nazareth, and now in the continuing transformation of the world.[20]

Atonement through the Cross

Early on, the Christian believers had to come to terms with the meaning of the humiliating and repulsive death that had been thrust upon the man they had now come to recognize as their Lord and God. The earliest layers of tradition reveal that the first Christian communities struggled with the "scandal" of the cross. At first, the early communities focused on the cross as Israel's rejection of the messiah, but gradually they came to see that Jesus' death was somehow expiatory and that the cross was a symbol of their redemption.[21] Paul uses one of the earliest traditions when he writes to the Corinthians that "Christ died for our sins" (1 Corinthians 15:3).

Of course, crucifixion itself would not be ample grounds to move people to view Jesus as a Savior. Martin Hengel points out that crucifixions had taken place over centuries, and not only were these not seen as being redemptive, most were not even noted by either the Jews or the Romans.[22] Greek and Roman literature contain accounts of heroes whose death brought exaltation for themselves and atonement for others. In ancient cultures a short and glorious life was generally seen as more desirable than a long and inglorious one. And the voluntary acceptance of death as a path to honor is dramatized in the stories of the Greek heros Heracles and Achilles.

The Greeks were familiar with the role of the martyr, whether it be Socrates dying for truth, or other heroes dying for the common good or for their friends. The Graeco-Roman world was also familiar with the idea that the death of an individual could carry the power to calm the wrath of angry gods and purify the land of sin.[23] The Roman writer Lucan writes of the death of young Cato, who says, as he expires, "This my blood will ransom all the people; this my death will achieve atonement for all that the Romans have deserved through their moral decline."[24] We also find examples of figures who atone for others through their sufferings in some of the Greek tragedies of Euripides and Sophocles.

There are some examples of expiatory suffering in the Jewish tradition, including the suffering servant in Isaiah 53 and the martyrs during the Maccabean period and after the destruction of Jerusalem in 70 C.E. Although the Isaiah passages seem eventually to have had influence on the Christian redemption tradition, it is debatable whether the later martyrs had any influence on the biblical material.[25]

In spite of all these parallels, there is really no story comparable to the one about Jesus the Christ. The Gentile world would have considered it "irrational and excessive" to think that a commoner who underwent a criminal's death had successfully expiated sin. Likewise, for many Jews, it was outlandish, even offensive, to accept as messiah one who was a craftsman from Nazareth and who was condemned and crucified as a messianic pretender.[26] Therefore, in order for such an unlikely person and story to become the new story of complete atonement of sin and the beginning of the new age, something extraordinary must have happened over and above the experience of the crucifixion.

Hengel has a fascinating suggestion for how the atonement theology developed around the death of Christ. It is his position, and there seems to be a growing consensus for it among scholars, that the resurrection experience is at the heart of this new awareness that Jesus Christ was the one who definitively brought expiation for sin and the restoration of atonement between God and people. According to this view, the crucifixion plunged Jesus' disciples into a state of confusion, disillusionment, and even guilt for having abandoned him in a time of crisis. The resurrection experience for them was one of forgiveness and atonement. It brought about a veritable "explosion" of faith in Jesus as the messiah, the one who expiated their sins, brought atonement, and was a signal of the dawning of a new era. Jesus was the "first fruits" of those who had died (1 Corinthians 15:20), the "firstborn of the dead" (Colossians 1:18), and the one who promised them the same destiny when he came again.[27]

Sacrifice

Because Jesus did die a bloody death on the cross, the sacrificial theme would be a predictable element in the development of the tradition. As they turned to the language of the Temple, the customs of sacrifice, and the image of Isaiah, the early Christians perceived Jesus as a victim offered to God. He would be described as "the Lamb of God who takes away the sins of the world" (John 1:29; Isaiah 53:7).

This does not mean that Jesus was a passive victim, but one who took a position against hypocrisy and oppression, and who preached a message of salvation that was unacceptable to many of the leaders of the time. Refusing to back off from his mission and his position, he faced death with resolve and courage. In other words, he chose to sacrifice himself throughout his life and in his death, thereby bringing forgiveness and atonement to all.[28] Nor was Jesus to be compared to some burnt offering passively consumed on the "altar" of the cross; he made himself the gift offering of praise and fidelity toward God. He undoubtedly saw his death as inevitable, not because of some divine knowledge, but because of the hostility and alienation he had received from some people from the very beginning of his public life.[29] Hence, his last trip to Jerusalem was not a "death wish." It came from Jesus' determination to take his message to the very heart of his religion in Jerusalem, and to refuse to back down no matter what the consequences.[30] The Abba, whom Jesus knew and experienced, was a saving God in solidarity with the suffering of Abba's people. It was appropriate that Jesus would be willing to face self-sacrifice, and understandable that he could see a saving purpose to this life and death.[31]

This notion of self-sacrifice would seem more true to the Jewish notion of sacrifice. The idea of sacrifice bribing or appeasing an angry god is really more Greek than it is Jewish. Moreover, the Christian version of sacrifice was not to offer animals, but, in imitation of the master, to offer themselves for others.[32] Jesus' sacrifice was the self-giving of love, not the sacrifice of the altar. He freely gave of himself, and so Paul calls upon Christ's followers to "present your bodies as a living sacrifice"(Romans 12:1).

For the early believers, then, Jesus is described in terms of a prophet-martyr, as the righteous sufferer of the Psalms and Wisdom literature, as the suffering servant of Isaiah, and as the Son of Man portrayed in Daniel 7:13, who represents the people. He is the righteous one of God who stands in our place and vicariously dies for us (2 Corinthians 5:18 ff). Yet the representative role he played should not be distorted and debased into a version of his being a scapegoat or of his taking on the sins of humanity as one who is cursed in our place. Although this "substitute" view did receive some attention in Paul (Galatians 3:31) and in later Reformers, such as Calvin and Luther, it presents a distorted image of God as well as the nature of Christ's mission if it is taken literally.[33]

In his person and mission, Jesus Christ represents the culmination of all that is positive in the prophetic, Davidic, Mosaic, and Son of Man traditions of Judaism.[34] He is the incarnation of the loving and forgiving Abba, not a burnt offering sent to appease an angry God. We, not God, are the ones who needed reconciliation. Moreover, in his person and mission, Jesus stands for the best of humanity, and not as one cursed for our sins or as one standing before a wrathful God in the place of sinful humanity.[35]

Justification

Justification was a key notion used by Paul to explain salvation to both the Galatians and Romans. Justification would eventually become central in Luther's debate with the Roman church and an important area of concern in the decrees of the Council of Trent (1563). Its earliest meaning seems to be the establishment of a person's cause as just in a court of law or in a business or some other kind of conflict. The just person becomes recognized as one dealing fairly with all, both externally and internally.[36]

For the Hebrew, it is unthinkable that sinful humans could ever really justify themselves before God. Only God could initiate the process and make it possible to be just in the sight of the Creator. In spite of this authentic tradition, however, a more legalistic notion—that one could, in fact, justify oneself in the sight of God by following laws—often prevailed in Judaism. This was certainly a chief source of conflict for Jesus, who insisted that loving service prevail over obedience to the scribal laws. For Jesus, the law was a means to becoming a loving, serving person. Those in conflict with him, however, often viewed the obedience of the law as an end in itself. This conflict was carried on among the early Christians. The importance of continuing to follow the Torah and the scribal laws was one of the first serious controversies of the early church.

The gospels seem to indicate that the early disciples saw Jesus as "the just one" (Acts 3:14), and that following him was the means of being justified before God. Jesus' person and cause had been justified before God in the resurrection; all those who now accepted him received the gift of justification before God. Paul tells the Romans of this gift: "But now the righteousness of God has been manifested...through faith in Jesus Christ for all who believe" (Romans 3:21–23). Paul sees justification as a gift from God that has been won by Jesus in the shedding of his blood for sin. Those who believe are therefore "justified freely by his grace through the redemption in Christ Jesus" (Romans 3:24). It is in Jesus that God is revealed as just, and through faith in Jesus that the disciples can appear just before God.[37]

Justification would, as we know, become an area of contention in the Reformation. Can salvation be merited? What is the value of good works for salvation? Need one accept the Roman church authority to be saved? Indeed, these questions have not been settled even today and are still a significant source of division among Christian churches.

Reconciliation

Another dimension of salvation is the goal of reconciling humankind with its maker and restoring the covenant between God and God's people. Paul tells the early Christian community in Corinth: "So whoever is in Christ is a new creation: the old things have passed away; behold, new things have come. And all this is from God, who has reconciled us to himself through Christ and given us the ministry of reconciliation, namely, God was reconciling the world to himself in Christ..." (2 Corinthians 5:17–20). Paul developed a theology wherein Jesus is a representative for us before God, reuniting us with the divine. Like the suffering servant in Isaiah and the Son of Man in Daniel, Jesus renews the ancient covenant.[38] His followers are to continue this work of reconciliation as the "ambassadors" of Jesus.

Liberation

Liberation, or giving of freedom, is another way of looking at salvation. Early in his ministry, Jesus is portrayed as identifying himself with the prophetic mission of freeing prisoners and liberating the oppressed (Luke 4:18). Matthew depicts Jesus as the new Moses, liberating his people in the new Exodus of Christian redemption.

Both John and Paul emphasize this theme of freedom. In John's gospel Jesus tells his disciples: "So if the Son set you free, you will indeed be free," and he assures them that the "truth has set you free" (John 8:32–36). And, indeed, Jesus' mission on earth did seem to free people from self-hatred, despair, fear, physical and psychological disabilities, oppression, and sinful ways of life.[39] Paul develops this theme in his letter to the Galatians. He tells them, "For you are called for freedom" (5:13), and "For freedom Christ set us free" (5:1). He then warns them that authentic freedom is not for selfishness but for loving service.[40] This theme of liberation has now taken on new political and social meaning and is the heart of a new and extremely influential liberation theology that will be discussed in the final chapter.

Patristic Interpretations

The biblical themes were carried forth during the patristic period and were often reinterpreted in terms of the Greek and Roman thought that was indigenous to the many Gentile converts entering the church. Here we will discuss some of the major themes of the patristic writing: the incarnation as redemption, divinization, victory through ransoming humankind from Satan, and the beginnings of the more juridical approach of satisfaction.

As we said in chapter ten, when we discussed the development of the early doctrines concerning Christ, the early fathers were much more concerned with the nature of Jesus Christ than they were with his saving actions. Their preoccupation with Christ's divinity and how this could be joined with humanity colored their approach to salvation. Thus, their discussion of redemption, even though it included the significance of the death and resurrection, often focused more on the saving power of the incarnation.

Many of the Fathers believed that we were saved more by the Logos becoming man than by any event in the life of Jesus. Clement of Alexandria's statement that "The Logos of God had become man so that you might learn from a man how a man may become God" was a commonly held belief among the fathers.[41] In addition, their concern for Christ being both God and man involved the very nature of salvation itself. "What was not assumed was not saved," and therefore salvation demanded that human nature be fully united to God in order to bring about redemption. Salvation, then, was often viewed both as restoration of what had been lost, as well as a new creation, a new deification of humanity.

Recapitulation

Irenaeus's theory of "recapitulation" is an excellent example of the central role incarnation plays in salvation. He argued that God's plan of salvation unfolds in three acts: the creation, the fall of human beings into sin, and the restoration of the world by Jesus Christ. God's purpose in creating was to share divinity with the world and with humanity. Adam's seduction, which Irenaeus seems to attribute to immaturity rather than malice, disrupted the plan. Moved by compassion, and not by wrath, God sent God's Son to be the new Adam so that he might restore or "recapitulate" the solidarity that God intended to have with humankind.[42] In assuming our human nature, said Irenaeus, God redeemed that nature and restored it to its original integrity. Redemption comes to our nature also by what Christ achieves in our human nature in his life, death, and resurrection. Irenaeus taught that the saving plan of God is "to sum up all things in Christ, in heaven and on earth (Ephesians 1:10).

Irenaeus's theory, which seems to be also reflected in the liturgies of his time as well in other patristic writings, accents the necessity of imitating Christ. God's cosmic plan called for the Logos to assimilate self to humans so that humans might, in turn, be united to God. By his obedience, especially by his obedience in his death on the cross, he negated all the damage done by Adam and provided justification and salvation for those who imitate him.[43]

Divinization

The Eastern fathers also liked to think of salvation in terms of divinization or deification, a notion with which many in the West would be uncomfortable. The West has always been more inclined to be juridical and legalistic in its approach to salvation, and not attracted to this more mystical approach of the East. The Eastern theological approach seems to reflect the Greek notion of God as the transcendent being more than the Hebrew God of history. It is a "high theology," wherein God is thought of as "sending down" the Son to take on human nature so that human beings might become like God.

Although the sinfulness of humanity is recognized in the Eastern tradition, for them the central human problem derived from the Fall is corruptibility in death. Thus Pelikan maintains that "the most widespread understanding of salvation in the Catholic church of the second and third centuries" was salvation from death and the gaining of eternal life.[44] Redemption overcomes this corruption in that, through Jesus, we become united to God, the incorruptible Spirit. The Eastern fathers were fond of speaking of this saving plan of God as "the economy" of salvation.

Victory Over the Devil

Another common salvation theme for the fathers was that of the victory over the devil. The early fathers took very seriously Jesus' struggle with Satan in the gospels. They attempted to use this drama as the central explanation for redemption, uniting this struggle with the gospel notion of ransom and concluding that the ransom has been indeed paid to Satan. In the writings of Origen, Gregory of Nyssa, and even Ambrose and Augustine we find variations on this interpretation. It was, no doubt, a highly allegorical interpretation for them, but it was often taken literally by the medieval mind. This view of the redemption as Jesus' victory prevailed until the middle ages, when it was replaced by Anselm's theory of satisfaction.

In the patristic allegory, Satan had gained certain proprietary rights over human beings as a result of the Fall. Origen developed this theory rather fully. In his drama, human beings had been under the power of Satan since the Fall, when humans sold themselves into slavery to the devil. The devil wrongly tried to take possession of Christ, but could not because Christ was without sin. In the process, the devil also lost possession of human beings. It was Christ who paid the ransom of his blood to liberate humankind and to defeat forever the forces of evil in the world.

Common in this approach was the notion that the redemption was achieved by tricking the devil. Gregory of Nyssa (d. 395) used the metaphor of fishing, suggesting that the divinity was the hook hidden in the bait, which was the humanity of Christ. When Satan went for the bait he was fooled and hooked by God, and his power over the world was defeated.[45] Origen wrote of how Jesus had been handed over by God to the devil, that master of death. It was only when the soul of Jesus was handed over as a ransom that the devil had to give up his possession of the human race.

Of course, not all the fathers pushed the metaphor to such bizarre limits. Gregory of Nazianzus (d. 389) thought that it was shameful to pay a ransom to the devil for all his tyranny, especially such an extravagant price as the blood of the Son of God.[46] Irenaeus settled for the more reasonable explanation that, while Satan had brought ignorance and darkness into the human heart, Jesus overcame all this as well as its effects of death and corruption by his passion. At the same time, Christ brought new life and truth to humans.[47] Irenaeus said that "to follow the Savior is to participate in salvation."[48] For some fathers, this seems to have meant participating in a salvation already accomplished. For others, salvation seems to have simply meant following the example of Jesus and listening to his teachings. This "exemplar" notion of salvation would recur later, especially in the nineteenth century in the thought of Protestant liberalism.

Satisfaction

Tertullian (c. 225), who wrote in Latin and seems to have been deeply influenced by Roman law, was most influential in bringing a more Western juridical slant to redemption theology. He developed the notion of satisfaction for sin, which he may have derived from Roman law. This law provided that, in private situations, amends could be made for not fulfilling an obligation, and that, in public matters, the court could decree a form of punishment. Tertullian, who did not explicitly connect satisfaction with the death of Christ, did point out that the Son of God died for sinners and thereby saved them from death.[49] When Tertullian did speak of satisfaction, it was more in the context of the Christian's way of making up to God for sin.[50]

It was Hilary who explicitly connected "satisfaction" with the death of Christ and who viewed the death as a sacrifice that made reparation to God on behalf of sinners.[51] (This later became a motif in the work of other fathers, such as Origen, Basil, Ambrose, and Augustine; in their works the death of Jesus was viewed as a satisfaction for sin.[52]) This notion of satisfaction would not become dominant, however, until the appearance of the great medieval theologian, Anselm of Canterbury.

Anselm

Anselm (d. 1109) wrote his famous treatise on redemption, *Cur Deus Homo*, in 1098 during his early years as archbishop of Canterbury. The work was actually finished during one of the exiles imposed upon him by the king as punishment for his views against lay investiture.[53] In this and several other works Anselm set down his well-known "satisfaction theory" of salvation, a theory that replaced the old "victory over Satan" approach and prevailed in Christian thought until modern times.

Anselm's theory of satisfaction has been often misinterpreted to mean that the crucifixion was the necessary means to satisfy the displeasure of an angry, vengeful, wrathful God, a God who required the death of his own Son to make up for the injustice of the sin of Adam.[54] Nothing could be more foreign to Anselm's dispassionate and highly reasonable "English" mentality, which was concerned with honor and love, and not expiation or ransom. If anything, Anselm had set out to put to rest the earlier notions of ransom, especially those concerning the transaction with the devil.

Much of *Cur Deus Homo* is, in fact, concerned with sin, and how the sinless Christ, because of his affinity with humans, could sacrifice himself for human sin. Convinced that faith and reason are mutually supportive, Anselm was confident that he could put together solid and absolutely certain arguments about the necessity of the cross to satisfy the justice of God. Moreover, it was his conviction that he could actually set aside the person of Jesus, as well as the events described in Scripture, and assemble a simple and lucid argument that could convince unbelievers as well as believers, the uneducated as well as the educated.[55] In actuality, Anselm's confidence was not far off, because his theory deeply influenced some of the greatest theologians (Aquinas, Luther, and Barth, to mention a few) and was the prevailing theory of salvation for nearly one thousand years.

As a medieval person caught up in the feudal system, Anselm thought of the universe as reasonable and orderly. This is the way creation was designed and it is the beauty of this order that gives such pleasure to the mind. Humans have been created as rational so that they can enjoy this beauty, and so that they can discriminate between good and evil, obey God's will, and keep things in order. Conversely, disobeying God's will disturbs the order and the beauty of the world.[56] The feudal system of the time also placed great value on honor. The Lord, strongly bonded in solidarity with his vassals, was in an honorable position, representing public order and peace and responsible for maintaining this public order for all.[57]

Anselm sets out to explain his theory, apparently under the impression that he is a mere middle person opening to others what God had implanted in his reason. Directly addressing his monastic companion (with the unlikely name of Boso), Anselm proceeds to relate how sin clouds the vision of the beautiful and orderly universe and offends the honor of the Lord God. Because this offense is indeed against God, it is an infinite offense and cannot be satisfied by mere finite human beings. Proper satisfaction, by necessity, could only be performed by one who could perform infinite satisfaction; namely, the Son of God. The satisfaction is not to appease an angry God, nor does it mean that the Son substitutes for sinful people. Satisfaction for Anselm is rather a restoration of harmony and beauty to a world disfigured through sin. Just as it was disturbed by an abuse of love and freedom, so it is restored by Christ who freely and lovingly sacrifices himself for us.

Abelard

Peter Abelard (d. 1142), another medieval theologian, put love rather than honor or justice at the center of his thinking on salvation. Very much influenced by the Johannine tradition, Abelard viewed the human problem as lovelessness rather than disorder. Redemption, therefore, comes from Christ's endurance of suffering out of love. As John writes, "No one has greater love than this, to lay down one's life for one's friends" (John 15:13). Jesus tells his followers to love each other in the same fashion, and gives them the power of a love that for all time enables people to put aside their fears and act as children of God.[58] In contrast to Anselm's thought, where redemption seems to be a transaction necessarily involving satisfaction, here it is a free act of love and mercy on the part of God and is carried out through God's Son.

Abelard has been accused of approaching salvation in a purely subjective fashion, limited to the emotions. Some think that it was his approach that influenced Friedrich Schleiermacher's (d. 1834) shift to "feeling" as central to salvation in nineteenth-century Protestant theology.[59] In actuality, however, there is an objective dimension to Abelard's notion of love. He argued that the love of Christ had an enduring effect on the world, and that it was "infused into his followers" as a continually creative force. As Teilhard often indicated, love is a universal energy that draws all things to God in Christ. It is not a mere inward feeling, but a transforming and liberating force that can transform the world. Perhaps that is why Schillebeeckx can say: "Essentially and substantially salvation is love."[60]

The "Classic" Position

In the early 1930s, Gustaf Aulén attempted to put theories on salvation in perspective and to ascertain what the truly classic position is.[61] Aulen maintained that the traditional division of redemption theories into "objective" (where redemption has in some fashion been already achieved) and "subjective" (where redemption is in some way applied to an individual) is not accurate. It was his position that the more accurate categories to describe the two mainstreams of Christian tradition on redemption are "Classic" and "Latin." The classic theory, according to Aulén, is that of the fathers who viewed Christ as "victor" over the devil. Aulén recognizes that one must demythologize the medieval images of Satan and ransom, but he maintains that salvation is indeed a dramatic struggle between good and evil. In this drama, God is the principal actor and, through Christ, conquers the demonic forces in the world.

It was Aulén's position that Tertullian, Cyprian, and others developed the "Latin" tradition of satisfaction. This culminated in the work of Anselm, and from then on a rationalistic and legalistic approach to redemption replaced the classic patristic tradition. Aulén maintains that Luther carried forward the classic tradition in his writings and should be credited with its restoration.[62] Aulén seems to suggest that this classic theory should be reclaimed over both the Anselmian theory that helped generate a "merit" system of justification in Catholicism, and nineteenth-century liberal Protestantism with its emphasis on sentiment and feeling.

Aulén's work certainly made an impact, especially among Protestants. Today, however, some feel that he did not give Anselm a fair reading and overlooked many departures from the "classic" theory in the works of Luther.[63] For many, the image of Christ as "victor" is medieval, and does not fit the contemporary images of the historical Jesus. Others would point to the irony that, several years after Aulén's work on redemption as victory over evil, the world was plunged into a war where there was enormous destruction and a demonic holocaust of the innocent.[64]

Further Developments

As we have seen, the church has never formally defined salvation, but has allowed multiple interpretations to develop within liturgy, creedal statements, and theology. Generally, these interpretations carried forward a number of biblical themes and reshaped these themes according .to the philosophical and cultural framework of the time.

This development seems to have centered around two main notions: 1) victory over Satan, which dominated from the patristic time until the middle ages; 2) Anselm's theory of satisfaction, which prevailed in the tradition, especially among Catholics, until recent times. In modern times the pace of the development of redemption theories hastened. There is only space here to mention some of the main trends of the recent past and give some indication of current emphases.

Some Important Directions

The formulation of redemption theories often places emphasis on either the objective or subjective dimension. In nineteenth-century liberal Protestantism, for example, the subjective dimension of salvation was emphasized. Schleiermacher, one of the most influential theologians of that time, reacted against both the Enlightenment's emphasis on reason and Emmanuel Kant's stress on moral judgment with regard to religion. Schleiermacher preferred to root his discussion of salvation in human experience, in particular in the "feeling of absolute dependence." He also rejected the Western emphasis on the death of Jesus as something owed to God as atonement for sin. Instead, he chose to stress the importance of the historical Jesus who serves as an example and who establishes a community that feels dependent on him. Here salvation seems to be something that happens to people more than a redeeming act by God.[65]

Karl Barth, the great theologian of Protestant orthodoxy, reacted against this subjective trend and against how Christianity had accommodated itself to culture in the nineteenth century. He insisted on the radical transcendence of God and of Christ's message. He rooted salvation not in personal experience but in the Jesus of history who revealed God's gracious election of all humankind to participate in his kingdom. Here the atonement of Jesus is a fulfilling work, linked to the whole saving process that has gone on since creation. Salvation is objectively gained for all, but subjectively possessed only in costly discipleship and concern for justice.[66]

Paul Tillich's theory of redemption arose out of the post-war period's existential approach to reality. Tillich reacted against the transcendent approach of Barth and proposed a theology of culture that would better link salvation to the experience of the world. For him, the problem was not sin so much as it was alienation from God, whom he describes as "the ground of being." Salvation for Tillich means reunion with the ground of being through Christ, who is the "New Being." Here, salvation by the Christ seems to be more of a metaphysical achievement than one of a free choice on the part of the historical Jesus to give himself in life and death for others.[67] Even though Tillich stresses the objectivity of redemption by the New Being, his constant emphasis on faith as "ultimate concern" links him to the subjectivity of Schleiermacher.

Current Emphasis on Experience

The contemporary person often feels autonomous and self-sufficient and really not in need of being saved from sin or estrangement. Theories based on "ransom" or "satisfaction," or even "re-grounding in being," often have little relevance to the contemporary person. At the same time, there are many constraints and dangers from which people today would like to be "saved." There is also often a feeling of helplessness in the face of these perils, an awareness that there is little that one can do on one's own. There are the threats of nuclear destruction, environmental catastrophe, the spread of violence and war, the menace of drugs, the hazard of AIDS, and the constant spread of hunger, homelessness, and disease. There is the contemporary experience of oppression on the part of women, minorities, gays, the disabled, and ethnic groups.

Today's world is generally not seen as populated by evil spirits, or "powers and principalities." It is not so much a battlefield where God wages war with the devil, or a fallen world looking for restoration. Rather, for many it is a world often plagued with addictions, a world with social and political structures that oppress and destroy. Often the contemporary experience calls for salvation in terms of healing and the struggle for justice. Any theories of salvation today will have to be relevant somehow to these contemporary experiences or they will find little response. Moreover, such theories will have to go beyond the individualized version of salvation that has been so common in both Catholicism and Protestantism. They will need to advocate a solidarity with people throughout the world and a concern for bringing them justice and peace.

Redemption today is often not thought of as coming from some remote God who sends a Savior "from above." Instead, it is seen as coming from a God within who is "part of" and " along with" people in their sins and suffering. This is the God who was personified in the historical Jesus, the God whose Spirit acts in the risen Christ to free people in all their personal and social struggles. As Schillebeeckx points out, salvation that is not connected to human experience loses its meaning and usefulness.[68]

Although salvation is initiated by God as a gift given in love and mercy, it "happens" in human experience where it is received and lived out in our human experience of nature, social life, cultural life, and religion.[69] Indeed, at the very heart of Schillebeeckx's extensive work on Jesus Christ seems to be an effort to discover how the historical Jesus was experienced as God's offer of salvation, as well as how the risen Lord brought this experience to fulfillment in his disciples through the resurrection event. Using the best in contemporary exegesis, Schillebeeckx attempts to uncover how this experience of salvation in the Christian Scriptures can be a guide for understanding salvation today.[70]

It would seem that a useful theology of salvation today would also link creation with redemption and view both as continuing processes. Such a theology would also value the saving mission of the historical Jesus as well as the redeeming power of the risen Lord. Here Jesus Christ would not only perform salvific acts, but would in fact *be* salvation in his person. Jesus the Savior is indeed the Son of God who chose to live and die for others, and who, in his resurrection, was glorified forever as the Savior of the world.

Is Jesus Christ Unique?

The recognition of religious pluralism and the need for religions to dialogue respectfully and learn from one another have raised a crucial question about Jesus as Savior. Is Jesus Christ *the* Savior through whom all humankind has been saved, or is he but one among a number of saviors that God has chosen? Some would feel that only the latter position provides a framework for open and fruitful dialogue among Christians and other religions.[71]

Certainly Catholicism has moved beyond its former exclusivist position that salvation resides only in the church. It was clearly stated at Vatican II that to be saved one must sincerely search for God and lead a good life. It was recognized that God's truth and salvation is accessible in other churches, other religions, and even outside of organized religions altogether.

At the same time, the council did not pull back from the traditional notion that salvation was gained for all by Jesus Christ. As Carl Braaten notes, the apostolic tradition in the Scriptures as well as the doctrinal pronouncements of the ancient church proclaim that Jesus is Lord and God and that he is worshiped as the Savior.[72] This makes it most difficult to view all these testimonies as mere confessional language or the exaggerated language of lovers.[73]

Nor does it seem plausible that the Christian belief in the uniqueness of Jesus as Savior is simply an enculturated statement from a different time and place and no longer relevant to today's more pluralistic and evolutionary period. Schillebeeckx points out that Jesus was exalted in resurrection and uniquely marked by God as the Savior of the world.[74] That was the message that the early communities preached to the world, and it was the same message that gave birth to Christianity. It is unlikely that religious pluralism or the laudable goal of interreligious dialogue will alter that good news.

We might conclude then, that while Christians have no grounds to feel that they are superior to those in other religions, they do have the prerogative to proclaim that Jesus Christ is their Lord and God, and that his life, death, and resurrection ushered in a new creation and somehow touched all people everywhere.

Summary

Although Christians have always looked to Jesus as their Savior, how he has saved us has been interpreted differently throughout the centuries. Yet, at the heart of it all, there seems to have been the recognition that through his life, death, and resurrection Jesus did reveal and bring to a new level of experience the saving power of God.

There have generally been two dimensions to this experience throughout the history of this belief: a saving *from* and a saving *for*. The Scriptures, the writings of the fathers, and the writings of theologians have, in different models (whether it be ransom from the devil, satisfaction, or some other model), stressed that Jesus Christ saved his people *from* fear, sin, attachment to things other than God, oppression, and even death itself. But God's people have also been saved *for* something. They have been saved for reconciliation and renewed covenant with God, for faithful service to others, especially the poor and outcast, and ultimately for life eternal in resurrection. And their model in all this is Jesus Christ, who in his very person *is* salvation.

Each age, according to its own needs and insights, seems to have a unique interpretation of salvation. In the next chapter, we will examine what might perhaps be the most significant shift in the understanding of salvation that has appeared in centuries. It is an interpretation that has emerged from the suffering and deprivation of the Third World. It is a cry from the "have-nots" and the dispossessed to Jesus Christ as their Liberator.

Questions for Reflection and Discussion

1. "What is beyond dispute is the fact that the first Christians pro-

claimed Jesus not merely as risen but as saving." If you agree with this statement, cite passages from the gospels and from St. Paul that reflect such early belief.

2. What, if anything, does "gospel salvation" add to the Hebrew notion of salvation?

3. Explain the differences among "ransom," "atonement," "justification," and "reconciliation."

4. What was Anselm's basic argument in his "satisfaction theory"?

5. What are some of the things from which people want to be "saved" today? Can "Christian salvation" somehow speak to these needs of our time?

CHAPTER TWELVE

The Liberator

So far we have examined many perspectives on the person of Jesus Christ. We have seen him as an actual person living an authentically human life at a specific time in history. We looked at Jesus as a teacher, prophet, healer, advocate for women, and as a person who loved the earth as God's creation. We have discussed how his early followers interpreted Jesus' birth, life, and death in light of their experience of his resurrection and with a faith that proclaimed him to be the Son of God, their messiah. Attention was given to the doctrinal formulations of the early councils, as the church of the first centuries strove to settle the many controversies over the divinity and humanity of Jesus Christ. In chapter eleven we reflected on the varied ways that Jesus' followers have looked upon him as their Savior over the centuries. Now we end by looking at one of the most recent, and perhaps most urgently needed images of Jesus for the next millennium, Jesus as Liberator. This image focuses on the strong yet compassionate side of Jesus Christ that struggles for peace and justice, is in solidarity with the poor and oppressed, and promises social, economic, and spiritual liberation.

We will begin by looking at this image in its sources: the struggles and suffering in the Third World and the formal religious reflections on these struggles in liberation theology. This theology seems to have arisen out of the oppression of Christians in Latin America. It reflects their hope in Jesus and his gospel as a means to overcome repression and injustice. We will discuss in some detail how liberation theology reinterprets the Jesus of history, his teachings on the kingdom, and his death and resurrection. Finally, we will consider how this image of Jesus is being used as a norm for liberating action, and describe how this movement is now rapidly spreading into other parts of the world.

Source of Liberator Image

The image of Jesus as Liberator emerges from Latin America, an area that for hundreds of years has known severe poverty, oppression, and violence. The story of the poor in these countries often has been a story of plunder, genocide, deprivation, and inequality, from the time of the Spanish Conquistadores four hundred years ago until the oligarchies and tyrannical governments so common in the modern era. In the early sixteenth century, Bartolomé de las Casas, a colonial official who later became a courageous churchman, sided with the Indians. He wrote passionate and indignant letters to Charles I, the King of Spain, about horrible atrocities where natives were hunted down with bloodhounds for sport, of how Indian men were taken from their families and made to work in the metal mines until they died from disease or exhaustion, and how the young maidens were kidnapped from their homes and forced into the harems of the wealthy colonialists.[1]

Similarly, present-day missionaries recount contemporary atrocities. Millions of peasants and urban residents are subject to starvation, inadequate medical care, dire poverty, unemployment, and bombings. Those who complain or rebel are often taken off in the night and executed by death squads.[2]

Various images of Jesus have been operative in these oppressed cultures. The image of Jesus the heavenly monarch has often been misused by the powerful to justify their tyrannical exercise of power over the natives and the peasants. This image was also abused by monarchs and the wealthy to justify their "God-given" right to pillage the native people and to destroy anyone who might challenge their power.[3] Even today many see no irony in attending church services and being orthodox Christian believers while at the same time abusing and oppressing the voiceless masses in their midst.

In the past a number of images of Jesus have prevailed among the poor in these areas. Missionaries often gave the native peoples images with which they could identify: Christ the prisoner of his enemy, one suffering at the hands of cruel persecutors, a defenseless innocent who was humiliated and killed, or a young person cut off before he had a chance to live out his life. Often this was the image of a passive, nonresistant Jesus, offering his sufferings to the Father and preparing to be in Paradise.[4]

There is, however, another image of Jesus that has been within the faith consciousness in Latin America, the image of a just and compassionate Jesus who was indignant over oppression and who confronted the religious and political leaders of his time.[5] Now this image is beginning to emerge strongly from the basic Christian communities throughout this region. These basic communities are local gatherings of Christians who come together to pray, to reflect on the gospels, and to consider how they might act to confront those who subjugate them. Their image of Jesus is of a person who identifies with the outcast and who stands with conviction and power against those who oppress them. Leonardo Boff has called this image Jesus the Liberator, the incarnation of a God who helps people struggle against enormous odds for peace and justice.

Liberation Theology

The theology surrounding this liberating image of Jesus, unlike much of traditional and progressive theology, refuses to accept the "status quo" of oppressive social structures. It takes a prophetic stance that points out the injustices that are incompatible with the teachings of Jesus. Moreover, it proposes imitation of Jesus in his vigorous action on behalf of the persecuted.[6]

This "liberation theology" seems to have been precipitated by Vatican II, which moved the church away from a posture of isolation from the world to one of solidarity with today's poor and suffering. The post-Vatican II church planted its feet firmly in the world and began to be more closely identified with the millions of poor who were without food, shelter, and health care. This commitment inspired the Latin American bishops gathered at historic meetings in Medellín, Colombia, in 1968 and in Puebla, Mexico, in 1979 to deplore the oppression and to declare that the church of Jesus Christ was in solidarity with the poor of the world. In between these two crucial meetings, a worldwide synod of Roman Catholic bishops in 1971 reminded the church that followers of Jesus should follow his lead in being in solidarity with the victims of abuse. This synod also pointed out that action on behalf of liberation from oppression was of the very essence of the church's mission.[7]

Liberation theology found its initial formulation in the now classic book by Gustavo Gutiérrez, *A Theology of Liberation*.[8] This was followed by an avalanche of writing on liberation theology, with a wide spectrum of views on how this approach to theology is to be understood and lived. In spite of this plurality, however, there seems to be a general agreement that liberation theology is "from below," coming from the lived experience of the gospel poor, and that it is committed to action against oppression and injustice.

At first, liberation theology concentrated on critiquing traditional approaches to Christian theology and pointing out the urgency for connecting the gospel with action on behalf of social justice. In these initial stages little attention was given to where the person of Jesus Christ fit into the liberation perspective. Eventually this deficiency was overcome by the work of theologians such as Sobrino, Segundo, Boff, Galilea, Ellacuría, and others.[9] In the following section we will explore some of the themes common in this developing Christology of liberation.

Concern for the Historical Jesus

Liberation theology's approach to Jesus shifts away from the classical "Logos" Christology of the early councils and focuses on the historical Jesus that underlies the gospels. Many liberation theologians maintain that the Logos theology of Nicea and Chalcedon bears too heavily the stamp of ancient Greek philosophy. They argue that this classical approach to Jesus is simply too abstract and speculative to be useful in confronting injustice and oppression. These theologians also criticize the traditional approach to Jesus for being too preoccupied with his nature, and not attentive enough to his saving mission, both in the past and present.[10] The Logos Christology, they point out, served a useful purpose in preserving both the divinity and humanity of Jesus Christ when these were challenged. This approach, however, came out of an individualistic society and appealed mainly to elite intellectuals. Today there are other pressing challenges, such as the oppression of and violence done to the poor. Thus the challenge of Christology today is to come to an understanding of Jesus that will enable his followers to answer the cries heard around the world for justice.

Liberation theology, therefore, seems to move away from the "high Christology," which accents God's coming "from above" and the divinity of Christ. In what has been called a "low theology" or a "theology from below," liberation theology focuses more on the humanity of Jesus and on his struggle to overcome oppression and injustice. One liberation theologian has remarked that today we need a "human logos," a flesh and blood Jesus with whom the poor and those walking with them can identify and from whom strength and courage can be derived to face the dangers of political and social protest.[11]

The inadequacy of past doctrines on Christ is not the only reason for renewed interest in the historical Jesus. Liberation theologians also seem concerned with reclaiming the memory of Jesus' own mission so that it can be carried on in the present. They hope that, if parallels can be found between the social struggles in his time and ours, Jesus' disciples will be able to learn better how to follow his example in dealing with these difficulties.[12] Jesus had to deal with corruption and oppression, just as many do today. His message and actions, therefore, have a certain universal element that can be applied to our current struggles.[13] The gospels themselves reveal the early Christian communities reinterpreting the teaching and practice of Jesus in order to deal with the problems they encountered. Similarly, today's disciples can regain the memory of Jesus and use it as a model for their mission in a world torn by violence and injustice. It is the historical Jesus who can concretely put people in touch with the means and method for liberating others.

The return to the historical Jesus also serves to put us in touch with the humanness of Jesus. Past Christology often put so much stress on the divinity of Jesus that many today seem to believe that Jesus only appeared to be human. From such a perspective, Jesus can be viewed as one who represents a God who stands at a distance from human suffering. To emphasize the historical Jesus, however, is to encounter a God gradually revealed in a person who is passionately involved in life. This is a personal God who can enter into human sufferings and reveal how people can be victorious over suffering and death, triumphant over those who persecute the innocent.[14] This is a God who is progressively revealed through the human decisions and actions of Jesus as a God who cares, a God who is actively involved in the historical struggle against injustice. Jesus is seen as a man who was deeply involved in the human scheme of things, a person who had to feel his way, like any other person, in ambiguity and even darkness. At the same time, in his fidelity and unswerving commitment to people, Jesus revealed the possibilities that exist for humans and offered a glimpse of what people can be at their best. He modeled how one might deal nobly with failure and disappointment, and how one's radical confidence in God would be ultimately vindicated.

It should be clear that this emphasis on the humanity of Jesus in no way denies his divinity. Rather, it sees the divinity as gradually being revealed in the history of a human life. Here Jesus gradually comes into the fullness of divine sonship, and thus serves as the model for others who aspire to be one with God.[15] Jesus' story becomes a human story, and thus serves as an inspiration for others who also experience suffering, pain, and even death for their opposition to tyranny.

The Problematic Search

Most liberation theologians seem to realize the hazards of searching for the historical Jesus. Few are so naïve as to think that they can find much biographical data about Jesus in the gospels or even recover much of his exact words and deeds. Most seem comfortable with many of the findings of the historical-critical approach to the gospels, and are satisfied with discovering the "kinds of things" that Jesus said and did that seem to be the substratum of the gospels.

Nonetheless, the impression is given at times that some liberation theologians are taking the gospel stories too literally and are making claims about the historical Jesus without sufficient evidence.[16] Indeed, in their search for the historical Jesus some of these theologians do need to be cautioned to avoid the pitfalls of the "searchers" of the last century, who often tended to make Jesus into their own image. In the extreme, for the purposes of rebellion, Jesus could be caricatured as an armed militant, deviously plotting the overthrow of the Roman government. Fortunately, the majority of liberation theologians avoid such extremes and generally shy away from the theories that Jesus was a supporter of the Zealots. Nor do these theologians commonly portray Jesus as one who had a concrete plan for social and political reform.[17]

A Listening Theology

A key method for discovering the historical Jesus in liberation theology entails listening to the poor as they relate the gospels to their experience of oppression. In a way, this approach recaptures the early Christian community spirit of applying the memory of Jesus to the daily experiences of their lives. Some of these early communities connected Jesus' teachings with their own persecution by the Pharisees or the Romans. Others attempted to apply his message to the critical questions connected with extending the gospel message to the Gentiles. The very construction of the gospels seems to reflect this process of a Christology "from below."[18]

This same phenomenon of seeing the message of Jesus in the light of modern conflicts comes through in liberation theology. One has only to read such moving books as *The Gospel According to Solentiname* or *Through Her Eyes* to become aware of the rich, new insights that are being brought to Christian consciousness today.[19] At the same time, it would seem necessary that these reflections be seen alongside the findings of biblical criticism, lest they become purely subjective and imaginative images of Jesus. Subjective insights on the gospels might be useful for promoting liberation, but they may have little connection with the Jesus of history or his original message.

Liberation theologians are sometimes accused of placing so much emphasis on the historical Jesus and his teachings on freedom and justice that they neglect the Christ of faith and the more traditional emphases on his divinity and redeeming mission. In response to this charge, Jon Sobrino answers that he sees the historical Jesus and the Christ of faith in continuity, the one coming to fullness of the other. It is through personal access to the Jesus of history than one gets access to the Christ of faith.[20] It is for this reason that liberation theologians are not generally satisfied with the Bultmannian approach to Jesus, which places little value on Jesus as a historical person and concentrates rather on discovering the Christian "message." Liberation theology wants, instead, to relate to a real person who can inspire them in their struggle. The message, or kerygma, is not enough. As Boff cleverly remarks: "In Bultmann's theology Christ is not the Word that was made flesh but flesh that was made Word."[21]

Was Jesus Political?

The activity of the historical Jesus is extremely important to liberation theologians. If he is to be a model for seeking social reform, one obvious question needs to be asked: Was Jesus political? It seems apparent that Jesus was not politically militant in the modern sense.[22] The gospels give us no indication that he engaged in disputes about the Roman occupation of his land, or that he devised some revolutionary program for his followers to carry out. Even though Jesus himself was probably crucified for political crimes, there is no evidence that such charges were true. Moreover, none of his followers was arrested with him, which certainly would have been the case had he actually been viewed as an insurrectionist. All the efforts by scholars to somehow link Jesus with the Zealot movement, if such a movement even existed at the time, have been unpersuasive.[23] There are no uprisings linked with Jesus' name or his teachings, and the later revolutions of the late 60s and early second century did not involve Christians. Making Jesus out to be an insurrectionist of his time, then, is not something that can be verified in the Scriptures. It is anachronistic and a distortion of his teachings of love, compassion, and forgiveness, to portray him in terms of a modern freedom fighter.[24]

After all this is said, however, it is still possible to see a very real political dimension to Jesus' teachings and actions. As Ellacuría has put it: "Jesus engaged in what was primarily religious activity; but it could not help appear to be political as well to those who held religious and political power."[25] It has to be kept in mind that the distinction between the secular and the sacred, the religious and the political was not as clear then as it is today. Many Jews still longed for a theocratic form of government where religion and politics were integrated. The Roman occupation of Palestine had both political and religious implications for them. Insurrections by Jewish rebels were religio-political actions, and crucifixions by the Romans carried both meanings. There is even a blending of politics and religion in the religious leaders. The high priests were appointed by Rome, and both they and the Sadducees were known to be collaborators with the Romans.

Jesus was born and raised in this highly charged religio-political situation. He grew up in Galilee, the northern province led by the corrupt Herodian family. This was an area inhabited by many displaced persons and tenant farmers. Rebellion against the burdensome taxes and repression gave the Galileans a reputation for being troublemakers. As for Jesus' attitude toward the Roman occupation of his land, it would be hard to imagine that he did not share the resentment and desire for freedom so prevalent among his people. To portray him as a naïve preacher moving about unaware of the religious and political oppression surrounding him would certainly be unrealistic.

Jesus of Nazareth was a conflictual person, and most of his confrontations had political implications. Early on he is described as being in conflict with the people of his own synagogue when he identified himself with the prophetic tradition. These must have been seriously threatening words if they provoked his own villagers to want to throw him off a cliff. Matthew portrays Jesus as telling the crowds and his disciples not to follow the example of the scribes and the Pharisees who lay heavy burdens on people's shoulders and make no efforts to be of help. In the gospels, he calls these leaders "hypocrites," "blind guides," and "white-washed tombs"—certainly inflammatory comments for the intelligentsia and political leadership of his religion.

At that time, to disturb the Jewish leadership was to also disturb the Romans, who wanted matters to be uncontentious and calm among the peoples they dominated. The passion stories also reveal that, throughout his public life, Jesus had built up tremendous animosity among the Sanhedrin, the Sadducees, and the high priests of the Temple, many of whom were nothing more than pawns of the Romans. His confrontations with these leaders had decidedly political implications for those within both religious and imperial circles.

If the way Jesus is portrayed as standing up to the high priests and to Pilate himself is any indication of the confrontational posture of Jesus, he most certainly must have been perceived as being politically dangerous. He publicly defied Herod, calling him a "fox," told his followers to give Caesar nothing more than the coin of tribute, challenged the corruption of Temple practices and worship, and even predicted the ultimate destruction of the Temple if such abuses continued. He characterized the hated Samaritan as being more compassionate and charitable than his own priests and doctors of the law. His triumphant entry into Jerusalem, as well as his riotous disruption of the Temple money exchange and sales area, deeply disturbed the Jewish and Roman authorities alike. Many among the Roman elite and the Jewish Sadducees may have seen their sumptuous lifestyles threatened by Jesus' outburst. Here Jesus was attacking the banking and commercial aspects of the Temple—an action that had serious religious and political implications.[26] In many ways, this was the culmination of many confrontations that Jesus had with the established order. It seems as though it was soon after this that he was arrested and put to death.

Although Jesus did not have a political program, he did teach a religious message that was aimed at the ultimate goal of all political activity, "the betterment of the human condition."[27] It was a message aimed at the sins of violence and injustice, a message meant to liberate both the oppressed and the oppressor. It was a message of universal love, even of one's enemy, of compassion for the outcast, and of forgiveness for unjust offenses. Jesus' words on the cross, as offered by Luke, underline the evil of unjust persecution and yet do not allow the bitterness to spread to the victim: "Father, forgive them, they know not what they do" (Luke 23:34).

Jesus' teachings also proclaimed the "blessedness" of the poor and the marginalized, blessedness because both he and the Father had taken up their cause. Jesus' outreach to the outcasts was designed to restore their dignity and self-esteem. To empower the masses in such a manner was indeed revolutionary. No doubt it presented a significant threat to those who disenfranchised the poor through religious and political domination. Jesus' prediction to his disciples that following him and his message would bring division among their synagogues and families, as well as persecution upon themselves, indicates the "dangerous" element of his teachings and actions. His own eventual execution as a political threat is a stark symbol of how threatening empowerment of the poor can be to those who see power only in terms of tyrannical domination. Furthermore, his teaching about a God of love and forgiveness was not acceptable to those who used a God of domination and destruction to intimidate the masses. And although Jesus refused to accept the political messiahship that many wanted to force upon him, he seems to have, instead, pursued a serving and self-sacrificing messiahship to which he felt called by his Father.[28] Such aspirations were totally unacceptable to those in power at the time.

The story of the freeing of Barabbas in place of Jesus also seems to symbolize that Jesus' non-violent confrontation was viewed as even more dangerous than the violent terrorism of a Zealot.[29] As Jesus stands before Pilate, the power of a kingdom not of this world seems to over-shadow the imperial power of Rome. In the passion stories Pilate had the imperial power to condemn Jesus to death, and yet seems dwarfed next to this Nazarean who stands before him beaten but unbowed, with an energy that is incomprehensible to the "mighty" procurator.

Jesus, then, never claimed to be an anarchist or a political revolutionary, but he did bring "good news" to the poor and marginalized, the kind of good news that cried out for social change. His message and ministry heralded the human dignity of all people and set in motion "a dynamism of socio-political change, for his time and for all history to come."[30] He gave worship only to the Father and not to the totalitarian power of the imperial and religious leaders of his time. He proclaimed a universal salvation for people that went far beyond either Jewish nationalism or Roman imperialism.[31] And for refusing to back down on these radical positions when threatened with execution, Jesus was scourged and crucified as "the king of the Jews."

In the Prophetic Tradition

Jesus' prophetic role also had its political implications. Luke indicates that Jesus identified himself early on with the prophetic tradition of Isaiah in bringing good news to the poor, release to captives, and freedom for the oppressed (Luke 4:18–19). Like the prophets of old, he lived austerely, had no official position in the religious or political establishments, and no membership in the parties of his time. Instead, he stands out as a charismatic figure who challenges and confronts. Apparently, Jesus was perceived by those who heard him as being in the tradition of Elijah, Jeremiah, and John the Baptist, all figures who challenged the corrupt leaders and institutions of their time. Even though he does not attempt to bring about structural change directly, he points out with prophetic indignation how inconsistent social disorder is with the will of God, and he challenges the abusers of the people.[32]

Religious and political structures that oppressed and caused poverty and suffering were unmasked by Jesus as sinful. Jesus challenged riches that were gained at the expense of others, and he pointed out how the wealthy were in grave jeopardy of self-destruction. Riches were not a blessing from God, as conventional wisdom had so often claimed. Too often they had been gained by making others destitute. Moreover, Jesus did not see poverty as a punishment from God but as a common result of subjugation. He strongly criticized those who caused such deprivation, and he offered the poor liberation through the power of God. Indeed, his words and actions must have been perceived as a menacing attack on both the religious and political leaders, who lived comfortably at the expense of others.

Jesus actually went beyond the traditional prophet's role. He did not claim any special call or visions, nor did he claim to communicate hidden truths. He openly proclaimed the love and intimacy he had experienced with Abba.[33] It might be said that he brought the prophetic tradition to its full climax. He would be the last of the great prophets.

Preference for the Poor

An important aspect of the historical Jesus for the liberation theologians is his own personal poverty and his identification with those who suffer deprivation. He had left the security of a craftsman's life and took to the road on a mission of preaching, healing, and service to others. Jesus had experienced first hand the plight of the common folk in his own tiny village of Nazareth and in the towns and villages that he visited throughout Palestine. He knew the frustrations and anguish of tenant farmers who barely eked out a living. These people often lived in fear of not being able to pay the exorbitant taxes and land mortgages, a crime often punished by being sold into slavery. He had witnessed the misery of the many who had become displaced persons under the Roman regime, as well as the suffering of the handicapped and diseased who did not have adequate health care.

The peasants in Central and Latin America see the circumstances of Jesus' times as parallel to their own situations. Millions live in dire poverty and often in fear of imprisonment or even death if they do not do what is required of them. Many are also keenly aware of the compassion that Jesus had for the marginal and the outcasts of his time, and those who lacked the basic necessities of life. These Christians somehow feel that Jesus understands their plight. They know how he reached out to people with compassion, concern, and healing. Moreover, they are convinced that they can expect the same kind of support and favor from the risen Lord in the crises that confront them daily. In imitation of Jesus, many of the liberation theologians live simple lives among the impoverished, and they identify with their struggles as friends.

Blessed Are the Poor

Jesus proclaimed that the poor were indeed blessed by God, and that there were indeed reasons for the poor to be happy. This, according to liberation theology, does not imply a naïve or simplistic idealization of poverty. There is nothing glamorous, much less blessed about the squalor and destitution in which so many in the world today have to live. Poverty is an evil that generally includes hunger, suffering, rejection, and anguish. It is neither a gift from God nor a condition willed by God so that people might gain heaven. Poverty is an evil sustained and often caused by the greed of the wealthy.[34] To tell the poor: "Don't worry; be happy" can well be taken as an insult.

If poverty is not blessed, then what are we to make of the beatitude: "Blessed are the poor"? First, it is important to note that Jesus described the poor as blessed, not poverty. The people who find themselves in poverty can consider themselves blessed in that God loves them, gives them strength to carry on, and can be counted on for support in their struggle for liberation. The poor are blessed, "happy," because God is in their midst. This is a central notion in liberation theology. For them, the life of Jesus bears witness that God always has and always will dwell in a unique manner among the poor. As Bishop Helder Camara has taught, the poor have a privileged position with God, especially in view of the fact that God became one of them and experienced their lot firsthand in Jesus of Nazareth, and continues to be in their midst.[35] In Jesus, God somehow struggles for justice with the poor, suffers with them, dies with them, and brings them to new life.

This unique preference that God has for the poor is one of the main reasons why liberation theologians see the poor as a primary resource for discovering Jesus Christ. To go into the midst of the faithful poor and to listen to them is to hear the Christ once again suffering oppression, rejection, torture, and death. It is to encounter the same Christ who has given hope and courage to the poor during centuries of repression, from the genocide and pillage of the Conquistadores to the ruthlessness of contemporary dictators. One can meet Jesus the Liberator in the voiceless of society, the exploited, the unemployed, the pushed aside. From the poor come prophetic voices who demand the very equity and justice for which Jesus labored and died. In marginal people, Jesus is found newly incarnated and in a contemporary confrontation with social and political evils. In the "outcasts," Jesus continues to carry on his mission of liberation.

God "poured out" the self, divested the self, and came to dwell as a workman in the original incarnation. Today, this process of "incarnation" continues amid the millions of the world's impoverished. Jesus died at the hands of those who grew to hate him for exposing the corruption and greed of the wealthy and for his solidarity with their victims. From the liberation perspective, Jesus continues this same mission today among those who are in need and those who give up their lives that others may be free.

Ministering with the Poor

Jesus not only worked among the poor, he also chose many of his disciples from among their ranks. Because they had little to which they were attached, perhaps Jesus believed they would be more free to move about with him and carry on his mission after his death. It would be the poor who would predominate in the first Christian communities. Perhaps this is why so many were able to move about the empire anonymously, have access to the large masses of poor in many areas, and know how to effectively communicate the gospel to them.[36]

Jesus would ask those who came to follow him, such as the rich young man, to divest themselves of their possessions and help carry out his mission of liberation. To free others, he taught, one must first free the self of all attachments. Once freed from sin and the accumulation of material things, one is free to serve others. Moreover, such detached persons also have the freedom to be critical of oppression and evil, because they have nothing that can be taken away as a punishment. Such persons have only their life, and they stand freely to give up even that life, if that be necessary in order to achieve peace and justice.

Liberation theologians thus see poverty and identification with the poor as an essential aspect of following the practice of Jesus. Many of them hold that only by living simply with the oppressed can one effectively walk with them and minister with them as did the Lord. Such poverty helps us to listen to the poor and also to bear witness to their suffering. Sobrino points out that the poor must indeed be the center of the newly emerging church, for it is they who best mediate for the rest of us who God is and what God expects of us in matters of justice.[37] The poor can speak Christ in ways that are not heard among the affluent and the comfortable.

The image of Jesus Christ that speaks most profoundly to most liberation theologians, therefore, is that of Jesus suffering and dying among the poor. This Christ calls his followers not only to belief but to "praxis," that is, to specific actions on behalf of those who are exploited. These actions are a direct result of careful reflection on the social and political causes of oppression, and a commitment to applying Jesus' message to the struggle for freedom.

The Kingdom of God

Liberation theologians also have some distinctive interpretations of

Jesus' teaching on the kingdom of God. Boff's description of the kingdom might be viewed as somewhat typical. He points out that the "the kingdom of God is the realization of a fundamental utopia of the human heart, the total transformation of this world, free from all that alienates human beings, free from pain, sin, divisions, and death."[38] In this description the kingdom seems to be a human horizon that stubbornly remains out of reach and yet is also at hand in the continuing transformation of human hearts and of the world in which they live. The kingdom is both here and there; in the present and yet still to be anticipated in the future.

The kingdom here is sharply distinguished from social reform, revolutions, or even from the church itself. Ultimately, the kingdom is "gift," the graced bestowal of the liberation of Jesus Christ upon his people. As such, the kingdom cannot be reduced to temporal progress or a just society or the overthrow of a tyrannical government. All of these might well be effective means for people to open themselves to the kingdom, but they are not the kingdom.

The kingdom cannot be equated with a just society, but that does not mean that Christians can stand by and ignore an unjust society. The kingdom can be realized only in a society where there is equality and justice. Thus the sins of exploitation and oppression are viewed as obstacles to the coming of the kingdom and must be rooted out of hearts and structures before the kingdom can take hold. The work of the kingdom is, therefore, comprehensive and all-inclusive. It entails not only purification of hearts, but a radical liberation of all levels of activity—social, political, even religious. It calls for a "new creation," not only in the spiritual sphere, but in all spheres of living. For the liberation theologian, spiritual transformation is not authentic unless it also includes political and social transformation. Gutiérrez writes: "... the salvation of Christ is a radical liberation from all misery, all despoliation, all alienation."[39]

Jesus the Liberator has a mission to the world, not merely to "souls." The Jesus of history is seen here not as some "icon" transcending the world, but as a flesh and blood man who engaged himself with his world and its problems. And it is in the Spirit of this Jesus that his followers, in turn, are now to assert themselves against social and political evils.

Thy Will Be Done on Earth

Liberation theology is adamant in its commitment to social reform. It relates the kingdom to such everyday problems as homelessness, hunger, unjust salaries and racial prejudice. The "at hand" dimension of

the kingdom of God is concerned with providing solutions to these social problems. Their notion of kingdom is far from Marx's caricature of
some "transcendent pie in the sky." Rather, it is a driving force within
the world, seeking to liberate the world from both personal and social
sin. It is the sovereign power of God that takes in all things, sacred and
secular, church and world, humans and cosmos, and draws all into harmony and union.

From the liberation perspective, the kingdom is also to be awaited in
a time ahead. This will be the time of ultimate fulfillment where there
will no longer be suffering and death, a time of "full and total liberation of all creation, in the end, purified of all that opposed it, transfig-
ured by the full presence of God."[40] Although there must be a constant
struggle to build the kingdom here through personal, national, and
even global conversion, ultimately the universal character of the kingdom transcends all of this.

Finally, the sovereignty of the kingdom does not imply the power of
domination or destruction that so often characterizes political realms.
Liberation theologians remind us that the power of God's kingdom is
the creative power of love, the power of healing and service. It is a
reign, therefore, that stands in protest to repression and violence.[41] It is
an invitation to turn from these toward a new sisterhood and brother-
hood in peace and justice.

The Death of Jesus

Death is much more visible and often more horrible among the poor of
the southern hemisphere. It comes sometimes to a child suffering from
malnutrition, to an elderly person without health care, or from a soldier's
bullet. It comes in the night with the arrival of a death squad or in the
afternoon from the sudden devastation of a bombing. Instantaneous,
premature, and often violent death has been the constant companion of
the peasant and the Indian for five centuries in the southern hemisphere.
Many of these people have clung to the cross of Jesus just to survive and
somehow keep alive. The crucified Jesus has been able to give meaning
to these deaths and keeps the movement for liberation going even
though the struggle is generally painful and seems at times hopeless.

Liberation theology has attempted to discover where God fits into
all this death that surrounds the people of Latin America. Influenced
by theologians like Bonhoeffer and Möltmann, they have begun to recognize that God can indeed be found in the midst of suffering and
death. This is evident in the writings of many of the liberation theologians who maintain that God cannot express love in a world of misery

without somehow being personally involved in that misery. A God of love cannot remain indifferent to the victims of violence and death. Therefore, somehow, God must be in solidarity with the victims.[42]

Liberation theology finds in Jesus the revelation of God's participation in the suffering of the innocent. The death of Jesus teaches that the will of God is not death but perseverance in the struggle for liberation, and that God will be faithful to God's people in their struggle for justice. Jesus chose to die rather than betray his mission to the poor. His death was not by divine decree but by the decree of those who could not accept him or his radically new message about God and the kingdom. In the death of Jesus, God is revealed as one who is in solidarity with those who suffer unjustly and who "opens up a hope and future through the most negative side of history."[43]

The cross is a symbol of how threatening those who proclaim justice are to those in power. Jesus' acceptance of this horrible death reveals an inner freedom, one that he offers to those who follow him. Jesus dies in anguish and yet also in peace and giving forgiveness. Violence can break the body but it need not break the spirit. This image of the dying Christ has indeed been a source of courage and hope to countless poor who have faced torture and death rather than give up their struggle for freedom.

It is important for the liberation cause to maintain that Jesus' death was not simply a result of false arrest or due to some trumped up charges of blasphemy or of claiming to be the messiah. From the liberation perspective, Jesus' arrest and execution were a result of his life and his teaching. Jesus died at the hands of those who were threatened by this message of compassion and freedom. He was killed by those who refused to accept God as "Abba" and who were angered by his prophetic charges against the religious and political abuses of his day. He was killed because his life stood in conflict with those who heavily burdened others while refusing to lift a hand to help them. He was put to death by those who thought that the power of violence could obliterate the power of love and freedom.

According to the liberation view, those who follow Jesus must be willing to denounce hatred, division, and the sinful social structures of our modern world. They have to be willing to sacrifice themselves in many ways, perhaps even to the point of sacrificing their lives in order to confront those who foster such oppression. A key liberation or freedom here is freedom from the fear of death. Many of those caught up in this movement know that their death will have meaning if they should die in the cause of freedom. Only the meaningless death of a person without commitment is a death to be feared. Liberation theologians often point to the many recent examples of Christian martyrs who were not afraid to face death if standing in solidarity with the poor required it. They speak of Archbishop Romero, who was gunned down while saying Mass, the four American women who were raped and murdered in El Salvador, the six Jesuits and two women who were murdered at the José Simeon Canas University of Central America, and the countless thousands of disciples of Jesus who were willing to stand against oppression and injustice. The crucifixion of Jesus continues, yet its agony and death are transformed constantly by a compassionate and loving God.[44]

Liberation and Resurrection

In liberation theology, resurrection often represents the vindication of both Jesus' teaching and actions with regard to peace and justice. Jesus' resurrection was the "definitive triumph of life and hope for a reconciled kingdom in which universal peace is the fruit of divine justice and the integration of all things in God."[45] The resurrection experiences of the early disciples, then, were glimpses of the "new creation," the ultimate future for the world and all humankind. Resurrection defeats oppression, suffering, and death. The mystery of resurrection reveals that the death of the innocent person in the struggle for justice has ultimate meaning. In resurrection the life given for others is glorified and exalted over the violence and brutality of those who inflict pain on others. It is an "eschatological event" because the risen Jesus entered into the final condition for which all creation has been destined: the condition of ultimate freedom from suffering and death.[46]

The resurrection is a source of hope for those who have lost many friends and loved ones in the struggle for justice and who themselves live daily with the threat of death. As in early Christian times, resurrection can free people from the fear of persecution and death and offer them the courage to continue Jesus' mission for freedom and equity. These people firmly believe that they "will never die," and that the risen Lord will ever be with his people in their quest for freedom. These were the thoughts of Romero before his own death, when he pointed out that no matter what happened to him, he would rise up again in the people.

There is a song from El Salvador that captures this belief. As the people sing their praises to God, a name is shouted out: Oscar Romero, or Tomás Gonzalez, or someone else in the community who has been killed in the cause of liberation. After each name is called, a resounding *Presente!* is sung to celebrate that that person is still present among the congregation. This is what the resurrection of the Lord and his people means to the people of liberation.

The resurrection of Jesus confirms the authenticity of his life of sacrifice and his message of the imminence of the kingdom. In his life he was himself free from material attachments, sin, legalism, and the fear of attack from those he confronted about their hypocrisy and lack of compassion. The resurrection validates this freedom and symbolizes the ultimate freedom, freedom from death itself. Thus resurrection becomes the "touchstone of Christian faith" in that it enables his followers to now recognize the divine nature of Jesus' person and revelation. It is here that Christian faith began, and it is here that Christians will find the commitment to continue to carry out Jesus' drive for social and religious reform.[47]

Jesus as a Norm for Discipleship

So far we have seen that liberation theology emphasizes a number of the aspects of Jesus' life: the "political implications" of his teachings and actions, the prophetic stand he took against the inequities of his time, his simple lifestyle and dedication to the poor, the urgency of his teaching about the dynamic and saving presence of the kingdom, his persistence in his position in the face of death, and his being raised from the dead so that his person and teaching might be confirmed by God.

This is the "total Christ" who calls others to discipleship and who serves as a model for their own mission. The call is a radical one, asking persons to divest themselves, cut any ties that might hold them back, and sacrifice themselves for others.[48] Discipleship calls for imitating Jesus by standing up to the corruption within religious, social and political systems. Here one follows Jesus with the same freedom he had, a freedom gained from experiencing God intimately as an "Abba" of love and goodness. It is a discipleship requiring a deep conversion of one's personal life as well as a conversion to social responsibility. It is a call to a ministry of reconciliation not only with God, but with fellow human beings.[49]

Liberation theology's notion of discipleship is much more demanding than what we often find in traditional Christianity. Here one speaks of conflict, confrontation, even rebellion against tyranny. Generally, liberation theologians are committed to such actions in a non-violent fashion. Liberation theology does not promote violent revolution. Instead, it imitates the non-violent yet conflictual ways of Jesus Christ. At the same time, while granting that Jesus did not permit harm to others, even one's enemy, the cause of freedom often knowingly runs the risk of having violence done to self. Here a new kind of "martyrdom" is described: not so much the traditional martyrdom of dying rather than giving up the faith, but the martyrdom of facing death rather than giving up the struggle for peace and justice.

Archbishop Romero spoke of such commitment during the very homily at the eucharist where he was gunned down. He said:

> You have just heard in Christ's gospel that one must not love oneself so much as to avoid getting involved in the risks of life that history demands of us, and that those who try to fend off the danger will lose their lives, while those who out of love for Christ give themselves to the service of others will live. The grain of wheat dies, but only apparently. If it did not die, it would remain alone. The harvest comes about only because it dies, allowing itself to be sacrificed in the earth and destroyed. Only by undoing itself does it produce the harvest.

Moments later a shot rang out from the back of the church and the archbishop who had spoken out for the poor lived out his own words.[50]

Spread of Liberation

Rosemary Radford Ruether, an American theologian, has pointed out that liberation theology is giving Christians universally a new starting point for understanding the messianic role of Jesus' action against political corruption.[51] Ruether maintains that Jesus' actions to transform the world in which he lived are the key to understanding his person as well as his message. Jesus was in solidarity with the poor and taught that the only hope of salvation for the wealthy was to divest themselves of the wealth and power they had gained by oppressing the poor.

From her perspective, Jesus' vision of the kingdom is social and political and includes undoing the unjust structures that keep people impoverished. Jesus is the messianic prophet who condemns poverty, suffering, and unjust death, and who stands in solidarity with those who are so afflicted. The privatized, other-worldly notion of Christian faith that has prevailed for so many centuries is no longer acceptable.[52]

Spread of Liberation Thinking

Liberation theology had its origins in the poverty, violence, and social injustice that have been the lot of the majority of people in Latin America. It is a radical interpretation of Jesus and the gospels that comes from a specific set of socioeconomic circumstances. As such, this theology cannot be easily transferred over to other countries and situations. At the same time, liberation theology has certain tenets that are universally applicable; thus it has begun to influence the religious thinking of other cultures and oppressed peoples. Its thrust for liberation of the poor has spread to the inner cities of Britain, to the struggle for racial justice in South Africa, and to many other countries on the same continent.[53] Its faith commitment to standing up for the poor has also spread to the East, to Japan, China, India, South Korea, and other Asian countries. Oppressed people throughout the world—whether they be women who struggle for equality and justice, the elderly who have been marginalized because of their age, or children who are unprotected from neglect and abuse—are turning to the teachings of Jesus in order to gain freedom. Those who have been excluded because of race, sexual orientation, ethnic background, or for whatever reason are standing up and calling for a new kind of socially concerned and active Christianity. We will end this chapter with just a sampling of some of the versions of liberation theology that seem to be emerging on other continents.

Liberation Theology in Africa

It has been extremely difficult to develop a substantial indigenous Christology on the African continent.[54] One of the obstacles has been Christianity's reluctance to integrate itself properly into the cultures and customs of that continent.

Only gradually is a theology of Jesus evolving that can be understood in these African cultures. For example, the process of initiation is associated with various stages of life—birth, puberty, marriage, death, and especially the entry of the adolescent into adulthood in the tribe. Unless Jesus can be understood as the "Master of Initiation," the elder brother bringing children into the same household, the sacraments of initiation are difficult for the African to relate to. Similarly, Africans are very concerned about rampant disease and the desperate need for health care. Many of them can easily relate to Jesus the Healer or *Nganga* (which means witch doctor or medicine man.) The exalted notion that many Africans hold toward their ancestors, whom they believe now exist in a state of closeness with the Supreme Being, can easily be extended to Jesus. As an exalted ancestor, he is now with God and acts as a mediator on their behalf.[55]

Jesus as Liberator

There does seem to be a type of liberation theology and a parallel

Christology throughout Africa. Here, of course, one must distinguish between the theology of South Africa and that of the rest of the continent. In South Africa, the theology within the movements opposing apartheid often seems to be influenced in good measure by the so-called black theology of North America. This may be partially because they are struggling more with dominant white churches from the First World than with African Christianity.[56] Some South Africans have criticized the liberation theology of Latin America for not being sufficiently aware of the racial dimensions of the struggle in their own nations. Seeing Jesus as the Liberator, they say, is still too often the product of European theology.[57]

Racial injustice is at the heart of the struggle in South Africa, and the Jesus who means most to those struggling is the black Christ, the Black Messiah. Allan Boesak, a prominent black theologian and leader in South Africa, writes: "To confess Jesus Christ as the Black Messiah is the only true confession of our time."[58] This is the Jesus Christ who walks with the people in the shanty towns of the so-called "home-lands" and suffers with them when they face torture and death at the hands of the police, the military, or even their own people. It is this Jesus who helps them actively and militantly rebel against the inhumane laws and social structures of South Africa.[59] Archbishop Desmond Tutu, a Nobel Prize winner and one of the most visible church leaders against apartheid, maintains that liberation theology has been having a notable effect in bringing freedom to South Africa.[60]

Liberation theology has a different set of difficulties to overcome in the many newly independent countries of Sub-Saharan Africa. The newly-established governments in these countries are African and the people are often still too much in the first flush of enjoying independence to be openly critical. Even though there are often grave injustices coming from these governments, it is difficult to construct a liberation theology with Jesus as an advocate of justice when this might mean moving against one's own people. As a result, the theology in these countries is often criticized for being more concerned with issues of indigenization than with liberation.[61]

Liberation in Asia
There is certainly ample need for liberation theology in Asia, where eighty-five percent of all the people suffer from abject poverty and oppression. The situation here, however, is also unique, for Christianity is a minority religion in Asia. Only three percent of the people are Christian. In addition, Christianity daily encounters other ancient and dynam-

ic major religions, such as Buddhism and Hinduism. Given this position, it has been difficult for Christian theologians to develop a liberation theology that will make an impact in the East. Yet there are beginnings.

Japanese Christian theologians have to articulate their theology amid religious pluralism and a rapidly growing secularism. Theologians like Kazoh Kitamori point out the human oppression in Japan. Kitamori believes that realizing the pain of others is a part of God's nature, and that coming to an understanding of how God suffers with God's people is a vital task for theology in Japan today. Another writer, Kosuke Koyama, speaks of a liberation theology in Japan that is "from below," or, in his terms, a "rice-roots" theology that comes out of the everyday experience of the farmers. Here Christianity can honor and listen to both Jesus and Buddha.[62] It is also a Christian theology that, for the first time in four hundred years, listens to the deepest aspirations and frustrations of the people. It reveres a God who moves, not at the Western speed, but with Oriental grace among the poor and the voiceless of the East.

The Asian Christian theologians seem to be at the point of learning the liberation theology of Latin America and searching for ways to use this Christian viewpoint to help more people stand up for the oppressed of Asia. Justice is desperately needed for the countless millions of peasants who live in destitution throughout Asia, for the many poor and untouchables of India, the desperate Boat people of South Asia, and the *minjung*, or millions of downtrodden in Korea.

Kim Chi-Ha, one of the best known poets in Korea, writes a story called "The Gold-Crowned Jesus," which symbolizes the difficulties that stand in the way of developing the image of Jesus the Liberator in Asia. It depicts Jesus as a figure in gold, imprisoned in concrete by an oppressor. A leper comes by and wants to liberate Jesus, and begins by taking off the gold crown and asking Jesus how he can be liberated from the concrete. Jesus tells about the terrible poverty and oppression around him and says that only action on the part of the poor will give him life again. In the end the leper finds that he cannot liberate Jesus. He is compelled by the forces of the state and church to restore the gold crown to Jesus' head, thereby imprisoning Jesus once again.[63]

Summary

Given the widespread poverty, starvation, and homelessness throughout the world, the image of Jesus as Liberator may well be the most prominent one in the future. The context for this image, liberation theology, seems to represent a major shift in Christian theology, perhaps comparable to those that occurred with Augustine in the early centuries, Aquinas in the medieval period, or Schleiermacher in modern times.[64]

This image of Jesus emerged from the impoverished people in Latin America and was articulated by a number of outstanding theologians who walked with these people in their oppression. It is an interpretation of Jesus and the gospels that stands as a serious critique of the European theology that has prevailed within Western Christianity and has often lacked awareness of the plight of the poor throughout the world. Liberation theologians look to the image of the historical Jesus in his struggle against those who put heavy burdens on the poor but do little to come to their aid. They follow a prophetic Jesus who cries out against violence and persecution.

This is a conflictual Jesus who confronts and yet loves his enemies, who takes such a relentless stand with the poor that he is executed for it. And yet this is a Jesus who forgives his enemies and prays for those who persecute him. He is the Lord and Savior who empowers people today to be willing to sacrifice themselves "for justice sake." There are many signs that this image of Jesus will continue to spread throughout the world. It seems that Christians in many areas will reclaim this image of the Christ and reinterpret his life, teachings, death, and resurrection in such a way as to empower them to identify with the poor and engage in their struggle for freedom and justice.

Questions for Reflection and Discussion

1. "The image which Africans have formed of Jesus Christ can be found in various parts of the world—African, the Americas, and in Suriname. It is an image bound up with the dramatic and turbulent history of black people." What kind of image of Jesus is indeed emerging here?

2. Liberation theology is a "listening" theology. Explain what this statement means to you.

3. Do you think that there is a valid basis in the gospels for thinking of Jesus as a liberator? If so, cite specific passages in the gospels which might justify such an image.

4. What possibilities do you see for developing a liberation theology in the United States? What would be some procedures for developing such a theology?

Notes

CHAPTER ONE

1. S. Applebaum, "Economic Life in Palestine," in *Compendium Rerum Judaicarum ad Novum Testamentum*, eds. S. Safrai and M. Stern (Philadelphia: Fortress Press, 1974) II, 623, 637. For more extensive background, see M. McNamara, *Palestinian Judaism and the New Testament* (Wilmington: Glazier, 1983) and John Riches, *The World of Jesus: First-Century Judaism* (Cambridge: Cambridge University Press, 1990).
2. Raymond E. Brown, Joseph A. Fitzmyer, and Roland E. Murphy, eds., *The New Jerome Biblical Commentary* (Englewood Cliffs, N.J.: Prentice-Hall, 1990), 75: 156–159.
3. For detailed studies of Herod the Great, see Michael Grant, *Herod the Great* (New York: American Heritage Press, 1971) and S. Sandmel, *Herod, Profile of a Tyrant* (Philadelphia: Lippincott, 1967).
4. Brown, Fitzmyer, Murphy, eds. *The New Jerome Biblical Commentary*, 75: 168. See also Paul Winter, *On the Trial of Jesus* (New York: de Gruyter, 1974), pp. 70–89.
5. Robert Schreiter, ed., *The Schillebeeckx Reader* (New York: Crossroad, 1984), p. 134.
6. Irving M Zeitlin, *Jesus and the Judaism of His Time* (New York: Polity Press, 1988), pp. 29ff.
7. For a detailed account of the theory that Jesus was intimately associated with the Zealot movement, see S.G.F. Brandon, *Jesus and the Zealots: A Study of the Political Factor in Primitive Christianity* (New York: Charles Scribner's Sons, 1967).
8. Sean Freyne, *Galilee, Jesus and the Gospels* (Philadelphia: Fortress Press, 1988), 135ff.
9. Joachim Jeremias, *Jerusalem in the Time of Jesus* (Philadelphia: Fortress Press, 1969), p. 119. The prevalence of such violence during the time of Jesus has been debated. Freyne in *Galilee, Jesus and the Gospels* does not seem to think that the times were as troubled as do R.A. Horsley and J. Hanson, *Bandits, Prophets and Messiahs* (New York: Winston Press, 1985), pp. 52–62.
10. John Riches, *Jesus and the Transformation of Judaism* (London: Darton, Longman and Todd, 1980), pp. 168ff. See also Geza Vermes, *Jesus and the World of Judaism* (Philadelphia: Fortress Press, 1983) and Carolyn Osiek, *What Are They Saying About the Social Setting of the New Testament?* (Mahwah, N.J.: Paulist Press, 1984).
11. Geza Vermes, *Jesus the Jew* (New York: Macmillan, 1973), p. 53.

12. Freyne, *Galilee, Jesus and the Gospels*, p. 2.
13. *Ibid.*, p. 154.
14. Applebaum, "Economic Life in Palestine," *Compendium Rerum Judaicarum ad Novum Testamentum*, Vol. II, 640ff. For more background, see Sherman E. Johnson, *Jesus and His Towns* (Wilmington: Michael Glazier: 1989).
15. S. Safrai, "Education and the Study of the Torah," *Compendium Rerum Judaicarum ad Novum Testamentum*, Vol. II, 953ff. See also Bruce D. Chilton, *A Galilean Rabbi and His Bible* (Wilmington: Michael Glazier, 1984).
16. See Jeremias, *Jerusalem in the Time of Jesus* for extensive details. Many have challenged the findings of Jeremias because he relies on later sources that are in fact questionable in their accuracy concerning the time of Jesus. For a more recent assessment, see James H. Charlesworth, *Jesus within Judaism* (Garden City, N. Y.: Doubleday, 1988), pp. 101, 140ff. See also J. Wilkinson, *Jerusalem as Jesus Knew It: Archeology as Evidence* (London, 1982).
17. Jeremias, *Jerusalem in the Time of Jesus*, p. 77.
18. S. Safrai, "Jewish Self-Government," in *Compendium Rerum Judaicarum ad Novum Testamentum*, Vol. I, 379ff.
19. Jeremias, *Jerusalem in the Time of Jesus*, pp. 56ff., and 75ff. See also Charlesworth, *Jesus Within Judaism*, pp. 117ff.
20. Schreiter, ed., *The Schillebeeckx Reader*, pp. 134ff.
21. Jeremias, *Jerusalem in the Time of Jesus*. pp. 93ff.
22. Zeitlin, *Jesus and the Judaism of His Time*, pp. 23ff. See also Charlesworth, *Jesus Within Judaism*, pp. 59ff. and E.P. Sanders, *Jesus and Judaism* (Philadelphia: Fortress Press, 1985), pp. 46ff., 193.
23. Zeitlin, *Jesus and the Judaism of His Time*, p. 25.
24. Edward Schillebeeckx, *Jesus: An Experiment in Christology* (New York: Seabury Press, 1979), p. 145.
25. For more background on the Essenes, see T. Gaster, *The Dead Sea Scriptures* (Garden City, N.Y.: Doubleday, 1977); G. Vermes, *The Dead Sea Scrolls: Qumran in Perspective* (World, 1978); and Samuel Sandmel, *Judaism and Christian Beginnings* (New York: Oxford University Press, 1978).
26. Sanders, *Jesus and Judaism*, pp. 174ff. This author thinks that Jesus' attitude towards sinners, including those that were still unrepentant, is a unique historical aspect of his ministry. See also his "Jesus and Sinners," *Journal for the Study of the New Testament* 19 (1983), 5–36.
27. *Ibid.*, pp. 44ff.
28. For further comparisons, see Ethelbert Stauffer, *Jesus and the Wilderness Community at Qumran* (Philadelphia: Fortress Press, 1964).
29. While not agreeing with radical views like those of Reimarus or Brandon, some scholars do see Jesus in the image of a vigorous liberator in conflict with the authorities of his time. See Albert Nolan, *Jesus Before Christianity* (Maryknoll, N.Y.: Orbis Books, 1978).
30. Jeremias, *Jerusalem in the Time of Jesus*, p. 119.
31. Bernard J. Lee, *The Galilean Jewishness of Jesus* (Mahwah, N.J.: Paulist Press, 1988), pp. 73ff.
32. Zeitlin, *Jesus and the Judaism of His Time*, p. 31.
33. William M. Thompson, *The Jesus Debate* (Mahwah, N.J.: Paulist Press, 1985), p. 32.
34. Zeitlin, *Jesus and the Judaism of His Time*, pp. 33ff.
35. Brown, Fitzmyer, Murphy, eds., *The New Jerome Biblical Commentary*, 81: 144.

See also J. P. M. Sweet, "The Zealots and Jesus," in Ernst Bammel and C.F.D. Moule, eds., *Jesus and the Politics of His Day* (Cambridge: Cambridge University Press, 1984), pp. 1–9. See also Oscar Cullmann, *Jesus and the Revolutionaries* (New York: Harper & Row, 1970).

36. Zeitlin, *Jesus and the Judaism of His Time*, pp. 11ff. See also Anthony J. Saldarini, *Pharisees, Scribes and Sadducees in Palestinian Society* (Wilmington: Michael Glazier, 1988).

37. See J. Kingsbury, "The Developing Conflict between Jesus and the Jewish Leaders in Matthew," *The Catholic Biblical Quarterly* 49 (1987): 57–73.

38. Jeremias, *Jerusalem in the Time of Jesus*, pp. 233ff.

39. Sandmel, *Judaism and Christian Beginnings*. p. 161.

40. Thompson, *The Jesus Debate*, pp. 158ff. For other perspectives on the Pharisees, see Harvey Falk, *Jesus the Pharisee* (Mahwah, N.J.: Paulist Press, 1985); Jacob Neusner, *Judaism in the Beginning of Christianity* (Philadelphia: Fortress Press, 1984), and *The Pharisees: Rabbinic Perspectives* (Hoboken, N.J.: KTAV, 1973), as well as John T. Carroll, "Luke's Portrayal of the Pharisees," *The Catholic Biblical Quarterly* 50 (Oct. 1988): 604–621.

41. Sanders, *Jesus and Judaism*, p. 49. See also J. Bowker, *Jesus and the Pharisees* (New York: Cambridge, University Press, 1973); Michael J. Cook, "Jesus and the Pharisees—The Problem as It Stands Today," *Journal of Ecumenical Studies* 15 (1978): 441–60.

42. Schreiter, ed., *The Schillebeeckx Reader*, p. 135.

43. Thompson, *The Jesus Debate*, p. 159ff.

44. Zeitlin, *Jesus and the Judaism of His Time*, p. 14.

45. Jeremias, *Jerusalem in the Time of Jesus*, p. 258.

46. Schreiter, ed., *The Schillebeeckx Reader*, p. 135.

47. Sanders, *Jesus and Judaism*, p. 49.

CHAPTER TWO

1. Brown, Fitzmyer, Murphy, eds., *The New Jerome Biblical Commentary*, 78.

2. For background on the origin of this approach to the gospels, see Harvey K. McArthur, ed., *In Search of the Historical Jesus* (New York: Charles Scribner's Sons, 1969), pp. 3ff. See also James Barr, *Fundamentalism* (Philadelphia: Westminster Press, 1978).

3. Thompson, *The Jesus Debate*, pp. 90ff.

4. For a readable introduction to biblical criticism, see Wilfred Harrington, *The New Guide to Reading and Studying the Bible* (Wilmington: Michael Glazier, 1978). See also Robert Grant with David Tracy, *A Short History of the Interpretation of the Bible*, 2nd ed. (Philadelphia: Fortress Press, 1984) and Pheme Perkins, *Reading the New Testament: An Introduction*, 2nd ed. (Mahwah, N.J.: Paulist Press, 1977).

5. See Brown, Fitzmyer, Murphy, *The New Jerome Biblical Commentary*, 70: 5–84.

6. For detailed information on this approach see, Gene Tucker, *Form Criticism of the Old Testament* (Philadelphia: Fortress Press, 1971) and Edgar V. McKnight, *What Is Form Criticism?* (Philadelphia, Fortress Press, 1969).

7. See Norman Perrin, *What Is Redaction Criticism?* (Philadelphia: Fortress Press, 1962).

8. Grant with Tracy, *A Short History of the Interpretation of the Bible*, pp. 174ff. For background on the so-called Gnostic gospels that were excluded from

the canon, see Pheme Perkins, *The Gnostic Dialogue: The Early Church and the Crisis of Gnosticism* (Mahwah, N.J.: Paulist Press, 1980) and Elaine Pagels, *The Gnostic Gospels* (New York: Random House, 1981).

9. Terence J. Keegan, *Interpreting the Bible: A Popular Introduction to Biblical Hermeneutics* (Mahwah, N. J.: Paulist Press, 1986), pp. 45ff.

10. See Richard A. Horsley and John Hanson, *Bandits, Prophets, and Messiahs: Popular Movements in the Times of Jesus* (New York: Winston Press, 1985) and Richard A. Horsley, *Jesus and the Spiral of Violence* (New York: Harper & Row, 1987).

11. See Fulton Oursler, *The Greatest Story Ever Told* (Garden City, N.Y.: Doubleday, 1949); Giuseppe Ricciotti, *The Life of Christ* (Milwaukee: Bruce Publishing Co., 1947); Ferdinand Prat, *Jesus Christ* (Milwaukee: Bruce Publishing Co., 1950), 2 vols.; Fulton J. Sheen, *Life of Christ* (New York: McGraw Hill, 1958).

12. Further studies on the contemporary Catholic biblical approach to doctrine and Christology are: The International Theological Commission: "Select Questions on Christology," (Washington, D.C.: USCC, 1980); John McKenzie, "American Catholic Scholarship: 1955–1980," in John J. Collins and John Dominic Crossan, eds., *The Biblical Heritage in Modern Catholic Scholarship* (Wilmington: Michael Glazier, 1986), Raymond E. Brown, *Biblical Exegesis and Church Doctrine* (Mahwah, N.J.: Paulist Press, 1985), and Gerald P. Fogarty, *American Catholic Biblical Scholarship* (San Francisco: Harper & Row, 1989).

13. For further discussion of Reimarus, see Gerald O'Collins, *Interpreting Jesus* (Mahwah, N.J.: Paulist Press, 1983), pp. 22ff.

14. See Walter Kasper, *Jesus the Christ* (Mahwah, N.J.: Paulist Press, 1976), p. 29ff.

15. See Michael L. Cook, *Guidelines for Contemporary Catholics: The Historical Jesus* (Chicago: Thomas More Press, 1986), pp. 16ff., and Dermot Lane, *The Reality of Jesus* (Mahwah, N.J.: Paulist Press, 1975), pp. 18ff.

16. Albert Schweitzer, *The Quest of the Historical Jesus: A Critical Study of Its Progress from Reimarus to Wrede* (New York: Macmillan, 1961).

17. For a thorough treatment of Strauss, see William Madges, *The Core of Christian Faith: D.F. Strauss and His Catholic Critics* (New York: Peter Lang, 1987) and the same author's "D.F. Strauss in Retrospect: His Reception Among Catholics," *Heythrop Journal* 30 (1989): 273–292.

18. See Rudolph Bultmann, *Jesus Christ and Mythology* (New York: Charles Scribner's Sons, 1958).

19. See Gustav Aulén, *Jesus in Contemporary Historical Research* (Philadelphia: Fortress Press, 1976), pp. 2ff. See Edward Hobbs, ed., *Bultmann, Retrospect and Prospect* (Philadelphia: Fortress Press, 1985).

20. For further discussion, see Cook, *Guidelines for Contemporary Catholics*, pp. 27ff.

21. See Leander E. Keck, *A Future for the Historical Jesus* (London: SCM Press, 1971), pp. 12ff. For a thorough overview of this question, see Elizabeth Johnson, "The Theological Relevance of the Historical Jesus: A Debate and a Thesis," *Thomist* 48 (1984): 1–43. See also Howard C. Kee, *What Can We Know About Jesus?* (Cambridge: Cambridge University Press, 1990); and James H. Charlesworth, "The Historical Jesus in Light of Writings Contemporaneous With Him," *Principat* 25/1(1982): 451–476.

22. Thompson, *The Jesus Debate*, pp. 106ff.

23. David Tracy, *The Analogical Imagination: Christian Theology and the Culture of Pluralism* (New York: Crossroad, 1981), pp. 234–235.

24. *Ibid.*, pp. 238, 245, 295

25. See David Tracy, *Blessed Rage for Order* (New York: Crossroad, 1975), p. 218.

26. For more information on this debate, see Raymond E. Brown, "After Bultmann, What? An Introduction to the Post–Bultmannians," *Catholic Biblical Quarterly* 26 (1964): 1–30, and Peter Stuhlmacher, *Historical Criticism and Theological Interpretation* (Philadelphia: Fortress Press, 1977), pp. 51–71.

27. For an overview of how the "new quest" has affected the study of Jesus Christ, see Randy L. Maddox, "The New Quest and Christology," *Perspectives in Religious Studies* 11(1984): 43–55; and David Cairns, "The Motive and Scope of Historical Inquiry," *Scottish Journal of Theology* 29 (1976): 335–355.

28. Karl Rahner, *Foundations of Christian Faith: An Introduction to the Idea of Christianity* (New York: Seabury Press, 1978), p. 238. See also his "The Position of Christology in the Church Between Exegesis and Dogmatics," in *Theological Investigations* (New York: Crossroad, 1982) II: 185–214 and "Remarks on the Importance of the History of Jesus for Catholic Dogmatics," *Theological Investigations*, XIII, 201–212.

29. Hans Küng, *On Being a Christian* (Garden City, N.Y.: Doubleday, 1976), p. 154.

30. This seems to be an underlying theme in the author's major work on Jesus; see Edward Schillebeeckx, *Jesus: An Experiment in Christology* (New York: Crossroad, 1979). This is volume 1 of a three-volume series.)

31. *Ibid.*, p. 70

32. *Ibid.*, p. 76. For a thorough critique of Schillebeeckx's work, see John Nijenhuis, "Christology without Jesus of Nazareth Is Ideology: A Monumental Work by Schillebeeckx on Jesus," *Journal of Ecumenical Studies* 17 (1980), 125–140. Other Catholic theologians who put value on the historical Jesus are Walter Kasper, *Jesus the Christ*; Jon Sobrino, *Christology at the Crossroads* (Maryknoll, N.Y.: Orbis Books, 1978); Dermot Lane, *The Reality of Jesus* (Mahwah, N.J.: Paulist Press, 1975), and Leonardo Boff, *Jesus Christ Liberator* (Maryknoll, N.Y.: Orbis Books, 1978).

33. Schillebeeckx, *Jesus*, pp. 72ff. Rahner, *Foundations of Christian Faith*, pp. 235ff.

34. Küng, *On Being a Christian*, p. 147.

35. See Sanders, *Jesus and Judaism*, p. 326 for his conclusions on what of Jesus is historical, ranging from the "certain" to the "incredible."

36. In G.K.A. Bell and D. Adolf Deissman, eds., *Mysterium Fidei* (New York: Longmans, Green and Co., 1930), p. 49.

CHAPTER THREE

1. Some examples are this approach are: S.G.F. Brandon, *Jesus and the Zealots: A Study of the Political Factor in Primitive Christianity* (New York: Charles Scribner's Sons, 1967); Harvey Falk, *Jesus the Pharisee* (Mahwah, N.J.: Paulist Press, 1985), and Morton Smith, *Jesus the Magician* (New York: Harper & Row, 1978).

2. F. Gerald Downing, "The Social Contexts of Jesus the Teacher: Construction and Reconstruction," *New Testament Studies* 33 (1987): 441ff. For an overview of the various kinds of Gentile teachers during Jesus' time and how Je-

sus might be compared and contrasted, see Pheme Perkins, *Jesus as Teacher* (Cambridge: Cambridge University Press, 1990) and George Nickelsburg, *Faith and Piety in Early Judaism* (Philadelphia: Fortress Press, 1983).

3. This position is explored in V.K. Robbins, *Jesus the Teacher* (London: SCM Press, 1985).

4. Irving M. Zeitlin, *Jesus and the Judaism of His Time* (New York: Polity Press, 1988), pp. 100ff.

5. Gerard Sloyan, *Jesus in Focus: A Life in Its Setting* (Mystic, Conn.: Twenty-Third Publications, 1983), 39. See also Paul J. Achtmeier, "'He Taught Them Many Things': Reflections on Marcan Theology," *Catholic Biblical Quarterly* 42(4) (1980): 465–481.

6. Samuel Sandmel, *Judaism and Christian Beginnings* (New York: Oxford University Press, 1978), p. 228.

7. J. Neusner, *Jesus and the Beginning of Christianity* (Philadelphia: Fortress Press, 1984), pp. 63–88.

8. Sandmel, *Judaism and Christian Beginnings*, p. 236.

9. A.E. Harvey, *Jesus and the Constraints of History* (Philadelphia: Westminster Press, 1982), p. 49.

10. Robbins, *Jesus the Teacher*, p. 87ff.

11. See Martin Hengel, *The Charismatic Leader and His Followers* (New York: Crossroad, 1981), pp. 53 ff., 80ff. and Bernard J. Lee, *The Galilean Jewishness of Jesus* (Mahwah, N.J.: Paulist Press, 1988), pp. 119ff.

12. Sandmel, *Judaism and Christian Beginnings*, p. 228. See also Lloyd Gaston, "Messiah of Israel as Teacher of the Gentiles: the Setting of Matthew's Christology," *Interpretation* 29 (Jan. 1975): 24–40.

13. Zeitlin, *Jesus and the Judaism of His Time*, pp. 105ff.

14. Charles H. Dodd, "Jesus as Teacher and Prophet," in G.K.D. Bell and D. Adolf Deissmann, eds., *Mysterium Christi* (New York: Longmans, Green and Co., 1930), pp. 55ff. See also Sloyan, *Jesus in Focus*, p. 39 and Joseph A. Grassi, "The Gnostic View of Jesus and the Teacher Today," *Religious Education* 77 (1983): 336–49.

15. Martin Hengel, *The Charismatic Leader and His Followers*, pp. 42ff.

16. Downing, " The Social Contexts of Jesus the Teacher," *New Testament Studies:* 443ff.

17. Abraham Heschel, *The Prophets* (New York: Harper & Row, 1962), p. x. See also Walter Brueggemann, *The Prophetic Imagination* (Philadelphia: Fortress Press, 1976).

18. Brueggemann, *The Prophetic Imagination*, p. 13.

19. *Ibid.*, pp. 62ff. See also John Riches, *Jesus and the Transformation of Judaism* (New York: Seabury Press, 1982), pp. 187ff.

20. See Bruce Vawter, *This Man Jesus: An Essay Toward a New Testament Christology* (Garden City, N.Y.: Doubleday, 1973), p. 183. See also John P. Meier, "John the Baptist in Matthew's Gospel," *Journal of Biblical Literature* 99 (3) (1980): 383–405.

21. Günther Bornkamm, "Jesus of Nazareth," in Harvey K. McArthur, ed., *In Search of the Historical Jesus* (New York: Charles Scribner's Sons, 1969), p.167.

22. A.E. Harvey, *Jesus and the Constraints of History*, p. 59. See also Fred Howes, *This Is the Prophet Jesus* (DeVorse and Co., 1983).

23. Edward Schillebeeckx, *Jesus: An Experiment in Christology*, pp. 472ff.

24. Rudolf Schnackenburg, *God's Rule and Kingdom* (New York: Herder and

Herder, 1963), p. 89. See also G.R. Beasley-Murray, *Jesus and the Kingdom of God* (Grand Rapids, Mich: Eerdmans, 1986), Henry M. Evans, "Current Exegesis on the Kingdom of God," *Perspectives in Religious Studies* 14 (Spring 1987): 67–77; Paul Ricoeur, "The 'Kingdom' in the Parables of Jesus," *Anglican Theological Review* 63 (April 1981): 165–169; Neal Fisher, *The Parables of Jesus: Glimpses of God's Reign* (New York: Crossroad, 1990); and Dermot A. Lane, *Christ at the Centre* (Mahwah, N.J.: Paulist Press, 1991): pp. 11-52.

25. Robert J. Schreiter, ed., *The Schillebeeckx Reader* (New York: Crossroad, 1984), pp. 137ff.
26. Quoted in Schackenburg, *God's Rule and Kingdom*, p. 11.
27. See John Reumann, *Jesus in the Church's Gospels* (Philadelphia: Fortress Press, 1968), p.147 and Schreiter, ed., *The Schillebeeckx Reader*, pp. 137ff.
28. Zeitlin, *Jesus and the Judaism of His Time*, pp. 115ff.
29. Wm. M. Thompson, *The Jesus Debate* (Mahwah, N.J.: Paulist Press, 1985), p. 182. See also Walter Kasper, *Jesus the Christ* (Mahwah, N.J.: Paulist Press, 1976), p. 16.
30. Hans Küng, *On Being a Christian* (Garden City, N.Y.: Doubleday, 1968), pp. 251ff.
31. Kasper, *Jesus the Christ*, p. 74.
32. Thompson, *The Jesus Debate*, p. 191.
33. Kasper, *Jesus the Christ*, p. 74.
34. Schillebeeckx, Jesus, pp. 258–63.
35. Karl Rahner, *Foundations of Christian Faith* (New York: Crossroad, 1987), p. 251.
36. See Schreiter, ed., *The Schillebeeckx Reader*, p. 138.
37. See Bernard Häring, *Free and Faithful in Christ*, vol. 1 (New York: Crossroad, 1984), pp. 117ff, Peter Hodgson, *New Birth of Freedom* (Philadelphia: Fortress Press, 1976), and Edward Schillebeeckx and Bas van Iersel, eds., *Jesus Christ and Human Freedom* (New York: Herder and Herder, 1974).
38. See John Dominic Crossan, "Parable as Religious and Poetic Experience," *Journal of Religion* 53(1973) 3: 330–358.
39. Reumann, *Jesus in the Church's Gospel*, p. 136.
40. Crossan, "Parable as Religious and Poetic Experience, *Journal of Religion:* 348.
41. See Pheme Perkins, *Hearing the Parables of Jesus* (Mahwah, N.J.: Paulist Press, 1981), p. 2. For other resources on parables, see John Drury, *The Parables in the Gospels* (New York: Crossroad, 1985), Bernard B. Scott, *Hear Then the Parable: A Commentary on the Parables of Jesus* (Minneapolis: Fortress Press, 1989), H. Brad Young, *Jesus and His Jewish Parables: Rediscovering the Roots of Jesus' Teaching* (Mahwah, N.J.: Paulist Press, 1989), Herman Hendrickx, *The Parables of Jesus* (San Francisco: Harper & Row, 1987).
42. *Ibid.*, p. 90.
43. *Ibid.*, p. 4.
44. Schreiter, ed., *The Schillebeeckx Reader*, p. 2.
45. Sallie McFague, *Models of God: Theology for an Ecological, Nuclear Age* (Philadelphia: Fortress Press, 1987), p. 46.

CHAPTER FOUR

1. Reginald Fuller, *Interpreting the Miracles* (London: SCM Press, 1963), pp. 8ff.
2. Herman Hendrickx, *The Miracle Stories* (San Francisco: Harper & Row, 1987), pp. 3ff.

3. Stephen Hawking, *A Brief History of Time: From the Big Bang to Black Holes* (New York: Bantam Books, 1988), pp. 20, 110.

4. René Latourelle, *The Miracles of Jesus and the Theology of Miracles* (Mahwah, N.J.: Paulist Press, 1988), p. 26.

5. Fuller, *Interpreting the Miracles*, p. 12.

6. See Latourelle, *The Miracles of Jesus and the Theology of Miracles*, pp. 36ff. for a critique of this. Latourelle takes many if not most of the miracles stories to be historical and goes to great pains to establish this. For a more contextual study, see Howard Clark Kee, *Medicine, Miracle and Magic in New Testament Times* (Cambridge, Mass.: Cambridge University Press, 1986), 75ff.

7. Hawking, *A Brief History of Time*, p. 172ff.

8. *Ibid.*, p. 175.

9. Hendrickx, *The Miracle Stories*, p. 6.

10. Kee, *Medicine, Miracle and Magic in New Testament Times*, p. 9ff.

11. See E.P. Sanders *Jesus and Judaism* (Philadelphia: Fortress Press, 1985), pp. 164ff. for a discussion of whether these miracles fit into the category of "magic" or prophetic symbol.

12. Kee, *Medicine, Miracle and Magic in New Testament Times*, p. 91.

13 *Ibid.*, p. 21.

14. A.E. Harvey, *Jesus and the Constraints of History* (Philadelphia: Westminster Press, 1982), p. 117.

15. Fuller, *Interpreting the Miracles*, 20ff.

16. Hendrickx, *The Miracle Stories*, p. 8.

17. Kee, *Medicine, Miracle and Magic in New Testament Times*, pp. 78, 84ff. Morton Smith in *Jesus the Magician* (New York: Harper & Row, 1978), pp. 84ff. attempts to parallel Jesus' healings with those of Apollonius.

18. See Smith, *Jesus the Magician* and G. Vermes, *Jesus the Jew: A Historian's Reading of the Gospels* (New York: Macmillan, 1973).

19. See Sanders, *Jesus and Judaism*, pp. 164ff. and Kee, *Medicine, Miracle and Magic in New Testament Times*, pp. 79, 112ff. for further discussion of how Jesus compares with the magicians of his time.

20. Harvey, *Jesus and the Constraints of History*, pp. 109ff.

21. Kee, *Medicine, Miracle and Magic in New Testament Times*, p. 86.

22. *Ibid.*, p. l.

23. Karl Rahner, *Foundations of Christian Faith* (New York: Crossroad, 1987), p. 264.

24. Jacob Neusner, *Judaism and the Beginning of Christianity* (Philadelphia: Fortress Press, 1984), p. 47.

25. Walter Kasper, *Jesus the Christ* (Mahwah, N.J.: Paulist Press, 1976), p. 90.

26. Hendrickx, *The Miracle Stories*, p. 20.

27. See Schillebeeckx, *Jesus*, pp. 183ff. and Fuller, *Interpreting the Miracles*, pp. 16ff.

28. H.J. Richards, *The Miracles of Jesus* (Mystic, Conn.: Twenty-Third Publications, 1986), pp. 11ff.

29. See John Paul Heil, "Significant Aspects of the Healing Miracles in Matthew," *Catholic Biblical Quarterly* 4 (April 1979): 283–84.

30. Kasper, *Jesus the Christ*, pp. 95ff. See also Peder Borgen, "Miracles of Healing in the New Testament," *Studia Theologica* 35(2) (1981): 91–106.

31. Fuller, *Interpreting Miracles*, pp. 42ff.

32. See G. Ebeling, *The Nature of Faith* (London: Collins, 1961), pp. 128–137. See also Mary Ann Beavis, "Mark's Teaching on Faith," *Biblical Theological Bulletin* 16(4) (1986): 139–142.

33. Rahner, *Foundations of Christian Faith,* pp. 263ff.

34. Richards, *The Miracles of Jesus,* pp. 11ff.

35. Schillebeeckx, *Jesus,* pp. 199ff.

36. Kasper, *Jesus the Christ,* p. 98.

37. See Michael L. Cook, *The Jesus of Faith: A Study in Christology* (Mahwah, N.J.: Paulist Press, 1981), p. 55. See also Earl S. Johnson, Jr., "Mark 10: 46–52: Blind Bartimaeus," *Catholic Biblical Quarterly* 40 (April 1978), 191–204.

38. Monika Hellwig, "The Miracles of Jesus," *Chicago Studies* 26 (Nov. 1987), 272–283.

39. *Ibid.,* p. 279.

CHAPTER FIVE

1. For a discussion of these views, see Rosemary Radford Ruether, "The Liberation of Christology from Patriarchy," *Religion and Intellectual Life* 2 (Spring 1985), 120. See also Mary Hembrow Snyder, *The Christology of Rosemary Radford Ruether: A Critical Introduction* (Mystic, Conn.: Twenty-Third Publications, 1988), pp. 59ff.

2. Leonard Swidler, *Biblical Affirmations of Women* (Philadelphia: Fortress Press, 1979), p. 13. See also his *Women in Judaism* (Metuchen, N.J.: Scarecrow Press, 1976).

3. Elisabeth M. Tetlow, *Women and Ministry in the New Testament* (Mahwah, N.J.: Paulist Press, 1989), pp. 5ff. See also Swidler, *Biblical Affirmations of Women,* p. 15.

4. Tetlow, *Women and Ministry in the New Testament,* pp. 10ff.

5. Swidler, *Biblical Affirmations of Women,* p. 17.

6. Tetlow, *Women and Ministry in the New Testament,* p. 18. See also Sarah B. Pomeroy, *Goddesses, Whores, Wives, Slaves* (New York: Schocken, 1972), p. 172ff.

7. Swidler, *Biblical Affirmations of Women,* p. 29. See also Rosemary Radford Ruether, ed., *Religion and Sexism: Images of Women in the Jewish and Christian Tradition* (New York: Simon and Schuster, 1974).

8. See Neusner, *Judaism and the Beginning of Christianity,* pp. 31ff.

9. Pheme Perkins, "Women in the Bible and Its World," *Interpretation* 42, 1 (Jan. 1988), 33ff. See also Elisabeth Schüssler Fiorenza, *In Memory of Her: A Feminist Theological Reconstruction of Christian Origins* (New York: Crossroad, 1984), pp. 118ff.

10. Ben Witherington III, *Women in the Ministry of Jesus* (London: Cambridge University Press, 1988), p. 3. See also Jeremias, *Jerusalem in the Time of Jesus,* p. 375.

11. Jeremias, *Jerusalem in the Time of Jesus,* p. 300.

12. Perkins, "Women in the Bible and Its World," p. 40ff.

13. Witherington, *Women in the Ministry of Jesus,* pp. 5ff.

14. See Jeremias, *Jerusalem in the Time of Jesus,* p. 370.

15. Swidler, *Biblical Affirmations of Women,* pp. 92ff.

16. Schüssler Fiorenza, *In Memory of Her,* p. 108.

17. Tetlow, *Women in Ministry in the New Testament,* p. 24.

18. Schüssler Fiorenza, *In Memory of Her,* pp. 142ff.

19. Alicia Craig Faxon, *Women and Jesus* (Philadelphia: United Church Press, 1973), p. 11.

20. Brown, Fitzmyer, Murphy, *The New Jerome Biblical Commentary*, 61: 115.
21. See Eugene Maly, "Women and the Gospel of Luke," *Biblical Theology Bulletin* 10 (3) (1980) 101ff.
22. Jane Kopas, "Jesus and Women: Luke's Gospel," *Theology Today* 43 (2) (July 1986), 195ff.
23. Witherington, *Women in the Ministry of Jesus*, pp. 18ff.
24. See Elisabeth Moltmann-Wendel, *The Women Around Jesus* (New York: Crossroad, 1982), p. 4; Anne E. Carr, *Transforming Grace* (San Francisco: Harper & Row, 1988), pp. 170 ff; and Bernard Cooke, "Non-Patriarchal Salvation," *Horizons* 10 (1) (1983), 22–31.
25. Witherington, *Women in the Ministry of Jesus*, p. 38.
26. Brown, Fitzmyer, Murphy, *The New Jerome Biblical Commentary*, 81: 149ff. See also Winsome Munro, "Women Disciples in Mark?" *Catholic Biblical Quarterly* 44(2) (1982), 25–241 and Ronald W. Graham, "Women in the Ministry of Jesus and in the Early Church," *Lexington Theological Quarterly* 18 (1) (1983), 1–42.
27. Witherington, *Women in the Ministry of Jesus*, pp. 80ff.
28. *Ibid.*, pp. 9ff.
29. Maly, "Women in the Gospel of Luke," p. 102. See also Carr, *Transforming Grace*, p. 173.
30. See Leonardo Boff, *The Maternal Face of God: The Feminine and Its Religious Expressions* (San Francisco: Harper & Row, 1987), pp. 114ff.
31. See Sandra M. Schneiders, "Women in the Fourth Gospel and the Role of Women in the Contemporary Church," *Biblical Theology Bulletin* 12(2) (1982), 35–45.
32. *Ibid.*, p. 43.
33. See Gerald O'Collins and Daniel Kendall, "Mary Magdalene as Major Witness to Jesus Resurrection," *Theological Studies* (48) (1987), 634. See also Elisabeth Schüssler Fiorenza, "Mary Magdalene: Apostle to the Apostles," *UTS Journal* (April 1975) 22ff.
34. *Ibid.*, p. 632.
35. See Raymond Brown, *The Community of the Beloved Disciple* (Mahwah, N.J.: Paulist Press, 1979), pp. 189ff.
36. George W. MacRae, *Faith in the Word: The Fourth Gospel* (Chicago: Franciscan Press, 1973), pp. 38ff.
37. Moltmann-Wendel, *The Women Around Jesus*, p. 136.
38. See Elisabeth A. Johnson, *Consider Jesus: Waves of Renewal in Christology* (New York: Crossroad, 1990), pp. 110ff. Johnson points to the number of ministries held by women in communities of Paul and Acts. See also Elizabeth Carroll, "Women in Ministry," *Theological Studies* 36(4) (1975), 660–687 and CBA Task Force on the Role of Women in Early Christianity, "Women and Priestly Ministry: The New Testament Evidence," *Catholic Biblical Quarterly* 41(4) (1979), 608–613.

CHAPTER SIX

1. N.M. Wildiers, *The Theologian and His Universe* (New York: Seabury Press, 1982), pp. 37ff.
2. Joseph Campbell, *The Power of Myth* (Garden City, N.Y.: Doubleday, 1988), p. 35.
3. Gibson Winter, *Liberating Creation: Foundations of Religious Social Ethics* (New

York: Crossroad, 1981), p. 76.

4. Jürgen Moltmann, *God in Creation: A New Theology of Creation and the Spirit of God* (San Francisco: Harper & Row, 1985), p. 32.

5. John Macquarrie, *Thinking About God* (New York: Harper & Row, 1975), pp. 142ff.

6. Winter, *Liberating Creation*, p. 116.

7. For a discussion of how the biblical perspective contributed to the emergence of science, see A.R. Peacocke, *Creation and the World of Science* (Oxford: Clarendon Press, 1979) pp. 10ff.

8. Christopher Mooney, *Teilhard de Chardin and the Mystery of Christ* (London: Collins, 1966), p. 65.

9. J.A. Lyons, *The Cosmic Christ in Origen and Teilhard de Chardin* (New York: Oxford University Press, 1982), p. 215.

10. Wildiers, *The Theologian and His Universe*, pp. 188ff.

11. Pierre Teilhard de Chardin, *Christianity and Evolution* (New York: Harcourt and Brace, 1969), p. 139.

12. Lyons, *The Cosmic Christ in Origen and Teilhard de Chardin*, pp. 153ff. See also George A. Maloney, *The Cosmic Christ: From Paul to Teilhard* (New York: Sheed and Ward, 1968) and Matthew Fox, *The Coming of the Cosmic Christ* (San Francisco: Harper & Row, 1988).

13. Mooney, *Teilhard de Chardin and the Mystery of Christ*, pp. 6ff.

14. Anne Lonergan and Caroline Richards, eds., *Thomas Berry and the New Cosmology* (Mystic, Conn.: Twenty-Third Publications, 1987), pp. 25–26.

15. Mooney, *Teilhard de Chardin and the Mystery of Christ*, p. 52.

16. Juan Luís Segundo, *An Evolutionary Approach to Jesus of Nazareth* (Maryknoll, N.Y.: Orbis Books, 1988), pp. 66ff.

17. See John Paul II, "Encyclical on Social Concerns," *Origins* 17, 38 (March 3, 1988): 645ff.

18. Jay B. McDaniel, *Earth, Sky, Gods and Mortals: Developing an Ecological Spirituality* (Mystic, Conn.: Twenty-Third Publications, 1990), pp. 135ff.

19. Evelyn Underhill, *Mysticism: A Study in the Nature and Development of Man's Spiritual Consciousness*, p. 141, quoted in Lyons, *The Cosmic Christ in Origen and Teilhard de Chardin*, p. 35.

20. Günther Bornkamm, *Jesus of Nazareth* (New York: Harper & Row, 1960), p. 177. This author was one of the first modern theologians to give attention to this dimension of Jesus.

21. William Thompson, *The Jesus Debate* (Mahwah, N.J.: Paulist Press, 1985), p. 201. See also Bornkamm, *Jesus of Nazareth*, p. 119.

22. John Dominic Crossan, "The Seed Parables of Jesus," *Journal of Biblical Literature* 92 (1973): 244–46.

23. Segundo, *An Evolutionary Approach to Jesus of Nazareth*, pp. 64ff.

24. C.F.D. Moule, *Man and Nature in the New Testament* (Philadelphia, Fortress Press, 1967), pp. 9ff. See also Brown, Fitzmyer, Murphy, *The New Jerome Biblical Commentary*, 41: 34ff.

25. *Ibid.*, 42, 97. See also Wesley Granberg-Michaelson, *A Worldly Spirituality: The Call to Redeem Life on Earth* (New York: Harper & Row, 1984), p. 95.

26. See *The New Jerome Biblical Commentary*, 41, 44 and S. Masuda, "The Good News of the Miracle of the Bread," *New Testament Studies* 28 (1982): 191–219.

27. R.A. Guelich, "The Beginning of the Gospel—Mark 1: 1–15," *Biblical Research* 27 (1982): 5–15.

28. B.D. Chilton, "The Transfiguration," *New Testament Studies* 27 (1980–1981), 115–124.

29. See Raymond E. Brown, *The Crucified Christ in Holy Week* (Collegeville, Minn.: Liturgical Press, 1986), pp. 30ff. for a discussion of the use of nature in the passion stories.

30. Lonergan and Richards, eds., *Thomas Berry and the New Cosmology*, pp. 15ff.

31. See Sallie McFague, *Models of God: Theology for an Ecological Nuclear Age* (Philadelphia: Fortress Press, 1987), pp. 111ff. for an incisive development of this image.

32. See Karl Rahner, "Christology and the Evolutionary View of the World," in *Theological Investigations* (Baltimore: Helicon Press, 1966) Vol. V, 172ff. See John F. Haught, *The Cosmic Adventure: Science, Religion and the Quest for Purpose* (Mahwah, N.J.: Paulist Press, 1984), p. 159. The author points out that Jesus is the embodiment of God's unconditional love of the cosmos. See also A.R. Peacocke, *Creation and the World of Science*, p. 311.

33. Jürgen Moltmann, *The Crucified God* (London: SCM Press, 1973), p. 195. See also A.P. Peacocke, *Creation and the World of Science* (New York: Oxford University Press, 1979), pp. 311ff.

34. Moltmann, *The Crucified God*, p. 270.

35. Lyons, *The Cosmic Christ in Origen and Teilhard de Chardin*, p. 169.

36. Peacocke, *Creation and the World of Science*, p. 244.

37. Teilhard de Chardin, *Christianity and Evolution*, pp. 146ff. This notion will be developed in greater detail in Chapter Eleven.

CHAPTER SEVEN

1. See Wilfred Harrington, *The Drama of Christ's Coming* (Wilmington: Michael Glazier, 1988), pp. 7ff. Also useful here is R. Rhys Williams, *Let Each Gospel Speak for Itself* (Mystic, Conn.: Twenty-Third Publications, 1987), pp. 29–47, and Reginald H. Fuller, "The Conception/Birth of Jesus as a Christological Moment," *Journal for the Study of the New Testament* 1 (1978): 37–52.

2. Raymond E. Brown, *The Birth of the Messiah* (Garden City, N.Y.: Doubleday, 1977), pp. 534ff.

3. *Ibid.*, pp. 26ff. See also Herman Hendrickx, *The Infancy Narratives* (London: Geoffrey Chapman, 1984).

4. *Ibid.*, p. 8.

5. See D.E. Nineham, "The Genealogy of St. Matthew's Gospel and Its Significance for the Study of the Gospel," *Bulletin of John Rylands University Library* 58 (1976): 421–44 and Brown, *The Birth of the Messiah*, pp. 57–95.

6. See H.C. Waetjen, "The Genealogy as the Key to the Gospel According to Matthew," *Journal of Biblical Literature* 95 (1976): 205–30.

7. See L. Cantwell, "The Parentage of Jesus: Mt. I, 18–21," *Novum Testamentum* 24 (1982), 304–15, Edgar W. Conrad, "The Annunciation of Birth and the Birth of the Messiah," *The Catholic Biblical Quarterly* 47 (Oct. 1985): 656–663, and A. Tosato, "Joseph Being a Just Man (Mt. 1,19)," *The Catholic Biblical Quarterly* 41 (1979): 547–51.

8. See Brown, *The Birth of the Messiah*, pp. 316ff.: and R.C. Tannehill, "The Magnificat as Poem," *Journal of Biblical Literature* 93 (1974): 263–75. See also Raymond E. Brown, ed., *Mary in the New Testament* (Mahwah, N.J.: Paulist Press, 1978) and Leonardo Boff, *The Maternal Face of God* (New York: Harper & Row, 1987).

9. Brown, *The Birth of the Messiah*, pp. 283ff.

10. Senior, *The Passion of Jesus in the Gospel of Mark*, p. 96.

11. Harrington, *The Drama of Christ's Coming*, pp. 38ff.

12. *Ibid.*, p. 32.

13. See O'Collins, *Interpreting Jesus*, pp. 195ff; Brown, *The Virginal Conception and Bodily Resurrection of Jesus*, p. 63ff., Joseph A. Fitzmyer, "The Virginal Conception of Jesus in the New Testament," *Theological Studies* 34 (1973): 541–75, Gerard Sloyan, "Conceived by the Holy Ghost, Born of the Virgin Mary," *Interpretation* 33 (1979): 81–84.

14. See Raymond E. Brown, "The Meaning of the Magi; The Significance of the Star," *Worship* 49 (1975), 574–82 and Brown, *The Birth of the Messiah*, pp. 188–200.

15. Brown, *The Birth of the Messiah*, p. 228. See also R.T. France, "The Massacre of the Innocents—Fact or Fiction?" *Novum Testamentum* 21 (1979): 98–120.

16. See Raymond Brown, "The Meaning of the Manger: The Significance of the Shepherds," *Worship* 50 (1976): 528–38.

17. See Brown, *The Birth of the Messiah*, pp. 485ff.

18. Richard A. Horsley, *The Liberation of Christmas* (New York: Crossroad, 1989), p. 45.

19. Paul L. Maier, "The Infant Massacre—History or Myth?" *Christianity Today* 19 (Dec. 1975): 9.

20. Horsley, *The Liberation of Christmas*, p. 85.

21. *Ibid.*, 23ff.

22. Brown, *The Birth of the Messiah*, p. 413. See also J. Thorley, "The Nativity Census: What Does Luke Really Say?" *Greece and Rome* 26 (1979), 81–84 .

23. Horsley, *The Liberation of Christmas*, pp. 85ff.

24. Maier, "The Infant Massacre–History or Myth?" p. 9. See Raymond Brown, *An Adult Christ at Christmas* (Collegeville, Minn.: Liturgical Press, 1985), pp. 26ff.

25. Brown,*The Birth of the Messiah*, pp. 226ff.

26. See Williams, *Let Each Gospel Speak for Itself*, p. 9.

27. Horsley, *The Liberation of Christmas*, pp. 100ff.

28. Brown, *The Birth of the Messiah*, p. 420.

29. Brown, *An Adult Christ at Christmas*, p. 21.

30. Brown, *The Birth of the Messiah*, pp. 451ff.

31. *Ibid.*, pp. 171ff.

32. Brown, *The Birth of the Messiah*, p. 167.

33. See Janice Capel Anderson, "Mary's Difference: Gender and Patriarchy in the Birth Narratives," *Journal of Religion* 67(2) (April 1987): 183–202.

34. *Ibid.*, pp. 183ff.

35. *Ibid.*, p. 188.

36. *Ibid.*, p. 191

37. Horsley, *The Liberation of Christmas*, pp. 110ff.

38. Brown, *The Birth of the Messiah*, p. 243.

CHAPTER EIGHT

1. Raymond E. Brown, *The Crucified Christ in Holy Week* (Collegeville, Minn: Liturgical Press, 1986). This is a popularly written, yet reliable exegesis of the four gospel accounts. See also Howard I. Marshall, "The Death of Jesus in

Recent New Testament Study," *Word and World* 3 (1983), 12ff. For detailed accounts see Donald Senior, *The Passion of Jesus in the Gospel of Matthew; The Passion of Jesus in the Gospel of Mark; The Passion of Jesus in the Gospel of Luke; The Passion of Jesus in the Gospel of John* (Wilmington: Michael Glazier, 1984–89).

2. See O'Collins, *Interpreting Jesus*, 1983, p. 82, and also Reginald H. Fuller and Pheme Perkins, *Who Is This Christ?* (Philadelphia: Fortress Press, 1983), p. 109.

3. See Brandon, *Jesus and the Zealots* for a full discussion of these theories.

4. A.E. Harvey, *Jesus on Trial* (Atlanta: John Knox Press, 1976), p. 32.

5. Lee, *The Galilean Jewishness of Jesus*, p. 75. For a detailed account of this theory on the Roman responsibility for the execution, see Ellis Rivkin, *What Crucified Jesus?* (Nashville: Abingdon Press, 1984).

6. Gerhard Lohfink, *The Last Days of Jesus* (Notre Dame, Ind.: Ave Maria Press, 1984), p. 28.

7. Sanders, *Jesus and Judaism*, p. 301.

8. Schillebeeckx, *Jesus*, p. 312.

9. Harvey, *Jesus on Trial*, p. 10. See also Sanders, *Jesus and Judaism*, p. 307.

10. Mackey, *Jesus, The Man and the Myth*, p. 57.

11. Donald Senior, *The Passion of Jesus in the Gospel of Mark* (Wilmington: Michael Glazier, 1979), pp. 20ff.

12. See David R. Catchpole, "The Triumphal Entry," in Ernst Bammel and C.F.D. Moule, eds., *Jesus and the Politics of His Day* (Cambridge: Cambridge University Press, 1984), pp. 319ff.

13. See Sanders, *Jesus and Judaism*, pp. 295ff. He maintains that the Temple event was extremely significant in gaining enemies for Jesus.

14. See O'Collins, *Interpreting Jesus*, p. 75, and Zeitlin, *Jesus and the Judaism of His Time*, p. 149.

15. Schillebeeckx, *Jesus*, pp. 294ff.

16. Senior, *The Passion of Jesus in the Gospel of Mark*, p. 15.

17. Lohfink, *The Last Days of Jesus*, p. 13.

18. Zeitlin, *Jesus and the Judaism of His Time*, p. 152ff. See also Paul Winter, *On the Trial of Jesus* (Berlin: Walter de Gruyter, 1961), chap. 3 and Gerard Sloyan, *Jesus on Trial* (Philadelphia: Fortress Press, 1973), pp. 63ff.

19. See John Galvin, "Jesus' Approach to Death: An Examination of Some Recent Studies," *Theological Studies* 41(4) (1980): 715ff.

20. Zeitlin, *Jesus and the Judaism of His Time*, p. 155.

21. See Sanders, *Jesus and Judaism*, p. 299, Harvey, *Jesus and the Constraints of History*, p. 17, and John T. Pawlikowski, "The Trial and Death of Jesus: Reflections in Light of a New Understanding of Judaism," *Chicago Studies* 25 (1) (1986): 79–94.

22. Sloyan, *Jesus on Trial*, p. 24.

23. *Ibid.*, p. 27.

24. Harvey, *Jesus and the Constraints of History*, p. 16.

25. Martin Hengel, *Crucifixion* (London: SCM Press, 1977), p. 21.

26. See Joseph A. Fitzmyer, *To Advance the Gospel* (New York: Crossroad, 1981), pp. 126ff.

27. Hengel, *Crucifixion*, p. 84.

28. Harvey, *Jesus and the Constraints of History*, pp. 11ff.

29. See Wm. D. Edwards et al., "On the Physical Death of Jesus Christ," *Journal of the American Medical Association*, 255, 11 (March 21, 1986), 1455–1463.

30. Fitzmyer, *To Advance the Gospel*, 126ff.

CHAPTER NINE

1. Gerald O'Collins, *Jesus Risen* (Mahwah, N.J.: Paulist Press, 1987), p. 21.
2. *Ibid.*, p. 24.
3. See F.X. Durrwell, *The Resurrection* (New York: Sheed and Ward, 1960) and D. M. Stanley, "Christ's Resurrection in Pauline Soteriology," *Analecta Biblica*, 13 (Rome: Pontifical Biblical Institute, 1961).
4. Pheme Perkins, *Resurrection: New Testament Witness and Contemporary Reflection* (Garden City, N.Y.: Doubleday, 1984), pp. 38ff.
5. *Ibid.*, p. 22.
6. Sandmel, *Judaism and Christian Beginnings*, pp. 200ff.
7. Perkins, *Resurrection*, p. 47.
8. *Ibid.*, p. 62ff. See also James D.G. Dunn, *The Evidence for Jesus* (Philadelphia: Westminster Press, 1985), p. 71.
9. Perkins, *Resurrection*, p. 62.
10. Kasper, *Jesus the Christ*, p. 125.
11. See Wm. P. Loewe, "The Appearances of the Risen Lord: Faith, Fact, and Objectivity," *Horizons* 6 (1979): 178ff. See also Lane, *Christ at the Centre*, pp. 90ff.
12. O'Collins, *Jesus Risen*, p. 8.
13. Perkins, *Resurrection*, p. 124.
14. O'Collins, *Jesus Risen*, p. 100.
15. *Ibid.*, p. 107.
16. Kasper, *Jesus the Christ*, p. 132.
17. See Willi Marxsen, *The Resurrection of Jesus of Nazareth* (Philadelphia: Fortress Press, 1970). For commentary on this theory, see O'Collins, *Jesus Risen*, p. 63.
18. See Dunn, *The Evidence for Jesus*, p. 59. See also Kasper, *Jesus the Christ*, p. 24.
19. Reginald H. Fuller, *The Formation of the Resurrection Narratives* (Philadelphia: Fortress Press, 1980), p. 47.
20. Mackey, *Jesus: the Man and the Myth*, p. 89.
21. See Raymond Brown, *The Virginal Conception and Bodily Resurrection of Jesus* (Mahwah, N.J.: Paulist Press, 1973), pp. 87ff.
22. Dunn, *The Evidence for Jesus*, p. 71.
23. Collins, *Jesus Risen*, p. 9.
24. *Ibid.*
25. Perkins, *Resurrection*, pp. 218ff.
26. See Mooney, *Teilhard de Chardin and the Mystery of Christ*, pp. 58ff. and Thompson, *The Jesus Debate*, p. 423.
27. Brown, *The Virginal Conception and Bodily Resurrection of Jesus*, p. 90.
28. Kasper, *Jesus the Christ*, p. 39. See also Fuller, *The Formation of the Resurrection Narratives*, p. 46.
29. See Perkins, *Resurrection*, p. 107 and Schillebeeckx, *Jesus*, p. 73.
30. Rahner, *Foundations of Christian Faith*, p. 277.
31. Kasper, *Jesus the Christ*, p. 184.
32. See Schillebeeckx, *Jesus*, pp. 346ff., 643ff.
33. See O'Collins, *Interpreting Jesus*, p. 124. See also Küng, *On Being a Christian*, p. 91.
34. See Brown,*The Virginal Conception and Bodily Resurrection of Jesus*, p. 128.
35. Mackey, *Jesus, The Man and the Myth*, p. 112.
36. See Monika Hellwig, *Jesus, The Compassion of God* (Wilmington: Michael Glazier, 1983), p. 101.

37. Brown, *The Virginal Conception and Bodily Resurrection of Jesus*, p. 76.
38. Dunn, *The Evidence for Jesus*, p. 72.
39. Brown, *The Virginal Conception and Bodily Resurrection of Jesus*, p. 75.
40. Fuller, *The Formation of the Resurrection Narratives*, p. 52.
41. Dunn, *The Evidence for Jesus*, p. 53.
42. See Fuller, *The Formation of the Resurrection Narratives*, p. 52.
43. See Brown, *The Virginal Conception and Bodily Resurrection*, p. 113.
44. Perkins, *Resurrection*, p. 94. See also W.L. Craig, "The Historicity of the Empty Tomb of Jesus," *New Testament Studies* 31 (1) (1985): 39–67.
45. Dunn, *The Evidence for Jesus*, p. 66.
46. *Ibid.*, p. 67.
47. See Perkins, *Resurrection*, p. 94.
48. See Brown, *The Virginal Conception and Bodily Resurrection*, pp. 108ff. See also Hubert Richards, *The First Easter: What Really Happened?* (Mystic, Conn.: Twenty-Third Publications, 1983), and Gerald O'Collins, *Interpreting the Resurrection* (Mahwah, N.J.: Paulist Press, 1989).

CHAPTER TEN

1. Richard A. Norris, Jr. ed., *The Christological Controversy* (Philadelphia: Fortress Press, 1987), p. 3.
2. Gerard H. Ettinger, *Jesus, Christ and Savior* (Wilmington: Michael Glazier, 1987), pp. 23 ff.
3. Jaroslav Pelikan, *The Christian Tradition*, vol. 1: *The Emergence of the Catholic Tradition (100–600)* (Chicago: University of Chicago Press, 1971), pp. 173ff.
4. See Maurice Wiles, *The Making of the Christian Tradition* (New York: Cambridge University Press, 1967), p. 54.
5. Pelikan, *The Emergence of the Catholic Tradition*, p. 173.
6. Leo Davis, *The First Seven Ecumenical Councils (325–787)* (Wilmington: Michael Glazier, 1987), p. 34. This author provides interesting historical background to the councils.
7. *Ibid.*, pp. 40ff.
8. Justo L. Gonzalez, *The Story of Christianity*, Vol. 1: *The Early Church to the Dawn of the Reformation* (New York: Harper & Row, 1984), pp. 58ff. See also Norris, *The Christological Controversy*, pp. 35ff.
9. Kasper, *Jesus the Christ*, p. 200.
10. Lane, *The Reality of Jesus*, p. 97.
11. *Ibid.*, pp. 95ff.
12. Kasper, *Jesus the Christ*, p. 166.
13. See Pelikan, *The Emergence of the Christian Tradition*, p. 186.
14. Earl Richard, *Jesus, One and Many: The Christological Concept of the New Testament Authors* (Wilmington: Michael Glazier, 1988), pp. 439ff.
15. Pelikan, *The Emergence of the Christian Tradition*, p. 188.
16. Wiles, *The Making of Christian Doctrine*, p. 117.
17. Pelikan, *The Emergence of the Christian Tradition*, p. 188.
18. Norris, *The Christological Controversy*, pp. 7ff.
19. *Ibid.*, p. 10.
20. Richard, *Jesus: One and Many*, p. 44.
21. Davis, *The First Seven Ecumenical Councils*, pp. 43ff.
22. Richard, *Jesus: One and Many*, p. 445.

23. Ettinger, *Jesus, Christ and Savior*, p. 69.

24. *Ibid.*, p. 70.

25. For background on this, see Rowan Williams, *Arius: History and Tradition* (London: Darton, Longman and Todd, 1987). See also Charles Kannengieser, "Arius and the Arians," *Theological Studies* 44 (Sept. 1983): 456–475.

26. See Joseph Lienhard, "The 'Arian' Controversy: Some Categories Reconsidered," *Theological Studies* 48 (Sept. 1987): 417ff., R.G. Gregg, ed., *Arianism: Historical and Theological Reassessments* (Cambridge, Mass.: Philadelphia Patristic Foundation, 1985), and Robert C. Gregg and Dennis E. Groh, *Early Arianism: A View of Salvation* (Philadelphia: Fortress Press, 1981).

27. Pelikan, *The Emergence of the Catholic Tradition*, p. 193.

28. *Ibid.*, pp. 198ff.

29. Gonzalez, *The Early Church to the Dawn of the Reformation*, pp. 160ff.

30. See Hubert Jedin, *Ecumenical Councils of the Catholic Church* (New York: Herder and Herder, 1960), p. 14.

31. Davis, *The First Seven Ecumenical Councils*, p. 57. See also Frances M. Young, *From Nicea to Chalcedon: A Guide to Literature and Its Background* (Philadelphia: Fortress Press, 1983).

32. Gonzalez, *The Early Church to the Dawn of the Reformation*, p. 162.

33. Richard, *Jesus: One and Many*, p. 452.

34. Jedin, *Ecumenical Councils of the Catholic Church*, pp. 28ff.

35. Richard, *Jesus: One and Many*, p. 464.

36. Lane, *The Reality of Jesus*, p. 101.

37. *Ibid.*, p. 100.

38. Pelikan, *The Emergence of the Catholic Tradition*, p. 247.

39. *Ibid.*, p. 231.

40. Davis, *The First Seven Ecumenical Councils*, p. 177.

41. *Ibid.*, pp. 181ff.

42. See Anthony Baxter, "Chalcedon, and the Subject of Christ," *Downside Review* (Jan. 1989): 1–21. For additional critique of Chalcedon, see Brian McDermott "Roman Catholic Christology: Two Recurring Themes," *Theological Studies* 41(2) (1980): 339–367.

43. For an engaging discussion of these images, see Jaroslav Pelikan, *Jesus Through the Centuries* (New York: Harper & Row, 1985).

CHAPTER ELEVEN

1. Carl E. Braaten, "The Christian Doctrine of Salvation," *Interpretation*, 35 (April 1981): 117–131. See also Franz J. van Beeck, "Ten Questions on Christology and Soteriology," *Chicago Studies* 25 (3) (1986): 269–278.

2. Russell Aldwinkle, *Jesus: A Savior or the Savior? Religious Pluralism in Christian Perspective* (Macon: Mercer University Press, 1982), pp. 99ff.

3. Gerard Sloyan, *Jesus: Redeemer and Divine Word* (Wilmington: Michael Glazier, 1989), pp. 43ff,

4. Edward Schillebeeckx, *Christ: The Experience of Jesus as the Lord* (New York: Seabury Press, 1980), p. 115.

5. Arland J. Hultgren, *Christ and His Benefits: Christology and Redemption in the New Testament* (Philadelphia: Fortress Press, 1987), pp. 160ff.

6. Edward Schillebeeckx, *Jesus: An Experiment in Christology* (New York: Seabury Press, 1979), p. 291.

7. Denis Edwards, *What Are They Saying About Salvation?* (Mahwah, N.J.: Paulist Press, 1986), pp. 1ff. See also Reginald H. Fuller, "Jesus Christ as Savior in the New Testament," *Interpretation,* 35 (April 1981): 151ff.

8. Hultgren, *Christ and His Benefits,* pp. 5ff.

9. *Ibid.,* pp. 47ff.

10. *Ibid.,* pp. 75ff.

11. Sloyan, *Jesus: Redeemer and Divine Word,* p. 46.

12. Hultgren, *Christ and His Benefits,* pp. 85ff.

13. *Ibid.,* pp. 137ff

14. *Ibid.,* pp. 16ff.

15. Fuller, "Jesus Christ as Savior in the New Testament," pp. 150ff.

16. Bruce Vawter, *This Man Jesus: An Essay Toward a New Testament Christology* (Garden City, N.Y.: Doubleday and Co.. 1973), p. 75.

17 Karl Rahner, *Foundations of Christian Faith* (New York: Crossroad, 1987), p. 288.

18. Xavier Léon-Dufour, *Dictionary of Biblical Theology* (New York: Desclee Co., 1967), p. 134

19. Edwards, *What are They Saying About Salvation?,* pp. 8ff.

20. Paul Fiddes, *Past Event and Present Salvation: The Christian Idea of Salvation* (Atlanta: John Knox Press, 1989), p. 17.

21. Fuller, "Jesus Christ as Savior in the New Testament," pp. 146ff. See also Martin Hengel, "The Expiatory Sacrifice of Christ," *Bulletin of the John Rylands Library* 62 (2) (1980): 454–475.

22. Martin Hengel, *The Atonement* (Philadelphia: Fortress Press, 1981), p. 1.

23. *Ibid.,* pp. 19ff.

24. Fiddes, *Past Event and Present Salvation,* p. 67.

25. Schillebeeckx, *Jesus,* p. 293. See also, Walter Kasper, *Jesus the Christ* (Mahwah, N.J.: Paulist Press, 1976), pp. 215ff.

26. Hengel, *The Atonement,* pp. 28ff; 46ff.

27. *Ibid.,* p. 65ff. See also Sloyan, *Jesus: Redeemer and Divine Word,* p. 42.

28. Gabriel Daly, *Creation and Redemption* (Wilmington: Michael Glazier, 1989), p. 179.

29. Hengel, *The Atonement,* pp. 71ff.

30. C. D. F. Moule, *The Origin of Christianity* (Cambridge: Cambridge University Press, 1977), p. 109.

31. Schillebeeckx, *Jesus,* p. 293, *Christ,* pp. 728ff.

32. Fiddes, *Past Event and Present Salvation,* p. 630.

33. Vawter, *This Man Jesus,* pp. 77ff.

34. Kasper, *Jesus, the Christ,* pp. 163ff.

35 Hans Küng, *On Being a Christian* (Garden City, N.Y.: Doubleday, 1976), pp. 424ff. For an overview of contemporary approaches to the saving dimension of Jesus' death, see John P. Galvin, "Jesus' Approach to Death: An Examination of Some Recent Studies," pp. 713–744.

36. Dufour, *Dictionary of Biblical Theology,* pp. 284ff.

37. Sloyan, *Jesus: Redeemer and Divine Word,* pp. 49ff.

38. Kasper, *Jesus, the Christ,* pp. 215ff.

39. Brennan R. Hill, *Key Dimensions of Religious Education* (Winona, Minn.: St. Mary's Press, 1989), pp. 86ff.

40. See Häring, *Free and Faithful in Christ,* vol. 1.

41. Jaroslav Pelikan, *The Christian Tradition: A History of the Development of Doc-*

trine. Vol. 1, The Emergence of the Catholic Tradition (100-600) (Chicago: University of Chicago Press, 1971), p. 155.

42. Daly, *Creation and Redemption*, p. 184. There seems to be the assumption here that Adam was a historical figure.

43. Pelikan, *The Emergence of the Catholic Tradition*, pp. 144ff.

44. *Ibid.*, p. 153.

45. Daly, *Creation and Redemption*, p. 186.

46. Sloyan, *Jesus: Redeemer and Divine Word*, p. 82.

47. Wm. Loewe, "Irenaeus' Soteriology: Christus Victor Revisited," *Anglican Theological Review* (Jan. 1985): 1–15.

48. Pelikan, *The Emergence of the Catholic Tradition*, p. 141.

49. *Ibid.*, pp. 147ff.

50. Sloyan, *Jesus: Redeemer and Divine Word*, pp. 79ff.

51. Pelikan, *The Emergence of the Catholic Tradition*, p. 147.

52. William M. Thompson, *The Jesus Debate* (Mahwah, N.J.: Paulist Press, 1985), p. 347.

53. G.R. Evans, *Anselm and Talking About God* (Oxford: Clarendon Press, 1978), pp. 126ff.

54. Gerald O'Collins, *Interpreting Jesus* (Mahwah, N.J.: Paulist Press, 1983), p. 150.

55. Evans, *Anselm and Talking About God*, pp. 133ff.

56. *Ibid.*, pp. 146ff.

57. Kasper, *Jesus, the Christ*, p. 220.

58. Thompson, *The Jesus Debate*, pp. 350ff.

59. Fiddes, *Past Event and Present Salvation*, p. 140.

60. Schillebeeckx, *Christ*, p. 745.

61. Gustav Aulén, *Christus Victor* (New York: Macmillan, 1969).

62. Daly, *Creation and Redemption*, p. 188.

63. See Pelikan's Foreword of Aulén's *Christus Victor*, p. xiv.

64. Fiddes, *Past Event and Present Salvation*, p. 112.

65. Colin R. Gunton, *The Actuality of Atonement* (Grand Rapids, Mich.: Eerdmans, 1989), pp. 12ff.

66. Donald G. Bloesch, "Soteriology in Contemporary Christian Thought," *Interpretation* 35 (?) (April 1981): 133ff.

67. For a discussion of Tillich's views, see Lee Snook, *The Anonymous Christ: Jesus as Savior in Modern Theology* (Minneapolis: Augsburg, 1986), pp. 60ff. See also Paul Tillich, *Systematic Theology*, Vol. II (Chicago: University of Chicago Press, 1963).

68. Schillebeeckx, *Christ*, pp. 64ff.

69. Snook, *The Anonymous Christ*, p. 105.

70. *Ibid.*, p. 116.

71. For a detailed discussion of these issues, see John Hick, *God Has Many Names* (Philadelphia: Westminster Press, 1982), Paul Knitter, *No Other Name?* (Maryknoll, N.Y.: Orbis Books, 1985), John Hick and Paul Knitter, eds., *The Myth of Christian Uniqueness* (Maryknoll, N.Y.: Orbis Books, 1987), and Franz J. van Beeck, "Professing the Uniqueness of Christ," *Chicago Studies* 24 (1) (1985): 17–36.

72. Braaten, "The Christian Doctrine of Salvation," pp. 117ff.

73. See Brennan Hill, Paul Knitter, and William Madges, *Faith, Religion & Theology* (Mystic, Conn.: Twenty-Third Publications, 1990), pp. 214ff. for Knitter's explanation of how the gospel language on Jesus' uniqueness might be the

language of family and relationship rather than a definitive position on Jesus' uniqueness.

74. Schillebeeckx, *Jesus*, pp. 516ff. See also Edward J. Miller, "Inclusivist and Exclusivist Issues in Soteriology: To Whom Does Jesus' Saving Power Extend?" *Perspectives in Religious Studies* 12 (2) (1985): 123–137.

CHAPTER TWELVE

1. Claus Bussmann, *Who Do You Say? Jesus Christ in Latin American Theology* (Maryknoll, N.Y.: Orbis Books, 1985), p. 11.
2. Leonardo Boff and Clodovis Boff, *Introducing Liberation Theology* (Maryknoll, N.Y.: Orbis Books, 1987), pp. 2ff.
3. Saul Trinidad, "Christology, Conquista, Colonization," in Jose Miguez-Bonino, ed., *Faces of Jesus: Latin American Christologies* (Maryknoll, N.Y.: Orbis Books, 1984), p. 32.
4. Michael L. Cook, "Jesus from the Other Side of History: Christology in Latin America," *Theological Studies* 44 (2) (June 1983), 279.
5. *Ibid.*, p. 284. See also David Batstone, *From Conquest to Struggle: Jesus of Nazareth in Latin America* (Albany: State University of New York Press, 1991).
6. Bussmann, *Who Do You Say?*, pp. 17ff. See also Russell Pregeant, "Christological Groundings For Liberation Practice," *Modern Theology* 5 (Jan. 1989): 113–132, and Robert McAfee Brown, *Theology in New Key* (Philadelphia: Westminster Press, 1978).
7. See "Justice in the World" in David J. O'Brien and Thomas A. Shannon, eds., *Renewing the Earth: Catholic Documents on Peace, Justice and Liberation* (Garden City, N.Y.: Doubleday, 1977), p. 391.
8. See Gustavo Gutiérrez, *A Theology of Liberation* (Maryknoll, N.Y.: Orbis Books, 1973).
9. See Jon Sobrino, *Jesus in Latin America* (Maryknoll, N.Y.: Orbis Books, 1989), *Christology at the Crossroad* (Maryknoll, N.Y.: Orbis Books, 1976), Juan Luís Segundo, *The Historical Jesus of the Synoptics* (Maryknoll, N.Y.: Orbis Books, 1985), Leonardo Boff, *Jesus Christ Liberator* (Maryknoll, N.Y.: Orbis Books, 1972), Segundo Galilea, "Jesus Attitude Toward Politics. Some Working Hypotheses," in J. Miguez-Bonino, ed., *Faces of Jesus* (Maryknoll, N.Y. Orbis Books, 1984), and Ignacio Ellacuría, *Freedom Made Flesh* (Maryknoll, N.Y.: Orbis Books, 1976).
10. Ignacio Ellacuría, "The Political Nature of Jesus' Mission," Miguez-Bonino, ed., *Faces of Jesus*, p. 80.
11. Ellacuría, *Freedom Made Flesh*, pp. 24ff.
12. Sobrino, *Jesus in Latin America*, pp. 65ff.
13. Boff, *Jesus Christ Liberator*, pp. 279ff.
14. Sobrino, *Jesus in Latin America*, p. 29.
15. *Ibid.*, pp. 65ff.
16. Cook, "Jesus From the Other Side of History," p. 272. See also Bussmann, *Who Do You Say?*, pp. 97ff.
17. The Vatican has published two statements on liberation theology. The second is more positive that the first. See Alfred T. Hennelly, ed., *Liberation Theology: A Documentary History* (Maryknoll, N.Y.: Orbis Books, 1990), pp. 393ff.
18. Christopher Rowland and Mark Corner, *Liberation Exegesis: The Challenge of*

Liberation Theology to Biblical Studies (Atlanta: John Knox Press, 1990), pp. 39ff.

19. Solentiname was a Christian community in Nicaragua that became radicalized through the gospel. It was destroyed by Somoza, but then restored after the Sandinista revolution. See Philip and Sally Scharper, eds., *The Gospel in Art by the Peasants of Solentiname* (Maryknoll, N.Y.: Orbis Books, 1984). For the viewpoints of Latin American women, see Elsa Tamez, *Through Her Eyes: Women's Theology from Latin America* (Maryknoll, N.Y.: Orbis Books, 1989).

20. Sobrino, *Jesus in Latin America,* pp. 65ff.

21. Boff, *Jesus Christ Liberator*, p. 11.

22. Gustavo Gutiérrez, "Jesus and the Political World," in Bussmann, *Who Do You Say?*, p. 39.

23. Segundo, *The Historical Jesus of the Synoptics*, pp. 27ff.

24. Galilea, "Jesus' Attitude Toward Politics," p. 93.

25. Ellacuría, *Freedom Made Flesh*, p. 46.

26. Rowland and Corner, *Liberation Exegesis*, p. 93.

27. See Bussmann, *Who Do You Say?*, p. 56.

28. Sobrino, *Christology at the Crossroads,* p. 214.

29. Ellacuría, *Freedom Made Flesh*, p. 75.

30. Galilea, "Jesus' Attitude Toward Politics," p. 96.

31. *Ibid.*, p. 97.

32. Harvey, *Jesus and the Constraints of History*, pp. 131ff. See also Gutiérrez, *A Theology of Liberation*, p. 170.

33. Boff, *Jesus Christ Liberator*, p. 82.

34. Ellacuría, *Freedom Made Flesh*, p. 32.

35. Rowland and Corner, *Liberating Exegesis*, p. 47.

36. Bussmann, *Who Do You Say?*, pp. 61ff.

37. See Jon Sobrino, *The True Church and the Church of the Poor* (London: SCM Press, 1985), p. 222.

38. Boff, *Jesus Christ Liberator*, p. 49.

39. Gutiérrez, *A Theology of Liberation*, pp. 176ff.

40. Boff and Boff, *Introducing Liberation Theology*, p. 52.

41. *Ibid.*, p. 228.

42. Segundo, *The Historical Jesus of the Synoptics*, p. 6. See also Sobrino, *Christology at the Crossroads*, p. 197.

43. Sobrino, *Christology at the Crossroads*, p. 224.

44. Segundo, *The Historical Jesus of the Synoptics*, pp. 3ff.

45. Boff and Boff, *Introducing Liberation Theology*, p. 54.

46. Boff, *Jesus Christ Liberator*, p. 290.

47. Leonardo Boff, "Images of Jesus in Brazilian Liberal Christianity," Miguez-Bonino, *Faces of Jesus*, p. 25.

48. Boff, *Jesus Christ Liberator*, p. 141.

49. Sobrino, *Christology at the the Crossroads*, p. 209.

50. Hennelly, ed., *Liberation Theology*, p. 304.

51. See Snyder, *The Christology of Rosemary Radford Ruether*, p. 51. See Ruether, "The Liberation of Christology from Patriarchy," *Religion and Intellectual Life* 2(3) (Spring 1985): 116–128.

52. Snyder, *The Christology of Rosemary Radford Ruether*, pp. 53ff.

53. Rowland and Corner, *Liberating Exegesis*, p. 89.

54. Raymond Maloney, "African Christology," *Theological Studies* 48 (3)(1987): 505.
55. See K. Appiah-Kubi "Jesus Christ: Some Christological Aspects from African Perspectives," in J.S. Mbiti, ed., *African and Asian Contributions of Contemporary Theology* (Bossey: World Council of Churches, 1977), 51–65, C. Nyamiti, *Christ as Our Ancestor: Christology from an African Perspective* (Gweru, Zimbabwe: Mambo, 1984), Boulaga Eboussi, *Christianity Without Fetishes: An African Critique and Recapture of Christianity* (Maryknoll, N.Y.: Orbis Books, 1984).
56. See James H. Cone, "Black Theology: Its Origin, Method and Relation to Third World Theologies," in William K. Tabb, ed., *Churches in Struggle: Liberation Theologies and Social Change in North America* (New York: Monthly Review Press, 1986), pp. 32ff.
57. Deane W. Ferm, *Third World Liberation Theologies* (Maryknoll, N.Y.: Orbis Books, 1985), pp. 59ff.
58. *Ibid.*, p. 67.
59. See Kortright Davis, "Jesus Christ and Black Liberation: Toward a Paradigm of Transcendence," *Journal of Religious Thought* 42, 1 (Spring-Summer 1985): 51-67.
60. Desmond Tutu, *Hope and Suffering* (Grand Rapids, Mich.: Eerdmans, 1984), p. 170ff.
61. Ferm, *Third World Liberation Theologies*, p. 61.
62. *Ibid.*, p. 78.
63. *Ibid.*, p. 98. See also Ahn Byung-Mu, "The Korean Church's Understanding of Jesus," *International Review of Mission* 74 (293) (1985): 81–91.
64. McFague, *Models of God*, p. 46.

Suggested Readings

CHAPTER ONE

Freyne, Sean. *Galilee, Jesus and the Gospels*. Philadelphia: Fortress Press, 1988.

Horsley, R.A. and J. Hanson. *Bandits, Prophets and Messiahs*. New York: Winston Press, 1985.

Johnson, Sherman. *Jesus and His Towns*. Wilmington: Michael Glazier, 1989.

Lee, Bernard J. *The Galilean Jewishness of Jesus*. Mahwah, N.J.: Paulist Press, 1988.

McNamara, Martin. *Palestinian Judaism and the New Testament*. Wilmington: Michael Glazier, 1983.

Osiek, Carolyn. *What Are They Saying About the Social Setting of the New Testament?* Mahwah, N.J.: Paulist Press, 1984.

Riches, John. *Jesus and the Transformation of Judaism*. London: Darton, Longman and Todd, 1980.

_____. *The World of Jesus: First-Century Judaism*. New York: Cambridge University Press, 1990.

Saldarini, Anthony. *Pharisees, Scribes and Sadducees in Palestinian Society*. Wilmington: Michael Glazier, 1988.

Vermes, Geza. *Jesus and the World of Judaism*. Philadelphia: Fortress Press, 1983.

Wilkinson, John. *Jerusalem as Jesus Knew It: Archaeology as Evidence*. London: Thames and Hudson, Ltd.,1982.

Zeitlin, Irving M. *Jesus and the Judaism of His Time*. New York: Polity Press, 1988.

CHAPTER TWO

Charlesworth, James H. *Jesus within Judaism*. Garden City, N.Y.: Doubleday, 1988.

Cook, Michael L. *Guidelines for Contemporary Catholics: The Historical Jesus*. Chicago: Thomas More Press, 1986.

Fitzmyer, Joseph. *A Christological Catechism*. Mahwah, N.J.: Paulist Press, 1982.

Harrington, Wilfred. *The New Guide to Reading and Studying the Bible*. Wilmington: Michael Glazier, 1978.

Keck, Leander E. *A Future for the Historical Jesus*. London: SCM Press, 1971.

Kee, Howard C. *What Can We Know About Jesus?* New York: Cambridge University Press, 1990.

Keegan, Terence J. *Interpreting the Bible: A Popular Introduction to Biblical Hermeneutics.* Mahwah, N.J.: Paulist Press, 1986.

McArthur, Harvey K., ed. *In Search of the Historical Jesus.* New York: Charles Scribner's Sons, 1969.

Perkins, Pheme. *Reading the New Testament: An Introduction.* Mahwah, N.J.: Paulist Press, 1977.

Sanders, E. P. *Jesus and Judaism.* Philadelphia: Fortress Press, 1985.

CHAPTER THREE

Beasley-Murray, G.R. *Jesus and the Kingdom of God.* Grand Rapids, Mich.: Eerdmans, 1986.

Boucher, Madeleine. *The Parables.* Wilmington: Michael Glazier, 1981.

Brueggemann, Walter. *The Prophetic Imagination.* Philadelphia: Fortress Press, 1976.

Falk, Harvey. *Jesus the Pharisee.* Mahwah, N.J.: Paulist Press, 1985.

Hengel, Martin. *The Charismatic Leader and His Followers.* New York: Crossroad, 1981.

Lane, Dermot A. *Christ at the Centre: Selected Issues in Christology.* Mahwah, N.J.: Paulist Press, 1991.

Neusner, Jacob. *Jesus and the Beginning of Christianity.* Philadelphia: Fortress Press, 1984.

Perkins, Pheme. *Hearing the Parables of Jesus.* Mahwah, N.J.: Paulist Press, 1981.

_____. *Jesus as Teacher.* New York: Cambridge University Press, 1990.

Robbins, V.K. *Jesus the Teacher,* London: SCM Press, 1985.

Sloyan, Gerard S. *Jesus in Focus: A Life in Its Setting.* Mystic, Conn.: Twenty-Third Publications, 1983.

Viviano, B. *The Kingdom of God in History.* Wilmington: Michael Glazier, 1988.

Willis, W., ed. *The Kingdom of God in 20th Century Interpretation.* Peabody, Mass: Hendrickson Publishers, 1987.

CHAPTER FOUR

Fuller, Reginald H. *Interpreting the Miracles.* London: SCM Press, 1963.

Helminiak, Daniel A. *The Same Jesus.* Chicago: Loyola University Press, 1986.

Hendrickx, Herman. *The Miracle Stories.* San Francisco: Harper & Row, 1987.

Kee, Howard C. *Medicine, Miracle and Magic in New Testament Times.* New York: Cambridge University Press, 1986.

Kelsey, Morton. *Healing and Christianity.* New York: Harper & Row, 1973.

Latourelle, René. *The Miracles of Jesus and the Theology of Miracles.* Mahwah, N.J.: Paulist Press, 1988.

Moule, C.F.D., ed. *Miracles.* London: Mowbray and Co., 1965.

Richards, H.J. *The Miracles of Jesus.* Mystic, Conn.: Twenty-Third Publications, 1986.

Theissen, Gerd. *Miracle Stories of the Early Christian Tradition.* Philadelphia: Fortress Press, 1983.

CHAPTER FIVE

Carr, Anne E. *Transforming Grace*. San Francisco: Harper & Row, 1982.

Craig Faxon, Alicia. *Women and Jesus*. Philadelphia: United Church Press, 1973. •

Johnson, Elizabeth A. *Consider Jesus: Waves of Renewal in Christology*. New York: Crossroad, 1990.

Moltmann-Wendel, Elisabeth. *The Women Around Jesus*. New York: Crossroad, • 1982.

Ruether, Rosemary Radford, ed. *To Change the World: Christology and Cultural Criticism*. New York: Crossroad, 1981.

Schneiders, Sandra. *Women and the Word*. Mahwah, N.J.: Paulist Press, 1986. •

Schüssler Fiorenza, Elisabeth. *In Memory of Her*. New York: Crossroad, 1984. •

Snyder, Mary Hembrow. *The Christology of Rosemary Radford Ruether*. Mystic, • Conn.: Twenty-Third Publications, 1988.

Swidler, Leonard. *Biblical Affirmations of Women*. Philadelphia: Fortress Press, • 1979.

Tetlow, Elizabeth M. *Women and Ministry in the New Testament*. Mahwah, N.J.: Paulist Press, 1989.

Wilson-Kastner, Patricia. *Faith, Feminism and the Christ*. Philadelphia: Fortress Press, 1983.

Witherington, Ben. *Women in the Ministry of Jesus*. London: Cambridge Univer- • sity Press, 1988.

CHAPTER SIX

Carroll, D. *Toward a Story of the Earth*. Dublin: Dominican Publications, 1988.

Fox, Matthew. *The Coming of the Cosmic Christ*. San Francisco: Harper & Row, 1988.

Johnson, Elizabeth A. *Consider Jesus: Waves of Renewal in Theology*. New York: Crossroad, 1990.

Lyons, J.A. *The Cosmic Christ in Origen and Teilhard de Chardin*. New York: Oxford University Press, 1982.

McDaniel, Jay B. *Earth, Sky, Gods and Mortals: Developing an Ecological Spirituality*. Mystic, Conn.: Twenty-Third Publications, 1990.

McFague, Sallie. *Models of God: Theology for an Ecological and Nuclear Age*. Philadelphia: Fortress Press, 1987.

Mooney, Christopher. *Teilhard de Chardin and the Mystery of Christ*. London: Collins, 1966.

Ruether, Rosemary Radford. "Ecological and Human Liberation," in *To Change the World: Christology and Cultural Criticism*. New York: Crossroad, 1981.

Teilhard de Chardin, Pierre. *Hymn of the Universe*. New York: Harper & Row, 1965.

Thompson, William M. *The Jesus Debate*. Mahwah, N.J.: Paulist Press, 1985.

CHAPTER SEVEN

Boff, Leonardo. *The Maternal Face of God*. New York: Harper & Row, 1987.

Brown, Raymond E. *An Adult Christ at Christmas*. Collegeville Minn.: Liturgical Press, 1985.

_____. *The Birth of the Messiah*. Garden City, N.Y.: Doubleday, 1977.

_____. *The Virginal Conception and Bodily Resurrection of Jesus*. Mahwah, N.J.: Paulist Press, 1973.

Harrington, Wilfred. *The Drama of Christ's Coming*. Wilmington: Michael Glazier, 1988.

Horsley, Richard A. *The Liberation of Christmas*. New York: Crossroad, 1989.

Williams, R. Rhys. *Let Each Gospel Speak for Itself*. Mystic, Conn.: Twenty-Third Publications, 1987.

CHAPTER EIGHT

Brown, Raymond E. *The Crucified Christ at Holy Week*. Collegeville, Minn.: Liturgical Press, 1986.

Grassi, Joseph A. *Rediscovering the Impact of the Death of Jesus*. Kansas City: Sheed and Ward, 1987.

Harvey, A.E. *Jesus on Trial*. Atlanta: John Knox Press, 1976.

Hengel, Martin. *Crucifixion*. London: SCM Press, 1977.

Rivkin, Ellis. *What Crucified Jesus?* Nashville: Abingdon, 1984.

Rosse, Gerard. *The Cry of Jesus on the Cross*. Mahwah, N.J.: Paulist Press, 1987.

Senior, Donald. *The Passion of Jesus in the Gospel of Mark; The Passion of Jesus in the Gospel of Matthew; The Passion of Jesus in the Gospel of Luke: The Passion of Jesus in the Gospel of John*. Wilmington: Michael Glazier, 1984-89.

Sloyan, Gerard S. *Jesus on Trial*. Philadelphia: Fortress Press, 1973.

CHAPTER NINE

Brown, Raymond E. *The Virginal Conception and Bodily Resurrection of Jesus*. Mahwah, N.J.: Paulist Press, 1973.

Dunn, James D.G. *The Evidence for Jesus*. Philadelphia: Westminster Press, 1985.

Durrwell, F.X. *The Resurrection*. New York: Sheed and Ward, 1960.

Fuller, Reginald. *The Formation of the Resurrection Narratives.* Philadelphia: Fortress Press, 1980.

Neyrey, Jerome. *The Resurrection Stories.* Wilmington: Michael Glazier, 1988.

O'Collins, Gerald. *Interpreting the Resurrection.* Mahwah, N.J.: Paulist Press, 1988.

_____. *Jesus Risen.* Mahwah, N.J.: Paulist Press, 1987.

Perkins, Pheme. *Resurrection: New Testament Witness and Contemporary Reflection.* Garden City, N.Y.: Doubleday, 1984.

Williams, R. Rhys. *Let Each Gospel Speak for Itself.* Mystic, Conn.: Twenty-Third Publications, 1987.

Chapter Ten

Carmody, Denise L. and John T. *Jesus: An Introduction.* Belmont, Cal.: Wadsworth Publishing Company, 1987.

Chestnut, D.F. *Images of Christ: An Introduction to Christology.* New York: Seabury Press, 1984.

Davis, Leo. *The First Seven Councils (325-787).* Wilmington: Michael Glazier, 1987.

Ettinger, Gerard H. *Jesus,Christ and Savior.* Wilmington: Michael Glazier, 1987.

Gonzalez, Justo L. *The Early Church to the Dawn of the Reformation.* New York: Harper & Row, 1984.

Hart, Thomas. *To Know and Follow Jesus.* Mahwah, N.J.: Paulist Press, 1984.

Neyrey, Jerome H. *Christ in Community: The Christogies of the New Testament.* Wilmington: Michael Glazier, 1985.

Norris, Richard A., ed. *The Christological Controversy.* Philadelphia: Fortress Press, 1987.

Richard, Earl. *Jesus: One and Many.* Wilmington: Michael Glazier, 1988.

Sloyan, Gerard S. *The Jesus Tradition: Images of Jesus in the West.* Mystic, Conn.: Twenty-Third Publications, 1986.

Wiles, Maurice. *The Making of Christian Doctrine.* New York: Cambridge University Press, 1967.

Chapter Eleven

Daly, Gabriel. *Creation and Redemption.* Wilmington: Michael Glazier, 1989.

Edwards, Denis. *What Are They Saying About Salvation?* Mahwah, N.J.: Paulist Press, 1986.

Fiddes, Paul. *Past Event and Present Salvation.* Atlanta: John Knox Press, 1989.

Hengel, Martin. *The Atonement.* Philadelphia: Fortress Press, 1981.

Hultgren, Arland J. *Christ and His Benefits.* Philadelphia: Fortress Press, 1987.

O'Grady, John F. *Models of Jesus.* Garden City, N.Y.: Doubleday, 1981.

Schillebeeckx, Edward. *God Among Us.* New York: Crossroad, 1983.

Sloyan, Gerard S. *Jesus: Redeemer and Divine Word.* Wilmington: Michael Glazier, 1989.

Snook, Lee. *The Anonymous Christ: Jesus as Savior in Modern Theology.* Minneapolis: Augsburg, 1986.

CHAPTER TWELVE

Boff, Leonardo and Clodovis. *Introducing Liberation Theology.* Maryknoll, N.Y.: Orbis Books, 1987.

Boff, Leonardo. *Jesus the Liberator.* Maryknoll, N.Y.: Orbis Books, 1972.

Brown, Robert McAfee. *Theology in a New Key.* Philadelphia: Westminster Press, 1978.

Bussmann, Claus. *Who Do You Say? Jesus Christ in Latin America.* Maryknoll, N.Y.: Orbis Books, 1985.

Clarke, Thomas. *Above Every Name: The Lordship of Christ and Social Systems.* Mahwah, N.J.: Paulist Press, 1980.

Ellacuría, Ignacio. *Freedom Made Flesh.* Maryknoll, N.Y.: Orbis Books, 1976.

Miguez-Bonino, J., ed. *Faces of Jesus.* Maryknoll, N.Y.: Orbis Books, 1984.

Segundo, Juan Luís. *The Historical Jesus of the Synoptics.* Maryknoll, N.Y.: Orbis Books, 1985.

Sobrino, Jon. *Christology at the Crossroad.* Maryknoll, N.Y.: Orbis Books, 1976.

_____. *Jesus in Latin America.* Maryknoll, N.Y.: Orbis Books, 1989.

Scripture Citations

Index